BIG FOOD,
BIG PHARMA,
BIG LIES

BIG FOOD,
BIG PHARMA,
BIG LIES

Exposing the Dangers Within the Pharmaceutical and Agriculture Industries

Martha Rosenberg

Essex, Connecticut

Prometheus Books

An imprint of Globe Pequot, the trade division of
The Rowman & Littlefield Publishing Group, Inc.
4501 Forbes Blvd., Ste. 200
Lanham, MD 20706
www.rowman.com

Distributed by NATIONAL BOOK NETWORK

British Library Cataloguing in Publication Information Available

Library of Congress Cataloging-in-Publication Data

The Library of Congress has cataloged the hardcover edition of this book as follows:

Rosenberg, Martha.
    Born with a junk food deficiency : how flaks, quacks, and hacks pimp the public health /
by Martha Rosenberg.
        p. cm.
    Includes bibliographical references.
    ISBN 978–1–61614–593–4 (cloth)
    ISBN 978–1–61614–594–1 (ebook)
    1. Health education. 2. Consumer education. I. Title.

ISBN 9781633889354 (pbk. : alk. paper) | ISBN 9781633889798 (epub)

∞™ The paper used in this publication meets the minimum requirements of American National Standard for Information Sciences—Permanence of Paper for Printed Library Materials, ANSI/NISO Z39.48-1992

To H. P.

CONTENTS

PART 2. BIG FOOD

FOREWORD

Can you imagine what would happen if Big Food stopped hawking junk and starting marketing healthier foods, like vegetables and fruits? I suspect Wall Street and shareholders alike would demand a change in management as soon as quarterly profits dropped.

Today, U.S. children see ten thousand commercials for food each year on television and countless more ads in print, at school, and on screens, and two thirds of our infants are being fed junk food before their first birthday. In the words of a former Kellogg's ad man, "Our primary goal is to sell products to children, not educate them." Why? According to the marketing executive, if a child doesn't get what he wants, he'll "throw himself on the floor, stamp his feet and cry. You can't get a reaction like that out of an adult."

It is not just the ubiquitous advertising of junk food—and its ubiquity in gas stations, drugstores, hardware stores, bookstores, and even clothing stores—that let food marketers get unhealthy products into our refrigerators and pantries. Industry-funded "research" downplays the dangers of cholesterol and saturated fat, the presence of contaminants and pharmaceutical drugs, and unhygienic food production practices in too much of the foodstuffs available to us 24/7. Did you know, for example, that intensive fish farming requires half a pound of antibiotics to produce just *one pound of salmon* and much of U.S. seafood has been found to be tainted with antibiotics? Eggs are now, inexplicably, presented as the "perfect food," though only half an egg has about 80 mg of cholesterol, which has been scientifically linked to premature aging.

As if that weren't bad enough, Big Food creates phony consumer groups with plasticky names like "Americans Against Food Taxes" to spin restrictions on the marketing of unhealthy, fattening food as violations of our "rights" and consumer choice. As a physician, I wonder if food consumers would *choose* the obesity, diabetes, hypertension, gallstones, heart and kidney disease, and more that are linked to consumption of processed junk food.

Big Food isn't alone. It follows Big Tobacco's playbook, and Big Pharma uses the same deceptive marketing tactics, sometimes even disease-mongering to hype up disorders and diseases to push their pills.

Sadly many, perhaps even most, medical associations accept money from drug makers no matter the obvious conflict of interest and bias. The nonprofit organizations I founded and work with—the American College of Lifestyle Medicine and NutritionFacts.org—have strict policies against that, of course, but we are among the exceptions to the norm.

I used to ask my medical colleagues when they so readily accepted invitations to so-called drug lunches from pharmaceutical representatives if they didn't think it would affect their prescribing. There is no such thing as a free lunch, and studies have shown that the feeling of indebtedness, even from something as small as a meal, can make the recipient want to reciprocate.

Like commercials for junk food, network and cable news shows receive so much revenue from direct-to-consumer "Ask Your Doctor" drugs ads, they may be less likely to cover drug safety scandals in an unbiased way. Vioxx and opioid over-prescribing jump to mind. Those are their advertisers. Seldom will they report that prescriptions kill more than a hundred thousand Americans a year.

There is an even more pernicious effect that comes from drug advertising: remedy messaging. When someone hears there is a "solution" to their obesity, hypertension, or other lifestyle-connected medical condition, the message can be subconsciously interpreted that the problem is manageable and the person often relinquishes personal responsibility. As a result, the condition may even get worse.

Big Food spends more money on advertising than any other sector, with Big Pharma nipping at its heels. Because of financial realities, both industries profit more when people are unhealthy and eating unhealthy foods. We should all beware.

INTRODUCTION

How do you launch a "disease" created for no other purpose than to sell drugs that are supposed to treat it?

- Issue a press release about how it is an "under-recognized" disease with many "barriers" and "stigmas" to treatment.
- Launch a TV campaign to "raise awareness" about the disease's symptoms and risk factors to help "sufferers" in the general public diagnose themselves.
- Create a website with a quiz for people to determine if they have the disease and a script for them to take to the doctor to be prescribed the intended drug.
- Hire doctors to warn people that the disease is progressive and silent and will only get worse if they ignore it and don't seek treatment.
- Create patient front groups to lobby the Food and Drug Administration (FDA) to approve expensive drugs for the disease and to lobby insurers to not substitute a lower-cost drug.
- Plant articles in respected medical journals about the hidden costs of the under-recognized disease in hospitalizations and quality-of-life of sufferers that total more than it would cost insurers to buy the drug.
- Develop a second drug that sufferers need to add to the first drug to boost its performance, either because the first drug doesn't work or because the people never had the disease in the first place.

How do you produce food that fattens and sickens instead of nourishes?

- Use taxpayer money to market unhealthy food directly to consumers to help Agribiz, ignoring the government's duty to protect public health.

13

- Dump unhealthy food into school lunch programs and other government programs where food consumers have little choice—also to help Agribiz.
- Pay dietitians to concoct protein, milk, or nutrient "deficiencies" in children and in the general public to unload the unhealthy food.
- Protect the identity of farms producing contaminated products and abusing workers, animals, and the environment.
- Refuse to prosecute perpetrator farms, except for slaps on the wrist, and *never* shut them down, because that would be anti-industry.
- Strip federal food inspectors of power to enforce laws, stop assembly lines, and report violations, making them pathetic figureheads who are openly ridiculed by plant managers.
- Remind people to wash their hands after handling raw food because food safety is their responsibility and federal food inspectors can't catch everything.
- Outlaw food labels that reveal production methods, dangerous ingredients, or genetic engineering associated with a product so consumers can't make informed purchasing choices.

Despite the wonder of Western medicine, the United States has some of the sickest people in the world, thanks to direct-to-consumer advertising—and most of it is self-diagnosed.

We "suffer" from seasonal allergies, asthma, seasonal affective disorder, social anxiety, depression, bipolar disorder, attention deficit hyperactivity disorder, erectile dysfunction, irritable bowel syndrome, dry eye, fibromyalgia, insomnia, migraines, mood disorders, obsessive-compulsive disorders, spectrum disorders, chronic fatigue, restless legs, excessive daytime sleepiness, osteopenia, perimenopause, and lactose intolerance. Many of the new diseases are "imbalances" from a "deficiency" of a drug that Big Pharma makes, and we will need them for the rest of our lives, say the marketing materials.

In addition to taking drugs for diseases (and deficiencies) that barely existed before drug ads came into being, we take drugs to prevent diseases we don't even have, like thinning bones and cardiovascular diseases.

And despite the wonders of the Western diet, the United States has the *least fit* people in the world. We develop high cholesterol, high blood pressure, high blood sugar, obesity, diabetes, heartburn, gastroesophageal and reflux disease from junk food—and aching backs, painful joints, poor circulation, and sleep apnea from the extra weight we gain from eating too much and poorly. Drugs we're already taking for "deficiency" diseases add to the obesity problem, and we treat that with *more drugs* for metabolism like statins, "purple pills," and blood sugar–lowering pills. The food leads us to drugs and the drugs lead us to food, in a vicious cycle.

The TV "teleprompter" telling us to eat junk food is not the only cause of our national obesity. Supersizing, free refills, and all-you-can-eat buffets encourage people to get their money's worth at the price of their waistlines and health. The family meal, where we learned portion control and restraint, is a dying cultural icon. Size inflation, which has caused women who were size sevens to now be size zeros, furthers adipose denial. And baggy and low-rider urban fashions seldom "don't" fit.

And there is the ubiquity of snacks themselves. Once upon a time, snacks weren't available in banks, bookstores, body shops, hardware stores, and hospitals. When some Europeans visiting a US mall saw people in the food court eating cheese fries at ten thirty in the morning, they asked, "What meal is that?" Good question.

When you consider the toll that cheap food and drugs take on the public health, it is obvious that there is nothing "cheap" about them. The billions that Big Food and Big Pharma make are simply transferred to the cost of treating a nation with chronic, expensive-to-treat, and often preventable diseases.

In fact, the junk food and drug "deficiencies" we're said to suffer from bring to mind the 1953 song, made popular by Burl Ives, "There Was an Old Lady Who Swallowed a Fly." After swallowing a fly, the old lady swallows increasingly larger animals to catch the previously swallowed animal. She swallows a spider to catch the fly, a bird to catch the spider, a cat to catch the bird, a dog to catch the cat, and so on. Every time she swallows a larger animal, the absurdity of her first act is repeated in the chorus: "I don't know why she swallowed the fly, perhaps she'll die." And, in the end, she does. It sounds a lot like US consumers in the age of aggressive junk food and drug advertising.

Part 1

BIG PHARMA

Chapter 1

WHEN THE MEDICATION IS READY, THE DISEASE (AND PATIENTS) WILL APPEAR— OR, WHEN TV MAKES YOU SICK

C an anyone remember life before "Ask Your Doctor" ads?

All you knew about prescription drugs came from the ads you peeked at in the *Journal of the American Medical Association* (*JAMA*) in your doctor's waiting room. They were full of vaguely ominous terms—*nulligravida? hemo-dialysis?*—as well as side effects and overdose treatments that you didn't understand and didn't *want* to understand. And they confirmed that the doctor knew more than you, more than he was *telling* you (and if this was more than twenty years ago, the doc probably *was* a "he"), and sometimes he was looking down on you.

In the 1950s, *JAMA* ads had a hokey feel to them, with cartoons and ads for soda pop, orthopedic shoes, and sickroom supplies. "Fifty million times a day at home, at work or while at play," says an ad, referring to the wide use of what *seems* to be a medicine but is actually Coca-Cola®.[1] "Why look at the *back* of a 7-UP® bottle?" says another soft drink ad.[2] "Here's why. On the back of the bottle are listed all the ingredients of this sparking, crystal-clear drink." Yes, soft drinks weren't just empty calories!

But by the 1960s, *JAMA* ads boasted slick, *Mad Men*–style ads for the tranquilizers Valium®, Librium®, and Miltown®; the antipsychotics Thorazine and Mellaril; the amphetamine Benzedrine; and antidepressants like Elavil®

and Triavil. Commensurate with the psychoanalytical times, before biological psychiatry, in which people with emotional problems had "shrinks," neuroses, and "complexes," many ads suggest patients are motivated by drives and impulses they deny.

"Do you have patients who try to hide frustration behind conformity?" asks an ad for the antidepressant nortriptyline, depicting a bored, upper-middle-class couple in Burberry®-like attire. "They may be unable to face the pain of their depression," says the body copy.[3] "Help them see behind the veneer and accept the reality" is the tag line. Other ads in the series accuse patients of "hiding their anger behind charm" and "hiding anguish behind arrogance."[4]

One ad lacquers ageism and sexism onto denial by showing an older, wrinkly woman in a bouffant wig with hair bows, gigantic sunglasses, and garish jewelry.[5]

The headline, "Lady, your anxiety is showing (over a coexisting depression)," is written across her nose to further the ridicule. "On the visible level, this middle-aged patient dresses to look too young, exhibits a tense, continuous smile and may have bitten nails or overplucked eyebrows," says the ad copy. "What doesn't show as clearly is the coexisting depression." The ad suggests the antidepressant and tranquilizer Triavil.

On the visible level, this middle-aged patient dresses to look too young, exhibits a tense, continuous smile, and may have bitten nails or overplucked eyebrows. Symptoms of anxiety are hard to miss. What doesn't show as clearly is the coexisting depression that often complicates treatment.

TRIAVIL offers effective tranquilizer-antidepressant therapy. TRIAVIL provides perphenazine to help allay anxiety and amitriptyline HCl to lift depressive mood and relieve the functional somatic complaints often encountered in patients of this age group.

FOR MODERATE TO SEVERE ANXIETY WITH DEPRESSION

TRIAVIL
containing perphenazine and amitriptyline HCl

TRANQUILIZER-ANTIDEPRESSANT

Patients who have received MAO inhibitors within two weeks should not receive TRIAVIL. Those on TRIAVIL should be warned that response to alcohol may be potentiated. The drug may impair alertness in some patients; operation of automobiles and other activities made hazardous by diminished alertness should be avoided. Contraindicated in glaucoma, in patients expected to experience problems of urinary retention, in CNS depression from drugs, and in bone marrow depression. Should not be given with guanethidine or similarly acting compounds. Not recommended in pregnancy. Since the possibility of suicide is inherent in any serious depressive illness, close supervision of patients is essential until you are satisfied that significant remission has taken place.

For additional prescribing information, please see following page.

A third patient-in-denial ad depicts an upper-middle-class breakfast scene. Under a chandelier, a smiling wife and mother in a flowered housedress has prepared a breakfast of cooked cereal, juice, milk, and percolated coffee (who remembers coffee percolators?) for her executive-type husband and their college "co-ed" daughter, who is wearing pearls. The headline says, "The pre-hysterectomy patient who wears a façade of unconcern." When you turn the page, the husband and daughter have left—and so has the woman's smile. It's all an act.[6]

Such ads elucidating the pathos of aging wives and mothers who are losing their looks, children, femininity, and purpose in life were rampant in 1960s and 1970s medical journals, before the women's liberation movement had taken hold. One such ad shows a woman at her child's graduation ceremony with the headline "Magna cum depression," referring to the empty-nest syndrome she will soon, presumably, experience.[7]

Ads for hormone replacement drugs like Premarin® were even more ruthless.

"When Women Outlive Their Ovaries" is the headline for one, showing a grandmotherly woman in a frumpy cardigan sweater. "There we were—my husband at the peak of his career . . . but no time for me," says the ad. "This wasn't a 'change,' it was a catastrophe."[8]

Journal ads during the 1960s and 1970s also pushed drugs on *men*, who were having trouble with gender roles. The contemporary businessman, said ads for the antipsychotic Mellaril, "is always fearful about his standing with the boss," "misses half of what is said at meetings," because he is so "emotionally upset," "loses his temper with colleagues and subordinates," and "goes home at night and takes it out on his family."[9] But ads of this era were still much harder on women who didn't comply with the social expectations of getting married, being a good wife, and having kids. Jan, we are told in an ad for Valium, is "psychoneurotic" because she is unmarried at age thirty-five. "You probably see many such Jans in your practice," says the ad—"The unmarrieds with low selfesteem. Jan never found a man to measure up to her father."[10]

Some ads are almost sympathetic to "housewives" who, before the women's liberation movement, were supposed to find fulfillment taking care of others and their homes, with no job or career of their own. But instead of

When women outlive their ovaries...

Here illustration shows artist's interpretation of cross section of brain symbolizing impulse transmissions from hypothalamic area to the pituitary and other neurohormonal target organs

"There we were—my husband
at the peak of his career—
busy, successful…but no time for me.
With that and all my other problems,
I'd lie awake night after night, more
depressed every day. This wasn't
a 'change,' it was a catastrophe."

JAMA 222, no. 6 (August 11, 1970): 498–500.

recommending freedom for women suffering from what early feminist Betty Friedan called the "problem that has no name" (the "problem" was suffered by women with material comforts but no intellectual outlet) the ads counseled tranquilizers and other psychiatric drugs. "Why is this woman tired?" asks the headline under a photo of a dissipated, bathrobe-clad young woman about to tackle a stack of dirty dishes.[11] She may just need more sleep, says the ad, but she also may be one of "many of your patients—particularly housewives—[who] are crushed under a load of dull, routine duties that leave them in a state of mental and emotional fatigue. For these patients, you may find 'Dexedrine' an ideal prescription."

"I'm restless, nervous, tired all the time and always nagging," says another "dirty dishes" ad, this one for the antidepressant Sinequan®.[12] (Maybe the women needed a dishwasher, not a prescription.) Another ad in the Sinequan series shows a clothesline with similar I'm-exasperated copy. "A lot of little things are wrong," says the ad. "Headaches, diarrhea, this rash on my arm. And sometimes I think I don't like being married."[13] Another Jan who can't find a husband to measure up to dear, old dad?

"Bad" wives—especially nagging wives—made a regular appearance in drug ads. "A sleeping pill for night squawks" was the sexist headline for an ad for the hypnotic sedative Doriden, in a 1969 issue of *JAMA*.

"She has insomnia . . . so he's awake," continues the copy. "Restless and irritable, she growls at her husband. How can this shrew be tamed?"[14] Ouch. Psychiatric drugs were not only the answer to maladjusted, nagging housewives, suggested ads published throughout the 1960s and 1970s; they were also the answer to bad employees.[15] "Sally Wilson has lost her reputation," floats the headline over a woman in reading glasses with a ream of papers, who appears to be a secretary. "In the last week or so, Sally Wilson's year-old reputation as an unpredictable grouch has melted away." Sally has also "been coming in on time and turning out more work," the ad goes on to say. "Sally's menopause had triggered symptoms that hormone therapy by itself apparently hadn't helped," but adjunctive Valium has "helped her relax."[16]

In the 1950s and 1960s, traditional psychoanalytical theories held that the birth of children, especially a son, would give housewives peace and fulfillment beyond their clothesline and kitchen sink. But drug ads of that era

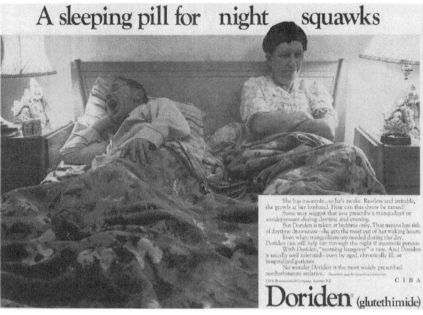

A sleeping pill for night squawks

She has insomnia...so he's awake. Restless and irritable, she growls at her husband. How can this shrew be tamed?
Some may suggest that you prescribe a tranquilizer or antidepressant during daytime and evening.
But Doriden is taken at bedtime only. That means less risk of daytime drowsiness—she gets the most out of her waking hours.
Even when tranquilizers are needed during the day, Doriden can still help her through the night if insomnia persists.
With Doriden, "morning hangover" is rare. And Doriden is usually well tolerated—even by aged, chronically ill, or hospitalized patients.
No wonder Doriden is the most widely prescribed nonbarbiturate sedative.

CIBA

Doriden (glutethimide)

JAMA 207, no. 10 (1969): 1942–44.

showing women with children often suggest otherwise. In a 1956 ad for Serpasil, brand name of the hypertensive drug resperine, once given as a mood leveler, a mother screams as her Davy Crockett–inspired son runs through the living room with a toy rifle.

Seated on a couch in a pinafore apron, with a canister-style vacuum cleaner at her feet, the harried mother appears to be screaming and resembles Lucille Ball crying "Awwww, Ricky" on the 1950s sitcom *I Love Lucy*.[17] "Raise the emotional threshold against everyday stresses," says the ad's headline. Serpasil "acts as a gentle mood-leveling agent [and] . . . sets up a needed 'tranquility barrier' for the many patients who, without some help, are incapable of dealing calmly with a daily pile-up of stressful situations."

Today, of course, little Davy Crocketts would be treated for attention deficit hyperactivity disorder (ADHD), oppositional-defiant disorder, conduct disorder, and bipolar disorder. (And husbands whose wives keep them awake would be given sleeping pills.) But today's tradition of giving kids adult medications that are sometimes dangerous was evident decades ago in medical journals.

RAISE THE EMOTIONAL THRESHOLD

against
everyday stresses...

Serpasil in a LOW, ONCE-A-DAY* dose acts as a gentle mood-leveling agent ...sets up a needed "tranquility barrier" for the many patients who, without some help, are incapable of dealing calmly with a daily pile-up of stressful situations.

*As little as 0.25 mg. Serpasil or less once daily may frequently maintain the average patient who is being treated for emotional strain, anxiety and overexcitability... with a minimum of side effects.

TABLETS, 0.1 mg., 0.25 mg. (scored), 1.0 mg. (scored), 2.0 mg. (scored), and 4.0 mg. (scored). ELIXIR, 0.5 mg. or 1.0 mg. per 4-ml. teaspoon.

Serpasil®
(reserpine CIBA)

C I B A *Summit, N.J.*

Psychosomatic Medicine 18, no. 4 (July 1956).

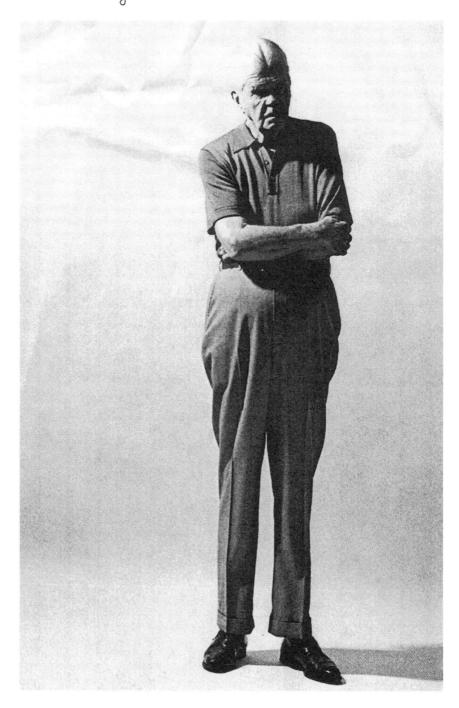

The Collector

At 65 he's collected, among other things, an ailing wife, a decreased income, grown children he seldom sees, and various physical symptoms—real or imagined.

when his collection leads to anxiety or mixed anxiety-depression

Mellaril®
(thioridazine)
25 mg. t.i.d.

JAMA 15, no. 1 (January 4, 1971).

As early as 1956, ads for the antipsychotic Thorazine said it "reduces hyperactivity and aggressiveness, decreases anxiety and hostility [and] improves mood, behavior and sleeping patterns . . . in belligerent, overactive children."[18] It was also advertised for childhood vomiting.[19] The tranquilizer Miltown was similarly advertised for "a wide range of tension/anxietyrelated disorders of children and adolescents, ranging from tics and tantrums to 'school headache' and stammering."[20] And it wasn't only kids whose minor conditions were medicated with major psychoactive drugs. Thorazine was advertised for treatment of alcoholism, asthma, bursitis, arthritis, cancer, the fear of cancer, ulcers, psoriasis, senility, menopause, and hiccups in adults.[21] Yes: hiccups.

The amphetamines and stimulants Benzedrine, Dexedrine®, and Ritalin® were similarly marketed for a breadth of maladies from depression, menopause, and alcoholism to "middle-age and senile let-down" that includes "a sense of frustration and inadequacy" and "waning gonadal function."[22]

Some ads confirm what patients often suspected: that they were a bother to doctors. An ad for the sleeping pill Quaalude said, "Now the physician has one less tired, sleepy and apprehensive patient to contend with."[23] Other ads, especially those addressing elderly and menopausal patients, unabashedly recommend palliation (drugs for what were really life problems not medical problems) with whatever works.

"At 65 he's collected, among other things, an ailing wife, a decreased income, grown children he seldom sees, and various physical symptoms—real or imagined," reads an ad for the Thorazine-like antipsychotic Mellaril, with a full-page photo of a wizened man who looks closer to ninety than sixty-five.[24]

DAWN OF A NEW MARKET

One night in 1997, as Americans were parked on the couch in front of an episode of *Touched by an Angel*, they were touched by something else unexpected: an ad for a prescription allergy pill called Claritin®, promoted directly to the consumer! Prescription drugs had never been sold directly to the public before, because, without a doctor's recommendation, how could people know if the medication was appropriate or safe? Soon, ads for Xenical®, Meridia®, Propecia®, Paxil®, Prozac®, Vioxx, Viagra®, Singulair®, Nasonex®, Allegra®, Flonase®, Pravachol®, Zyrtec®, Zocor®, Flovent®, and Lipitor® followed. By 2006, the pharmaceutical industry (a.k.a. Pharma) was spending $5.5 billion a year on direct-to-consumer (DTC) advertising—as much as the US government was spending for an entire month on the Iraq War.[25]

Although DTC advertising was never illegal, according to the Food and Drug Administration (FDA), it was widely thought to be until the FDA issued guidelines for advertisers in 1997. A push for DTC advertising also came from AIDS patients who wanted greater involvement in their own care and to know what their doctors knew about the drugs they were taking. A funny thing happened as Americans viewed all these pill ads. People discovered they weren't as healthy as they thought. Suddenly, they suffered from seasonal allergies, social anxiety, high cholesterol, depression, bipolar disorder, ADHD, erectile dysfunction, low testosterone, gastroesophageal reflux disease (GERD), irritable bowel syndrome, dry eye, fibromyalgia, chronic fatigue syndrome, seasonal affective disorder (SAD), restless legs syndrome, and worse. In fact, the parade of symptoms and diseases was so all encompassing, comedian Chris Rock said he was ready for a DTC ad asking, "Do you fall asleep at night and wake up in the morning?"

"Yeah, I got that!" he joked.[26]

Before the advent of DTC advertising, gastroesophageal reflux disease,

or GERD, was a hidden epidemic. This condition vaulted Nexium® to the fourth-best-selling drug in the country, once the drug's marketing campaign made people realize they suffered from the problem.[27] "The implication in the direct-to-consumer ads is if you have heartburn you're well on your way to cancer of the esophagus," says Marcia Angell, MD, a former editor of the *New England Journal of Medicine* and author of *The Truth about the Drug Companies*. "For most people who have heartburn, the best way to treat it is probably to lose a little weight, get out and take a walk or drink a glass of milk, but that somehow is seen as less good than taking a prescription drug."[28]

The fact that DTC advertising debuted at the same time as the World Wide Web doubled its power. Even if ads and websites weren't advertising drugs directly to consumers, the world of diseases and prescription drugs, once tucked into *JAMA* ads, was suddenly open to anyone who could operate a mouse. You could even buy drugs online, no doctor or prescription necessary.

Theoretically, all the newly and readily available medical information created a better-informed patient. It was the same reason the trailblazing feminist book *Our Bodies, Ourselves* was published thirty years earlier—patients have the right to know and be participants in their own healthcare. But three features of DTC advertising did more harm than good—unless you were Pharma. Diseases were created or overplayed, sometimes called disease du jours. Risks of disease—fears of getting a condition or the condition getting worse—were whipped up to sell drugs. And extreme drugs were marketed when milder and cheaper drugs would do. The best example of this last point is Vioxx, which was billed as a "super-aspirin" for everyday arthritic or menstrual pain but ended up causing twenty-seven thousand heart attacks and sudden cardiac deaths before its removal from the market in 2004.[29] Yet before Merck even settled the Vioxx cases, the dangerous epilepsy drugs Lyrica®, Topamax®, Neurontin, and Lamictal® and the antidepressant Cymbalta® were similarly marketed for simple pain, even though all carried suicide warnings and Topamax is also linked to birth defects.[30] It was obvious that no lessons had been learned from Vioxx.

Other examples of DTC advertising excess are antipsychotics like Seroquel®, marketed for simple depression and to *children*, and costly, genetically engineered, injected drugs like Prolia®, Humira®, Enbrel, and Remicade®, marketed as first, rather than last, choices in autoimmune conditions. The lucrative but dangerous new drugs, called monoclonal antibodies (moAbs) and tumor necrosis factor (TNF) blockers invite cancers and lethal infections because they suppress the body's immune system, and it can't fight infections.[31] They are even pushed for asthma. In 2008, the FDA announced that forty-five people died from fungal diseases from taking Humira, Enbrel, Remicade, and Cimzia®—20 percent of the 240 patients who got sick.[32] Humira, in particular, was investigated by the FDA in 2008 for thirty reports of childhood cancer and its links to lymphoma, leukemia, and melanoma in children. In 2011, the FDA warned that Humira can cause "a rare cancer of white blood cells"[33] in young people. The same year, five patients died during Humira trials in Italy, and the entire drug class was found to be linked to heart risks.[34]

But when a drug like Humira earns a company an average of $20,000 per patient per year—that's potentially $7 billion a year—cancer, fungal infections, and heart side effects are but details. The deaths might not have been Humira-related but rather "bad luck," said a researcher with the Italian trials, and an avalanche of Pharma articles disputed the heart findings.[35] Meanwhile, Abbott Laboratories is seeking to broaden Humira indications, including an approval for ulcerative colitis.

In addition to normalizing dangerous drugs like Humira, the advent of DTC advertising and health websites led to disease glamorization, a "sickness culture," symptom chasing (cyberchondria), the exchange of incorrect information, and self-diagnosis (the latter because so many sites had "symptom checkers" and self-quizzes). It also changed the doctor/patient relationship forever.

Like the old proverb that whenever a man and a woman are alone together, the third party in the room is the devil, by the late 1990s, whenever a patient and a doctor were alone together, the third party in the room was the web. Patients often asked the doctor for a drug they had self-prescribed for a disease they had self-diagnosed, reducing the doctor to a mere order taker or gatekeeper. And, even though the DTC-demoted doctors could push back and ask, "What medical school did *you* go to?" they *also* went to the web get information.

To prevent snake oil selling, the FDA required that DTC ads mention risks and dangerous side effects associated with a drug. Pharma detested the risk mandates because it needed to buy twice the air time—sixty-second TV spots instead of the thirty-second spots most advertisers bought. Pharma preferred online "reminder ads" that showed only the drug's name and indication, piggybacking off all the advertising to date but without risk data. But the FDA ruled in 2009 that reminder ads *also* had to show risks—within the ad, not "one click away," on the drug's website. This forced Pharma to add a scroll window for risk information, since the side effects would take up too much room if displayed at once.

Risk information often amounted to a second ad that seemed to be created by the drug's evil twin. While health warnings can obviously fail, as with cigarettes, some wondered if the parade of drug side effect risks—"brain bleeds, sudden death, difficulty breathing, stomach bleeding, liver failure, kidney failure, muscle breakdown, fainting, hallucinations, cataracts, seizures, gout, severe and debilitating pain, skin rash, difficulty swallowing"—could actually *sell* the drug by tapping into some kind of national death wish. After all, buried skulls and the word *death* in ad copy subliminally sold consumer products in the 1950s, according to the bestseller *The Hidden Persuaders* by Vance Packard.[36]

People generally like DTC drug advertising for the same reason they like advertising in general—it's entertaining and designed to be liked and relevant. Ad agencies, after all, brim with writers and artists talented enough to be in fine arts or academia, if they weren't selling Drāno® and Turtle Wax. As far as whether the DTC ads work, most believe that the ads make the *other guy* desire and ask for a drug, but not them. (The same thing medical professionals say about "gifts" from Pharma—that they make other doctors prescribe a drug, but not them.)

GO ON, BE HAPPY

From the debut of Prozac in 1988, ten years before DTC advertising, one of the top-performing drug categories was depression drugs. In fact, the discovery that people with real-life problems with their jobs, the economy, and their families would term it "depression" sailed Pharma through the 1990s and 2000s. Unlike drugs like Valium and Librium, which were taken as needed—which the new antidepressants replaced (because anxiety was now "really depression")—the new antidepressants were taken every day, for years.

In fact, ten years after DTC advertising began, the number of Americans on antidepressants had doubled to twenty-seven million, or 10 percent of the population.[37] During the same time period, the number of doctor visits where individuals were prescribed antidepressants even though they had no psychiatric diagnoses increased from 59.5 percent to 72.7 and accounted for four out of five antidepressant prescriptions.[38] A growing number of people were also prescribed antipsychotics, and the number of people undergoing psychotherapy shrank.[39] Both insurers and patients preferred pills to psychotherapy because they were quicker, easier, and fun. Who says advertising doesn't work? But three things began to dry up the depression gravy train for Pharma. Blockbusters like Prozac, Paxil, and Zoloft®, called SSRIs (or selective serotonin reuptake inhibitors), went off patent (meaning they were no longer protected by lucrative brand-name patents and were now open to competition from the same drugs, manufactured as generics and costing a fraction of their patent prices), antidepressants were linked with gory and unpredictable violence, and they *didn't even work* in many cases, according to medical articles in *JAMA*.[40]

Even before a *JAMA* article in 2010 suggested that in mild depression, antidepressants don't work, reports of "Prozac Poop-out" in which patients develop a tolerance to the antidepressants and they quit working surfaced in the medical and general press. "Prozac wears off within a year for about one-third of those who take it," said *Harvard* magazine.[41]

Human nature might be a contributor to poop-out, too, said psychiatrist Phillip Sinaikin. "An antidepressant not working anymore is no different from getting used to anything that used to thrill us," said Sinaikin in an interview about his book *Psychiatryland*.[42] "We buy our dream house with two bedrooms and a garage, and after a while it doesn't make us happy anymore, and we are eyeing the house with three bedrooms and a pool. Another example, of course, is falling in and out of love."

Ineffective antidepressants and poop-out are no doubt the reason DTC ads began spinning the idea of "add-on" drugs and "treatment-resistant con-

ditions," which supported the lucrative but inexact practice of polypharmacy, or drug "cocktails."

Ads for the atypical (referred to as such because they were thought to be different from older antipsychotics like Thorazine) antipsychotic Abilify® unabashedly hawked it as an add-on drug to the antidepressants Prozac, Paxil,

Zoloft, Effexor®, and Lexapro, saying that "approximately 2 out of 3 people being treated for depression still have unresolved symptoms."[43] The ads don't say why people should stay on the original drugs that don't work.

"Treatment-resistant depression" similarly kept people taking iffy drugs. Your first expensive and dangerous drug needed to be coupled with *more* expensive and dangerous drugs because monotherapy, one drug alone, wasn't doing the trick. It wasn't that the drugs didn't work (or you didn't have depression in the first place), you had "treatment-resistant depression."

You've got to admire Pharma's audacity with this upsell strategy— also known as trying to get people to spend more money. Adding drugs to a treatment-resistant depression triples its take; patients don't know which drug is working, so they'll take all of them, and the defective drugs are exonerated— because the problem is the patient! Entire new psychiatric drug approvals were based on nothing more than this add-on use.

Of course, if people were paying for the drugs out of their pocket, and they were told to add a drug that costs almost $500 a month because the first one isn't working, they would say the only thing "treatment resistant" is your sales pitch—and to go find another fool. But since third-party payers carry the freight, no one seems to mind the scheme—or even notice it. In fact, psychiatric drug cocktails of eight, ten, and twelve drugs are common now, even though the drugs have seldom been tested when taken together—unless you count the patients taking them now.

There was another trick to keep the antidepressant boat afloat. Your depression is "progressive," said DTC ads. Once upon a time, when depression was neither seasonal, atypical, bipolar, nor treatment resistant, it was considered to be a self-limiting disease. In fact, just about the only good thing you could say about depression was that it wouldn't last forever. But, by 2010, DTC ads were giving depression the same "don't wait" scare treatment used to sell statins, add-on asthma controller drugs, and bone drugs. If you don't hurry and take medication, your depression will get worse!

"Depressive episodes become more easily triggered over time," floats an article on the doctor education website Medscape (flanked by ads for the antidepressant Pristiq®). "As the number of major depressive episodes increase, the risk for subsequent episodes is predicted more from the number of prior episodes and less from the occurrence of a recent life stress."[44] Translation: your depression gets worse on its own, regardless of the stress in your life. The article, unabashedly titled "Neurobiology of Depression: Major Depressive Disorder as a Progressive Illness," was written by Vladimir Maletic, MD, who has served on Eli Lilly and Company's Speakers Bureau, says the disclosure information, and whose coauthors are each employees and/or Eli Lilly shareholders.

An article on WebMD, sister site to Medscape, also "sells" depression. An article called "Depression: Recognizing the Physical Symptoms," smothered with five ads for the Eli Lilly antidepressant Cymbalta, submits, "Most of us know about the emotional symptoms of depression. But you may not know that depression can be associated with many physical symptoms, too."[45] Depression may masquerade as headaches, insomnia, fatigue, backache, dizziness, lightheadedness, or appetite problems, mongers the article. "You might feel queasy or nauseous. You might have diarrhea or become chronically constipated."[46] And you thought it was something you ate!

The danger with these symptoms, says the article, is that you would fail to diagnose yourself as suffering from a psychiatric problem and buy an over-the-counter drug like a normal person. "Because these symptoms occur with many conditions, many depressed people never get help, because they don't know that their physical symptoms might be caused by depression. A lot of doctors miss the symptoms, too."[47]

To prevent such loss of potential market share, the article counsels worry and fear about your symptoms. "Don't assume they'll go away on their own." Symptoms may "need additional treatment" and "some antidepressants, such as Cymbalta and Effexor, may help with chronic pain, too."[48] The article's content was "selected and controlled by WebMD's editorial staff" and "funded by Lilly USA," says disclosure information. Eli Lilly was an original WebMD financial partner, according to the *Washington Post*.[49]

Millions of children were on ADHD medication even before DTC advertising. But since DTC advertising, adults have also been told they have concentration and attention problems. "Can't stay awake at work? Working odd hours or a shift schedule?" asked radio ads in 2011. "You could be suffering from shift work sleep disorder!" Shift work sleep disorder (SWSD), said the campaign from Cephalon, who makes the Schedule IV (the category most

highly controlled) stimulants Provigil® and Nuvigil®, affects one out of four people working nontraditional schedules. That would be a lot of people—if anyone had a job today.

Shift work sleep disorder (a disruption of the natural circadian sleep rhythms) is characterized by trouble focusing, increased irritability, and poor work performance—think ADHD (though perhaps lacking the hyperkinesis)—says a website called the Wake-Up Squad.[50] But don't think the answer is a simple renegotiation with your alarm clock, says the site. "Just improving your sleep may not improve your ability to cope with shift work."[51] The site offers a self-quiz to see if you have SWSD and does not mention any drug name.

Of course, it's not too difficult to sell speed. As the street dealers say, "The first taste is free." Stimulants are so addictive, mothers confess to pilfering from their ADHD-diagnosed kids. But DTC ads give people other reasons to take uppers (besides the high), like excessive daytime sleepiness (EDS), sleep apnea, narcolepsy, and non-restful sleep (NRS). Notice how a best-selling disease ideally has catchy initials?

In fact, the only reasons for wakefulness problems that the ads *don't blame* are not getting enough sleep and doing something boring. Remember the slogan on T-shirts that used to say, "I drink to make other people more interesting?" The same claim is made for speed, which is why it's a favorite with factory workers, long-distance truck drivers, and students—it makes repetitive tasks more interesting. Only recently did people doing boring work start having a "disease."

"You may 'suffer from Excessive Daytimes Sleepiness,'" said ads in college newspapers in Chicago trying to recruit students for clinical trials to test stimulants. "Being sleepy throughout the day is more than just a nuisance, it's a heavy burden."[52] "Struggling to Fight the Fog?" asks an ad for the stimulant Provigil® that shows a judge in his black robe, nodding out on the job. ("Yo! Your Honor! I'm trying to plead!") An ad for Vyvanse in *Men's Fitness* magazine shows a family happily engrossed in TV—because Dad has speed for his "adult ADHD."[53]

Of course, you can't very well discuss daytime sleepiness without talking about insomnia. Not getting enough sleep certainly contributes to excessive daytime sleepiness, but "wakefulness drugs" also contribute to insomnia. Sleeping pills have not been Pharma's finest hour. In the 1960s, barbiturates were immortalized by Marilyn Monroe's death and by the 1967 movie *Valley of the Dolls*, which starred Sharon Tate, Patty Duke, and Barbara Parkins.

In 1970, sleeping pills known as "reds" were indicted for "sweet Jane's" downfall in the Grateful Dead song "Truckin'": Jane was "livin' on reds, vitamin C, and cocaine."[54] In 1993, the sleeping pill Halcion® was banned in the United Kingdom and other countries for causing amnesia, paranoia, depression, hallucinations, and violence in users. Travelers, among its biggest users, would find themselves on the other side of the Atlantic Ocean and not remember boarding a plane.[55] And in 2001, a similar pill, Dalmane, was said to "increase the risk of an injurious accident more than five times normal," at FDA/National Transportation Safety Board hearings.[56]

Still-newer sleeping pills like Ambien®, Lunesta®, Sonata®, and Rozerem are a gold mine for Pharma because everyone sleeps or watches TV when they can't. Even though in FDA documents, one sleeping pill, Rozerem, was no better than a placebo, its sales shot up 60 percent because of its DTC advertising, reported the *New York Times*.[57]

To churn the insomnia market, Pharma rolled out subcategories like it did with depression. There was chronic, acute, transient, initial, delayedonset, middle-of-the-night, waking up four to five hours after falling asleep and not being able to get back to sleep, and early-morning wakening; menopausal insomnia; and, of course, non-restful sleep. In India, the sleeping pill Zolfresh® is advertised as making *people live longer*, with no medical evidence and in spite of the fact that DTC advertising is illegal there, says pharmaceutical reporter Ed Silverman.[58]

Thanks to former Rhode Island representative Patrick Kennedy, many became aware of the downside to sleeping pills. Who can forget how the congressman drove to Capitol Hill to "vote" at 2:45 a.m. in 2006 on Ambien and crashed his car (he had also been taking Phenergan, a gastroenteritis drug that can cause drowsiness)?

Kennedy's apparent blackout may have been from more than Ambien, but blackouts caused just by Ambien soon came to the attention of authorities. The FDA issued warnings about the potential of "complex sleep-related behaviors" that may include "sleep-driving, making phone calls and preparing and eating food (while asleep)" while on Ambien and twelve other sleeping pills in 2007.[59]

Law enforcement officials reported that traffic accidents increased because of Ambien with some drivers not even recognizing the police officers there to arrest them.[60] Horror stories also began to circulate about svelte dieters waking up amid mountains of pizza, Krispy Kreme® donuts, and Häagen-Dazs® cartons consumed by their evil twins when they took Ambien. Sanofi-

Aventis, Ambien's manufacturer, was forced to publish ads telling people if they were going to take Ambien, to get in bed and stay there.

But the can't-sleep-because-of-the stimulants/can't-wake-up-because-of-the-sleeping-pills blues was not really new. The nation had done the same yin-yang dance with "bennies" (Benzedrine) and "barbs" (barbiturates) during the 1960s.

BUT THEY COULDN'T SAY IT IF IT WEREN'T TRUE . . .

In 1962, the same year thalidomide was given to pregnant women for morning sickness outside the United States, Congress strengthened drug laws and added the concept of effectiveness to the definition of "new drug." That meant drug manufacturers couldn't market a drug for non-approved indications, known today as "off-label" marketing. "The initial claim would tend to be quite limited," said a group of senators, led by Tennessee's Estes Kefauver. "Thereafter, the sky would be the limit. Extreme claims of any kind could be made."[61]

Indeed. Most of the huge fraud and/or wrongdoing settlements in recent years against drug giants like Pfizer, AstraZeneca, and Eli Lilly center on offlabel marketing—selling drugs for conditions they have not been proven safe or effective to treat.[62] Because it's legal for doctors to prescribe a drug for non-FDA-approved uses—but it's not legal to advertise it for such uses—a lot of such advertising is disguised as journal articles and continuing medical education (CME) courses offered by Pharma. Scores of journal articles promoting hormone therapy for menopausal women to prevent heart disease and cognitive decline, for example (non-FDA uses and erroneous) were planted by Wyeth-paid functionaries, according to court-obtained documents.[63]

And even though the epilepsy drug Neurontin (also used for nerve pain) is only FDA-approved for postherpetic pain (pain that follows shingles) and as an add-on drug for partial seizures (and even though Pfizer settled off-label marketing Neurontin charges in 2004), it is still brazenly promoted for off-label uses. A CME course on Medscape asserts that Neurontin "appeared to be well tolerated and effective as migraine prophylaxis," and that epilepsy drugs in general may have a role in "treating headache, facial pain, and mood disorders."[64]

Before the Vioxx scandal in 2004, and the big fraud settlements and loss of patents a few years later, being a Pharma rep was probably the next best thing to working on Wall Street. Direct-to-consumer advertising did your presell for you, and all you had to do was show up with your snappy Vytorin® tote bag and samples case. Some Pharma reps had their own reception room with ice water, swivel chairs, and laptop ports at medical offices, and most waltzed in ahead of waiting and sick patients. Pharma usually hires "hotties" for sales reps—women often sporting spike heels and cleavage, men often "beefcake"—which also helps their reception by office staff.[65]

But, by 2011, the bloom had fallen off the Pharma reps' roses. The number of prescribers willing to see most reps fell almost 20 percent, the number refusing to see all reps increased by half, and eight million sales calls "could not be completed," reported ZS Associates.[66] Pharma was also discovering that online advertising, "speakers bureaus" (in which one doctor is hired to present to others), and continuing medical education courses were a better bang for the buck than old-fashioned shoe leather sales reps. Not all doctors hide their antipathy toward Pharma sales reps. Salt Lake City family doctor Ross Brunetti estimated that six reps called on his office every morning, and six more in the afternoon. "In a week, I might see three people trying to sell me the same thing," he says, adding, "On Friday, when they want to get out early and go skiing, they're all here, all in the morning. There are more drug reps than patients. It's like a minefield."[67]

While Brunetti said the reps are only tolerated for the drugs they leave, "for people who can't pay," there is a growing movement among medical professionals concerned about Pharma influence to refuse even free samples. Not only are they an inducement to prescribe more expensive drugs, not necessarily appropriately; the samples seldom go to needy patients and are often more free gifts to the doctors, their staff, and their families to use, critics say. The backlash against free samples and Pharma gifts in general coalesced in 2007, when the sixty-two-thousand-member American Medical Student Association (AMSA) debuted its "scorecard" program, which grades the nation's 150 medical schools on their policies toward Pharma gifts, consulting and speaker fees, and disclosure information.

"The scorecard program has changed the landscape because medical schools really understand grades," said Nitin Roper, MD, then a recent graduate and AMSA member.[68] "Schools which originally wouldn't give us their policies suddenly thought their grades were unfair. In a revealing turn of the tables, one medical school contacted our student organization to request its D grade be changed to a C+."

At the 2010 American Psychiatric Association meeting, there were fewer Pharma-funded classes, not to mention less entertainment and free food. "They used to wine us and dine us," one participant complained.[69] "An SSRI maker flew my entire group to a Caribbean island," remembered a psychiatrist from the East Coast who did not want to be identified. Exhibition displays on the sales floor were still pretty gee-whizzy—an entire children's bedroom was constructed to sell an ADHD medication—but where "take one" signs had once appeared, there were now signs explaining the new "no gift" policies.[70]

Pharma marketing might be further dampened by a proposed "Pharmaceutical Inverse Benefit Law" that two researchers have devised based on the premise that the more heavily a drug is promoted, the less its benefits compare with its risks. The law's authors, Howard Brody, MD, and Donald W. Light, PhD, warn of six marketing strategies "that create an environment in which prescribing certain drugs could undermine, rather than promote patient safety and public health."[71] The marketing strategies include exaggerating safety and efficacy claims, relying on surrogate end points (assumptions from short studies), encouraging off-label use, reducing "thresholds for diagnosing diseases," and actually *creating new 'diseases.'*"[72]

Then Harvard professor Jerry Avorn, MD, author of *Powerful Medicines*, also cited surrogate end points (which suggest but don't prove a drug's safety and effectiveness) at a conference about Critical Prescribing Skills in Chicago. "We are spending billions on Vytorin to lower cholesterol, yet the drug has not been proven to prevent heart disease and Avandia [a diabetes drug] causes a 40 percent increase in heart attacks," he said.[73] The research projects presented at the Critical Prescribing Skills conference were funded by a Pfizer settlement for off-label marketing of Neurontin and intended to help medical centers and other health groups develop training products for prescribers to prevent *future* Neurontins. One training product to help doctors defend against unapproved uses is a "pharmaceutical marketing elective" at the University of Illinois—

Chicago, in which former sales reps demonstrate their sales techniques to medical students. A project at University of Vermont College teaches doctors *refusal skills* for patients who come in waving direct-to-consumer ads.

Even though writing a prescription may seem quicker, "explaining to a patient why a highly advertised drug might not be appropriate only takes three minutes," said Richard Pinckney, MD, then professor at the University of Vermont College of Medicine, "and the insurance savings could pay for programs like these." The Vermont project included "secret shoppers" asking doctors for a brand-name insomnia drug to see how well training worked.[74] "Doctors have a hard time saying no if a drug is effective, even if it is expensive," agreed Audiey Kao, MD, then vice president of ethics at the American Medical Association, which also created training products shown at the conference.[75] A video developed by Consumers Union, which publishes *Consumer Reports*, for patients to view before receiving a prescription resulted in one-third asking to speak to their doctors or pharmacists after viewing it. Fifteen percent of patients changed the drug they requested.[76]

Another gray marketing area in DTC advertising is what might be called off-label *distribution*—advertising a drug for a disease that affects a small part of the population to a much larger general population, in case there are more "takers" who think they might have the disease or want the drug. A good example is the genetically engineered, injected drug Humira, first used to treat rheumatoid arthritis. Despite the FDA's clear warnings about its dangers, inserts advertising Humira to treat the intestinal tract condition known as Crohn's disease, a subsequent approval, which affects only 1 percent of the population, were inserted in Chicago college and weekly newspapers.[77] Humira ads reading "Hate psoriasis. Love clearer skin," run in weekly celebrity magazines like they are selling skin moisturizers instead of a subcutaneous drug that suppresses the immune system.

When a reporter asked the then Abbott vice president of specialty operations Heather Mason why a drug that costs up to $20,000 a year and treats rare conditions was advertised to general audiences on TV, she said, "Rheumatoid arthritis is a market where people often don't know what they have for a while" and it is often "misdiagnosed."[78] A condition is so subtle people don't know they have it, but it is so serious it needs an immune-suppressing drug?

The FDA's Division of Drug Marketing, Advertising, and Communications (DDMAC) is in charge of monitoring Pharma materials for fraudulent and off-label marketing claims and undisclosed risks. At least in theory. But the staff of thirty can only spot-check the avalanche of marketing pieces it receives per year—more than seventy thousand, said Amy Toscano, then a DDMAC pharmacist.[79]

Since drug companies do not have to get permission for new marketing claims in their advertising and promotional materials—they only have to *inform* DDMAC of what they are doing—misleading ad campaigns can and do run. And what happens when they do? Companies get love letters like this one, sent to Eli Lilly: "DDMAC requests that Lilly immediately cease the dissemination of violative promotional material for Cymbalta, Evista and Gemzar, such as those described above," DDMAC wrote the drug giant in 2009.[80] "Please submit a written response to this letter on or before April 9, 2009, stating whether you intend to comply with this request." *Whether you intend to comply?* Maybe the DDMAC should be running the IRS!

Why would an FDA warning letter about illegal advertising influence Pharma when billion-dollar settlements over Zyprexa® and Bextra marketing haven't? asked Bruce L. Lambert, PhD, then a professor in the Department of Pharmacy Administration at the University of Illinois–Chicago, at the Critical Prescribing Skills conference. "Doesn't the FDA have the authority to take stronger actions?"[81] Why are "disease awareness" ads allowed to begin with? asked Women's Health Network executive director Cindy Pearson at the conference. They "appear to 'educate' but really create and monger diseases to sell drugs."[82]

In 2010, the FDA, under President Obama–appointed commissioner Margaret Hamburg, announced a whistle-blowing program to widen DDMAC's net. Anyone seeing misleading ads that market a drug for off-label uses and/or that hide the drug's risks can report them directly to DDMAC through a dedicated e-mail address, badad@fda.gov. But the biggest users of the turnin-a-bad-ad program so far are not patients or doctors but competing drug companies, says DDMAC's Amy Toscano.[83] They certainly know the rules.

SELLING SOAP, COLA, AND . . . PSYCHIATRIC DRUGS

Like consumer-product advertising in general, DTC advertising relies on the time-tested triad of positioning ("the King of Beers"), benefit ("Healthy Choice," "SnackWell"), and repetition. Repetition is so important to product recall, some broadcast ads repeat immediately, literally running back-to-back, causing consumers to think it's a mistake. It's no mistake, and the very fact that consumers notice it means the repetition works. Medication ads are so much like other consumer-product ads that the wacky "Can Your Beer Do This?" Miller Lite campaign of the 1990s came back to life to sell the antidepressant Wellbutrin XR®. In a glossy, color magazine ad, a young man rows his girlfriend on a scenic lake and lists the benefits of his Wellbutrin XR. "Can your medicine do all that?" he asks.[84] When an ad affixes a "your" in front of the noun it is trying to sell—"your mouthwash," "your pain reliever," "your engine treatment," "your teeth whitener"—it implies that if you don't already have a mouthwash or engine treatment, *you should*. What does it say about the saturation of psychiatric drugs in the community that "antidepressants" have joined mouthwashes and engine treatments as something people are assumed to have?

Another snappy way to sell a product is to elevate it to an experience. Who remembers ads for the "Kodak Moment," the "Maalox® Moment," and even the "L&M® Moment" from years ago? Sure enough, the sleeping pill Lunesta deploys such "experience" advertising with "Lunesta Sleep. Have You Tried It?" in a 2007 *Parade* magazine ad.[85]

Taking on the competition is also a revered advertising tradition ever since Avis Rent-A-Car called itself "Number Two" in relation to Hertz, and 7-UP® called itself the "Uncola." "I asked for one good reason to stick with Actonel®. My doctor gave me seven," says a full-page color ad for a bone drug in the *New York Times*, depicting a fifty-something woman in a denim jacket with arrows pointing to her collarbone, spine, upper arm, wrist, pelvis, hip, and leg—the seven reasons.[86] "What about the new osteoporosis medicine, Boniva®?" the Actonel copy asks, referring to its competitor and the drug the woman won't switch to. "Boniva is not proven to prevent fractures beyond the spine," says the ad, answering its own question. What is really going on in the ad, according to *Advertising Age*, is Actonel's manufacturer is getting back at the makers of Boniva because "once-monthly" Boniva stole market share from once-weekly Actonel.[87] Patients don't like having to wait sixty minutes before eating or drinking anything and remaining completely upright, as they have to do after swallowing the bone drugs. So the Actonel ad seeks to find an area where Boniva is inferior—like not preventing other fractures, as it charges.

Unfortunately, the joke was on both Actonel and Boniva when the FDA issued a warning in 2010 that all the drugs in their class could cause the very fractures they were supposed to prevent, and Evista, a bone drug that worked differently, slammed them both. "You can take Evista at any time of day, with or without food," said full-page ads in the *New York Times*.

When DTC advertising began, it relied on the product-marketing work-horse of celebrity endorsement. Television personality Joan Lunden and baseball player Mike Piazza pushed the allergy pill Claritin; model Lauren Hutton, hormone replacement therapy; singer Wynonna Judd, the diet drug allī®; actresses Sally Field and Brooke Shields, Boniva and Latisse®, respectively; skater Dorothy Hamill and track star Bruce Jenner, the pain pill Vioxx; former Sen. Bob Dole, Viagra; and Dr. Robert Jarvik, Lipitor. NASCAR figure Bobby Labonte even endorsed Wellbutrin XL in a print ad in 2004.[88]

But unlike regular advertising in which a celebrity could taint a product with an ethics scandal or jail sentence (like Tiger Woods or Martha Stewart), the opposite was occurring: *pills* were becoming the bad actors, like Vioxx, which increased heart attacks, and hormone replacement therapy, which increased cancer, according to a large federal study.[89] So many blockbuster drugs seemed to be recalled, Pharma even declared an advertising moratorium for drugs under one year old in a "don't regulate us; we'll police ourselves!" plea to the government.[90] The moratorium was so short; it also seemed to last under one year. Meanwhile, celebrity ads like a ubiquitous Lipitor commercial with Robert Jarvik, MD, the inventor of the Jarvik artificial heart, drove congressional hearings in 2008. "In the ads, Dr. Jarvik appears to be giving medical advice, but apparently, he has never obtained a license to practice or prescribe medicine," said former senator John Dingell (D-MI), then chairman of the House Committee on Energy and Commerce.[91]

Celebrity/Pharma links are not always disclosed. When actress Kathleen

Turner shared her battle with rheumatoid arthritis on CNN in 2002, she didn't share the names of the arthritis drug manufacturers who were funding her, says the *Philadelphia Inquirer*.[92] And who knew that TV talk show host Meredith Vieira's zeal against osteoporosis was augmented by the money that bone-drug maker Merck & Co. was giving her?[93]

THE BLACK HAND OF UNBRANDED MESSAGES

It's happened to anyone who's attended an open-mike session at an FDA advisory committee hearing. A queue of patients seems to materialize out of nowhere to testify, often in tears, about the need for *crucial approval* of a drug that the public has often not even heard of. Sometimes the drug has not been approved by the FDA at all, but often it has been approved but just not for the use the patients want, and so it's available, but the cost is not reimbursable from insurance companies. "When insurers balk at reimbursing patients for new prescription medications, these groups typically swing into action, rallying sufferers to appear before public and consumer panels, contact lawmakers, and provide media outlets [with] a human face to attach to a cause," writes Melissa Healy, then a reporter at the *Los Angeles Times*.[94]

Psychiatric groups like the Depression and Bipolar Support Alliance, which gets half its funding from Pharma and the National Alliance on Mental Illness (NAMI), which received $23 million in just two years from Pharma, are often the most vocal because of the huge cost of psychiatric medicines.[95] "For years, the alliance [NAMI] has fought states' legislative efforts to limit doctors' freedom to prescribe drugs, no matter how expensive, to treat mental illness in patients who rely on government health care programs like Medicaid," says the *New York Times*.[96] "Some of these medicines routinely top the list of the most expensive drugs that states buy for their poorest patients." But mental health groups have plenty of company. Of twenty-nine nonprofit patient-advocacy groups studied by *New Scientist*, most, including the American Heart Association and Colorectal Cancer Coalition, accepted funds from companies making drugs the patients use.[97]

And Pharma has another use for fake groups besides stumping for expensive drugs. It uses them as front groups for "disease awareness" campaigns that establish a condition or disorder as a looming public health problem. So-called unbranded advertising seeks to convey the breadth and heartbreak of a hitherto unpromoted disease without mentioning any drug by name, like the Shift Work Sleep Disorder campaign. It is often disguised as a public service announcement (PSA), which radio and TV stations run for free, like "smoke detectors save lives" messages, in the interest of the "public good."

One such PSA campaign, funded by the Depression and Bipolar Support Alliance, NAMI, and other groups, likens depression to cancer, heart disease, and "other life-threatening diseases," because it kills, and then it compares the disease to diabetes because it doesn't go away. "Nobody ever says, 'it's nothing serious, it's just heart disease.' So why do some say that about depression?" ask the free ads, which played on major radio stations in 2011.[98]

Thanks to unbranded advertising, almost anytime you hear that a disease is more serious than people think, or more widespread, you can start being suspicious. Whether it's an "educational campaign" from one of Pharma's advertising and public relations firms or a medical article or CME course by Pharma-paid doctors, the hallmarks of unbranded advertising are (1) the disease is "underdiagnosed," "misdiagnosed," and "underreported," (2) there are "stigmas" and "barriers" that keep patients from treatment, and (3) there are "hidden costs" to society.

Joel M. Kremer, MD, then a consultant to Humira-maker Abbott, gave a good example of "hidden cost" spin when he defended the drug's high price for treating rheumatoid arthritis to the *New York Times*.[99] "Inadequately treated rheumatoid arthritis typically leads to multiple joint replacements, lost productivity, lost tax revenue and a greatly diminished quality of life, as well as an increased risk of life-threatening infections and cardiovascular disease," he said. "You have to consider what it costs to fix a bridge against what it will cost when the bridge collapses." He does not mention the cancers and lethal infections that could also be considered. Stephen Hanauer, MD, then another Abbott consultant, agrees that early Humira treatment reduces "overall costs" and enhances "patients' quality of life" in a medical journal.[100] Abbott gave Humira free to elderly patients in 2003 ("first taste, free") while it lobbied Congress to get the drug covered by Medicare. Look at all the patients who crave this drug! The stunt worked, too.[101] The Cochrane Collaboration, a not-for-profit international organization, says drugs like Humira are linked to "adverse events and TB reactivation" and need "long-term safety" studies.[102]

A multipage advertising supplement in the *New York Times* magazine reveals classic unbranded advertising from a Pharma public relations firm.[103] First, the article, funded by "assorted advertisers," trumpets that the percentage of adults with bipolar illness is "significantly higher than was previously estimated" and that "as many as 80 percent of individuals with bipolar disorder go undiagnosed—and untreated." Then the supplement segues into the hidden financial toll. "The indirect costs of bipolar disorder were estimated to be $26 billion." "A third of all spouses of patients with bipolar illness develop serious depression and anxiety themselves."[104] And when caretakers and patients don't get prescription drug help, another groups suffers too: Pharma.

Sometimes Pharma conducts an awareness campaign in advance of a drug's approval to build buzz. In 2010, Germany-based Boehringer Ingelheim Pharmaceuticals told the world about the major public health problem of female "hypoactive sexual desire disorder" (HSDD)—for which it happened to have a drug candidate under FDA consideration, flibanserin.[105] Flibanserin, dubbed the Pink Viagra by the press, is an antidepressant-like drug, chemically closer to older antidepressants like Buspar and Serzone® than Prozac and Paxil. It was rolled out at the European Society for Sexual Medicine's annual meeting in Lyon, France, in 2009 as an exciting new treatment for libido-impaired women. Volunteers reported the number of "satisfying sexual encounters" per month almost doubled.

In 2010, Boehringer-Ingelheim launched a "Sex Brain Body: Make the Connection" campaign to raise HSDD "awareness," starring TV personality Lisa Rinna. Despite her sexy appearance, reported *CBS News*, the actress says "she suffered from sexual dysfunction and wants to help other women with the condition, which is widely accepted for men, but not for women."[106] "The new educational campaign will focus on female sexual health and highlight the role the brain is thought to play in desire."

As hypoactive sexual desire disorder took off as a disease, the Discovery Channel launched a CME course for credit called Understanding Female

Sexual Desire: The Brain-Body Connection.[107] A web article blared, "If There is No Desire to Get Physically Romantic, You Could Be Suffering from HSDD," with a racy boudoir photo. And ads on the inside cover of a major medical journal hyped the new public health problem of women's lack of sexual desire without mentioning a specific drug treatment. Some gynecologists, sex researchers, and women welcomed the attention to female sexuality. Why should men have all the fun with drugs like Viagra? they asked. But others saw HSDD marketing as another way of pathologizing women when they didn't comply with male ideals and expectations—no different from early Pharma ads recommending drugs for women who failed to be good mothers and wives.

"I have long had a problem with the tendency of the healthcare system, aided and abetted by the pharmaceutical industry, to diagnose as a problem a symptom or sign experienced by the majority of people," wrote Ingrid Nygaard, MD, in an *Obstetrics & Gynecology* editorial, citing HSDD as one example.[108] The escalating diagnoses might be driven by grants, stock shares, and providers' need for income, she wrote.

There were safety questions about the Pink Viagra, too; clinical trials were marred with side effects like dizziness, nausea, fatigue, and somnolence.[109] And there were dosing questions. Would women want to change their bodily chemistry every day for a few enchanted nights? Unlike Viagra, the Pink Viagra would have to be taken every day—and women had largely rejected a similar prospect when Sarafem® (Prozac) was recommended for the days they had premenstrual syndrome (PMS) symptoms, because it would have to be taken every day.

Despite HSDD's audacious unbranded advertising and the billions of dollars a true Pink Viagra would earn Pharma, when it came to the drug's approval, the FDA had a headache. Flibanserin was rejected for use in treating HSDD not because of safety concerns but because it was not effective, said the FDA. Still, Boehringer Ingelheim remained a believer. "We remain convinced of the positive benefit-risk ratio of flibanserin for women suffering with HSDD," said Professor Andreas Barner, then professor with the board of managing directors at Boehringer Ingelheim.[110]

Before direct-to-consumer advertising, the healthcare system was devoted to preventing overtreatment and assuring patients they were probably okay. Who remembers "Take two aspirin and call me in the morning"? But whereas ads once told doctors that their patients had hidden "coexisting depression," patients now tell their doctors they have hidden "coexisting depression" and come into the office clutching coupons and demanding prescriptions. DTC advertising works so well, it practically does the drug-sales reps' jobs for them. The fact that the doctors have to be taught "refusal skills" shows the great pressure, even if doctors know the drug isn't appropriate.

Of course, hypochondria is not new, but a national hypochondria of people self-diagnosing a disease and self-prescribing a drug treatment is. So are disease "clubs" that people can join, like Sally Field's "My Boniva" and Nuvigil's "Wake-Up Squad." Does having a disease give people a feeling of identity, importance, or drama in their lives, like the little French girls in the children's book *Madeline* who want their appendices removed like the heroine? Or is experimenting on yourself with prescription drugs just a new kind of "recreation"?

Either way, promoting diseases to sell more drugs is not innocent or harmless. Prescription drugs kill more people a year than traffic accidents—and that doesn't count traffic accidents *caused* by prescription drugs.[111] And while DTC advertising may look like a free lunch for TV, radio, magazines, websites, medical journals, ad agencies, public relations agencies, pharmacies, and benefits managers—it's as "free" as the subprime mortgage. Both the ads and the drugs are ultimately paid for by taxpayers, through government entitlement programs and private insurance policy holders. The only free lunch is Pharma's.

Chapter 2
FRAGILE
HANDLE WITH RISPERDAL . . . AND SEROQUEL AND ZYPREXA AND GEODON

In his book *Psychiatryland*, psychiatrist Phillip Sinaikin recounts reading a scientific article in which it was debated whether a three-year-old girl who ran out into traffic had oppositional-defiant disorder or bipolar disorder, the latter marked by "grandiose delusions" that she was special and cars could not harm her.[1]

How did the once modest medical specialty of child psychiatry become the aggressive "pediatric psychopharmacology" that finds ADHD, pediatric conduct disorder, depression, bipolar disorder, oppositional defiant disorder, mood disorders, obsessive-compulsive disorders, mixed manias, social phobia, anxiety, sleep disorders, borderline disorders, assorted "spectrum" disorders, irritability, aggression, pervasive development disorders, personality disorders, and even schizophrenia under every rock? And how did this branch of psychiatry come to find the answer to the "psychopathologies" in the name of the discipline itself: pediatric psycho**pharmacology**? Just good marketing. Pharma is wooing the pediatric patient because that's where the money is. Just like country-and-western songs about finding love where you can when there is no love to be found at home. Pharma has stopped finding "love" in the form of the new blockbuster drugs that catapulted it through the 1990s and 2000s. According to the *Wall Street Journal*, new drugs made Pharma only $4.3 billion in 2010 compared with $11.8 billion in 2005—a two-thirds drop.[2]

Doctors have a "growing fear of prescribing new drugs with unknown side effects,"[3] explains the *Journal*, and the government is cracking down on illegal marketing. But also, private and government insurers are less willing to "cough up money for an expensive new drug—particularly when a cheap and reliable generic is available.[4]

It's gotten so bad, AstraZeneca, whose controversial Seroquel® still makes $5.3 billion a year though it is no longer new, now conducts "payer excellence academies" to teach sales reps to sell insurers and state healthcare systems on its latest drugs.[5] No wonder Pharma is finding "love" by prescribing drugs to the nation's youngest (and oldest) patients, who are often behavior problems to their caregivers, who make few of their own drug decisions, and who are often on government health plans.

"Children are known to be compliant patients and that makes them a highly desirable market for drugs," says former Pharma rep Gwen Olsen, author of *Confessions of an Rx Drug Pusher*.[6] "Children are forced by school personnel to take their drugs, they are forced by their parents to take their drugs, and they are forced by their doctors to take their drugs. So, children are the ideal patient-type because they represent refilled prescription compliance and 'longevity.' In other words, they will be lifelong patients and repeat customers for Pharma."

Just as it used to be said in obstetric circles, "Once a cesarean, always a cesarean," it's also true that "once a pediatric psychiatric patient, always a pediatric psychiatric patient." Few, indeed, are kids who start out diagnosed and treated for ADHD, bipolar disorder, and other "psychopathologies" who end up on no drugs, psychologically fine, and ready to run for class president. Even if they outgrow their original diagnoses—a big "if" with a mental health history that follows them—the side effects from years of psychoactive drugs and their physical health on mental, social, and emotional development take their toll. Even children on allergy and asthma drugs, which are promoted for kids as young as age one, are now known to develop psychiatric side effects according to emerging research.[7]

Kids who start out with psychiatric diagnoses are often lifers; when they are *expensive* lifers on psychiatric drug "cocktails" that exceed $1,000 a month, they are usually shuttled into government programs. What private insurer will pay $323 for an atypical antipsychotic like Zyprexa®, Geodon®, or Risperdal®, when a "typical" antipsychotic costs only about $40 without a fight?[8]

Not all medical professionals agree with the slapdash cocktails. Panelists at the 2010 American Psychiatric Association (APA) meeting assailed Pharma for such "seat of the pants" drug combinations and called the industry nothing but a "marketing organization."[9] In a symposium about comparative drug effectiveness, a Canadian doctor castigated the FDA's Jing Zhang, who had served then as a panelist at the symposium, for his agency's approval of drugs for "competitive reasons" rather than for patient health or effectiveness.[10] Research presented at the 2010 APA meeting also questioned the psychiatric cocktails. When twenty-four patients on combinations of Seroquel, Zyprexa, and other antipsychotics were reduced to only one drug, there was no worsening of symptoms or increased hospitalizations (except in one case), and patients' waist circumferences and triglycerides improved (a large waist circumference and high levels of triglycerides [fat] in the blood heighten one's risk of developing diabetes and cardiovascular diseases).[11] The drug cocktails were not working and were making patients worse by creating new medical problems.

But pediatric psychopharmacology is a billion-dollar business that sustains Pharma, Pharma investors on Wall Street, doctors, researchers, medical centers, clinical research organizations, medical journals, Pharma's PR and ghostwriting firms, pharmacy benefits managers, and the FDA itself—which judges its value on how many drugs it approves. The only losers are kids given a probable life sentence of expensive and dangerous drugs, the families of these children, and the taxpayers and insured persons who pay for the drugs.

The father of pediatric psychopharmacology, child psychiatrist Joseph Biederman, is often called Joseph "Risperdal" Biederman, because he is credited with ballooning the diagnosis of bipolar disorder in children by as much as fortyfold.[12] In 2008, Biederman, a prolific author who has written five hundred scientific articles and seventy book chapters, was investigated by Congress for allegedly accepting Pharma money he didn't disclose, and he agreed to suspend his industry-related activities.[13] After a three-year investigation, Harvard, where Biederman worked, "threw the book" at him and two other professors: they were required to "refrain from all paid industry-sponsored outside activities for one year and comply with a two-year monitoring period afterward, during which they must obtain approval from the Medical School and Massachusetts General Hospital before engaging in any paid activities." What a deterrent. They also face a "delay of consideration for promotion or advancement."[14]

When it comes to grandiosity, Biederman seems a lot like the three-year-old who ran out in traffic. He not only served as the head of the Johnson & Johnson Center for the Study of Pediatric Psychopathology at Massachusetts General Hospital, whose stated goal was to "move forward the commercial goals of J. & J."—the facility was his idea![15] According to court-obtained documents, Biederman approached J. & J. with the money-making scheme.[16] Biederman also promised the drug maker that upcoming studies of its popular child antipsychotic Risperdal would "support the safety and effectiveness of risperidone [Risperdal] in this age group."[17]

The Johnson & Johnson Center for the Study of Pediatric Psychopathology netted a cool $700,000 in one year of operation, according to published reports, but a spokesman for Harvard Medical School said Harvard isn't involved with the Johnson & Johnson Center, even though the hospital where it operates, Massachusetts General, is a Harvard teaching hospital. "Harvard Medical School does not 'own' any of its teaching hospitals," he told *Bloomberg News*. "While we are affiliated with them through academic appointments, all teaching hospitals are individually governed."[18]

Many people are aware of such Pharma/academia arrangements, since the 1980 Bayh-Dole law allowed universities to operate as patent and profit mills for industries "commercializing and transferring" technology. Biederman received $14,000 from Eli Lilly the same year he got a grant from the National Institutes of Health (NIH) to study Lilly's ADHD drug, Strattera®. Why does the government fund researchers already funded by Pharma? Not only do these researchers not need our tax dollars; working for Pharma is an overt conflict of interest that contaminates scientific results.

Another master at playing both the Pharma and government sides of the street is psychiatrist Charles Nemeroff, former head of psychiatry at Emory University and also investigated by Congress for unreported Pharma money. Nemeroff's NIH grant was terminated after the probe, something that is rarely done with a government grant.[19]

According to the *Chronicle of Higher Education*, when Nemeroff was later under consideration to be the head of psychiatry at the University of Miami, the former director of the National Institute of Mental Health (part of the NIH), Thomas Insel, MD, assured the medical school dean that if Nemeroff were hired, NIH money would follow, his prior problems notwithstanding. What's a little congressional investigation? The reason for the largesse, according to the *Chronicle*, was that Nemeroff had gotten Insel a job at Emory when Insel lost his NIH position in 1994. Nor does the cronyism and revolving door stop there. Nemeroff served on two NIH peer-review advisory panels that decide who else receives grant money, says the *Chronicle*, and Insel is personally involved with revising the National Institute of Mental Health's "conflict of interest" rules.[20]

Insel is also known for advancing Pharma's "SSRI deficiency/suicide hypothesis," in which a decrease in antidepressant sales was—according to Pharma—resulting in suicides because people weren't getting their drugs. "[The National Institute of Mental Health is] looking at whether the decrease in SSRI [antidepressant] utilization might be associated with an increase in suicidality rather than a drop in suicide, and my expectation is that we may see an increase," Insel told *Psychiatric News*, lamenting "the focus on risk and a neglect of benefit."[21]

ANTIPSYCHOTICS FOR EVERYONE

When the atypical antipsychotics Zyprexa, Geodon, Risperdal, Abilify®, and Seroquel, for use in stabilizing schizophrenia, came into being in the 1990s, they were like the credit default swaps and collateralized debt obligations of the pharmaceutical world. No one knew exactly how they worked, how *long* they would work, or what the final effects of their wide use would be (as with many withdrawn drugs, FDA gives approval on the basis of information from short-term trials). But they could make a lot of quick money easily compared with old-fashioned products; they had government's backing, and everyone was doing it!

Drug reps especially swarmed state agencies with many mentally disabled patients, including children. For example, Texas's Medicaid program spent $557,256 for two months of pediatric Geodon prescriptions in 2005, according to court documents, and Geodon was not even approved for children at the time.[22] Eighty-five percent of the state's Risperdal prescriptions were paid by the state government, court documents also show.[23] And Florida's Medicaid program spent $935,584 for one year of Geodon.[24] One hundred and eighteen prescriptions for Geodon were written *in one day*, according to the *Tacoma News Tribune*, at Western State mental hospital in Washington State. Asked why Pfizer reps made almost two hundred visits to the facility in four years, then Pfizer spokesman Bryant Haskins told the *Tribune*, "That's where our customers are."[25]

Mental institution psychiatrists were not the only ones targeted. United States Department of Veterans Affairs psychiatrists said in a survey that they were contacted an average of fourteen times per year by Pharma reps and were invited to attend company-continuing medical education seminars.[26] And court documents unsealed in South Carolina in 2009 show that Eli Lilly sales reps even used golf bets to push their atypical antipsychotic Zyprexa; one doctor agreed to start new patients on Zyprexa "for each time a sales representative parred."[27]

But as state outlays for atypical antipsychotics grew twelvefold between 2000 and 2007, some states and whistle-blowers began bringing Pharma to court. In 2007, Bristol-Myers Squibb settled a federal suit for $515 million, brought by whistle-blowers in Massachusetts and Florida, which charged that the company marketed the antipsychotic Abilify for unapproved uses in children and the elderly, bilking taxpayers in the process.[28] And the next year, Alaska won a precedent-setting $15 million settlement from Eli Lilly in a suit to recoup medical costs generated by Medicaid patients who developed diabetes while taking Zyprexa. Atypical antipsychotics are known to cause weight gain and glycemic changes that can lead to diabetes.[29] Soon Idaho, Washington, Montana, Connecticut, California, Louisiana, Mississippi, New Mexico, New Hampshire, Pennsylvania, South Carolina, Utah, West Virginia, Arkansas, and Texas took Pharma to court for the atypical "prescribathon," which hit the poor, the mentally ill, children, and the elderly the hardest.[30]

Of course, as with credit default swaps and collateralized debt obligations (or the cases of Bernie Madoff or BP's Deepwater Horizon or Enron), there were voices of dissent about the atypical revolution if people chose to listen. A National Institute of Mental Health study of children ages eight to nineteen with psychotic symptoms found Risperdal and Zyprexa were no more effective than the older antipsychotic Moban, but it caused such obesity that a safety panel ordered the children off the drugs.[31] In just eight weeks, children gained an average of thirteen pounds on Zyprexa, nine pounds on Risperdal, and less than one pound on Moban.

"Kids at school were making fun of me," said study participant Brandon Constantineau, who put on thirty-five pounds on Risperdal.[32]

Other studies, like one on Risperdal in the British medical journal *Lancet* and one on Zyprexa, Seroquel, and Risperdal in Alzheimer's patients reported in the *New England Journal of Medicine*, also found that atypicals work no better than placebos.[33] One study in the *British Medical Journal* found that Seroquel not only did not relieve agitation in Alzheimer's patients, but that it "was [also] associated with significantly greater cognitive decline" than placebos.[34] Yes, atypical antipsychotics made patients worse.

"The problem with these drugs [is] that we know that they are being used extensively off-label in nursing homes to sedate elderly patients with dementia and other types of disorders," testified then FDA drug reviewer David Graham, MD, during a congressional hearing.[35] Graham is credited with exposing the dangers of Vioxx and other risky drugs approved by the FDA. "But the fact is, is that it increases mortality perhaps by 100 percent. It doubles mortality," said Graham. "So I did a back-of-the-envelope calculation on this, and you have probably got 15,000 elderly people in nursing homes dying each year from the off-label use of antipsychotic medications. With every pill that gets dispensed in a nursing home, the drug company is laughing all the way to the bank."[36]

Just like Wall Street and banking lobbyist and cronies "advised" the government on how to write the credit default and derivative rules under which they would be regulated, Pharma helps states regulate—and buy—its brand-name drugs. An Eli Lilly–backed company named Comprehensive Neuroscience has "helped" twenty-four states to use Zyprexa "properly," reports the *New*

York Times.[37] "Doctors who veer from guidelines on dosage strengths and combinations of medications for Medicaid patients are sent 'Dear Doctor' letters pointing out that their prescribing patterns fall outside the norm," it reports. Doctors are also notified if patients "are renewing prescriptions," lest they have "setbacks in their condition." One such program sends registered nurses to the homes of patients who are on expensive brand drugs to ensure "compliance"; that is, to make sure patients have not stopped taking the drugs.

Some states say they have saved money under Pharma's guidance, but Wisconsin found that once it "placed restrictions on Zyprexa and three other antipsychotic drugs" and scrapped the Lilly-funded program, it lowered its antipsychotic bill by $4 million.[38]

And then there's the Texas Medication Algorithm Project, a "decision tree" developed by Pharma and Johnson & Johnson's Robert Wood Johnson Foundation in 1995 to "help" the state buy its drugs. The algorithm rules required doctors to treat patients—surprise!—with the newest, most expensive drugs first, which ballooned Risperdal sales as well as other atypical antipsychotics.[39]

But in 2008, the Texas attorney general's office charged Risperdal maker Janssen Pharmaceuticals, Inc., Johnson & Johnson's antipsychotic drug unit, with fraud.[40] Janssen defrauded the state of millions, said a civil suit, "with [its] sophisticated and fraudulent marketing scheme," to "secure a spot for the drug, Risperdal, on the state's Medicaid preferred drug list and on controversial medical protocols that determine which drugs are given to adults and children in state custody." In addition to lavishing trips, perks, and kickbacks on Texas's mental health officials to win drug sales, and disguising marketing as scientific research, the attorney general's office charged that Janssen "paid third-party contractors and nonprofit groups to promote Risperdal . . . to give state mental health officials and lawmakers the perception that the drug had widespread support."[41]

Such faux grassroots support from phony front groups has been cited in other lawsuits against Pharma. Whistle-blowers charge that Pfizer funded the National Alliance on Mental Illness (NAMI) to serve as a "Trojan horse" to sell Geodon in a complaint that led to forty-three states receiving givebacks and the largest criminal fine ever imposed in US history—$2.3 billion in 2009.[42]

The National Alliance on Mental Illness calls itself a "nonprofit, grass-roots, self-help, support and advocacy organization of consumers, families, and friends of people with severe mental illnesses,"[43] but it has been investigated by Congress for undisclosed Pharma money and is considered by some to be a front organization. The Geodon complaint even cites physician Richard Borison, who was jailed because of research fraud, in the corruption.[44]

Of course, to lock in taxpayer funding of psychoactive drugs, especially for children, it takes more than "helping" state officials at the point of purchase (and sending zealous drug reps to state facilities where the "patients are"). Pharma also finances continuing medical education (CME) courses that reward credits doctors need to retain their state licenses. A CME course called Individualizing ADHD Pharmacotherapy with Disruptive Behavioral Disorders taught by then Johnson & Johnson–funded Robert L. Findling, MD, refers to Risperdal thirteen times.[45] Another CME course that promoted Seroquel was "taught" by AstraZeneca staff and Dr. Nemeroff but was scrapped after the Accreditation Council for Continuing Medical Education found it "lacked sufficient information about possible adverse effects of treatment with atypical antipsychotic drugs; and failed to emphasize sufficiently the efficacy of alternative treatments."[46] The course was called Atypical Antipsychotics in Major Depressive Disorder: When Current Treatments Are Not Enough.

Pharma doctors also spread confidence about the drugs by publishing in medical journals like a Johnson & Johnson–subsidized article that upheld the "long-term safety and effectiveness of risperidone [Risperdal] for severe disruptive behaviors in children" in the *Journal of the American Academy of Child & Adolescent Psychiatry*. Despite thirty-one recorded child deaths, the drug was found to be safe, according to the article, on the basis of a one-year study.[47]

MOLECULES THAT KEEP ON GIVING

Of course, Pharma also has the help of sophisticated ad agencies to "move product." An Eli Lilly ad campaign called Viva Zyprexa sold forty-nine thousand new prescriptions in just three months using profiles of patients who doctors were told needed Zyprexa even though they clearly didn't have either of the diseases the drug was legally approved for—schizophrenia or bipolar disorder.[48] One character in an ad, for example, is a woman named Martha who "lives independently and has been your patient for some time," and who has agitation and disturbed sleep. But Martha does *not* have symptoms of paranoia or mania that would make her a candidate for Zyprexa, said doctors reviewing the campaign.[49] Viva Zyprexa's off-label marketing gambits were so lucrative that Michael Bandick, then Zyprexa brand manager, lauded the top sales reps who "maxed out on a pretty sweet incentive" and called Zyprexa "the molecule that keeps on giving" at a national sales meeting. It was reminiscent of Wyeth's CEO telling sales reps in pep rallies that hormone replacement therapy was going to be the next revolution.[50]

Pharma campaigns for younger people are even slicker. The London-based ad agency Junction 11 (GSW Worldwide) hired noted Welsh oil painter Mark Moran to create the award-winning Risperdal "Living Nightmares" campaign.[51] The paintings were designed to "capture physicians' attention and communicate patients' agony and need for treatment," said its originators, while helping Janssen to "own the relapse/prevention space." Some titles of paintings include, *Dog-Woman*, *Witches*, *Rotting Flesh*, and *Boiling Rain*.[52]

Another Risperdal campaign, called "Prescribe Early," uses a macabre abandoned wallet, a teddy bear, and keys on a barren street "to reposition a drug that was being used too late to achieve its maximum benefits," said its advertising agency, Torre Lazur McCann.[53] Seroquel brand managers even considered creating *Winnie-the-Pooh* characters like Tigger (bipolar) and Eeyore (depressed) to sell Seroquel, according to published reports, at an Astra-Zeneca sales meeting.[54] Parents say they have seen toys emblazoned with Seroquel logos.[55]

Creating kid-friendly figures to sell psychoactive drugs for children is not just a US phenomenon. A lime-green kids' brochure for Zyprexa, published by Britain's National Health Service (NHS), shows cartoons of happy children skating, Rollerblading®, and playing soccer, and says, "Many children, teenagers and young people need to take medicines prescribed by doctors to help them stay well and healthy."[56] Similar NHS brochures exist for Risperdal and Strattera, an ADHD drug, although the necessity and safety of such drugs in kids is widely disputed.

Like the emergence of "spectrum" disorders in which a child does not necessarily have to have symptoms of a disease to have the disease, Pharma's "Prescribe Early" campaigns double and triple sales by playing on parental fears. Your child is exhibiting signs of severe mental illness, says the marketing copy, which will only get worse if you don't put your child on drugs now (before the symptoms go away and we can't make any money, joke critics who are skeptical of Pharma marketing). Needless to say, parents will not necessarily know if their children would have gotten the psychiatric disease if they hadn't treated it with drugs. Nor will they know if "symptoms" that surface are from the drug(s) or the "disease."

Only one child in ten thousand has pediatric schizophrenia—some say one in thirty thousand—but that didn't stop Gabriele Masi, MD, then with the Stella Maris Institute for Child and Adolescent Neuropsychiatry at the University of Pisa in Italy from seeing it as a public health problem.[57] In an article titled "Children with Schizophrenia: Clinical Picture and Pharmacological Treatment," in the journal *CNS Drugs*, Masi writes, "Awareness of childhoodonset schizophrenia is rapidly increasing, with a more precise definition now available of the clinical picture and early signs, the outcome and the treatment strategies."[58] Symptoms of childhood schizophrenia include "social deficits" and "delusions . . . related to childhood themes," writes Masi.[59] What child doesn't have "social deficits"? Do delusions include imaginary playmates?

Masi lambastes the "hesitancy on the part of clinicians to make a diagnosis of schizophrenia," instead of prescribing early.[60] Masi "has or has received research funding from Eli Lilly; serves or has served as an advisor for Eli Lilly and Shire; and serves or has served on speakers bureaus for Sanofi Aventis, AstraZeneca, GSK, and Janssen, all of which manufacture many of the leading psychiatric drugs for children. She has received funds from Zyprexa maker, Eli Lilly," reports the American Academy of Child & Adolescent Psychiatry.[61]

Another prescribe-early buff is Joan L. Luby, MD, then director of the Early Emotional Development Program at Washington University School of Medicine in St. Louis. In an article in the *Archives of General Psychiatry*, she alerts the world to the public health problem of child psychiatric illnesses—in this case, toddler depression.[62] Researchers used to believe that "young children were too cognitively and emotionally immature to experience depressive effects," she writes in the article "Preschool Depression," which was widely picked up by the nonscience press—but those researchers now believe preschoolers can and do suffer from major depressive disorder (MDD)! "The potential public health importance of identification of preschool MDD is underscored by the established unique efficacy of early intervention during the preschool period in other childhood disorders," says Luby in a passage that should send chills down parents' spines. (Dear parent. Your three-year-old exhibits symptoms of major depressive disorder. Please report to . . .) "Based in part on the recurrent course and the relative treatment resistance of childhood MDD, there has been increased interest in the identification of the disorder at the earliest possible stage of development."[63]

It's tempting to make jokes about "preschool depression"—students get it every time their alarms ring—or to ridicule a scientist who finds "relapses," "chronicity," and "treatment resistance" in people who have been on the planet for forty months. But pathologizing three-year-olds isn't funny.

Both four-year-old Rebecca Riley of Hull, Massachusetts, and three-year-old Destiny Hager of Council Grove, Kansas, died in 2006 from psychiatric drugs that included Geodon and Seroquel to treat their "bipolar disorders."[64] And in 2009, seven-year-old Gabriel Myers of Broward County, Florida, a child in a state facility, hung himself while on Symbyax®, a pill that combines Zyprexa and Prozac®.[65]

In an interview, psychiatrist David Healy, author of the books *The Creation of Psychopharmacology*, *The Antidepressant Era*, and *Let Them Eat Prozac*, and then professor at Cardiff University in Bangor, Wales, says that the diagnosis of pediatric bipolar disorder is so entrenched, it's cited by women who say their baby kicked too much in utero. It is even diagnosed by sonographers who say they can't get a good picture of a baby's face because it moves too much, and by obstetricians who say they can't sample amniotic fluid.[66] The diagnosis precedes the baby! "One might ask if we are not witnessing a variant of Munchausen's syndrome, wherein significant others derive some benefit from someone else being ill," Healy said. Munchausen syndrome by proxy is a disorder in which caregivers deliberately exaggerate, fabricate, and/or induce health problems in others for the attention they (the caregivers) receive.

Luby admits that instead of having the "anxiety disorders" usually associated with major depression, the toddlers she studied had "disruptive disorders," possibly normal sharing and waiting-your-turn problems. But she still maintains the disruption "might be associated with social impairment and peer rejection that lead to later MDD," and that preschoolers should be screened. She recommends intervention at "the earliest possible stage of development."[67] Luby "has received grant/research support from Janssen, has given occasional talks sponsored by AstraZeneca, and has served as a consultant for Shire Pharmaceutical," according to an earlier journal article she co-wrote.[68]

Then there is Mani Pavuluri, MD, who "founded the now nationally recognized Pediatric Mood Disorders Clinic" that, according to University of Illinois–Chicago's website, "grew into [a] combined clinical and research program, and now the Pediatric Brain Research and Intervention Center at UIC."[69] Like Masi and Luby, Pavuluri finds serious drug deficiencies in tots resulting in conditions like pediatric mania and bipolar disorder, which, according to an article she co-wrote, says is "a complex illness with a chronic course, requiring multiple medications over the longitudinal course of illness, with limited recovery and high relapse rate."[70] And, again like Masi and Luby, Pavuluri pathologizes childhood itself, saying that "emotional impulsivity" in pediatric bipolar disorder is driven by "ventral frontostriatal circuitry dysfunction" instead of, perhaps, being five years old.[71] But instead of being a Zyprexa or Risperdal fan, Pavuluri favors Lamictal® for the pediatric problems, perhaps because she receives money from its maker, GlaxoSmithKline.[72] Like Biederman, Nemeroff, and many other Pharma-financed doctors, Pavuluri supplements her Pharma income from GlaxoSmithKline, Abbott Pharmaceuticals, and Johnson & Johnson with taxpayer money from the NIH.[73] Why should that be allowed?

"There is a growing body of literature supporting lamotrigine's [Lamictal] superiority over other mood stabilizers in not exacerbating or causing cognitive dysfunction ([ages] 6–10) or resulting in marked cognitive improvement" in young people, she writes in a GlaxoSmithKline-funded paper.[74] Lamictal is an epilepsy drug with clear warnings for life-threatening skin rashes called Stevens-Johnson syndrome, blood disorders, aseptic meningitis, "clinical worsening" of bipolar disorder, and risk of suicide. How is this appropriate for kids?

Still, a few psychiatric voices ring out against the idea of early treatment in children. At the 2010 American Psychiatric Association (APA) meeting, Mark Zimmerman, MD, then director of outpatient psychiatry at Rhode Island Hospital, submitted that the very fact that bipolar disorder is a lifelong disease is reason for sufferers to delay treatment until they are sure. His research, published in the *Journal of Nervous and Mental Disease*, finds a link between unconfirmed, overdiagnosed cases of bipolar disorder and . . . the receipts of disability payments. One possible reason for patients "embracing the diagnostic label is the secondary gain accrued from receiving disability payments," write the authors.[75]

HELP! MY ONE-YEAR-OLD HAS GERD!

Toddlers are not just under attack from people who think they have psychopathologies. In addition to ADHD and the rich spectrum of conduct and mood disorders they are labeled with, children are increasingly diagnosed with nonpsychiatric disorders, as well. Twenty-five percent of children and 30 percent of adolescents now take at least one prescription for a chronic condition, said Medco, then the nation's largest pharmacy benefit manager.[76] Use of prescription drugs is rising among children four times faster than in the overall population. In fact, more than five million children under age nineteen are likely on antihypertensives, drugs used to treat high blood pressure, reports the *Wall Street Journal*.[77]

Use of other drugs to treat conditions once considered "adult diseases" is also skyrocketing. In addition to high blood pressure medications, the use of which has risen by 17 percent among kids, respiratory medications have risen 42 percent, heartburn and gastroesophageal reflux disease (GERD) medications have risen 147 percent, and diabetes medications have risen by 150 percent, according to Medco.[78] Fifty percent of pediatricians also say they prescribe insomnia drugs to kids.[79]

Of course, one reason for the use of adult medications is that the pediatric population is suffering from "middle-age spread" just like adults—too many calories and not enough exercise. Over one-third of US kids are overweight, and 17 percent are obese—which, for a four-foot-ten-inch child would be 143 pounds. Obesity predisposes someone to diabetes, hypertension, high cholesterol, sleep apnea, gallbladder disease, osteoarthritis, and musculoskeletal disorders. It is also linked to a shorter life and to cancer. But rather than telling kids to unplug the TV or video games or to go outside and don't come back until dinner, parents and medical professionals enable the deleterious lifestyles with the easy-out of a pill. In fact, the statin Lipitor®, already the world's topselling medication in adults, was approved for US children in 2008 and was recently approved in a chewable form in Europe.[80] Statins are a popular drug that lowers cholesterol levels by inhibiting a liver enzyme involved in the production of cholesterol.

While statins can reduce cardiovascular risks in those who need them, they are overprescribed, expensive, and less desirable, according to clinicians, than lifestyle changes to lower cholesterol. Worse still, adults on statins are six times more likely to develop liver dysfunction, acute kidney failure, cataracts, and muscle damage, says a 2010 article in the *British Medical Journal*.[81] "Plenty of adults down statins regularly and shine off healthy eating because they know a cheeseburger and steak can't fool a statin," writes Michael J. Breus, PhD, on the *Huffington Post*. "Imagine a 10-year-old who loves his fast food and who knows he can get away with it if he pops his pills."[82]

And it gets worse. Gastroesophageal reflux disease, or GERD, already an adult epidemic that sells the "purple pills" Nexium® and Prilosec®, may be the next big disease in infants. "The number of acid-blocker prescriptions for colicky infants recently quadrupled," wrote pediatrician Darshak Sanghavi on *Slate*.[83] Studies regularly show that acid blockers do nothing to help reflux in babies, says Sanghavi, and "proton pump inhibitors" like Nexium may "increase brain bleeds and gut damage in preterm infants as well as the risk of food allergies in older infants."[84]

Reflux drugs, sometimes called Purple Crack, are so overprescribed, says Sanghavi—half of hospital inpatients are on them—that the head of Medicaid and Medicare admonished American Medical Association doctors that they should be "embarrassed" to prescribe them because the drugs increase "costs with no medical benefits."[85] They are even prescribed for intestinal tract pain where no hydrochloric acid exists for them to block, says Sanghavi. And the absence of heartburn doesn't necessarily mean you don't have GERD, just as the presence of heartburn doesn't necessarily mean you do. Protein pump inhibitors (PPIs) are also linked to hip fractures and community-acquired pneumonia, according to Public Citizen's *Worst Pills*, and to intestinal infections with a stubborn intestinal bacterium called *Clostridium difficile*, according to two recent studies.[86] Like psychoactive drugs, sleeping pills, and even asthma "control" drugs like Advair and Accolate®, reflux drugs can also cause the exact conditions they are supposed to prevent—heartburn and GERD—when people try to quit the drug.

OPEN HEARINGS; CLOSED MINDS

It takes a lot of chutzpah to request approval for something you are already doing. But that's just what Pfizer, AstraZeneca, and Eli Lilly did as they walked into FDA hearing rooms in June 2009 to request permission to market Geodon, Seroquel, and Zyprexa to children. Lilly had pled guilty to off-label promotion of Zyprexa three months earlier, and AstraZeneca and Pfizer would agree to huge off-label marketing settlements of Seroquel and Geodon the following year.[87] The charges against the three drug companies included the child indications they now sought. At the June hearings, the Psychophar-macologic Drugs Advisory Committee members would be considering

- whether Seroquel should be approved for, in the FDA's language, "acute treatment of schizophrenia in adolescents 13 to 17" and "acute treatment of bipolar mania in children 10 to 12 and adolescents 13 to 17,"
- whether Geodon should be approved for the "acute treatment of manic or mixed episodes associated with bipolar disorder, with or without psychotic features, in children and adolescents ages 10 to 17," and
- whether Zyprexa should be approved for the "acute treatment of manic or mixed episodes associated with bipolar I disorder and acute treatment of schizophrenia in adolescents."[88]

At the hearings, there were two ominous signs for patient advocates and safe drug activists. The Pharma doctors outnumbered the FDA doctors two to one. And the so-called patient representatives were Margy Lawrence, a member of NAMI, and Gail Griffith, who'd been a keynote speaker at a NAMI "Heroes" dinner.[89] Since much of NAMI's funding comes from Pharma and because some consider it a front group, this was a case of the fox guarding the henhouse.

When the black-box warning (the strongest warning possible) that the FDA put on SSRI antidepressant packages for suicide risk for young people in 2004 resulted in a sales drop of 20 percent for kids' prescriptions, patient representative Gail Griffith said, "This picture is disastrous," and questioned whether it was due to "physician reluctance" and "lack of education or fear of liability or malpractice. If the reluctance is coming from the public, then we have an opportunity here to provide evidence and educate," she added.[90]

Pharma doctors seemed to have an impossible task at the meeting. They needed to convince advisory committee members to ignore atypical anti-psychotic side effects like heart problems, diabetes, weight gain, metabolic syndrome, and unexplained deaths—and also to dispel the growing aware-ness among some doctors that kids are already overmedicated and probably don't need additional "treatment options." Why, for example, is a drug that can add an extra eight heartbeats a minutes in pediatric patients—as Pfizer doctors admitted about Geodon during the hearings—even under consideration? The extra heartbeats are the same side effect that convinced the FDA to reject Geodon as a new drug for adults in 1997, until Pfizer conducted further studies! Isn't doing the same thing and expecting different results the definition of insanity? Maybe both Pharma and the FDA need to take Geodon.

Some committee members refused to give Geodon a pass. "There [were] eight percent of the children or young people who had a pulse over 120," said Marsha D. Rappley, MD, then dean of the College of Human Medicine at Michigan State University. "If I had a fifteen-year-old who had a sustained pulse of 120, I would worry about that."[91] Edward L. C. Pritchett, MD, then with Duke University's Cardiology and Clinical Pharmacology Department agreed. If you subscribe to the theory that humans are allocated a finite amount of heartbeats in life, Geodon would actually shorten a life, he observed.[92]

Both Pritchett and Christopher B. Granger, MD, then director of Duke University Medical Center's Cardiac Care Unit, focused on the fact that Geodon's tendency to increase heart rate doesn't indicate that blood pressure is going down, as is the indication with most drugs. "You know, the interesting thing here is that the patient's blood pressure has actually gone up, so we have the curious situation of heart rate and blood pressure both going up," said Pritchett.[93] No one seemed reassured when Tom Tensfeldt, MD, then with Pfizer's pharmacokinetics group offered, "There may be a bit of a plateau in the effect, at least on average here." In other words, the number of extra heartbeats might not keep increasing.[94]

And what about Pfizer's post-marketing slides for Geodon "that revealed cardiopulmonary failure and stroke in children three to seventeen?" asked Kenneth Towbin, then with the NIH.[95] "We had ten reports of death in our postmarketing database in pediatric subjects. One of these subjects was a sixteen-year-old male who died of cardiopulmonary failure," said Susan Anway, MD, then with Pfizer safety and risk management.[96] "The second case you referred to was a case of stroke—cerebrovascular effects—or event. This was a subject who had many other comorbidities, [and was] on a number of other concomitant medications."

But that reassured no one! Pediatric patients are often on "cocktails of seven or eight medications," in the real world, observed committee member Rochelle Caplan, MD, then a psychiatry professor with Semel Institute for Neuroscience and Human Behavior, UCLA.[97] Still, Thomas Laughren, then FDA director of the Division of Psychiatry Products, tried to move the hearing forward. There's a "hazard in drawing too much from subsetting the data," interjected Laughren, known as an avid Pharma supporter.[98]

Geodon was not the only iffy drug assessed at the hearings. AstraZeneca's Liza O'Dowd, MD, had to assure committee members that the huge weight, glucose, and prolactin elevations, which are linked to cardiovascular and orthopedic problems and diabetes, seen with Seroquel could be "controlled and monitored" in patients.[99] They "didn't lead to discontinuation of the study," she said. Let's hope not—when a trial is only three weeks long, there won't be too many dropouts. Frank Greenway, MD, an endocrinologist and then medical director and professor at Pennington Biomedical Research Center in Baton Rouge, observed that the prolactin elevation seen with all atypical antipsychotics—which can cause men and boys to grow breasts—was at a level less than seen [in] a "prolactin secreting tumor," with Seroquel.[100] It's not saying much when a drug is safer than a tumor.

But cardiologist Christopher Granger confessed to "real discomfort" approving drugs that generate metabolic syndrome in adolescents in a very short period of time for "indefinite treatments" on the basis of three- or six-week trials.[101] "Hopefully we're not exposing someone for decades," he cautioned, which, of course, is exactly what Pharma is doing. His cardiology colleague, Pritchett agreed.

The *s* word also came up at the hearings. Pharma wasn't even going to bring it up until O'Dowd was asked to show the Seroquel suicide slide by an advisory committee member. Yes, five child suicides occurred during Seroquel trials, she admitted. AstraZeneca presenter Lili Kopala, MD, said she was sure the suicides stemmed from patients who were "still on the recovery curve," meaning the suicides were caused by their psychiatric disease and not by the drug.[102] But when Granger asked how she knew that, she abandoned scientific certitude and flip-flopped. "They may be random," she said.

Committee members also had questions about Pharma's "early treatment" theory, which dictates that suspected mental illness should be treated with medication immediately. "Tissue loss is related to time spent psychotic," said AstraZeneca's Ihor Rak, MD, meaning if a person is left untreated with pharmacological drugs, then their brain shrinks.[103] "The progression in frontal tissue loss is related to the number of psychotic relapses." But when advisory committee member Marsha Rappley, MD, asked if there was a "risk in not treating these manic episodes, and is this a cumulative risk—if it is not treated at the time of onset, but allowed to continue, will it get worse?" NIH's Towbin said no. The "kindling theory," which holds that bipolar episodes get more frequent or worse if a patient is not treated with drugs is "very much in doubt right now," said Towbin, and mania could be "somewhat self-limited."[104]

Benedetto Vitiello, MD, also with the NIH at the time, concurred. The danger of not treating early is not the risk of what happens to brain matter or volume but the behaviors that occur, like "poor judgment, poor insight," and risks "to others, due to the aggression that can be related to this condition," he said.[105]

Psychiatrist Grace Jackson, author of *Drug-Induced Dementia* and *Rethinking Psychiatric Drugs*, who was not at the meeting, agrees and takes the thinking further. "There is *no* evidence that failure to medicate 'harms' a psychotic person but there is evidence from neuroimaging studies in humans that old and new antipsychotics contribute to brain tissue loss, especially in the frontal lobes," she said in an interview.[106] "Moreover, people who were never psychotic or mentally ill can start to experience psychological symptoms upon the withdrawal of these drugs," and it is not uncommon for the drugs' withdrawal effects to be assigned to the "disease." In fact, when the state of Florida began requiring doctors to get approval for atypical antipsychotics before giving them to kids under age six on Medicaid, prescriptions for atypicals went from 3,167 in 2008 to 844 in 2007.[107] (Geodon, Zyprexa, and Seroquel were prescribed for children even though the drugs weren't approved until after the meeting described above.) Seventy-five percent of the kids were "cured." Forty percent fewer doctors prescribed the drugs, reported the *St. Petersburg Times*.[108]

Despite the FDA advisory panel's probing questions about early treatment, overmedication, and risks, it voted *for* the drugs, as often happens even when committees have been harsh.[109] Why do FDA committees "cosign" Pharma drugs even when members note dangerous side effects and are not

Pharma-funded? The Food and Drug Administration culture judges itself on how many medicines it approves, not how many it rejects, and a "new treatment option" is considered, by definition, positive. Also, doctors do not want to appear to be anti-progress, anti-Pharma, or at odds with their peers, and few know enough about Pharma marketing to realize that diagnostic categories grow from the drugs they approve, thanks to "disease mongering." (Once upon a time, there was practically no such thing as pediatric depression, bipolar disorder, or schizophrenia.) So, the committee voted that Geodon, Seroquel, and Zyprexa are effective and "acceptably safe" at treating schizophrenia and/or bipolar disorder in younger patients, and they are now used, with FDA approval, in kids.[110] Those who felt strongly about the dangers and about Pharma's drug offensive against children took the courageous step of voting "abstain" as opposed to "no."

Meanwhile, in 2011, there was more bad news about atypical antipsychotics used in adults: the Department of Veterans Affairs had spent $717 million on Risperdal to treat posttraumatic stress disorder in troops in Afghanistan and Iraq and those returning from these regions with PTSD over a period of nine years, only to discover that the drug worked no better than a placebo.[111] Veterans Affairs doctors wrote more than five million prescriptions for risperidone, the generic of Risperdal, from 2000 through June 2010 for naught, says a 2011 paper in the *Journal of the American Medical Association* (*JAMA*).[112] Where did clinicians ever get the idea that Risperdal could be used for such off-label purposes?

But despite the wasted millions in the apparent Pharma dupe and the abuse of the government, taxpayers, and especially the veterans, the Department of Veterans Affairs was not done with Risperdal. Less than two weeks after the *JAMA* study was published, the VA awarded a contract for more than two hundred thousand bottles of generic risperidone, said published reports, containing more than twenty million pills.[113] As with children, apparently, just because the antipsychotics don't work and do harm is no reason to not prescribe them.

Chapter 3

WEAPONS OF
HORMONAL THERAPY

How did menopause become a "disease" and hormone replacement therapy (HRT) the "cure"? A bestselling book in 1966 called *Feminine Forever* by Robert A. Wilson, a Wyeth-funded gynecologist, certainly helped. It referred to postmenopausal women as "flabby," "shrunken," "dull-minded," and "desexed," and warned that "no woman can be sure of escaping the horror of this living decay."[1]

This attitude was supported by a medical establishment that had already cast women as "neurotic" if they were divorced, didn't have children, were too attached to their dads, didn't keep clean houses, used the phone too much, bit their fingernails, or nagged their husbands. Many medical journal ads in the 1960s, '70s, and '80s, when doctors were still mostly men, degraded and trivialized women with headlines like "If She Calls You Morning . . . Noon . . . and Night Day After Day," recommending psychoactive drugs.[2] One ad for an antidepressant suggests that the graduation of a woman's child may signal the start of a "pathological depression" because it's the end of "feeling needed and useful."[3]

So it is no wonder that special derision was reserved for older women going through menopause or past it, who were said to have "outlived their ovaries" and to have lost their "symbol of femininity."[4] In fact, electroconvulsive therapy was prescribed for menopausal symptoms in the United States. A 1946 Smith, Kline & French ad in *Psychosomatic Medicine* calls electric shock and "estrogenic therapy" "fundamental measures" (when used in conjunction with Benzedrine Sulfate) for menopause.[5]

While some medical marketing campaigns claimed to want to spare women the "suffering" of menopause, others evinced undisguised contempt for women who weren't fertile or youthful in a society that didn't have any other role for them, depicting them frowning in aprons and peeling potatoes. Wyeth's high-budget TV ads in the early 2000s with model Lauren Hutton underscored the message that aging for women was terrible—and voluntary, just like ads, which also ran in the early 2000s, with figure skater Dorothy Hamill, which told people to take Vioxx for the aches and pains that accompanied old age. Menopause, the ads said, "contributes" to heart disease and other "age-related diseases," and hormone replacement therapy (HRT) was a youth elixir that would prevent diminished memory, loss of sight, and tooth loss. According to these ads, women didn't lose hormones because they aged; they aged because they lost hormones.

Of course, most people know by now that the "H" in HRT stood for *hoax* because not only didn't the drug prevent the "age-related diseases" the Hutton ads and other marketing warned of, but rather it *caused* many of them. A huge federal study in 2002 found that HRT increased the risk of breast cancer by 26 percent, heart attacks by 29 percent, stroke by 41 percent, and it doubled the risk of blood clots. In a related study published the next year, HRT doubled the risk of dementia in women, and in a separate study, the brains of older women who were given HRT actually shrunk.[6] These statistics did not exactly support the preservation of memory, as the ads promised. And, after the federal study, called the Women's Health Initiative (WHI), was terminated in 2002 because it was considered unethical to expose women to the obvious and known risks, subsequent studies widened the swathe of HRT-related harm.[7] Women on HRT are more likely to lose their hearing; to develop gall bladder disease, urinary incontinence, asthma, and melanoma; and to need joint replacement, said medical journals.[8] They are at greater risk for ovarian, endometrial, and lung cancers, and for non-Hodgkin's lymphoma.[9]

And not only did HRT increase the risk of breast cancer, but it also made detecting cancer more difficult. In 1995, an article in the journal *Radiology* said that "an increase in mammographic density" was demonstrated in most subjects undergoing continuous combined HRT.[10] By 2008, the abnormal mammograms associated with HRT were so well known, researchers warned that, "this adverse effect on breast cancer detection should be incorporated into risk-benefit discussions with women considering even short-term combined hormone therapy." Hormone replacement therapy increased the risk of lobular breast cancer in just three years and also increased the risk of fatalities among women with lung cancer.[11] Not exactly the fountain of youth.

Until the WHI study, being treated with HRT, later called hormone therapy (HT), for "estrogen deficiency" was a rite of passage for American women, just like getting their first bra or using Tampax®. In fact, in 2001, before HRT was discredited, sixty-one million prescriptions were written in the United States for HRT—enough to treat a third of all women. For New Jersey–based Wyeth, now merged with Pfizer, it was a two-billion-dollar-ayear business.[12]

In addition to preventing heart disease; memory, sight, and tooth loss; and other age-related diseases, HRT was prescribed to prevent osteoporosis and bone fractures—which it actually does. But the effects on bone issues last only as long as women take HRT, and, as a result of the Women's Health Initiative, that's supposed to be for as short a time as possible.[13]

Originally, Wyeth's estrogen drug Premarin® was the medication of choice for hormone replacement therapy.

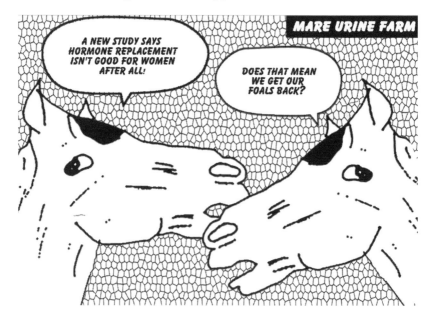

Named after pregnant mares' urine from which it's derived, Premarin cornered the market and still has no competing generic competition. But as early as the 1970s, Premarin had a "side effect" that eerily foreshadowed the WHI news in 2002: it caused endometrial cancer, a type of uterine cancer. While women on Premarin whose uteruses were removed through hysterectomies were not at risk, clinicians began prescribing a synthetic progestin called Provera® (medroxyprogesterone acetate) with Premarin to women who *did* have uteruses, because it seemed to prevent the risk of endometrial cancer. Provera was manufactured by Pfizer, which merged with Wyeth in 2009.

But in 1994, long before the merger, Wyeth created one pill that combined Premarin and Provera called Prempro®. Prempro was such a moneymaker for Wyeth that former CEO Robert Essner would host pep rallies called "Prempro parties" at which he would declare that Wyeth was creating an "HRT revolution." Women are now accepting the need to stay on hormone replacement drugs from menopause to death, Essner would say, and there should be "no boundaries, no limits to your selling effort," recount former salespeople.[14]

Like Wall Street CEOs who packaged worthless mortgage securities, or egg producers who sold salmonella-infected eggs, Wyeth both didn't know about the risks and warned the public about the risks, depending on when and whom you ask.

In some of the thirteen thousand lawsuits over HRT-caused cancer and other problems that have come to court, Wyeth has claimed that the warnings were clearly on the label. But Wyeth also stood by other benefits it shilled until the WHI findings, like reduced risks for heart, teeth, eye, brain, and memory issues. Natalie de Vane, a Wyeth spokesperson, said, "All of our communications to patients have always been based on science."[15]

Hormone replacement therapy is approved only for vasomotor symptoms, vaginal atrophy, and postmenopausal osteoporosis, and was never approved for cardiac benefits, despite Wyeth's strenuous attempts.[16] Moreover, advertising a drug for unapproved benefits is illegal.[17] In addition to the false HRT benefits advertised illegally to the public, Wyeth and its marketing firm, Design-Write of Princeton, New Jersey, operated a decade-long ghostwriting scheme conveying the same fabricated benefits to doctors and clinicians in the scientific press. In 1985, Lila E. Nachtigall, MD, then a professor at New York

University and director of the Women's Wellness Center (and who served on Wyeth's Speakers Bureau),[18] was doing damage control about HRT's cancer risks.[19] In a preemptive article titled "Is Estrogen Replacement Therapy Necessary?" she wrote, "Despite continuing controversy, the risks of ERT [HRT] are now considered minimal. With individualized therapy and appropriate monitoring, ERT with progestin supplements appears to be safe and effective for the great majority of postmenopausal women."[20]

By 1990, Nachtigall was addressing "compliance" problems due to "fears of cancer" in journal articles and asserting that even the administration of HRT for twenty-two years "did not increase the incidence of breast cancer" in a studied group.[21] HRT was not only safe; it "may even reduce the risk of atherosclerosis," wrote Nachtigall in the same article, floating the heart benefit. Most "studies have shown that replacing estrogen in the menopausal woman reduces cardiovascular disease," she wrote in a *Geriatrics* article titled "Protecting Older Women from Their Growing Risk of Cardiac Disease."[22] The article still stands. The shameless heart-benefits mongering and the denial of cancer risks was supplemented by other Wyeth HRT claims, like the prevention of Parkinson's disease and of macular eye disease.[23]

The Wyeth and DesignWrite ghostwriting documents led to an investigation by Sen. Charles Grassley of Iowa in 2009 when they were unsealed by a New York judge. The documents are posted on the University of California–San Francisco's Drug Industry Document Archive, which hosted the originally unsealed documents related to tobacco industry suits. Even though "unethical research" and "data fabrication" are grounds for retraction of medical journal articles according to the Committee on Publication Ethics (COPE), none of the over fifty articles that Wyeth and DesignWrite planted has been retracted.[24] Neither journal editors nor the authors want to admit their industry stenography, and so the bogus, bought papers stand and are cited in the medical literature, misleading future doctors.

"Is There an Association between Hormone Replacement Therapy and Breast Cancer?" asks an unretracted article in the *Journal of Women's Health* by "author" William T. Creasman, MD.[25] Is the earth flat? According to unsealed documents, Creasman neither wrote nor initiated the article, which was written by a DesignWrite employee named Karen Mittleman. The article finds there is no "definitive evidence" of a cancer link.[26] Also unretracted— despite the findings that HRT doubled the risk of dementia—are the articles "The Role of Hormone Replacement Therapy in the Prevention of Alzheimer Disease" in the *Archives of Internal Medicine* and "Mild Cognitive Impairment: Potential Pharmacological Treatment Options" in the *Journal of the American Geriatrics Society*.[27] And despite the 29 percent escalation of heart attack risk attributed to HRT, articles saying the drug was good for the heart also appear in the *Archives of Internal Medicine* and in *Cardiology in Review*.[28]

Nor was it just journals where Wyeth planted HRT misinformation. In 1998, former *McCall's* magazine editors Hilary Macht Felgran and Ann Hettinger said they received "a twenty-two-page pamphlet titled 'Take Charge! A Woman's Guide to Fighting Heart Disease,'" as part of an American Heart Association campaign sponsored by Wyeth. The top risk factor given for heart disease, they said, was "loss of estrogen."[29] Similar sales scare tactics appeared in "The Pharmacist's Guide to Women and Menopause" and "The Good Housekeeping Guide to Women's Health," according to evidence at one of the first HRT breast cancer trials.[30]

In 2002, the same year HRT was discredited by the federal Women's Health Initiative, Wyeth audaciously established a $12 million Council on Hormone Education at the University of Wisconsin School of Medicine and Public Health, which was "designed to provide OB/GYNs and primary care doctors access to the most up-to-date and fair balanced [*sic*] scientific and educational information about postmenopausal hormone therapy."[31] It was run by DesignWrite and a faculty of forty-four Wyeth-funded doctors, including Lila Nachtigall. Under the cloak of a legitimate medical school, the Council on Hormone Education offered continuing medical education (CME) courses to doctors. One course, called Quality of Life, Menopausal Changes, and Hormone Therapy, argued that all the heart and cancer data from the Women's Health Initiative "did not include any of the most commonly accepted, validated instruments for assessing menopause-related QOL [quality of life]."[32] As if quality of life could be weighed against the risk of cancer.

Credit for the Wyeth courses was available until 2008, and the course offerings themselves disappeared from the web only in 2009, after a *Milwaukee Journal Sentinel* exposé about the Pharma-funded courses at the University of Wisconsin.[33] One Council on Hormone Education doctor at the time, Leon Speroff, says that HRT-produced breast cancer (which he doesn't deny happens) is a *good* thing because it's a "better" cancer![34] "Evidence indicates that hormone users develop smaller, better-differentiated (lower grade) tumors," he writes in the journal *Menopause*. "Exposure to combined estrogen and progestin is beneficial, causing greater differentiation and earlier detection of breast cancers," he writes, amazingly.[35]

Other doctors on the council recommended HRT for breast cancer survivors. "The reluctance to provide postmenopausal hormone therapy to breast cancer survivors derives from the unsubstantiated belief that dormant malignant cells will be activated by exogenous hormone therapy; however, no clinical or research evidence supports this belief," says one Wyeth medical course.[36]

DÉJÀ VU AND FOOL ME TWICE

The philosophical nail in HRT's coffin probably came in late 2006 when researchers announced that in the one year since women quit HRT—2003— the incidence of breast cancer in the United States fell 7 percent. It fell 15 percent among women whose tumors were fed by estrogen (contrary to what the Council on Hormone Education asserted).[37] It was the first time breast cancer rates had ever fallen significantly, reported the *New York Times*.[38] According to Peter Ravdin, MD, then with the MD Anderson Cancer Center, it was the largest one-year drop that he could remember. The National Cancer Institute reported a "huge decline in breast cancer incidence" the year women quit HRT.[39] Fourteen thousand women who were expected to get breast cancer didn't, reported researchers, and the largest breast cancer reductions, 11 percent in California, correlated with the highest HRT use.[40]

The results were probably embarrassing to cancer researchers and public health officials. Not only was a major cause of cancer hidden in plain sight (and in medical journals and in CMEs), but the war on cancer should apparently have been a war on cancer-causing drugs! It was especially embarrassing since the entire sequence had happened before. In 1975, an FDA panel found a link between Premarin and endometrial cancer, and the *New England Jour-*

nal of Medicine (*NEJM*) indicted estrogen therapy for increasing the risk of endometrial cancer by at least five times.[41] Estrogen-caused cases of US endometrial cancer between 1971 and 1975 were estimated to be fifteen thousand by other researchers. "Long-term use of conjugated estrogen increases the risk of both localized and widespread endometrial cancer," reported the *NEJM*.[42]

And when women quit Premarin en masse in the 1970s because of its cancerous side effects (like they did with Prempro in 2002), what happened? "There was a sharp downward trend in the incidence of endometrial cancer that paralleled a substantial reduction in prescriptions for replacement estrogens," reported the *NEJM* in 1979.[43] Results were seen almost immediately, as in 2003. As in, "fool me twice!"

Then and now, Wyeth and Wyeth-related doctors disputed the charges that threatened the company's hormone franchise. In the 1970s, Wyeth's medical director wrote a letter to doctors claiming, "It would be simplistic indeed to attribute an apparent increase in the diagnosis of endometrial carcinoma solely to estrogen therapy," and maintained that Premarin still had "proven benefits" at the "the lowest maintenance dose"—a letter the FDA said was "intended to obfuscate the issues."[44]

And, in 2006, Wyeth and Wyeth-related doctors sought to spin the rises and drop in cancers as a phenomenon of *detection*—women getting more or fewer mammograms—and not HRT. But experts disagreed. "From 1975 to 2000, breast cancer incidence increased rather dramatically. While part of that increase was clearly due to the introduction of screening mammography, once you take out that effect, there is still a rather astounding increase of 30 percent," said Donald Berry, MD, then chairman of the department of biostatistics at the University of Texas MD Anderson Cancer Center in Houston. "While there have been a number of theories put forward to explain the increase [in breast cancer], it now looks like some of that increase is due to the use of HRT. When women stopped using HRT, it looked kind of like a market correction and the numbers went back down."[45]

HRT defenders also contended that cancer couldn't appear, or disappear, so quickly that relevant statistics would be reflected in the first year that one-half of US women who had been using HRT quit. But researchers said that small cancers already in the breast but "deprived of estrogen" could definitely regress, *or never start at all*, that quickly. "It's not like smoking where you have to wait 10 or 15 years for the risk to come down," said Claudine Isaacs, MD, then with Georgetown University's Lombardi Comprehensive Cancer Center.[46] When all the numbers were in, HRT was not just guilty of elevating breast cancer rates in women; it also elevated heart attacks and ovarian cancer in women, according to statistics, and those rates *also* fell when women quit HRT.[47]

Certainly US drug consumers are used to prescription drug scandals and cons. They may not be old enough to remember DES, Propulsid®, fenphen, Baycol, or Trovan, but they probably remember Vioxx, Avandia®, and Chantix®, and how the risks surfaced only once the drugs were marketed and in wide use. But the HRT scandal differs from hoaxes-as-usual in three ways.

1. After a respectful pause in marketing (and changing the term "hormone replacement therapy" to "hormone therapy"), HRT is *still* marketed to women as if nothing happened, predicated on a new generation of naive patients and clinicians. In fact, in 2009, Wyeth/Pfizer spent over $2 million funding estrogen courses at Duke, Penn State, and the University of Oklahoma medical schools; the Cleveland Clinic; and on leading doctor education websites like Medscape.[48] That doesn't sound like a therapy that's on its way out.
2. HRT's harmful side effects, whether heart attacks and stroke or increased dementia, were not peripheral but were marketed as its *benefits*. (Like marketing Vioxx to prevent heart attacks when it caused them.)
3. The entire sequence of HRT marketed as a youth elixir, but causing cancer and cancer rates dropping when women quit had occurred before.

Needless to say, after the 2002 WHI findings, as in the 1970s, prescriptions for HRT tanked. Wyeth announced it would close its Rouses Point, New York, plant where it manufactured its Prempro products and would eliminate twelve hundred jobs.[49] Sales reps were canned, and Pfizer's stock was also punished because it made Provera.

As the first of thousands of breast cancer lawsuits filed by HRT users began to emerge, the depth of the Wyeth deception was revealed. In a 2006

Little Rock, Arkansas, trial, Charles Payne, a former Wyeth salesman, disclosed that in 2000 he had written company executives, saying that "the desire for increased sales has overruled our company's ethical responsibility to promote our products safely." In a letter made public in 2010 along with two others, he wrote, "We are not selling used cars. We are selling pharmaceuticals that affect the lives of women who take them."[50]

Also in 2000, Wyeth sales rep Carl Whatley Jr. wrote the company that he was given a "scripted, written presentation" to sell Premarin for Alzheimer's disease and that "such off-label promotion could conceivably lead to Premarin [being] prescribed by a physician who was influenced by the Alzheimer's Disease Data and in a [worst-]case scenario, the patient develops breast cancer, a thrombosis, or any other medical problem."[51] Cynthia Waldrep, another Wyeth rep, wrote, "My most critical concern is the lives of the women in Alabama and Georgia that may be at risk due to these promotions. Many physicians have been persuaded to use these products for uses that have not been proven on the masses of postmenopausal women in Alabama and Georgia. I fear that their lives may be placed in serious potential danger."[52]

But at the 2006 Little Rock trial of breast cancer and mastectomy survivor Linda Reeves, age sixty-seven, the first to come to court, it was obvious Wyeth was going to play hardball. Even though Reeves was kept on Prempro and Premarin for eight years to "prevent osteoporosis," Wyeth lawyer Jane Bockus said that Wyeth and her doctor should have known that HRT was not supposed to be used for more than one year without a one-year follow-up.[53] The doctor, it turned out, gynecologist David Caldwell, MD, was a *paid Wyeth speaker* who said he stood by the treatment he gave Reeves and that he still prescribes Prempro.[54] Reeves lost her case.

Wyeth also played hardball with plaintiff Donna Scroggin, who Wyeth attorneys said had a history of breast cancer on both sides of her family and who would have gotten the disease anyway.[55] (Scroggin's cancer was hormone-receptor positive and fed by external hormones—not genetic, said her attorney.) And Wyeth played hardball with plaintiff Helen Rush, who Wyeth attorneys got to admit she didn't read the patient information before taking HRT, which led to her losing her case.[56]

Wyeth also lashed out against bioidentical hormones, which are compounded by pharmacies from plants like yam and soybeans and are often mar-keted against HRT as being more natural. Wyeth filed a complaint in 2005 asking the FDA to restrict the sale of bioidenticals, which it partially did.[57] Leon "the good cancer" Speroff devoted an entire newsletter at the University of Wisconsin's Council on Hormone Education to the bioidentical menace. "The marketing of bio-identical hormones preys on emotions," charges the newslet-ter (titled "Don't Confuse Marketing with Science") without a trace of irony or sheepishness about Wyeth's HRT marketing. "Clinical decision-making, in contrast, must be based on a foundation of knowledge," said the newsletter.[58]

Wyeth also played hardball in its marketing, after the cancer risks sur-faced, saying that women, instead of not using HRT or using it for the short-est period of time as the FDA now directs, should *take it earlier*—this just two years after the WHI study.[59] The hurry-up-and-treat/don't-wait-for-symp-toms advice fell into line with similar Pharma messages for bone, asthma, metabolic, and psychiatric drugs. "The benefits of HRT may outweigh the risks if treatment is given to younger women, but the risks may outweigh benefits if treatment is started at a later age," wrote Wyeth-linked Shelley Salpeter, MD, in a medical journal in 2004, in an early version of what came to be known as the HRT "timing theory."[60]

The same year, the National Institute on Aging (NIA), part of the

National Institutes of Health (NIH), invited Wyeth-funded researchers and Wyeth employees themselves to a workshop called Perspective on the WHI: Where Are We Now? Two years after the WHI cancer revelations, it was like inviting Philip Morris to weigh in on tobacco risks.[61] Included in the Wyeth guests were Eileen Helzner, MD, then Wyeth executive director; Ginger Constantine, MD, then with Wyeth's Women's Health Care; Darleen Deecher, PhD, then with Wyeth Ayerst Pharmaceuticals; and Jeannemarie Durocher, then assistant vice president of Wyeth's Women's Health Care. (Durocher, who was so involved with the DesignWrite machinations, was deposed for an early trial brought against Wyeth by a cancer patient.[62])

The same year, official "timing theory" clinical trials were begun at Albert Einstein College; Columbia; Harvard; Yale; the Mayo Clinic; and the Universities of California–San Francisco, Utah School of Medicine, and Washington School of Medicine. The four-year studies to test if estrogen protects against coronary vascular disease if started closer to menopause per the timing theory (and in defiance of the WHI results)—called Kronos Early Estrogen Prevention Study, or KEEPS—were privately funded and not linked to Wyeth or Pharma, according to administrators. But seven of the study's principal investigators were linked to Wyeth.[63] Nanette Santoro, MD, was a Wyeth consultant; Eliot Brinton, MD, and Hugh Taylor, MD, were on Wyeth's Speakers Bureau; Frederick Naftolin, MD, worked with DesignWrite on Wyeth ghost-writing projects; Sanjay Asthana, MD, and Rogerio Lobo, MD, were Wyeth grant recipients; and Thomas Clarkson, DVM, was a consultant on Wyeth's advisory board.[64] One timing theory trial, called "Alzheimer's Disease: Therapeutic Potential of Estrogen," was also taxpayer-funded by the NIA.[65]

At the NIA's "WHI: Where Are We Now?" workshop, one presentation, given by Wake Forest's Thomas Clarkson, DVM, also a KEEPS investigator, raised ethical and oversight questions. Slides from his research presentation, titled "Cardiovascular Health and Cognition: Perspectives on Using the Primate as a Model," depict an orangutan in an aqua-colored flannel dress, its face contorted in apparent terror with a comic strip–style balloon coming out of its mouth that says, "I just don't know what to think."[66] Another mirthful photo shows a chimpanzee who has apparently typed a page on a typewriter to illustrate the "cognition research" being performed in the lab. A third photo shows a capuchin monkey dressed in big, black eyeglasses that are barely supported by its little head, who is also apparently commenting about the ongoing research in the lab.

When asked about the appropriateness of the images on a government research site, it was communicated that NIA does not fund research by Clarkson except for a grant to organize a meeting related to the twentieth annual scientific meeting of the North American Menopause Society in September 2009. Furthermore, it was suggested that queries regarding the images should have been directed to the speaker. The images were promptly taken down from the site after the query.

Dr. Clarkson, an early promoter of the HRT timing theory, told the Wake Forest University publication *Visions* that "all experimental evidence from animals says that if you go longer than six post-menopausal years before you begin to give estrogens, you pass the window of opportunity for seeing benefit."[67] This statement was made soon after the WHI findings. "If women have been deriving prevention benefits, as I and others believe they have, and suddenly there is a 48 percent reduction in prescriptions [for HRT medicine], it could have an adverse effect on the extent and severity of cardiovascular disease in the population." Clarkson's fear of an "estrogen deficiency" in the aging women can be compared to the Pharma creation of an "SSRI deficiency," in which public health allegedly suffered when black-box warnings were added to antidepressants and prescriptions subsequently fell.[68]

Because there is so much money in developing drugs for half of the population as it ages, research into primate "menopause"—often conducted with tax dollars—is booming at Wake Forest, Mount Sinai, and other medical centers, despite fundamental questions about whether primates are even appropriate models.[69] In one experiment, Clarkson and others removed the ovaries of four adult female cynomolgus monkeys after treating the animals with a drug that causes ovarian failure for twenty-seven days.[70] In another experiment (reminiscent of macabre experiments conducted by Harry Harlow, who was known for cruel maternal-separation and social isolation experiments on monkeys), called "Social Deprivation and Coronary Artery Atherosclerosis in Female Cynomolgus Monkeys," Clarkson and others kept primates in stark isolation and chronicled their health decline.[71]

In other research at Wake Forest, monkeys donated by Clarkson "were restrained with ketamine (15 mg/kg im [or intramuscular]), deeply anesthetized with sodium pentobarbital (35 mg/kg, iv), and perfused transcardially [killed by washing out their blood] with cold 0.1 M PBS (pH 7.4) [a fixative]. The brains were rapidly removed and sliced into 1-cm slabs with the aid of a monkey brain matrix."[72] The research was funded by the NIA. You don't have to be against animal research to see the banality in treating "menopausal" primates with pregnant mare urine to create drugs already *proven to give women cancer* for the disease of "aging"—which is not a disease at all. In addition to human cancers and suffering of the primates, the mares who produce the urine used for Premarin are tethered to "pee lines" with the offspring from their pregnancies sent to slaughterhouses.

Still, the timing theory sparked a third wave of HRT fever. Wyeth's Joseph Camardo, MD, former senior vice president of global medical affairs, told the press at a medical conference that women are starting to use HRT at a younger age and that the "same risks may not apply with the new patterns of use."[73]

A 2008 continuing medical education course at the University of North Texas Health Science Center titled A Fresh Look at Hormone Therapy proposes to reconsider HRT heart benefits. "Epidemiologic and observational studies demonstrate that estrogen lowers coronary heart disease (CHD) rates by 40 percent to 50 percent," say materials from the course, as if the WHI study had never occurred. The materials also fail to mention the decreased acute myocardial infarction rate among women in the US when women quit HRT. James Simon, MD, then a Wyeth consultant and Speakers Bureau member who listed fifty other financial links to Pharma in the course disclosures, "taught" the course.[74]

Exciting "menopause" research about primates given ovariectomies was also cited at a hormone symposium at the 2010 American Psychiatric Association meeting, led by Wyeth-funded C. Neill Epperson, MD, and Claudio Soares, MD.[75] Unfortunately for the leaders, some women psychiatrists in the audience who had actually suffered from breast cancer said they were more interested in relief from their chemo drugs than new breakthroughs in more HRT.[76]

The mainstream and medical press also embraced the timing theory and hormone redux, agreeing to misremember both the 2002 WHI findings of just a few years earlier and the endometrial cancer wave in the 1970s and 1980s.

When then University of British Columbia's Joseph Ragaz, MD, announced at the 2010 San Antonio Breast Cancer Symposium that estrogen has "been largely ignored" and can protect women against breast cancer, no one disputed his remarks. Nor did anyone ask why women with uteruses (who are still at risk for endometrial cancer, just as they were in the 1970s) would want to trade breast cancer for endometrial cancer[77]—or why there are so many unnecessary hysterectomies, for that matter. The alleged heart benefits of HRT were also cited by doctors at a menopause conference in the Philippines in 2009 where they claimed, falsely, that "HRT has been approved by the US FDA for symptom management such as treatment of moderate to severe hot flushes and night sweats, treatment of moderate to severe vaginal dryness, and for the prevention of chronic diseases, osteoporosis, cardiovascular disease, cognitive disorders, dementia and skin atrophy."[78]

The *Washington Post* saw fit to reprint an entire pro-HRT article lifted intact from the Massachusetts General Hospital website, where it was posted next to an article by several Wyeth-funded KEEPS researchers who touted HRT "heart benefits" in 2009.[79] And the *New York Times* magazine ran a protiming theory piece the following year titled "The Estrogen Dilemma" by Cynthia Gorney, which quoted five HRT "experts" with their financial links to Wyeth *nowhere to be found*. Oops. The "experts" were Claudio Soares, MD, who extolled hormones at the 2010 American Psychiatric Association meeting; Louann Brizendine, MD; Roberta Diaz Brinton, PhD, an animal researcher; and Clarkson and Asthana from KEEPS, the trials investigating the use of HRT closer to menopause.[80] Several letters to the *Times* editor and public editor went unheeded.

REPLACING HORMONE REPLACEMENT

Even before the major medical centers reported on their "timing theory" trials, the theory itself was given a setback. A new analysis from the Million Women Study, sponsored by England's National Health Service, found that the women who observed the timing theory and took hormones the earliest—before or soon after the onset of menopause—were at the greatest risk of getting breast cancer.[81] Whereas the incidence of breast cancer for women fifty to fifty-nine years was 0.30 percent if they had never taken hormones, it was 0.46 percent if they started hormones five or more years after the onset of menopause—and 0.61 percent if they started hormones *less than five years after the onset of menopause*.[82]

The Million Women Study analysis stood the "timing theory" on its head: the sooner HRT was begun, the more harmful it was. (In fact, this was the second time HRT benefits had been stood on their head—the first had been the Women's Health Initiative in 2002.)

Luckily for Pharma, plenty of other medications can be marketed in HRT's place—and are. One of the first classes of drugs to benefit from HRT's downfall was bone drugs like Fosamax®, Boniva®, and Actonel®, which are known as bisphosphonates. Hormone replacement therapy prevents postmenopausal osteoporosis only if patients *remain* on the drugs. Unfortunately for bone-drug makers, remaining on bisphosphonates is discouraged, thanks to emerging links to heart problems, intractable pain, jawbone death (osteonecrosis), esophageal cancer, and some reports that the bone drugs caused the very bone fractures they were prescribed to prevent.[83]

Postmenopausal women have also been put on statins, like Pfizer's Lipitor®, to reduce coronary heart disease, and epileptic drugs like Lyrica® and Topamax® for hot flashes. But statins and epileptic drugs have risk profiles all their own.[84] Women are put on antidepressants, not just because of neurological actions that could treat hot flashes, but also because menopause still carries mental and emotional stigma. For sleeplessness and a new disease category called "menopause insomnia," women, of course, are given sleeping pills.[85]

Soon after the WHI findings were published, Wyeth was also exploring

HRT alternatives. In 2007, the company was trying to retrofit Pristiq®—an antidepressant molecularly related to the antidepressant Effexor XR®—as a nonhormonal menopause treatment, thereby playing both sides of the street. Pristiq was already approved as an antidepressant. But the FDA, noting that two women in Pristiq clinical trials had had heart attacks, three had needed procedures to repair clogged arteries, and others had had serious liver problems, asked Wyeth for more studies.[86] The FDA also asked for *longer* drug trials, since 604 of the 2,158 test subjects took Pristiq for only six months. (There were also seventeen suicides reported in Pristiq's post-marketing data—not a surprise, since suicide was a known risk with Effexor.)[87]

Smelling blood in the water at Wyeth's setback, drug industry reps in the snarky web chat room Cafepharma, piled on. "Pristiq is not a good drug by any standard," wrote one anonymous poster. "We tried to get 100 mg approved as the standard dose. But our patients got so sick that they [couldn't] care less about the efficacy. They just couldn't tolerate the drug long enough to see any improvement."[88] "No study exists showing any anti-depressant including Pristiq works any better than a placebo for reducing hot flashes, which are subjective anyway and only last a few minutes long at worst," wrote another anonymous poster. "That is a heavy price to pay to take a heavy duty drug 24/7 for a few minutes of daily relief that a sugar pill also provides. FDA is crazy (or bought) if they allow this unproven drug travesty on the market."[89] A third poster predicted women wouldn't trade "hot flashes for decreased libido, nausea, increased blood pressure and incredible withdrawal issues" found with Pristiq. "Women and their physicians are not as gullible as they were back in the Premarin days."[90]

Even psychiatrist Daniel Carlat, who wrote a 2007 *New York Times Magazine* exposé about working as a Wyeth-paid spokesman selling Effexor to other doctors, dissed Pristiq.[91] "Every patient who takes Effexor produces Pristiq in their own body, at no additional charge," he wrote in a blog article titled "Top 5 Reasons to Forget about Pristiq."[92]

Wyeth was also trying to play both sides of the street—hormone and "nonhormone"—with a new menopause drug that added bazedoxifene, an antiestrogen similar to the breast cancer drug tamoxifen, to Premarin. "Aprela was designed as an alternative to combination estrogen and progestin

therapy to treat the vasomotor symptoms associated with menopause without the potential safety concerns associated with combination estrogen/progestin therapy, and with better tolerability," read a 2010 journal article.[93] Of course, the "safety concerns" are cancer, and Wyeth/Pfizer hopes that bazedoxifene will counteract the estrogen and keep cancer from developing—just like adding Provera (medroxyprogesterone acetate) to Premarin was supposed to do when it created Prempro.[94]

Michelle Warren, MD, who ghostwrote a paper for Wyeth and Design-Write in 2004 (unretracted), also sees promise in adding bazedoxifene to Wyeth's original HRT drug.[95] Women "who are reluctant to take combination hormone therapies because of the publicity after WHI," she writes in the journal *Menopause* (as if cancer were nothing but a public relations problem), might find "improvement in their quality-of-life scores, including that for sleep" by adding bazedoxifene.

Meanwhile, Pharma is eyeing a demographic just as big as aging women and probably with more money: aging men. Increasingly, the moodiness, low libido, metabolic shifts, and other physical changes that come with age are attributed to "Low T," or low testosterone, in men. Will men be the next targets of weapons of hormonal therapy, having outlived their testes?

Chapter 4

THE WAR AFTER THE WAR
HOW A SCANDAL-LINKED DRUG IS
ADDING TO COMBAT TROOPS' WOUNDS

- It wasn't Sotheby's or Christie's, but the auction hall in Augusta, Georgia, in December 1998 that was packed. Georgians had come to gawk at antiques, paintings, and even suits of armor with which local researcher *noire* Richard Borison, MD, had planned to furnish his eleven-thousand-square-foot castle—that is, until he was cuffed and sent off to prison like a common criminal.

- Borison, former psychiatry chief at the Augusta Veterans Affairs (VA) medical center and Medical College of Georgia, and his partner had lured vulnerable veterans into risky psychoactive drug trials and pocketed the money, stealing more than $10 million from Georgia's only state medical school in the 1990s.[1] Despite the fifteen-year prison term to which Borison was sentenced, his 1996 US Seroquel® Study Group research, funded by AstraZeneca, is unretracted and still cited in 173 works, including current medical textbooks.[2]

- The buzz at the 2000 American Psychiatric Association meeting was the new drug Seroquel, which was reportedly "significantly superior" to older psychiatric drugs and was to be a "first-choice antipsychotic," according to research conducted by Charles Schulz, MD.[3] The then up-and-coming University of Minnesota psychiatry chief was plucked by London-based AstraZeneca to spin Seroquel after its 1997 approval.[4] But when AstraZeneca memos revealed that the superiority data was fabricated, Schulz told the *Star Tribune* that what he meant by "superior" was that the drugs worked "about the same." Schulz's research also cited Borison's work.[5]

- Seroquel's "beneficial effects on cognitive skills, particularly verbal reasoning, fluency skills, immediate recall, executive skills, and visuomotor tracking," got big billing in the *Journal of Clinical Psychiatry* in 2002. Patients were said to "receive significant neurocognitive benefit from being switched" from other drugs to Seroquel, effused Henry A. Nasrallah, MD. Some of Nasrallah's zeal, though, may derive from having been an AstraZeneca consultant, paid speaker, and grant recipient, as the article discloses.[6] He also worked with Borison in the original Seroquel study group research.

How did a drug approved for a limited number of psychiatric conditions become the *fifth-best-selling* medication in the United States? Exceeded only by Lipitor®, Nexium®, Plavix®, and Advair Diskus®? Earning AstraZeneca over *five billion dollars* in 2010?[7] A drug that Florida's Department of Juvenile Justice spends twice as much on as Advil®?[8] How did Seroquel become the VA's second-most prescribed drug, accounting for $125.4 million of the VA budget in 2009?[9] Prescribed not just after combat but *on the battlefield* by the Department of Defense (DOD) for the non-FDA-approved use of sleep?[10]

And why have the FDA, Inspector General, Surgeon General, and Congress enabled the VA and the DOD's Seroquel spree—despite eight corruption scandals, two illegal marketing settlements, and escalating troop deaths?[11]

Just good marketing!

When antipsychotic drugs like Seroquel were discovered in the 1990s, they seemed to be so free of the stigmatizing side effects of the older antipsychotics, like Haldol® and Thorazine (which often caused tremor, muscle rigidity, and repeated movements called tardive dyskinesia, the "Thorazine Shuffle"), they were hailed as "atypical" antipsychotics. But the honeymoon was short lived.

First, the same side effects as the older, "typical" drugs began to emerge with atypicals as patients used them for longer time periods than the eightto twelve-week trials for which they were approved.[12] Seroquel's label now warns of tardive dyskinesia, and some clinicians ask if the drugs should be called "atypicals" at all.[13] Next, a big government study found that atypicals work no better than typicals, though they cost ten times as much.[14]

Then safety questions surfaced. Before Seroquel even hit pharmacy shelves, its team leader at the FDA, Thomas Laughren, MD, noted that in a safety update since original data were reviewed, "there were 16 additional deaths" and "16 additional overdoses with quetiapine [Seroquel] revealing a similar profile of adverse events as seen with overdoses in the original database."[15] Yet it was approved. Soon afterward, an article in the *South Dakota Journal of Medicine* questioned Seroquel's long-term safety and its safety when combined with eleven other drugs.[16] And three years after Seroquel's approval, researchers—including some at the Cleveland Clinic—began questioning Seroquel's effect on the heart's electrical activity.[17] By 2005, Seroquel was causing the secondhighest number of "deaths due to poisoning involving antipsychotics" in England and Wales, according to the *Journal of Psychopharmacology*.[18]

Meanwhile, the AstraZeneca marketing plan for Seroquel, which pledged to "demonstrate safe and effective use in special populations: treatment resistant, elderly, Parkinson's disease, children and adolescents within 3 years of launch" was in full swing.[19] By 2001, the promotion and subsidized research of Michael Reinstein, then a Chicago psychiatrist, was "worth half a billion dollars," to AstraZeneca, according to its internal memos.[20] Reinstein prescribed Seroquel for over one thousand Chicago-area Medicaid patients per year, while subsidized by AstraZeneca, says the *Chicago Tribune* and *Propublica*, at a total cost of $7.6 million to taxpayers.[21]

By 2002, research from two female medical professionals promoting Seroquel—one a researcher at London's Institute of Psychiatry, and the other a ghostwriter at medical communications firm Parexel—might have owed its glow to the extracurricular research these women were conducting with AstraZeneca's US medical director for Seroquel.[22] Wayne MacFadden, MD, left the company in disgrace in 2006, after sexual affairs with the two women surfaced, but his hormonally enhanced work is unretracted and was even part of Seroquel's FDA approval package for bipolar disorder.[23]

During the same time period, a voting member of the FDA advisory committee charged with *recommending* Seroquel approvals, Jorge Armenteros, MD, was a paid AstraZeneca speaker! He even served as chairman of the committee in 2009.[24] The Florida child psychiatrist left his post only when the *Philadelphia Inquirer* exposed the extreme conflict of interest in 2009, and now there is barely a clue in FDA online records that he was ever there, much less that he was a committee chair. Jim Dailey, a former policy director and board member of the National Alliance on Mental Illness (NAMI), a group that was supposed to speak for "citizens," was also a paid consultant for AstraZeneca's Seroquel marketing team, according to *BNET*.[25]

Seroquel was approved by the FDA for schizophrenia in 1997, as a single or as an add-on drug for manic episodes associated with bipolar I disorder in 2004, and for "major depressive episodes associated with bipolar disorder" in 2006, the latter thanks to the study MacFadden headed before departing AstraZeneca.[26] In 2008, it was approved as an add-on drug for maintenance of bipolar I disorder, and the next year, for kids ages thirteen to seventeen with schizophrenia, and for kids ages ten to seventeen with bipolar mania. Not only is Seroquel's approval path a classic example of "indication creep"—once a drug is in use, subsequent approvals are easier—but who remembers when kids that age didn't get schizophrenia and bipolar mania?

In 2009, Seroquel got out of the "mentally ill" drug niche altogether and became a prescribed drug for the general population with depression—that's where the real bucks are. The FDA approved Seroquel XR® (an extendedrelease version of Seroquel) as an add-on drug to antidepressants, boosting its potential market from 1 or 2 percent of the population to 10 percent.

Some lauded the push for "add-on" psychiatric drugs, which seemed to begin when Abilify® was marketed for people as an add-on drug to antidepressants when "an antidepressant alone is not enough."[27] Those supporters said that adding a drug would be safer than going to higher doses of the current drug. But others asked why more drugs would be layered on top of a drug that isn't working in the first place. Who would or could take a cocktail of drugs that may not even be working—especially if those patients were paying out of their pockets?

By 2009, Seroquel had become the number-two drug at the VA, where more than one-half of all veterans from the Afghanistan and Iraq Wars being treated were getting psychiatric care.[28] Its use had leapt by *700 percent* within the DOD since 2001.[29] And Seroquel had become the unofficial drug of choice for sleeplessness and posttraumatic stress disorder (PTSD) in the military—though it was approved for neither. The Army Surgeon General's 2010 Pain Management Task Force Report lists Seroquel right next to Ambien® as a "sleep med." According to Nextgov, deployed troops are allowed a 180-day supply of Seroquel "for sleep" *in the theater of combat.*[30]

Elspeth Ritchie, then medical director of the army's Strategic Communications Office in 2008, legitimized Seroquel for unapproved PTSD use when she told the *Denver Post* that the medication "is proving very useful for the treatment of anxiety and combat-related nightmares. Thus it has been increasingly utilized as an adjunct for PTSD, in both the civilian and military worlds."[31]

You wouldn't think a government official would promote a non-government-approved use (PTSD) for a drug. But you also wouldn't think a government official would appear in a Pharma-funded video promoting the drugs. Yet in a continuing medical education (CME) webcast for Massachusetts General Hospital Psychiatry Academy, funded by AstraZeneca and Eli Lilly and Company, Ritchie calls antidepressants "very helpful for PTSD," and said that soldiers are "maintained" on long-term antidepressants. They are "sophisticated" psychiatric medicines used "on the battlefield," she claimed.[32]

A quick glance at government administrators shows other military financial links to Pharma. At the same time Mark Hamner, MD, directed PTSD clinical care at Ralph H. Johnson VA Medical Center in Charleston, South Carolina, he was publishing research funded by AstraZeneca about . . . *PTSD clinical care!*[33] Talk about a conflict of interest. "Significant improvements were noted in subjective sleep quality, latency, duration, sleep disturbances, episodes of terror, and acting out dreams," wrote Hamner and his coauthors from the VA hospital in the *Journal of Clinical Psychopharmacology*. "Sleep duration increased from 4.0 ± 1.0 to 6.0 ± 1.8 hours per night. Results also suggest a decrease in the level of anxiety and anger experienced during the memories and nightmares of the trauma."[34]

The AstraZeneca-funded study was titled "Quetiapine Improves Sleep Disturbances in Combat Veterans with PTSD: Sleep Data from a Prospective, Open-Label Study," which sounds more like advertising than "research." Hamner also taught an AstraZeneca-funded CME on the medical education site Medscape, with Charles "superior means about the same" Schulz, which had a similar advertising-not-research tone. "Broadening the Horizon of Atypical Antipsychotic Applications" examined the use of Seroquel and similar drugs, Zyprexa® and Risperdal®, for PTSD and sleep disorders.[35]

Doctors are required to earn a certain number of CME credits a year to keep their state licenses. But the dumbed-down courses, usually funded by Pharma, have become associated so much with huckstering that they were investigated by Congress in 2008.[36] Hamner lists his disclosures for the CME course as: "Grant Support: AstraZeneca Pharmaceuticals, Bristol-Myers Squibb, Eli Lilly and Company, Forest Laboratories, Janssen Pharmaceutica; Speaker: AstraZeneca Pharmaceuticals, Bristol-Myers Squibb, Forest Laboratories, Janssen Pharmaceutica; Consultant: AstraZeneca Pharmaceuticals, Bristol-Myers Squibb, Janssen Pharmaceutica; Stock: Pfizer, Inc. Schultz lists his disclosures as: Grant Support: Abbott Laboratories, AstraZeneca Pharmaceuticals, Eli Lilly and Company, Janssen Pharmaceutica; Speaker and Consultant: AstraZeneca Pharmaceuticals, Eli Lilly and Company."[37]

Hamner particularly likes Janssen's Risperdal and says that researchers "noticed a reduction in intrusive memories on a patient checklist for PTSD, and also a reduction in irritability on the Overt Aggression Scale," with the drug.[38] In 2011, a large study found that Risperdal worked no better than a placebo for PTSD, and that the $717 million the VA spent over nine years using Risperdal to treat the PTSD of troops in Afghanistan and Iraq was a waste of taxpayers' money and a major disservice to soldiers.[39] Researchers speculated that Seroquel was just as worthless. Where did clinicians ever get the idea that Risperdal and Seroquel would work for PTSD?

Hamner, an original member of Borison's Seroquel study group, is hardly the only fox guarding the henhouse. Lori L. Davis, MD, chief of research and development of the Tuscaloosa VA Medical Center's Human Research Protection Program, and who collaborated with Hamner on two Seroquel trials, lists sixteen financial links to Pharma—including AstraZeneca—in a medical journal article.[40]

And then there is Matthew Friedman, MD, who was both executive director of the VA's entire National Center for PTSD and a self-declared AstraZeneca consultant, according to VA materials published in 2010.[41] He also served as a "Pfizer visiting professor" in 2011, teaching the course "Post-Traumatic

Stress Disorder and Traumatic Brain Injury: The Phenomenology, Neurobiology and Treatment of Invisible Wounds," according to the Pfizer Fellowships website.[42]

One of the CMEs taught by Friedman on the VA website in 2011 promised to teach doctors "the current evidence regarding the effectiveness of different medications for PTSD." "Pharmacological interventions for PTSD are common, and considerable research has been conducted on the effectiveness of such treatment," he writes, unblinkingly.[43] Friedman is also a coauthor of the American Psychiatric Association PTSD guideline, which says there's evidence that atypicals like Seroquel work as "adjunctive treatment" in PTSD when antidepressants aren't effective.[44] Where did clinicians ever get the idea of using atypicals for PTSD?

It is illegal for Pharma to market off-label uses of drugs, and AstraZeneca's $520 million settlement in 2009 included a charge of illegally promoting Seroquel for PTSD. But it's not illegal to "float" such uses in CMEs and journal articles and distribute them as "research." The reprints they generate are confidence-inspiring sales tools (because they come from medical journals): "See, Doc? It says right here . . ."—especially when researchers are with the government.

For example, Pfizer bought and distributed thirty thousand reprints of a *Journal of the American Medical Association* (*JAMA*) article that made the drug Celebrex® look safe, even though an FDA medical officer ruled the findings misleading (and the FDA later investigated the distribution), reports the consumer advocacy group Public Citizen.[45] But the faux reprinted article was cited 169 times in the medical literature, and Celebrex's sales catapulted from $2.62 to $3.1 billion.

HORRORS ON THE BATTLEFIELD—AND AFTERWARD

Warrior Transition Units (WTUs) were created by the DOD in 2007 to provide intensive aftercare for troops after a shocking exposé by the *Washington Post* about substandard care at Walter Reed Army Medical Center. The units were intended to return wounded soldiers to duty or to civilian life but have devolved into "warehouses of despair, where damaged men and women are kept out of sight, fed a diet of powerful prescription pills, and treated harshly by noncommissioned officers," says the *New York Times*.[46]

Headed by traditional army officers, not healthcare professionals, soldiers at the WTUs are simultaneously accused of being "crazy," and of faking their PTSD, says the *Times*. They are drugged to the point where they can barely "exercise, wake for morning formation, and attend classes"—which then earns them further abuse. "Medications are so abundant that some soldiers in the unit openly deal, buy or swap prescription pills," reports the *Times*. The report continues to say that "some soldiers have become addicted to their medications or have turned to heroin readily available in the barracks."[47]

At least thirty-two soldiers and marines at WTUs died of accidental prescription drug overdoses between 2007 and 2010, reported the *Army Times*. "Most of the troops had been prescribed 'drug cocktails,' combinations of drugs including painkillers, sleeping pills, antidepressants and anti-anxiety drugs," wrote the military paper of the deaths. "In all cases, suicide was ruled out." An army internal review into the noncombat deaths found the "biggest risk factor" was "putting a soldier on numerous drugs simultaneously, a practice known as polypharmacy," reported *Military Times* news website.[48]

One of the deceased was Sgt. John Conant, thirty-six, who had mixed morphine and Ambien and had stayed at a WTU. A coroner ruled his death a result of natural causes, reported the *Army Times*. Conant received only medication and no "meaningful" therapy at the Fort Carson, Colorado, WTU after he returned from Iraq, said his wife.[49] "These kids change their medication like they change their underwear," said an unidentified psychotherapist at the Fort Carson WTU. "They can't even remember which pills they're taking."[50]

This type of medical abuse of servicepeople with PTSD is hardly limited to WTUs. After returning to Fort Carson from service in Iraq and requesting counseling for PTSD, Pfc. Michael Nahas of Reidsville, North Carolina, was confined by his commanders and ordered to "kill himself" over a period of eight months, "so we [the military] don't have to pay for your welfare later," charges his mother, Mary Galione-Nahas. He was given "a cocktail of powerful psychiatric drugs and sleep aids," which, combined with the badgering, succeeded in causing Nahas to attempt suicide, she says.[51] After being released from a private Colorado Springs hospital after the unsuccessful attempt, Nahas was confined again to the barracks, where the psychological abuse continued, provoking him to leave without authorization. He was apprehended by a group of sergeants and specialists at his nearby apartment with such force he had to again be hospitalized for injuries. He has since been diagnosed with a brain injury, says Galione-Nahas.[52]

When the same group of men sought to remand Nahas to the barracks a second time, Galione-Nahas feared for her son's life and posted a frantic letter on Facebook®, which prompted nationally known soldier advocate Andrew Pogany to intervene.

Pogany is a staff sergeant who volunteered to serve in Iraq in 2003, but after experiencing PTSD-like panic symptoms and hallucinations related to violence in theater, he was sent back to Fort Carson and charged with "cowardly conduct as a result of fear."[53] Pogany and his attorney were able to prove that his reaction probably stemmed from Lariam®, a malaria drug with effects "similar to Post-traumatic Stress Disorder," according to the VA. Lariam "should not be given to anyone with symptoms of a brain injury, depression or anxiety disorder," reported *Army Times*, when the army began to phase out the drug in 2009. These symptoms describe "many troops who have deployed to Iraq or

Afghanistan." Lariam effects can last for "weeks, months, and even years," after it's stopped, says the VA, and the malaria drug was investigated after several soldiers murdered their wives at Fort Bragg, North Carolina, in 2002.[54]

After charges against Pogany were dropped and he was honorably discharged, he became a vehement advocate for the rights of soldiers with PTSD, especially when psychoactive drugs were involved. And, when Pogany saw Mary Galione-Nahas's SOS on Facebook, he lost no time in blocking the sergeants and specialists seeking to apprehend Nahas from the hospital. Galione-Nahas says that Pogany, along with Vicky Ray, the Texas state representative for the severely wounded at the DOD who also intervened, saved her son.[55]

Galione-Nahas's father and Michael's grandfather was Private John M. Galione, who is credited with discovering the Mittelbau-Dora concentration camp in Nordhausen, Germany, in 1945, and helping to liberate its prisoners. Galione-Nahas has written a book about her father's dogged pursuit of the camp and the fortuitous events that led to the rescue operation. What an irony, said Galione-Nahas, that the grandson of a war liberator would end up like a prisoner himself.[56]

Sgt. Bryan Lampe, a seventeen-year marine veteran who had deployed twice to Iraq and once to Afghanistan and Puerto Rico, also developed extreme PTSD while serving in Afghanistan in 2009.[57] "He went from being loving on the phone, to saying he never wanted to see me and our daughter again," said his wife, Erica, in an interview. "He said not to even bother coming to the airport to meet him, because he would walk right past us." When the couple did reunite, Bryan was frail and thin, and "the whites of his eyes were brown," says Erica.[58] He was both ridiculed and overmedicated for PTSD by his commanders, and the formerly competent drill instructor became increasingly unpredictable, suicidal, and violent. Lampe was incarcerated in the brig at Camp Lejeune, North Carolina, for assault in 2011, with neither his PTSD nor probable exposure to Lariam factored into his behavior, says his wife and soldier advocates. He was also given Seroquel in the brig, says Erica.[59]

Corporal Chad Oligschlaeger of Austin, Texas, also encountered ridicule and overmedication for his PTSD by superiors at the Twentynine Palms Marine Base after his service in Iraq. Instead of being given the opportunity to work through the trauma he experienced and witnessed, he was put on a drug cocktail of Zolpidem®, a sleeping pill; Trazodone®, an antidepressant; Prozac® and Zoloft®, both antidepressants; propranolol, a blood-pressure drug; lorazepam and clonazepam, anxiety pills; Chantix®, an antismoking drug with many warnings; and Seroquel, says his mother, Julie Oligschlaeger, of Houston, Texas. At a PTSD "therapy" session, he was admonished not to talk about a firefight that had been haunting him because "you can only discuss Iraq on Wednesdays," the group leader said, according to Oligschlaeger's mother. In an interview, Julie Oligschlaeger says she implored officers at Twentynine Palms to check on Chad because of the heavy drug cocktail, his severe memory problems, and the fact that he was living alone in the barracks. He was found four days later by two marines in what was later classified as an accidental death due to multiple-drug toxicity.[60]

The hurt and confusion did not end there for the Oligschlaeger family. "I was not even allowed to talk to the doctor when I flew to Twentynine Palms. Even his barracks-mates were instructed not to talk to me," says Julie. "When I showed his medical records to a doctor from Texas A&M University, she said to me, 'You realize the military killed your son, don't you?' The drugs Chad was taking should only have been prescribed in a clinical setting, and even then, not prescribed together."[61]

LEST WE FORGET

It is spring in Charleston, West Virginia, and yellow forsythia blossoms unfold as the temperature reaches seventy degrees. Red-winged blackbirds buzz above, scoping their spring nesting territories. As dusk settles, cars and trucks pull up to the one-story Unitarian Universalist church along the Kanawha River for a Thursday night PTSD support group. This night, they are letting a reporter attend.

Around the table are veterans of the Iraq and Afghanistan Wars; their wives and mothers; older veterans, including those who served in Vietnam; and people with PTSD from nonmilitary causes. The informal group, publicized through local fliers at high-traffic sites like Walmart, differs from PTSD support offered by the VA in several ways, says retired S.Sgt. Tom Vande Burgt, who founded the group with his wife. "There are no strings attached. We don't have a drug-company or VA or church message. You can come and talk about what's bugging you and no one's going to write it down or use it against you."[62]

"We include the family. That's another huge difference," adds Tom's wife, Diane, a mother of four. "When Tom tried to get PTSD help from the VA, they acted like it was none of my business. They didn't even want me in the room, until Tom overruled them. We also offer childcare, which seems pretty basic, except other PTSD support groups don't."[63] In 2011, Diane received the West Virginia Jefferson Award for her devotion to veteran causes and went on to represent the state in Washington, DC, proceedings.

Originally, meetings of the two-year-old Lest We Forget group, funded by the Council of Churches' Care-Net, were held in a VA building, until turf battles broke out. "'You're stealing my patients! You're not professionals!" an emotionally distraught VA counselor reportedly exploded at an early meeting, convincing Tom and Diane the group had to have a thick firewall between itself and the VA.[64] Lest We Forget offers support, not therapy, the Vande Burgts are quick to point out. But its message of peer-support advocacy, like telling vets to bring a support person to doctors' appointments to write down instructions and ask treatment questions, still ruffles the feathers of professional therapists at the VA.

But it was just such questions that saved Tom's life, says the couple. Veterans Administration psychiatrists had so overmedicated Tom's PTSD from his tour in Iraq—adding drugs to treat side effects of other drugs in an expanding, risky cocktail—that he tried to strangle Diane when she showed up at his workplace. That's when the Vande Burgts resolved to balance VA care and its "pills forever" stance with answers they find on their own and from other families dealing with PTSD.

"PTSD can resemble domestic violence," says Diane. "I tell women, if he wasn't violent before, then it's the PTSD. It's not your marriage and it's not you. And that goes for intimate issues too. VA counselors tried to tell us our problems were our marriage and not the PTSD, and they were flat out wrong."[65] Tonight, Diane shares a letter that Tom received from the VA yesterday, urging him to get help for his "mental illness" of PTSD to preserve family "safety," which, she says, proves her point. "A husband would never show this letter to his family," she vents. "It's calling him mentally ill and dangerous! PTSD is not an illness, it is a condition. I liken it to my bee phobia. I'm fine all winter, but when it's warm and there are bees around me, I can't concentrate on anything else. I am hypervigilant. It's no different than a veteran scoping for dead dogs and piles of trash on the side of the road because that's where they hid the IEDs that they used on them in theater."[66]

Doctors say PTSD resembles extreme sleep deprivation, with symptoms like anxiety, mood changes, impulsivity, suspicion to the point of paranoia, illusions and hallucinations, amnesia, mental befuddlement, extreme sleepiness, and craving for drugs and mood-altering substances. And, like alcoholism, PTSD tends to gets worse over time, says the group. "I was a police officer after Vietnam, and it never dawned on me when I stuck a Magnum in someone's face and told them I would kill them and *meant it*, that it was the PTSD talking," says a regular group member, who now works with other vets. "You can't shoot at people and be shot at by people, and *not* get PTSD.[67]

A mother in the group, who gives her name as Mary Ellen, is worried about her son. Since returning from Iraq, he is getting worse—unable to hold a job, irritable, and avoiding people. These are classic PTSD symptoms, which often don't even appear in the first year, the group says. "Your son needs an advocate to go to doctors' appointments with him," says Tom. "PTSD fries the short-term memory, so he won't remember doctors' instructions. And if they give him drugs and he develops side effects, you'll be the first one to see it, not him."[68]

"When I got involved in my daughter's care, they ended up demonizing me and retaliating against Lindsay," says Lest We Forget member Robin, whose daughter developed PTSD after serving as an MP (military police) in Iraq in 2010. "Medical staff stonewalled me even though I am her medical power of attorney, and she was actually threatened because of 'what your Mom is doing.'"[69]

There are many reasons why involvement in the wars in Iraq and Afghanistan produce extreme PTSD, says Tom Vande Burgt, starting with soldiers being under fire for an entire year, "port-o-potties made into swiss cheese," by enemy fire, unarmored Humvees, unclear civilian loyalties, and no safe place but the base.[70] "Even though everyone in the West Virginia Guard has been deployed, except the band, 99 percent of the country has no stake in the war and doesn't care," says Tom. "In past wars, 20 percent of the population sent someone or knew someone who was lost. Now you return to your job after being mortared, rocketed, and watching tracers for a year, and nothing's different. It's like it never happened."[71]

And the e-mail and Skype® exchanges that are supposed to keep soldiers closer to the family? "It adds to your problems and feelings of isolation," says Tom, who recounts arguing with an appliance repairman while in the deserts of Iraq.[72]

The military's treatment for PTSD, recounted by Lest We Forget members, sounds like a joke. Anger-management meetings can be held on weekday afternoons when working people probably can't attend, or at inconvenient locations eighty miles away. Alcoholic treatment programs, says the group, sometimes exclude patients because the troops are on the very drugs the VA gives them, placing the soldiers in an incomprehensible catch-22. The group also complains about therapists who are so out of touch with war realities; they think an RPG is a *car*, not a rocket-propelled grenade. There are also complaints of therapists who barely speak English. Drug refills, they say, arrive in the mail with no explanation, no doctor supervision, and sometimes no diagnosis, almost ensuring self-medication and overdoses.[73]

Upon her return from duty in Iraq, Lindsay's PTSD was also simultaneously underrecognized and overmedicated at Fort Richardson in Alaska, says her mother, Robin. "I went to the command and said I can't even wake her up because of all the medicine she's on." This occurred during a visit, three months after she returned from Iraq. "How is she supposed to do PT [physical therapy] and even get out of bed?" Lindsay's drug cocktail included, at various times, Seroquel, the seizure drug Lyrica®, Robaxin®, muscle relaxers, painkillers, antidepressants, and high blood pressure drugs, according to Robin.[74] After Lindsay fell more than once from the drug cocktails and was blocked by her command in seeking counseling and Judicial Advocate General services, Robin opened a congressional investigation with the help then of West Virginia senator Jay Rockefeller and Congresswoman Shelley Capito, which got Lindsay the care she needed—literally through an "act of Congress."

Tales of similar overmedication are the rule, not the exception at Lest We

Forget meetings. One veteran describes standing on a bridge over the Kanawha River after a drug cocktail left him suicidal. Member Mary Ellen says her son is highly medicated.[75] And Cpl. Andrew White, whose father, Stan White, is known as the patriarch of Lest We Forget, was on four antidepressants, two drugs for seizures, three pain medications, and an astounding 1,600 milligrams of Seroquel when he died in 2008 at the age of twenty-three.[76]

LIVING WITH LOSS

With its flat-screen TV, thick carpeting, and portraits over the mantel, Stan and Shirley White's basement family room in their Cross Lanes home near Charleston, West Virginia, seems right out of the American Dream. Until you realize both of the young men whose pictures hang over the fireplace are gone.

Five days after Andrew returned from Iraq, where his duties included locating and deactivating explosive devices, the news came that his older brother Robert had died in Afghanistan. Thirty-four-year-old Robert, a staff sergeant, was riding in a Humvee when it was hit by a rocket-propelled grenade. His ashes were spread over Fort Bragg, where a monument now commemorates his life. The White's oldest son, Will, is in the navy, and the baby of the family, Christina, is in college, majoring in criminal justice.[77]

Like many sufferers of PTSD, Andrew seemed fine at first, going back to school and working as a line cook and a car salesman. But after a year and a half, he began to feel angry, depressed, and reclusive—especially as the dosage of the PTSD drugs the VA prescribed him was increased. Andrew's mother, Shirley, a soft-spoken former elementary schoolteacher, began to call Andrew's clinicians and to accompany him on appointments, asking if the symptoms they were treating weren't, at least partially, from the drugs themselves. "You need to do what we say," replied Dr. Marlin Schauland, then Andrew's primary doctor at the VA hospital in Huntington, West Virginia. And when Andrew sought the services of a private psychiatrist, Schauland admonished him that he had to "deal with the VA and no one else."[78]

Andrew got worse, not better. He gained so much weight that his boots wouldn't fit. A private endocrinologist prescribed a testosterone patch to counteract the feminizing effects—like testicular atrophy—of the drug cocktail he was on. And on February 12, 2008, the day after a VA appointment found him to be fine, Andrew died at home. When Stan and Shirley drove to Huntington to personally tell Schauland the news, the VA doctor said he was sorry, but he wouldn't have "done anything differently."[79]

"There's nothing wrong with our soldiers; they are reacting normally to what happened to them!" says Georgeann Underwood, a friend of the Whites who has taken a break from selling real estate in the Charleston area to have a midmorning cup of coffee at the White's kitchen table.[80] Underwood, whose spiky white hair belies her seventy-plus years, is sympathetic to soldiers who have had trouble processing their war experiences and who have been given heavy PTSD drug cocktails. Her grandson, Private First Class Derek Johnson of Hurricane, West Virginia, died of such a cocktail.

When the twenty-two-year-old returned from Afghanistan in 2005 with PTSD and injuries, he was put on Seroquel, Paxil®, and Klonopin®, first by military doctors, and then by private ones. Like Andrew White, Derek also got worse instead of better. "He was the kindest of my three grandchildren, and I raised him until he was eleven, but his whole personality changed," says Georgeann.[81] "It was like having an ADHD child around. He would wrap everything up in duct tape. He'd have emotional outbursts. He'd be so drugged he couldn't stand, but he'd still try to drive his kids somewhere."

Derek was so agitated, says Georgeann, that he couldn't even wait at the VA hospital to receive his drugs, so she and her husband "privately paid for his drugs, thinking we were helping eliminate some of the stress and going on the assumption that the doctors know best." Finally, though, the effect of the drugs dawned on Georgeann, and she said to her husband, "I think the drugs are killing him. He's getting worse."[82]

Derek died in May of 2008, three months after Andrew. A "shoebox" of Seroquel and Klonopin was found in his room, says Georgeann. As of 2011, the Underwoods still have not seen the toxicology report.[83]

In 2009, one year after Andrew died, the Whites drove to Capitol Hill to visit the offices of members of the VA committee. They left packets of information detailing the suspicious deaths of Andrew and other military personnel but were allowed only to meet with then committee chairman Sen. Jay

Rockefeller and West Virginia congresswoman Shelley Capito. Later that year, the Whites mailed over fifty information packets to the Senate and House Veterans Affairs committees, to First Lady Michelle Obama, and to major news networks. Only the First Lady and L. Tammy Duckworth, then VA assistant secretary for public and intergovernmental affairs—and also an Iraq War veteran—responded, says Stan White, which was discouraging.[84]

But the results of a department of VA Office of Inspector General investigation into the deaths of Andrew White and another veteran were even more disappointing. "There was no apparent signal to indicate increased mortality for patients taking the combination of quetiapine [Seroquel], paroxetine [Paxil], and clonazepam [Klonopin] when compared with patients taking other similar combinations of psychotropic medications," said the report. "The direct impact of non-prescribed medications in these patient deaths cannot be determined."[85]

AN ELEPHANT IN THE ROOM CALLED BIG PHARMA

Since the Whites' visit to Washington, DC, the government has increased awareness about PTSD while still ignoring the elephant in the room called Big Pharma. For example, the DOD and the VA are finally acknowledging that traumatic head injuries (TBIs), which are so common in Iraq and Afghanistan combat and which can permanently change brain structure and behavior, are linked to PTSD.[86] But the military agencies miss the crucial biological corollary that TBIs increase the permeability of the blood-brain barrier and make the drug given for PTSD several times as potent.

The government is also in denial about Iraq- and Afghanistan-era suicides, although, by its own admission, more "young men and women die in combat than die by their own actions."[87] According to a *CBS News* investigation in 2005, there were 120 suicides "each and every week, in just one year."[88] Prescription drugs were involved in almost one-third of active-duty suicides, reported an army-named suicide-prevention task force, which indicts the shift from talk therapy and counseling to medication-centered treatment seen in both the military and society in general for the rising suicides.[89] "Research needs to be done to determine those specific medications that will reduce anxiety and depression without increasing suicidal risk," the task force's report states.[90]

But the long-anticipated 2010 army report, "Health Promotion, Risk Reduction, Suicide Prevention," blames the economy, the stress of nine years of war, family dislocations, repeated moves and deployments, lowered entrance standards, and the "high-risk-behavior" of troops for the rash of military suicides since the wars began, without looking at its own prescription drug spree.[91] Elspeth Ritchie, in her AstraZeneca-funded video, similarly blames "dear John e-mails" and access to loaded weapons as opposed to the psychoactive medications she admits soldiers are given.[92]

Atypical antipsychotics like Seroquel are not the only dangerous drugs prescribed for troops. In the 2010 army suicide report, then Gen. Peter W. Chiarelli acknowledges that there is "fair quality evidence that second generation antidepressants (mostly SSRI) increase suicidal behavior in adults aged 18 to 29 years."[93] But he omits mentioning the suicide-linked seizure drugs that have also become military darlings, like Klonopin, Lyrica, Neurontin, Topamax, Depakote®, Lamictal®, Tegretol®, and Depakene®. In fact, the government wasted $51 million on Lamictal in 2009, says the American Enterprise Institute, instead of buying the generic version.[94]

Former Vice Army Chief Peter Chiarelli also omits mention of the asthma drug Singulair®, the acne drug Accutane®, and the antismoking drug Chantix, all of which are linked to suicide, according to the FDA.[95] Worst of all, he leaves out the malaria drug Lariam, which, according to the Associated Press, is still in use and even has increased in use in the military.[96] In the nonfiction *Murder in Baker Company*, author Cilla McCain asks whether the use of Lariam might explain the actions of the soldiers accused in the grisly death of Army Specialist Richard Davis.[97]

Instead of indicting the PTSD "prescribathon" that Pharma set in motion, the army report blamed troops' illicit use of street drugs and risky behavior for the suicides. (The report doesn't even explore if the deaths *are* suicides.) For example, the report reveals that 21 percent of eight thousand urine samples with prescription drug traces show "illicit" drugs—as if the shocking figure is 21 percent, and not eight thousand.[98] And when Robert Siegel, then an announcer for National Public Radio flat-out asked General Chiarelli if the high number of troops on psychoactive medication was a factor in the suicides, the general said, "The good thing about those numbers is the prescriptions were all made by a doctor."[99] The word *illicit* appears 150 times in the report, and the word *psychiatrist* appears twice.[100]

The army is so convinced that the daily meds being dispensed are not the problem that a new "suicide form" suggested in the "Health Promotion, Risk Reduction, Suicide Prevention" report does not even have a box for the military's medical professionals to check for "adverse effects" or "drug interactions." Instead, boxes on the proposed new form ask how long before a suicide a patient was "compliant" with a prescription, and whether the medication was taken as prescribed, whether it was "skipped," or whether it was used in "excess."[101] What if the medicine, taken exactly as prescribed, was the cause? Still, by the end of 2011, there were some winds of DOD change. President Barack Obama announced that condolence letters will now be sent to families of service members who kill themselves while serving in combat overseas. "They didn't die because they are weak," said the president.[102] And a health advisory group to the secretary of defense suggested the department reexamine its policy of allowing troops in combat zones to use Seroquel "in low doses as a sleep aid, despite its connections to the deaths of two Marines who died of drug overdoses," reported the federal IT site Nextgov.[103]

SPINNING SEROQUEL-RELATED DEATHS

In addition to Seroquel's published side effects, like high blood sugar, diabetes, weight gain, increased LDL ("bad") cholesterol, decrease of white blood cells, cataracts, and tardive dyskinesia, the drug can also cause heart problems. In fact, Seroquel's link to sudden cardiac death, which some noncombat deaths appear to be, was even on the docket when Diane Vande Burgt and Stan and Shirley White attended FDA hearings in April of 2009 to consider expanding Seroquel's approvals to include depression.

Testifying at the hearings was Wayne Ray, PhD, then professor of preventive medicine at Vanderbilt University, who had just published research in the *New England Journal of Medicine* suggesting that patients on antipsychotics like Seroquel showed double the risk of a "sudden, fatal, pulseless condition, or collapse."[104] The article was titled "Atypical Antipsychotic Drugs and the Risk of Sudden Cardiac Death." Asked by Tom Laughren, director of the FDA's Division of Psychiatry Products, why AstraZeneca's own drug trials didn't "pick up a difference in sudden cardiac death," Ray replied that Astra-Zeneca's methodology suffered from "Simpson's paradox," pooling data from all clinical trials into one large data set with no allowances for the differences in the trials. It is the same distortion that made drugs like Vioxx look safe, said Ray.[105]

Couldn't the death certificates that said "sudden cardiac death" be inaccurate? asked Marc Stone, an FDA medical reviewer present at the hearings. "Paramedics are more likely to identify some deaths as sudden cardiac deaths," he said, then asked, "How do we know smoking wasn't a factor in the deaths?" There were other explanations for the deaths besides Seroquel, said Stone. The patients might have been "less likely to seek medical attention or disclose to anyone symptoms of a potentially rapidly fatal condition such as infection, pulmonary embolism, anaphylactic shock or drug overdose, to name a few," dissembled Stone. "Prescription of an antipsychotic drug, and even the dose of an antipsychotic drug, may simply correlate with the risk of dying alone."[106]

Despite Ray's testimony about sudden cardiac death with drugs like Seroquel, its add-on use for depression sailed through the advisory committee and was approved later in the year by the FDA. Seroquel was also approved later in the year for children, though the news seems to have been buried. Not only was it announced between Christmas and New Year's (by AstraZeneca, not the FDA); the new pediatric indication was noted as a mere "label change" on the FDA website—though the change represents millions in insurance reimbursements.

So it came as quite a surprise that, after FDA hearings dismissed "possible risks of sudden cardiac death" with Seroquel, the FDA announced there were indeed heart risks associated with Seroquel and that Seroquel and Seroquel XR "should be avoided" in combination with at least twelve other medications![107] The combinations were linked to a heart arrhythmia that can cause sudden cardiac arrest, said the new FDA warning. Seroquel was unsafe to take with some heart rhythm drugs, synthetic opioids like methadone, antibiotics, antiinfectives, and other antipsychotics, including Geodon® and Thorazine—just as many medical reports and clinicians had originally said.[108]

In fact, Seroquel was so unsafe the new FDA label cautioned that it probably should not be used at all by the elderly or by people with heart disease. The decision to reevaluate Seroquel's safety stemmed from "reports of arrhythmia in 17 people who took more than the recommended doses," reported the *New York Times*.[109] But the FDA announcement raised other questions (beyond why Seroquel was mass-prescribed to troops for off-label uses to begin with—and why it is *still* being prescribed.) Why, for example, did the FDA, specifically its Center for Drug Evaluation and Research (CDER), stonewall Seroquel safety questions for years, even as the number of casualties rose?

Just three months before the label change, Janet Woodcock, MD, then director of CDER, dismissed concerns from the watchdog group Project on Government Oversight over potentially lethal interactions between methadone and Seroquel.[110] "At this point, there is agreement within CDER that an interaction between quetiapine [Seroquel] and methadone that confers unreasonable risks to patients is exceedingly unlikely and, therefore, no further action is indicated regarding the labeling for these products or for related communication initiatives,"[111] she writes in a rambling, defensive letter.

When a reporter asked the FDA why Woodock's decision was followed by an unexplained policy reversal three months later, there was more FDA defensiveness. Sandy Walsh, an FDA spokesperson, said Woodcock's conclusions were still correct, "because the F.D.A. had found no biological basis for a problem or unusual numbers of deaths at normal dosages."[112] Deaths occurred only from drug interactions and overdoses?

STILL MARKETED, STILL A WONDER DRUG

On the surface, 2011 looked like a bad year for Seroquel. Not only did it receive new warnings about heart risks—finally, said many critics—but the atypical antipsychotics were found to be worthless for PTSD in a *JAMA* study.[113] Undaunted, AstraZeneca began marketing Seroquel for its newly approved depression indication and rolled out a campaign titled "Still Trying to Get Ahead of Your Depression."

Why does AstraZeneca want more people to use Seroquel when it has already settled almost twenty-five thousand personal injury suits, according to the Associated Press—and is probably settling them as fast as they are brought?[114] Is AstraZeneca's marketing strategy "Sue us, please!" as *BNET* charges?[115] Of course, everyone knows the answer. It's cheaper for AstraZeneca to hype Seroquel until its patents run out and clean up damages later because wrongful death payouts are built into the business plan. AstraZeneca has paid $1.5 billion, so far, in Seroquel settlements, which is equal to one good year of Seroquel sales.[116] There's plenty of money left over for researchers, doctors, and VA administrators. Especially with Borison himself out of prison.

Meanwhile, despite the 2011 recommendation of the Defense Health Board (which advises the secretary of defense) that the use of Seroquel and other atypicals for sleep in combat zones should be "discouraged" because of metabolic and cardiac risks, especially in unmonitored combat zones, and a "lack of supportive evidence," the military reaffirmed its commitment to Seroquel a short time later.[117] Lower doeses of Seroquel "can still be safely and effectively used as a sleep aid" in theater, said then Army Maj. T. G. Taylor, a spokesman for US Central Command (CENTCOM), and Seroquel "is particularly useful for patients with insomnia who do not respond to conventional sleep aids."[118]

If you didn't know better, you'd think the military decision makers were consulting to Pharma.

Chapter 5

A SIDE EFFECT FROM WHICH THERE IS NO RECOVERY

Y ou don't have to look hard to find Neurontin horror stories.

Two months after taking Pfizer's epilepsy drug for pain—not an FDA-approved use—Richard Smith, a seventy-nine-year-old retired Church of Christ minister, shot himself. Neurontin made him feel "not himself," said his family, who called the death inexplicable because he "was a godly man and he knew suicide was wrong."[1]

Nor do you have to look hard to find horror stories associated with the antidepressant Cymbalta®.

Who can forget the macabre Cymbalta-related death of Carol Anne Gotbaum, who accidentally strangled herself in police custody at Phoenix's Sky Harbor Airport in 2007?[2] Or the suicide on Eli Lilly's own campus of nineteen-year-old Traci Johnson, a drug-trial volunteer who had been switched to a placebo after one month of taking high doses of the drug?[3]

Suicide in the post-Prozac® era is such an epidemic that it's even struck Eli Lilly itself, which, of course, created Prozac and Cymbalta. Shortly after Lilly CEO Randall Tobias resigned as deputy secretary of state in 2007 because of a prostitution scandal, the alleged madam, Deborah Jeane Palfrey, killed herself.[4] Thirteen years earlier, Tobias's wife, Marilyn, had killed herself.[5] And in 2009, former Lilly president August Watanabe, MD, who had been at the bedside of Marilyn Tobias when she died, killed *himself*.[6]

Psychiatric drugs are not the only medications to have shocking side effects. Carter Albrecht, a musician with Edie Brickell & New Bohemians, was shot to death by a neighbor while acting aggressively on Chantix®, the antismoking drug banned by the FDA for use by pilots, air traffic controllers, and interstate drivers after 227 reports of suicidal acts and 28 suicides.[7] And fifteen-year-old Cody Miller of Queensbury, New York, took his own life while on the widely used asthma and allergy drug Singulair®, whose suicidal side effects the FDA subsequently publicized.[8]

In fact, there have been more than five thousand published reports of murder, suicide, and other violence linked to prescription psychoactive drugs since 1988. These reports are archived on a website called SSRI Stories. (SSRIs are antidepressants like Prozac, Zoloft®, and Paxil®, which debuted about twenty-five years ago.) But even though a shocking number of murders, mass murders, and suicides are linked to prescription drugs—including the shootings at Columbine High School in Colorado; Red Lake reservation in Minnesota; Northern Illinois University; and Virginia Tech—Pharma and the medical centers, researchers, ad agencies, research organizations, and government cronies it lobbies keep the drugs on the market.

Doug Alsberge, MD, practiced occupational medicine near Seattle.[9] A devoted father of two sons, he enjoyed hiking, sailing, swimming, and golf, and liked to write and play his acoustic guitar, says his wife Debbie. But when back pain from a preexisting condition began to interfere with being able to stand for prolonged periods at work, Doug sought treatment from a pain specialist to whom he sent his own patients. The doctor gave him a narcotic analgesic and the recently approved Neurontin that was heavily marketed for pain, though only FDA approved for use in epilepsy. "There was nothing in the medical literature to alert his physicians that it might not be effective, or worse, cause further harm," says Debbie.[10]

He stopped taking the narcotics, but Doug's entire demeanor continued to change while on Neurontin. He was agitated, couldn't concentrate, couldn't sleep, and had tremors, says Debbie. The Alsberges attributed the symptoms to Doug's bipolar disorder, diagnosed in the 1990s. But whereas that disorder had always stabilized with treatment, Doug now went into a psychological free fall that began to affect his ability to work. His appearance degenerated, he stopped eating normally, and police had to be called to the house for his emotional volatility.[11] "We didn't know his extreme internal restlessness was akathisia, which is linked to suicide in medical journals, or that it was from Neurontin," says Debbie. In his last, dark days, Doug drove for miles "searching for a knife to end his life," buying one at a nearby hardware store and another at a culinary store hours away, says Debbie.[12] On Palm Sunday, April 13, 2003, in an apartment he had rented away from his family, Doug died of multiple, self-inflicted stab wounds to the chest. He was fifty-two.

His death was "surreal, bizarre, and horrific," says Debbie. But it was only after she saw an article about Neurontin suicide links that she requested Doug's pharmacy records and realized the increases in drug dosages correlated with his symptoms and personality changes. "I just stood there in the parking lot outside of the pharmacy holding the documents in stunned disbelief," she remembers.[13]

Douglas Briggs, MD, was a Princeton graduate who practiced family medicine near Charlotte, North Carolina. Dedicated to his patients, wife, and two sons, he also coached soccer, headed the PTA, played tennis, and enjoyed running in what sounds like a storybook existence. Briggs never visited a psychiatrist or mental health professional. But after back surgery, Briggs was put on Neurontin for the pain it was widely marketed to treat, says his wife, Robin, a former nurse. "Medicine had been Doug's passion and his whole life. But after a few months on Neurontin, his bedside manner became curt. He stopped reading his journals and just lay on the couch. He had always been a stoic and he became whiny about his backache. We had never fought and we began fighting. He became a different person."[14]

Doug was a conservative prescriber and grilled his Pfizer sales rep about Neurontin's safety more than once, remembers Robin. He was so attuned to his responses to medications, when he took Vioxx before its dangers were known, he noted heart palpitations—and discontinued its use. A week later, Vioxx was pulled from pharmacy shelves for causing heart problems in some patients. But thanks to Neurontin-linked akathisia, a syndrome characterized by internal restlessness and severe agitation, Doug's ability to detect his own mental changes on the drug disappeared. "He did not know his suicidal thoughts were drug-induced and not his own," says Robin.[15] On Christmas Day 2004, after opening presents, Doug urged Robin and the boys to go to a movie. At first hesitant to leave Doug alone on a holiday, Robin says she remembered an *Oprah* episode about how men should get the chance to be alone in the house, to unwind, so the three went see the movie *Meet the Fockers*. When they returned, they found that Doug had hung himself in the foyer. He had been on Neurontin for ten months. He was fifty-four.

Like Debbie Alsberge, Robin Briggs's "aha!" moment came some time after her husband's suicide. Two weeks after Doug's funeral, a distraught patient literally drove up on the Briggs's lawn, saying he couldn't accept the uncharacteristic suicide and demanded to know what antidepressant Dr. Briggs was on. Even though she had been asked the question countless times and always responded, "He wasn't on an antidepressant, he just took Neurontin," this time Robin says a lightbulb went off in her head, and she ran upstairs to the medicine cabinet to read the Neurontin patient information for the first time.[16] It did not list suicide as a side effect, but it did list "emotional lability" recounts Robin. "So I called my sister who is a nurse and asked her to look up Neurontin in the nurse's desk reference. In bold letters it said 'suicidal tendencies, sudden unexplained deaths and psychoses.' I was sickened. Pfizer deliberately hid the risk from patients and doctors!"[17]

After Kate Miller of Queensbury, New York, lost her fifteen-year-old son, who had been given Singulair for hay fever, she also had an "aha!" moment. She knew nothing about Singulair's suicide side effects, she says, until her sister found them, weeks later, on the Internet. She suspects the pediatrician was also "completely unaware" of the risks.[18] It was months later that a prominent warning was added.[19]

WHAT'S IN A LABEL?

The label information that Debbie Alsberge, Robin Briggs, and Kate Miller did not necessarily see is part of the "horse-trading" that goes on at the FDA over iffy drugs. Rather than withdraw approval from a drug about which there are serious doubts—or even withdrawing one when its dangers are obvious—the FDA usually chooses to simply put more warnings on the label.

There are several reasons why the FDA favors Pharma's desire to market a drug over the public's desire to be protected from drugs. In the past, the agency has been assailed both by industry and by severely ill patients for its delay in approving important new drugs. This pressure, including large protests at the FDA headquarters by AIDS activists in the late 1980s, led to the passage of the Prescription Drug User Fee Act (PDUFA) in 1992, which authorizes the FDA to collect fees from Pharma to expedite its drug approvals—yes, Pharma is literally paying for approvals.

But the other reason for the industry leanings, say FDA insiders, is that the agency judges its value and effectiveness on how many drugs it gets to market—not how many it rejects. According to an FDA drug reviewer who requested anonymity, one FDA director asked, "Where are the dead bodies?" when accused of waving through dangerous drugs. Maybe he should visit SSRI Stories.

Of course, warnings on a prescription drug's label, like on any consumer product, indemnify the manufacturer against personal injury lawsuits, and to that extent, Pharma *wants* such labels on medications that could otherwise land it in court. But warnings of life-threatening side effects on drug labels that tell users to "seek medical help immediately" also give patients and doctors second thoughts—which, of course, is the point. (Though some say there are so many warnings on products that the public has vigilance fatigue and heeds none of them.) So Pharma also *dislikes* warnings—and when the FDA added black-box warnings about suicide risks in young people taking SSRI antidepressants in 2004, Pharma doctors began circling the wagons.[20] Figures released from the Centers for Disease Control and Prevention (CDC) showed that child- and teen-suicide rates rose in 2004—and doctors declared the deaths were from . . . an *SSRI antidepressant deficiency.*[21]

"The concerns about antidepressant use in children and adolescents have paradoxically resulted in a reduction in their use, and this has contributed to increased suicide rates," said Charles Nemeroff, MD, who has links to Eli Lilly, Pfizer, Wyeth-Ayerst, Pharmacia-Upjohn, and five other drug makers, and was investigated by Congress for undeclared Pharma income.[22]

Even though blaming patients' suicides on falling drug sales is as absurd as blaming obesity on the withdrawal of diet drugs like Meridia® or fen-phen, the "theory" got big play in the medical and mainstream press. The warnings create a "barrier" to treatment, said David Shern, PhD, then president of Mental Health America, "by scaring young people and parents away from care" that may be linked to the rise in suicide, reported Med Page Today.[23] ("Barrier" as it's used here, typically means "we're not making enough money" in Pharmaspeak.) Mental Health America is heavily subsidized by Pharma, according to congressional investigators.[24] Charles Nemeroff also used the *b* word: "The past history of such FDA warnings has revealed that they create barriers to care and unnecessarily frighten families away from seeking treatment," he told *ABC News*.[25] Soon, the *New York Times* got its feet wet with a story about people dying from antidepressant deficiencies.[26] Except that it wasn't true. While the statistics of rising suicides were correct, the black-box-warning-caused drop in SSRI prescriptions occurred the *following year*, and the number of prescriptions in the *cited* year were "basically unchanged and did not drop substantially, according to data from the study," said the *Times*.[27]

Asked about the statistical about-face (which probably proved the FDA was right about the warnings after all), the lead author of the paper that drove the deficiency news stories, Robert D. Gibbons, PhD, then a professor of biostatistics and psychiatry at the University of Illinois–Chicago, did not sound the statistician. Acknowledging to the *Times* that the data did not support a causal link between prescription rates and suicide in 2004, he said, "We really need to see the 2005 numbers on suicide to see what happened."[28] Doesn't it make sense to do that *before* writing a paper? The paper itself, in the *American Journal of Psychiatry*, was supported by $30,000 from Pfizer, wrote Alison Bass, author of *Side Effects: A Prosecutor, a Whistleblower, and a Bestselling Antidepressant on Trial*, in the *Boston Globe*.[29] Why? And Gibbons had published similar findings about veteran suicides two months earlier.[30]

Yet the "SSRI deficiency" paper, which reached false conclusions on the basis of the wrong data, was not retracted. Nor were Gibbons's financial links to Wyeth and Pfizer, which appear in the *British Medical Journal* and on the Center for Science in the Public Interest website, mentioned by the mainstream press—including the *Times*.[31]

Unfortunately, Gibbons's promise (or threat) to get next year's data was taken up by his colleagues. The following year, Gibbons's coauthor on the "SSRI deficiency" paper, Joel Greenhouse, MD, and two other authors published a research letter in the *Journal of the American Medical Association*

(*JAMA*) about the 2005 statsitics.[32] Except that in the first year that prescriptions actually *did* fall because of the black-box warnings—so did the suicide rate. Again, the FDA warnings were vindicated.[33]

Still, the medical and mainstream press picked up on the reissuance of the "SSRI deficiency" theory as if last year's wasn't a statistical belly flop, and this one wasn't too. "We've seen this increase as soon as these warnings started, and it is what we were most worried about," said Kelly Posner, PhD, in the *Wall Street Journal*.[34] "If you look at the whole evidence puzzle, it points in one direction—antidepressants save lives." The *Journal* reported that Posner "says she doesn't have any financial ties to drug companies," but the *Journal of the American Academy of Child & Adolescent Psychiatry* says she's "received research support from GSK, Forest, Eisai, Z Pharmaceuticals, Johnson & Johnson, Abbott Laboratories, Wyeth-Ayerst Research, Organon USA, BMS, SanofiAventis, Cephalon, Novartis, Shire Pharmaceuticals, and UCB Pharma.[35] Posner's links also went unnoticed by the *New York Times* when she similarly defended the antidepressant Paxil against suicides links.[36]

Pharma's aggressive Center for Medicine in the Public Interest (CMPI) also lauded the "SSRI deficiency" redux. "Now let's wait and see what the anti-SSRI mafia has to say," wrote then CMPI president Peter Pitts. "You can bet it'll be vitriolic pharma-bashing with a heaping measure of junk science."[37]

Still, other voices appreciated the irony of a drug that causes what it is supposed to prevent. "I would love to hear a doctor explain to me and my parents that yes, you have depression and that the answer to the problem is a prescription that could heighten or worsen the problems," wrote Sam Dunbar, then opinion editor of the *Collegian*. "This means, potentially, a patient who suffers from acute depression could suffer from suicidal tendencies after treatment begins."[38]

PFIZER PFACTS

Both Pfizer and its epilepsy drug Neurontin have checkered pasts. During one week in 2010, Pfizer[39]

1. agreed to pull its ten-year-old leukemia drug, Mylotarg®, from the market because it caused more, not fewer, patient deaths;

2. suspended pediatric trials of the antipsychotic Geodon® after the FDA said children were being overdosed;

3. suspended trials of tanezumab, an osteoarthritis pain drug, because patients got worse, not better; some even needed joint replacements;

4. was investigated by the House of Representatives for illegal marketing of the kidney-transplant drug Rapamune® and for specifically targeting African Americans for its use;

5. bid Scott Reuben, MD, who helped established its Bextra, Celebrex®, and Lyrica® as best-selling pain drugs, off to prison for research fraud pertaining to the same drugs;

6. was sued by Blue Cross Blue Shield to recoup money it overpaid for Bextra and other drugs;

7. received a letter from Sen. Charles Grassley (R-IA) requesting its whistle-blower policy; and

8. had its appeal to end lawsuits by Nigerian families who accuse it of illegal trials of the antibiotic Trovan® (in which eleven children died) rejected by the Supreme Court.[40]

Pfizer, the world's biggest drug company, despite having been in so much trouble with the government, sometimes seems to be thumbing its nose at regulators. According to court documents, Pfizer illegally marketed Neurontin while under probation for illegal activities related to Lipitor®. And it illegally marketed the seizure drug Lyrica (called Son of Neurontin) and three other medications *while* entering into a probation for illegally marketing Neurontin.[41]

Does Pfizer *like* trouble? It bought Neurontin's original company, Warner-Lambert, knowing the firm's drug-marketing practices were under criminal investigation. And it bought Wyeth, despite Wyeth's long history of personal-injury suits over fen-phen, the withdrawn diet drug, and Prempro®, the cancer-linked hormone replacement therapy drug.[42]

Neurontin's suicide links were known as early as 1992 from clinical trials and FDA review data.[43] But Robert Temple, MD, the then FDA's associate director for medical policy for the Center for Drug Evaluation and Research, blamed the *patients*, not Neurontin, for hundreds of emerging suicides. "These are the sorts of people who are complicated to think about because they tend to be at risk already," he told the *Boston Globe* in an early version of the "SSRI deficiency" theory.[44] Reports of adverse events, he said, "can't really tell you whether the suicidal event is because of the drug or despite the drug." Temple even legitimized Neurontin's widespread off-label uses for pain, migraines, and bipolar disorder by referring to them as if they were legitimate and legal, according to the *Globe* article.[45]

Of course, one of the problems—or benefits, if you are Pfizer—with illegal marketing is that the bell, once rung, cannot be unrung. Doctors and patients remember the illegal messages, like that of Neurontin treating bipolar disorder, even if they are disavowed and found false. So despite the fact that Neurontin is approved for only postherpetic neuralgia, pain after shingles, and epilepsy, it made Pfizer $387 million in 2008, and over 90 percent of sales were for its illegally marketed off-label uses.[46] Who says crime doesn't pay?

In court-released confidential memos, Pfizer (then Parke-Davis) admits the planned deceptions. "The U.S. market for Bipolar Disorders is an attractive commercial opportunity that warrants clinical development of Neurontin®. Based on the current patent situation, an investment in full clinical development is not recommended at this time since completion of two pivotal trials and regulatory filing and approval would occur close to patent expiration," says the memo. *Translation:* It would take too long to get legal approval—our patent would expire. Instead, says the memo, "it is recommended to implement only an exploratory study in outpatients with bipolar disorders with the results highlighted through a peer reviewed publication."[47] *Translation:* Let's not do the studies and plant some info in medical journals that looks like we did.

The FDA should have known about the con because Public Citizen, the national consumer advocacy organization, called attention to it in a 2002 docket filing. "It was not sufficiently profitable for Parke-Davis to obtain FDA approval for gabapentin's [Neurontin] alternative uses," Public Citizen wrote. "Instead, company officials developed a strategy that would allow Parke-Davis to avoid the costs of proving gabapentin's safety and effectiveness for these other uses."[48]

Pfizer's big Neurontin study, called the STEPS trial ("Study of Neuron-tin: Titrate to Effect, Profile of Safety"), was also a con, said reports that broke in 2011.[49] It was a "seed" trial orchestrated to convince the 772 investigators who were recruited to participate to personally prescribe the drug—not a legitimate trial to establish effectiveness and safety.

"In a typical seeding trial, a pharmaceutical company will identify several hundred doctors and invite them to take part in a research study. Often the doctors are paid for each subject they recruit," wrote Carl Elliot in a *New York Times* column.[50] "As the trial proceeds, the doctors gradually get to know the drug, making them more likely to prescribe it later." Nor was the vanity pyra-mid scheme innocent: 11 subjects out of 2,600 in the trials died, and 73 expe-rienced severe adverse reactions.[51] With similar impunity, Pfizer/Parke-Davis planted thirteen ghostwritten articles in medical journals promoting the faux Neurontin uses. One, a supplement in the prestigious *Cleveland Clinic Jour-nal of Medicine*, was made into forty-three thousand reprints by Pfizer/Parke-Davis to mail to the journal's "psychiatry audience" and for sales reps to give to doctors.[52]

Even Scott Reuben, MD, referred to as the "Bernie Madoff of medicine" because the clinical trials he published never existed, stumped for Neurontin. "Gabapentin would seem to be the ideal analgesic for managing acute and chronic pain following breast cancer surgery," effused the researcher *noire*, who was a member of Pfizer's Speakers Bureau and recipient of five Pfizer grants in five years before being sentenced and sent to the gated community known as Club Fed for six months in 2010 for the scam.[53] Amazingly, the ghostwritten articles, including some by Reuben, were not retracted. (Richard Borison, MD, who also went to prison, published articles on Neurontin, Seroquel®, and Geodon, which remain unretracted.) In fact, of all the publications that ran fraudulent Neurontin articles, the US Cochrane Group, which reviews healthcare interventions, is the only organization to retract them (except for an unrelated pain study in rats, conducted by a pharmaceutical company other than Pfizer, and published in the journal *Pain Medicine*).[54]

Of course, no one in scientific publishing likes retractions. Editors look dumb or duped, authors look sneaky and bought, and academic institutions—whose prestige and grants rely on publishing in journals—get major egg on

their faces. But what's the alternative? Leave the articles unretracted and hope readers forget? Mislead future clinicians?

Pfizer's newer epilepsy drug, Lyrica, is developing the same macabre trail as Neurontin. Lyrica was discovered by then Northwestern University chemist Richard Silverman in 1989 and was sold to Pfizer for $700 million, funding a new $100 million research facility, called the Richard and Barbara Silverman Hall for Molecular Therapeutics & Diagnostics.[55] In 2001, Lyrica had a setback when test mice developed cancerous tumors and Pfizer had to freeze pain trials and patient use. (Lyrica was also associated with ventricular tachycardia in a human subject, a potentially life-threatening fast heart rhythm, and with "sudden death in animal studies," as was revealed by internal company documents marked confidential.[56]) But when test rats did not develop the same cancers, Toni Hoover, then a vice president with Pfizer's labs in Ann Arbor, Michigan, sounded the all-clear. "The FDA has found that the benefit of taking the drug outweighs any risk," she told the *Detroit News*.[57]

Like Neurontin, initial articles about Lyrica were positive. Not surprising, since they were written by Pfizer-paid doctors.

"Well tolerated," said *Arthritis & Rheumatism*. "Durability of effect for relieving FM [fibromyalgia] pain," said the journal *Pain*. "The pregabalin [Lyrica]/celecoxib combination was the most effective treatment for reducing pain," said Scott "Madoff" Reuben. "Fewer patients experienced nausea in the pregabalin/celecoxib group compared with that in the placebo group."[58]

Like its "father" drug Neurontin, Lyrica is also linked to suicide. Pfizer created a ninety-two-page document for FDA advisory committee members to try to dispute the connections. The report calls suicide statistics "an exaggeration of risk" that could "over-warn" patients and prescribers and make them "underestimate the risks of declining treatment," per the SSRI deficiency theory.[59] And speaking of SSRI deficiencies, the Pfizer document to the FDA quotes none other than Robert Gibbons and Charles Nemeroff, the doctors who predicted increased suicides if SSRIs had strict warnings.[60] Small world. And there was more Lyrica spin. By 2011, articles in medical journals suggested Lyrica for the non-approved uses of generalized anxiety disorder and irritable bowel syndrome. It was starting to look like the planted Neurontin articles all over again.[61]

WHEN MEDICATION MAKES YOU WORSE, NOT BETTER

It is obvious that psychoactive drugs can bring about suicidal tendencies, but *why?*

One theory is that, when the slowed-down mental state of depression lifts, people have the energy or volition to act out suicidal impulses. "But this cannot explain the appearance of suicidality in healthy volunteers," writes David Healy, MD, a professor at Cardiff University in Wales, who is considered the leading international expert on SSRIs and suicide. Nor does it explain why SSRI "warnings explicitly apply to not only depressed patients but also people being treated for anxiety, smoking cessation, or premenstrual dysphoric disorder." The more likely causes of the violence, writes Healy, are "akathisia, emotional disinhibition, emotional blunting, and manic or psychotic reactions to treatment."[62] Robert Whitaker, who wrote *Mad in America*, quotes author Jack Henry Abbott's description of akathisia (a syndrome characterized by unpleasant restlessness) in Abbott's book *In the Belly of the Beast*, which he wrote while in prison.

> These drugs, in this family, do not calm or sedate the nerves. They attack. They attack from so deep inside you, you cannot locate the source of the pain. The muscles of your jawbone go berserk, so that you bite the inside of your mouth and your jaw locks and the pain throbs. For hours every day this will occur. Your spinal column stiffens so that you can hardly move your head or your neck and sometimes your back bends like a bow and you cannot stand up. The pain grinds into your fiber. . . . You ache with restlessness, so you feel you have to walk, to pace. And then as soon as you start pacing, the opposite occurs to you; you must sit and rest.[63]

Akathisia is also referred to on drug labels as agitation, emotional lability, and hyperkinesis, says Healy. Patients describing it say, "I don't feel myself" or "I'm afraid of some of the unusual impulses I have."[64]

Edward S. Friedrichs, MD, then a practicing community physician with some psychiatric training, agreed that a patient's preexisting mental condition is not necessarily the explanation for suicide, though it is often given as such. "It is best to remember that it is not common 'depression' that triggers suicide, it is panic/agitation, often associated with acute dire sleeplessness or persistent sleep deprivation," he says. "Sleep deprivation alone, even in normal brains, can produce hallucinosis and delusional thinking."[65]

One person who does not have to be convinced of the role of psychoactive drugs in suicides is the late Rosie Meysenburg, the founder and manager of

the website SSRI Stories. "The kind of energy, rage and insanity seen in a lot of crimes today was not seen before SSRIs appeared," says Meysenburg. "There are two cases of women on the site who stab a man close to 200 times and a case of a man who stabs his wife over 100 times and then goes next door to the neighbor's house and stabbed the neighbor's furniture about 500 times. There are also cases of kleptomania, pyromania and a strange kind of nymphomania in which women school teachers molest their minor male students."[66]

Meysenburg, who is retired, began SSRI Stories as a message board in 1997 after experiencing side effects from Prozac, which had been prescribed to help her quit smoking. The side effects were so severe, she was hospitalized.

Not long after establishing her website, she was joined by two other anti-SSRI activists (one whose daughter had killed herself while on the antidepressants) and they began posting stories from news sources. Soon, they could barely keep up with all the information available.[67]

The thousands of news reports on the site provide such strong evidence of drug-related violence that the site was mentioned in the *Journal of the American Physicians and Surgeons.* "Since no clinical trial involving multiple homicides is ever likely to be run, no firmer evidence is likely to be found," wrote Joel M. Kauffman, PhD, referring to the link between violence and psychoactive drugs.[68] In fact, the only thing more shocking than the number of newspaper stories on the site is the number of previously healthy people who committed violence with no precipitating events. Twenty people mentioned on the site set themselves on fire. Ten bit their victims (including a biter who was sleepwalking, and a woman on Prozac who bit her eighty-seven-year-old mother into critical condition). Three men in their seventies and eighties attacked their wives with hammers. A Midwest City, Oklahoma, woman accepted a cup of tea from an elderly nurse she'd just met—and then strangled her. A twelve-year-old boy left in his cousin's car while she shopped at Target killed her five-week-old daughter, who had also been left in the car. All were under the influence of psychoactive drugs.[69] Did events like these ever happen before the psychoactive drug revolution?

In one month of reports on the site, a fifty-four-year-old respiratory patient with a breathing tube and an oxygen tank and no previous criminal record held up a bank in Mobile. An enraged man in Australia chased his mailman and threatened to cut his throat . . . for bringing him junk mail. A fifty-eight-year-old Amarillo man with no criminal history tried to abduct three people and killed an Oklahoma grandmother in the process. A sixty-year-old grandmother in Seattle killed three family members and herself.[70] And fourteen parents drowned their children, a crime no one had heard of before the 2001 case of Andrea Yates, who was on the antidepressant Effexor®.[71]

In fact, so many older people arrested for violence are listed on the site that the warnings on SSRI labels for only young people seem to be an error.

There are also plenty of celebrities, some since deceased, represented on the site like actors and personalities Winona Ryder, Heath Ledger, Brittany Murphy, Anna Nicole Smith, Heather Locklear, Carrie Fisher, Sharon Osbourne, singer Glen Campbell, Lynyrd Skynyrd's harmonicist, actor and comedian Phil Hartman, and the mayor of Coppell, Texas, Jayne Peters.[72]

THE PHARMACOBATTLEFIELD

By now, most people are aware of the high suicide rate among military personnel since the Iraq and Afghanistan Wars, rates that sometimes exceed one soldier per day. In just one month—July of 2011—there were thirty-two suspected suicides, twenty-two of which were among active-duty troops, and ten among reservists. In one report, 36 percent of the troops who killed themselves had never even been deployed.[73]

Of course, the Iraq and Afghanistan Wars had stressors that didn't exist with other wars, like back-to-back deployments, long periods away from families, and no designated front lines. But they also had *drugs* that didn't exist during other wars and the dark practice of "polypharmacy," loading one drug on top of another in experimental drug cocktails until something worked. The Iraq and Afghanistan Wars are also the first wars to include the generation of men and women who grew up on psychoactive drugs like medications for ADHD and bipolar disorder and to who were prescribed or permitted drugs in combat zones—pharmacobattlefields.[74] So you don't have to be a cynic to ask if the reason so many troops are killing themselves is, at least partially, because the government is giving them drugs that make them kill themselves. In fact, from 2001 to 2009, the army's suicide rate increased more than 150 percent, and the Marine Corps's suicide rate increased 50 percent—both parallel the use of psychiatric drugs, reports *Military Times* website publication. Graphs of the suicide rates and the rise of prescribed drugs are so similar that they could be laid over each other.[75]

At Fort Hood, where 48,000 troops and their families are stationed, 6,000 soldiers were on antidepressants, and 1,400 were on antipsychotic drugs in 2009, reported *USA Today*.[76] At Fort Bragg, where 50,000 are stationed, 4,994 troops were on antidepressants, and 664 were on antipsychotics in 2010, reported the *Fayetteville Observer*, adding that "many soldiers take more than one type of medication."[77]

Military Times puts the psychoactive use even higher. "At least one in six service members is on some form of psychiatric drug," the site reported in 2010. And "many troops are taking more than one kind, mixing several pills in daily 'cocktails' for example, an antidepressant with an antipsychotic to prevent nightmares, plus an anti-epileptic to reduce headaches—despite minimal clinical research testing such combinations."[78]

In fact, between 2005 and 2009, half of all TRICARE (the military health plan) prescriptions for people between eighteen and thirty-four were for antidepressants and epilepsy drugs like Topamax®, and Neurontin prescriptions increased 56 percent, reports *Military Times*.[79] In 2008, according to *Military Times*, 578,000 epilepsy pills and 89,000 antipsychotics were prescribed to deploying troops.[80] In addition to suicides, what do the psychoactive drugs do to reaction time, motor skills, coordination, attention, and memory among troops on the battlefield? It's hard to believe the military doesn't see the correlations. Eighty-nine percent of troops with posttraumatic stress disorder (PTSD) are given psychoactive drugs, and 34 percent are given antipsychotics—drugs with clear suicide warnings.[81] A study of 887,859 VA hospital patients recommends "close monitoring" for suicide "after an antidepressant start."[82]

"Completed suicide rates were approximately twice the base rate following antidepressant starts in VA clinical settings," says psychiatrist Peter Breggin, who has testified at congressional hearings. SSRI antidepressants "can cause or worsen suicidality, aggression and other dangerous mental states."[83]

But oblivious to the risks and clear statistics, the VA's Iraq War Clinician Guide says, "We recommend SSRIs as first line medications for PTSD pharmacotherapy in men and women with military-related PTSD," and "Findings from subsequent large-scale trials with paroxetine [Paxil] have demonstrated that SSRI treatment is clearly effective both for men in general and for combat veterans suffering with PTSD."[84]

PSYCHOACTIVE DRUGS THAT ARE NOT SUPPOSED TO BE PSYCHOACTIVE

When well-adjusted fifteen-year-old Cody Miller, who played high school football, took his own life after being on the allergy drug Singulair for just seventeen days, his community was galvanized.[85] State senator Elizabeth Little was incredulous that Singulair ads declaring that "side effects are mild and vary by age" were still running on TV after the tragedy. And former New York representative (now senator) Kirsten Gillibrand assembled FDA representatives in her Washington, DC, office to hear the testimony of Cody's parents, Kate and Dave Miller.[86]

In connecting with parents of other apparent drug victims, Kate Miller says she discovered numerous Singulair casualties, like the eleven-year-old daughter of a family of non-English speakers who took her own life, "while still in her Catholic school uniform."[87]

And even as the FDA instructed makers of the asthma drugs Singulair, Accolate®, Zyflo®, and ZyfloCR®—which all have the ingredient montelukast—to add warning labels about behavior and mood changes that could lead to suicide, months after Cody's death, more unsavory news about the bestselling asthma drugs surfaced.

A sub-investigator who worked on the drugs' original clinical trials reported audacious fraud, raising questions about the drugs' FDA approvals.[88] Robert Davidson, MD, who worked at the Tucson, Arizona, facility of Vivra Asthma & Allergy, where clinical trials of Singulair, other asthma drugs, and antibiotics were conducted, says a "patient mill" was operated at the facility to pocket the lucrative compensation that trials paid per subject, regardless of the appropriateness of the subjects.[89]

In trials conducted for drug giants like Forest Pharmaceuticals, Novartis, Roche, Sepracor (now Sunovion Pharmaceuticals), Merck, GlaxoSmithKline, and Boehringer Ingelheim, patients with coronary artery disease, arrhythmia, pulmonary embolism, and other serious conditions were randomized into trials—despite the risks to them and corruption of safety data, says Davidson.[90] Unwilling patients were often coerced to participate, patients were serially enrolled (again, corrupting data), and the drugs being studied were "unblinded" to staff. Neither subjects nor clinical staff members are supposed to know which subjects are getting active study drugs versus placebos in clinical trials because such knowledge biases results. That's why studies are "double-blinded."

In trials comparing montelukast (Singulair) with salmeterol (found in Advair® and Serevent®) conducted at Vivra and other testing sites, more than 40 percent of subjects treated with both drugs experienced a "clinical adverse event."[91] Why were these drugs approved? What's worse: two subjects on salmeterol withdrew from trials because of "worsening asthma," and "one died as a result of bronchial asthma."[92]

Yet despite the death, worsening asthma, and the adverse events, the researchers wrote, "Both montelukast and salmeterol were well tolerated" in the *Annals of Internal Medicine*.[93] What would happen if they *weren't* well tolerated? No wonder Pharma-sponsored drug trials like this one, sponsored by Merck, are considered suspect.

(There has been additional negative news about the ingredient in Advair and Serevent. The Salmeterol Multicenter Asthma Research Trial was ended early after there were sixteen deaths, forty-four intubations and 369 hospitalizations in people taking the drugs, the majority in African Americans. Some doctors have called for a complete ban of the drugs.[94])

The "irregularities" at the Vivra facility did lead to an onsite FDA inspection at which falsified patient diaries with post hoc changes were found. "Three study coordinators stated that they saw diary card blank prior to subject entering exam room with P.I. [principal investigator] for visit 2," reads a report from a May 5 through June 28, 1999, inspection. "Five to ten minutes after, the diary had approximately two weeks of diary symptoms and peak flow entered."[95] Nor was patient safety apparently protected. "On multiple occasions over the last 8 months the P.I. strongly counseled the S.I. [sub-investigator] to NOT mention potential risks of study participation to potential study subjects (such as arrhythmia, drug-drug interaction, etc.) so as to not 'scare them away,'" the FDA inspection report reads elsewhere.[96]

Pressure was also apparently put on patients to participate. "Coordinator stated that subject called to say she could not participate in a 12-hour a day study due to her schedule. P.I. called the subject's estranged husband to say that they had to get the disease under control."[97]

To protect the safety of the subjects (and to ensure the validity of the test results), subjects were not supposed to be using "maintenance inhaled corticosteroid therapy" or other asthma and allergy drugs during trials. Yet, according to one passage in the FDA inspection reports, they clearly were. "P.I. enrolled subject into study despite subject having a clear study exclusion (maintenance inhaled corticosteroid therapy)," says a report. "Subject subsequently experienced a SAE [severe adverse event] (hospitalized) while in the study. Moreover, this subject had recently participated in a prior study [for] which she required multiple prednisone bursts and multiple courses of antibiotic therapy for several bouts of acute sinusitis with asthma exacerbation."[98] Translation: the first time the subject participated in the study, her asthma got worse and she got a sinus infection, which required corticosteroids and lengthy antibiotics to treat. The second time the subject participated, she became so sick from the study drugs she had to be hospitalized. The subject should have never been recruited, much less twice—and the drug being tested worsens rather than helps asthma, at least in some cases!

Food and Drug Administration reports also document missing informed consent forms (even drug companies complain about missing consent information), clinical records changed to minimize alcohol and cigarette consumption (for which patients would likely be excluded), records rewritten, and records actually ripped up by the principal investigator in front of witnesses.[99]

There were also insurance and billing irregularities at the Vivra testing facility, says Davidson.[100] All patients were screened as if they were going to be trial subjects to prevent "screening failures" at a later date if they did participate—which amounted to a gratuity to Pharma, footed by insurers. In fact, Gambro, which acquired Vivra in 1997, agreed to a $40 million settlement for submitting false claims to Medicare, Medicaid, and TRICARE in 2000 and to another Medicare fraud settlement for $350 million in 2004.[101]

It's hard to believe that medical professionals would risk patients' health for money and that the FDA would approve drugs tested under such circumstances for public use, thus perpetuating the risks. Among the tested drugs at Vivra was the antibiotic Raxar®, which was withdrawn from the market for causing fatal heart rhythm abnormalities, and the genetically engineered Xolair®, which has a black-box warning for anaphylaxis and was investigated

by the FDA for heart attack and stroke links.[102] Yet the FDA neither shut down the Vivra facility nor delayed related drug approvals. In fact, *inspections* were delayed to accommodate the drug tests, charges Davidson, thereby putting the cart before the horse.[103]

Likewise, the Arizona Board of Medical Examiners did not investigate

Vivra when Davidson presented it with fifty-one irregularities.[104] "It takes time to obtain a properly administered, formal informed consent with full disclosure of risks and benefits and that slows study-subject recruitment and ultimately, delays the time to obtain market approval from FDA," says Davidson. "It is virtually certain that there have been deaths of US citizens because of the fraudulent or seriously-flawed clinical research PDUFA [Prescription Drug User Fee Act] encourages. Nor is FDA likely to revoke expedited market approvals because that would be tantamount to admitting that they 'goofed.'"[105]

And there are more questions about the FDA's approval of Singulair, besides trials like Vivra's. FDA scientists, upon reviewing early Singulair trials, noted that subjects' "asthma control deteriorates when switched from low dose inhaled corticosteriods" to Singulair.[106] Again—patients' asthma got worse, not better, on an asthma drug.

There are also clear signals of Singulair risks among children, even though the drug is widely prescribed for them. FDA drug reviewers cautioned in the *New England Journal of Medicine* that, before the drug was in use, adult trials of Singulair "may not be predictive of the response" in children.[107] And FDA reviewers wrote in their early reports that infant monkeys given Singulair had to be euthanized because "infants may be more sensitive to the toxicity" of Singulair.[108] Monkeys are expensive and are euthanized only in extreme situations. FDA reviewers also wrote that many human subjects withdrew from Singulair trials because of "worsening asthma."[109]

In 2010, *Fox News* reported that Singulair may be producing aggression, hostility, irritability, anxiety, hallucinations, and night terrors in children, and that the symptoms are being diagnosed as ADHD (leading to *more* medications).[110] More than one hundred parents on the drug-rating website Ask a Patient agree—citing hyperactivity, tantrums, depression, crying, school trouble, facial tics, and "strange eye movements" in their children, some as young as one year old, after being put on Singulair.[111] "Do NOT recommend this drug to other parents," writes one mother. "4 year olds that suddenly talk about killing themselves are influenced by a DRUG!!" Parents of a nine-year-old boy on Singulair say, "he stated that he was depressed and attempted to stab himself with a knife. He has been hallucinating and feeling unsafe with scary dreams." "THE GOVERNMENT SHOULD BE ASHAMED OF THEMSELVES FOR APPROVING THIS!!!!" writes another mother.[112]

Any why are so many young kids on asthma drugs? National Asthma Education and Prevention Program (NAEPP) guidelines written by Pharma consultants recommend "initiating long-term control therapy" in children from birth to age four "who had four or more episodes of wheezing in the past year that lasted more than 1 day and affected sleep" and who have "risk factors" like food allergies and parents with asthma. The drugs, say the guidelines, will reduce "impairment."[113] Putting toddlers on maintenance asthma drugs before they develop asthma is not just an obscene waste of money—likely $1,000 a year—it's also extreme child abuse, on the basis of *Fox News* and Ask a Patient reports. "I would never have given my son a drug that causes depression for a simple allergy," says Kate Miller, whose child was put on Singulair for *hay fever*. "But my choice was taken away by a company that buried the risks in 'post marketing adverse events' while it made billions," she says. "Cody was never mentally ill nor did he have ongoing problems."[114]

Miller says she is not worried about jeopardizing a legal settlement by speaking to the press—it is the "least" of her concerns—and that she "wants change."[115] Debbie Alsberge and Robin Briggs feel the same way. "Suicide is deeply stigmatizing and devastating. But when families stay silent, we cede power to corporations that put profit ahead of human lives and we become part of the problem," says Alsberge.[116]

"Suicide has always been looked at as a choice, but for many people on psychoactive drugs, it's a chemical path they are on and not a choice at all," says Briggs.[117] "My husband would be alive today if this information were available and not hidden." Both Alsberge and Briggs have a son in medical school and don't want to see the tragedy of drug-induced suicides continue.

Kate Miller continues to work with elected officials on safe prescription legislation and better notification systems for patients and pharmacies when safety alerts about drugs are issued.[118]

Still, the blame-the-victim Pharma machinery continues unabated. In a consolidated case in 2011 of many plaintiffs who claim that Neurontin is linked to suicidal behavior, judges allowed Robert Gibbons—yes, *that* Gibbons—to testify in favor of Neurontin's safety. The judges allowed the testimony despite Gibbons's receipt of "several hundred thousand dollars" from Pfizer.[119] (Gibbons also faces the question of whether or not Neurontin causes suicide head-on in a 2010 article in *Pharmacoepidemiology and Drug Safety*.[120] Guess what he finds.)

Meanwhile, the FDA approved a new version of gabapentin (Neurontin) in 2011 called Horizant® to treat "restless legs syndrome."[121] Restless legs syndrome is also known as akathisia—an actual side effect of Neurontin.[122]

Chapter 6

PROTECTING BONES FROM PRODUCTS THAT PROTECT BONES

The year 1999 was a good one for the drug company Merck. In its sixty-four-page annual report, it predicted that the arthritis medicine Vioxx ("Our Biggest, Fastest, and Best Launch Ever!") would also prevent Alzheimer's disease and colon cancer. It announced it was seeking approval to market the asthma drug Singulair® to two-year-olds. And it forecast that forty million women would take its new osteoporosis drug, Fosamax®, as Merck continued to "help educate both doctors and patients" about the bone disease.[1]

Unfortunately for Merck, Vioxx was withdrawn in 2004 for doubling stroke and heart attacks in long-term users; Singulair now carries FDA warnings about neuropsychiatric events; and Fosamax is suspected of doubling the risk of esophageal cancer, *causing* bone fractures instead of preventing them, as well as causing heart problems, intractable pain, and jawbone death.[2]

The year 1999 was also a good one for milk producers. The secretary of Health and Human Services herself, Donna Shalala, was posing in "milk mustache" ads and stumping for the traveling "milk mobile." Soon she'd shill for rBGH, milk producers' new, genetically engineered bovine growth hormone product, assuring skeptics it was so safe, her "own kids" drank it."[3]

By 2010, most dairies had phased out rBGH due to popular demand, and a US Department of Agriculture (USDA) panel had found that milk did not prevent osteoporosis single-handedly, but it *did* increase prostate cancer and heart disease risks.[4]

There's plenty of ka-ching in selling "strong bones" products for the same reason there was plenty of ka-ching in selling "hormone replacement" products: one-half the population is female, and no one wants to look old. Of course, "avoiding hot flashes" really means "still looking hot" in hormone marketing terminology, and "avoiding fractures" really means "still looking hot" in bone product–marketing lingo. That's why attractive women like Meredith Vieira from the *Today* show, former Charlie's Angel Cheryl Ladd, and actress Sally Field push bone drugs, just as model Lauren Hutton pushed hormone replacement therapy.[5]

PAY NO ATTENTION TO THE SENSATION IN YOUR THROAT

Like its trouble-laden drug Vioxx, Merck's Fosamax, the first bisphosphonate bone drug approved for osteoporosis, flew out of the FDA. It received only a sixmonth review before its 1995 FDA approval to be used (or tested, as it turned out) on the public. And like Vioxx, Fosamax's wheels soon came flying off.[6]

First the drug's penchant for causing esophageal "irritation" (acid regurgitation, dyspepsia, dysphagia, erosive esophagitis, esophageal hemorrhage, esophageal perforation, and more) was unmasked by researchers only *after* it was approved, perhaps because of the rush to get the drug to market. The FDA, no doubt feeling duped, tried to unapprove Fosamax, says *Fortune* magazine, but Edward Scolnick, MD, then head of Merck research, "wrote to doctors in his own hand" and got the FDA to agree to "let Merck keep Fosamax on the market, albeit with a warning label that told patients to sit upright for an hour after taking the drug."[7] (Scolnick sounds like a pistol. He also threatened to "personally pressure" FDA senior officials if the FDA took unfavorable action toward Vioxx, according to the *New York Times*.[8]) After taking Fosamax, patients also had to wait an hour before eating or drinking anything except water—avoiding mineral water, coffee, juice, all other beverages, and even pills.

If patients did not stay upright for one full hour after taking Fosamax, the results were not pretty. One woman who took Fosamax but remained upright for only thirty minutes had to be admitted to the Mayo Clinic with "severe ulcerative esophagitis affecting the entire length of the esophagus" and had to be fed intravenously, according to the *New England Journal of Medicine* (NEJM).[9]

In fact, six months after Fosamax was approved, 1,213 adverse-effect reports had been relayed to Merck, which included information about thirty-two hospitalized patients with adverse esophageal effects, seventeen with "severe" effects, and two who were "temporarily disabled," said the report, written in conjunction with Merck and the Mayo Clinic.[10]

To make sure clinicians understood that the FDA and Merck had passed the information of serious risks on to the patient (portending the beginning of the many "we-warned-you" drug approvals that followed), then Merck senior vice president for medical and scientific affairs Louis M. Sherwood, MD, sent a "Dear Doctor" letter after approval, urging compliance.[11] "We believe that the risk of esophageal irritation can be substantially decreased with adherence to these recommendations," said the letter, which admitted that Merck was seeing patients "with difficulty or pain on swallowing, and/or retrosternal pain" (pain under the breastbone), both of which were "consistent with a chemical irritation of the esophagus."[12]

In addition to Fosamax's esophagus "perks," dentists and oral surgeons discovered as early as 2003 that after simple tooth extractions and other inoffice dental work, the jawbone tissue of patients who had been given bisphosphonates intravenously would sometimes not heal but become necrotic and die. "Up to this point, this rare clinical scenario was seen only at our centers in patients who had received radiation therapy and accounted for 1 or 2 cases per year," said the authors of an article titled "Osteonecrosis of the Jaws Associated with the Use of Bisphosphonates: A Review of 63 Cases," published in the *Journal of Oral and Maxillofacial Surgery*.[13] None of the patients had received radiation in the jawbone area, said the surgeons, and the lesions were unhealed by antibiotics. Most patients needed surgery to remove all of the involved bone.

The condition, known as jawbone death or osteonecrosis of the jaw (ONJ), was similar to an occupational disease of the 1800s with the strange name of "phossy jaw," which workers got from working with phosphorus, wrote Michael Donoghue, MD, in the *Medical Journal of Australia*, when cases were first beginning to emerge.[14] "It was the most distressing of all the occupational diseases because it was very painful and was accompanied by a foul fetid discharge that made its victims almost unendurable to others," Donoghue quotes a British doctor saying of phossy jaw. "It was obstinate and chronic, the treatment was agonizing and the final result was a distressing disfigurement."[15]

Osteonecrosis of the jaw didn't exactly take a long time to manifest—though it slipped through Fosamax's two, three-year clinical trials on which its FDA approval was based.[16] "Even short-term oral use of alendronate [Fosamax] led to ONJ in a subset of patients after certain dental procedures were performed," read a study in the *Journal of the American Dental Association.*[17]

By 2005, thousands of bisphosphonate-related ONJ cases emerged, and the FDA added a warning to Fosamax that ONJ "can occur spontaneously" and that "for patients requiring invasive dental procedures, discontinuation of bisphosphonate treatment may reduce the risk for ONJ." Dentists and oral surgeons reported that "further surgery in an effort to correct the problem only exacerbates it, leaving the patient with even more exposed bone and even more disfigured."[18] They requested waivers to work on bisphosphonate patients because of the risks. Jaw removal, bone grafts, and even tracheostomies were seen.[19]

Doctors, dentists, and pharmacists were enraged at what looked like deliberate obfuscation by Merck. There had been no warning in the Fosamax literature, Roger Lam, then owner of Lam's Pharmacy, told the *Review-Journal.* Merck reps selling Fosamax in his office made no mention of ONJ, echoed Russ Neibaur, a Nevada internist. But then Merck spokesman, Chris Loder, said there was a good reason that dentists, oral surgeons, and pharmacists were not notified of the risks: they are not the medical professionals who would prescribe Fosamax.[20]

Meanwhile, women told to keep looking young by using bisphosphonates were ending up *disfigured* in an eerie parallel to the women who were told to keep looking young by using hormone replacement therapy and who ended up with mastectomies.

Unfortunately for Merck and for the women taking bisphosphonates, ONJ was just the beginning of the emerging new risks. Reports in the *NEJM* in 2007 and in the *Archives of Internal Medicine* in 2008 said that patients on bisphosphonates faced an increased risk of developing atrial fibrillation, or a chronically irregular heartbeat.[21] And Fosamax and the other bisphosphonates, Actonel®, Boniva® and Reclast®, could cause severe bone, joint, or muscle pain, said the FDA in a 2008 press release.[22] "In the most serious cases, the pain was so severe that patients could not continue their normal activities," wrote the FDA, referring to reported cases. "Some patients have complete relief of symptoms after they stop taking the drug, while others have reported slow or incomplete resolution." Clearly, the FDA was trying hard to avoid the word *irreversible*.[23] In fact, the pain complication was serious enough that the FDA cautioned clinicians to "consider whether musculoskeletal pain in patients on bisphosphonates might be caused by the drug, and consider discontinuing it either temporarily or permanently."[24]

Could there be any more dangerous side effects with Fosamax? How about cancer? The esophageal effects Merck said it had not "observed in our controlled clinical trials" morphed into actual cancers, as reported by Diane Wysowski, PhD, then an epidemiologist with the FDA. In a 2009 *NEJM* article, she reported twenty-three incidences of Fosamax-associated esophageal cancer in the United States and eight deaths, as well as twenty-seven incidences of cancer in Europe and Japan and six deaths.[25] The following year, an article in the *British Medical Journal* said that patients double their risks of developing esophageal cancer by taking bisphosphonates.[26]

As the wheels fell off the Fosamax machine, a team of paid medical spokespersons rushed in to save the franchise. Don't get any ideas about stopping Fosamax, scolded then Merck consultant Stuart L. Silverman, MD. For patients to "obtain the medication benefit observed under trial conditions, they must be adherent and persistent with their osteoporosis therapies."[27]

Another group of doctors, with seven finance-related links to Merck, said the ONJ patients were reporting might not be from bisphosphonates at all but from "bad oral hygiene." The damage-control continuing medical education (CME) course on the doctor education website Medscape was called, "Postmenopausal Osteoporosis: Putting the Risk for Osteonecrosis of the Jaw into Perspective."[28]

Other doctors with finance-related links to Merck wrote of the urgency to "increase patients' awareness of the need to use osteoporosis medication as directed in order to benefit from them fully," in an article titled "Poor Adherence to Bisphosphonate Treatment and Its Consequences" in *Expert Opinion on Pharmacotherapy*.[29] Why would there be poor patient adherence? And, in the

American Journal of Medicine that same year, doctors with six finance-related links to Merck dismissed the dangerous side effects attributed to bisphosphonates as what one "would expect given the anecdotal and biopsy experience that has been reported."[30] Translation: patients are lying or they were already sick.

Meanwhile, Merck continued its campaign to get all the undiagnosed, at-risk women on bone drugs and presented a research poster at the National Osteoporosis Foundation's Sixth International Symposium on Osteoporosis titled "Underuse of Osteoporosis Treatment in Postmenopausal Women."[31] All the bad news about Fosamax was creating what? A barrier to use, as Pharma public relations calls its drugs that are not selling as fast as desired.

The *NEJM* published an article called "Ten Years' Experience with Alendronate [Fosamax] for Osteoporosis in Postmenopausal Women" that actually took a bow for Fosamax's track record! Nine of the eleven authors were funded by Merck, and one, Arthur C. Santora, MD, reported "holding equity in Merck" and receiving "several US and international patents as inventor related to the use of bisphosphonates that are assigned to Merck."[32]

Once the Fosamax/cancer revelations surfaced in 2009, public relations efforts began to reach the television audience. Merck-linked Nicholas Shaheen, MD, assured the public on *NBC News* that the drug was safe and actually rolled his eyes at the overreaction to a few cancer stories. Fosamax is "well tolerated" in the stomach, said Shaheen, once it gets past the esophagus where it "can irritate or burn the tissue."[33]

But the anticancer-public-relations spin was short lived. In 2010, the actual benefit to bisphosphonates, *prevention* of fractures, was shattered (pun intended) when studies revealed that bisphosphonates were sometimes *causing*, not preventing, fractures. "Long-term use of osteoporosis drugs linked to hip breaks," said *USA Today*.[34] "Increased risk of fracture with bisphosphonates," said the Associated Press.[35] "Possible increased risk of thigh bone fracture with bisphosphonates," said the FDA in a 2010 warning.[36] "Not a buy," said Wall Street advisers, no doubt about Merck stock.

The thigh bones of patients on bisphosphonates have "simply snapped while they were walking or standing," after "weeks or months of unexplained aching," reported the *New York Times* in an article titled "Drugs to Build Bones May Weaken Them."[37]

How could drugs supposed to strengthen bone weaken it? By suppressing the body's bone-remodeling action, bisphosphonates stop bone loss—but since the bone is not renewed, it becomes brittle, ossified, and prone to fracture. In normal bone, there's a balance between the action of osteoblast cells, which make bone, and osteoclast cells, which break down bone. Bisphosphonates reduce the life span of osteoclasts, thus increasing osteoblasts' action.

At the 2010 American Academy of Orthopaedic Surgeons annual meeting in New Orleans, doctors were actually shown the qualitative differences in bisphosphonate-treated bone and were able to see how the bone had degraded over four years of treatment. When asked, one-half of the doctors at one presentation said they'd personally seen patients with bisphosphonatecompromised bone, reported the *Los Angeles Times*.[38]

In a sense, the mainstream media was the last to know about the fractures. As early as 2004, Gordon Strewler, MD, in the *NEJM*, and Susan M. Ott, MD, in the *Annals of Internal Medicine*, warned that the actions of bisphosphonates could paradoxically make bones brittle and cause fractures.[39] Reports in the *Journal of Clinical Endocrinology & Metabolism*, *Journal of Orthopaedic Trauma*, and *Injury* followed.[40] And in 2008, Phuli Cohan, MD, appeared on CBS TV in Boston with x-rays of a woman whose hip had shattered after years on Fosamax. "There is actually bone death occurring," said Cohan, and her worst fears—"that we'd be seeing spontaneous fractures"—had been realized.[41]

Patients also reported bone-drug fractures, often before the media or clinicians did so. (Of course, their stories were considered "anecdotal.") "I broke the left femur (shattered it 2 times in 2006 and 2007)," while on Fosamax, wrote a seventy-two-year-old patient on Ask a Patient, a medicine-rating site, in 2010. "I now walk with a walker and the Dr. says it can never be repaired."[42]

"I twisted my left leg while shopping & broke left femur in two places, requiring surgery, pins and a rod," wrote a sixty-one-year-old patient on the same site, saying she had been taking Fosamax for thirteen years. "Then in 2/08 I jarred same side foot coming off a step & developed a stress fracture that won't heal. I now have a stress fracture on the right side femur after walking on the beach."[43]

"After six years of taking Fosamax, I slipped in ice in my driveway and broke my femur (thigh bone). Two years later, still taking Fosamax, I fell in the snow and my other femur snapped before I hit the ground," wrote another woman on the site.[44] "I did nothing really physical except water therapy, yet I have a break" in the third lumbar vertebrae, posted a sixty-seven-year-old patient, who said she'd been taking Fosamax for fourteen months.[45]

Ask a Patient and other patient-information sites must be, for Pharma, like having all your exes in the same room. Like feminist, consciousness-raising groups, patients compare notes, discover they have the same symptoms and side effects, and find out they have the same clinicians who dismiss them. And they get angry. All the ask-your-doctor ads, self-quizzes on websites, and Pharma-paid doctor pitchmen in the world won't dilute a posting like this one, about bisphosphonates: "Only have osteoPENIA in my wrist [have never fallen or broken a bone], but doctor insisted I take it even though it is not recommended for osteopenia," wrote a woman on Ask a Patient about Boniva.[46] "Started with Fosamax; when I complained of significant discomfort, doctor switched me to Boniva. Stupid. I did not realize they are basically the same. I started reading. Threw the Boniva out. My friend stood up and got a vertical femur fracture. I connected my other symptoms. Now I am really angry. How would you NOT have achy, brittle bones when your body is only keeping old bone and not making new flexible bone??!! Bisphosphonates should be banned and we should be compensated for being guinea pigs. Shame on the doctors for being pawns for the pharmaceutical companies."[47]

Or how about this one from the same site: "My mother was taking Fosamax from 1995 until 2005 for osteoporosis. I believe she was part of a clinical trial. She had severe esophageal ulcerations, nausea, jawbone loss and vertigo from the inner ear. She was told to continue the drug. October 2005, she began to have trouble swallowing, she was initially told it was anxiety, but was then diagnosed with esophogeal [*sic*] cancer and died nine months later in July 2006, she was 80 years old."[48]

Not all drugs are bashed on Ask a Patient. The average score on the site, founded in 2000, on a 5.0-point scale is 3.0, or "somewhat satisfied." ("Fiorinal w/Codeine No.3" continually gets scores of 5.0.) But the bisphosphonates are another matter. Fosamax has a lowly 1.5 on the site, and the highly advertised Boniva has been the lowest scorer of over four thousand drugs, rated with a score of 1.3.

How does a drug with a ten-year trail of serious and obscured side effects that is *universally panned* by patients become a best seller? Just good marketing.

While osteoporosis is a real disease that needs treating, osteopenia, the risk of getting osteoporosis, was made up by Pharma to sell its product, according to published reports.[49] Then Dartmouth Medical School professor Anna Tosteson, MD, says she attended the 1992 World Health Organization

(WHO) meeting in Rome, where the term was first invented, and that *osteopenia* was never meant as "a disease in itself to be treated."[50] The scientists in the room were simply tired and agreed on a definition of the term because they wanted to adjourn for the night, she told National Public Radio (NPR).

And the bone-density units called "T scores" that were used to define osteopenia were not even considered to be valid benchmarks, writes Susan Kelleher in the *Seattle Times*: they had "boundaries so broad they include more than half of all women over 50."[51]

In 1994, one year before Fosamax was even approved, Merck decided to market osteoporosis "far beyond ailing old ladies," at the behest of Edward Scolnick, and launched major awareness campaigns, reports *Fortune*.[52] And when the drug didn't move off pharmacy shelves after its approval the way Merck expected (maybe because it wasn't moving down throats the way *patients* expected), it hired former drug researcher Jeremy Allen to whip up osteopenia fears and demand, says NPR.[53]

Allen's company planted bone density–measuring machines in medical offices across the country, created the faux "Bone Measurement Institute" to establish osteopenia as a health epidemic, and even pushed through the Bone Mass Measurement Act, which transferred the cost of bone scans onto tax-

payers by making them reimbursable by Medicare.[54] Apparently, it takes a lot to sell a disease these days.

The legislation was written by then Rep. Constance A. Morella (R-MD), who appeared with Secretary of Health and Human Services Donna Shalala at a National Dairy Council rally kicking off free bone-density screenings to be offered in one hundred cities in 1998.[55] Getting bone scans (which, in turn, sell Fosamax prescriptions) paid for by the public dime was such a windfall to Pharma that when the Medicare reimbursement became threatened, a *Cleveland Clinic Journal of Medicine* article dropped all pretense of scientific and academic objectivity and exhorted readers to "lobby your legislators!" because bone scans served as such a "presell" for Fosamax.[56] "To assure patient access to diagnostic services for assessment of skeletal health, advocates are focusing on legislation to restore DXA (a type of scan) reimbursement to a level that would allow outpatient DXA facilities to avoid financial losses and continue operating," says the article, titled "Managing Osteoporosis: Challenges and Strategies." Patients are "likely to be harmed by limited access to DXA testing because of fewer instruments in operation and greater distances to travel to reach them."[57] The article's author, E. Michael Lewiecki, MD, was on Merck's scientific advisory and speakers board and had received grant and research funds from Merck.[58] *Cleveland Clinic Journal of Medicine* editors did not respond to requests from a reporter for a statement about the apparent embedded commercial.

Television host Meredith Vieira also dropped any pretense of professional objectivity in huckstering bone scans. "When I became menopausal, my doctor recommended I get a bone mineral density test. I had never even heard of it, to be quite honest. I thought, 'I'm in great health, great shape. I have no symptoms. Why do I need this?' But I went ahead and did the test anyway," she told *USA Today*.[59] "To illustrate how ignorant I was when I had the test done, I asked where I could change and the nurse told me I didn't need to take off my clothes. They did a test on my heel, hip and spine, which only took a matter of five minutes. And it was totally painless. It's so simple to do."[60]

By 1999, there were ten thousand bone density–measuring machines in medical offices and clinics when there had been only 750 before bisphosphonates, and the diagnosis of the "disease" of osteopenia had increased *sevenfold*.[61]

In fact, treating the disease of osteopenia had become so lucrative, Fosamax had competition. In 2000, the bisphosphonate Actonel, from Procter & Gamble (P&G) and Sanofi-Aventis, was approved for osteoporosis, and in 2003 Boniva, from Roche Pharmaceuticals and GlaxoSmithKline (GSK), was approved. It wasn't long before Actonel was drawing bad ink of its own.

In 2002, Aubrey Blumsohn, MD, then a senior medical professor at Sheffield University in England, and his research dean signed a $250,000 research contract with P&G to help in a marketing war against Fosamax, reported Slate.[62] Fosamax's global sales were $3 billion a year, and Actonel's were only $1 billion. But even though P&G used Blumsohn's name and research, he was originally denied access to the final data, says Slate. And when Blumsohn *did* see the data at the company's Surrey headquarters, 40 percent of the patient data he had provided was missing.[63] According to P&G statistician Ian Barton, Blumsohn was told the results were removed because they would have harmed Actonel's marketing stance against Fosamax.[64]

"Clearly, this is an example of an American drug company running roughshod over good science to gain product credibility," stated Mark Cohen, then Food and Drug Safety director for the Government Accountability Project. "If drug companies and universities can't be trusted to conduct honest research, the government needs to step in to protect doctors and consumers from this sort of fraudulent ghost science."[65]

P&G's extreme marketing did not stop there, according to unsealed court documents. Because P&G expected Boniva to outperform Actonel due to its once-monthly dose (Actonel was once-weekly), P&G sales reps were told to "show how Actonel 'differentiates' itself from other products, even when it doesn't,"[66] reports *Advertising Age*. One way that reps showed Actonel "differentiation" was to claim that Boniva may prevent spinal fractures, but it doesn't work as well as Actonel on non-spinal fractures like wrists, hips, and collarbones. P&G even took Boniva manufacturers to court when Boniva ads claimed the medication did in fact work on these types of fractures.[67]

And it got meaner. Boniva's manufacturers then took P&G to court in a counterlawsuit, claiming that P&G reps told doctors that Boniva "actually caused fractures and they could be sued for malpractice if they prescribed it."[68] (Of course, the charge would turn out to be right, to a limited extent.) P&G

came to regret its aggression toward Boniva, though. The company lost its injunction against the Boniva's ad claims in court, and Roche Pharmaceuticals rolled out a powerful new Boniva campaign using actress Sally Field.[69] In fact, in their first year, the Field ads, from ad agency Euro, netted double the media impact of the Fosamax and Actonel ad campaigns, reported *Advertising Age*.[70]

"You have only one body and one life," says Field, who starred as a family matriarch in the TV drama *Brothers and Sisters*, in the ads as she exhorts women to treat their bones. But after a litany of warnings about kidney disease, trouble swallowing, severe pain and jaw problems, you might expect her to finish with "so don't take Boniva."

MORE OSTEOPOROSIS DRUGS . . . AND MORE DANGEROUS SIDE EFFECTS

Bisphosphonates aren't the only drugs chasing the lucrative bone patient market. Evista®, a hormone-related drug called a Selective Estrogen Receptor Modulator (SERM), was approved by the FDA in 1997 to prevent osteoporosis. It didn't cause the notorious esophageal problems experienced with bisphosphonates.

"Fosamax has to be taken on an empty stomach in the morning, while Evista can be taken with food and at any time during the day," exalted Bruce Ettinger, MD, lead Evista investigator at the launch of the drug.[71] Evista was likely to become the "wonder drug for the next century," said the *Chicago Tribune*.[72]

Evista had other possible selling points, too, according to its manufacturer, Eli Lilly. The company had noted fewer incidences of breast cancer in an Evista trial and wanted to market the drug for both prevention of breast cancer and prevention of osteoporosis. But a group of doctors that Lilly consulted at an oncology conference said the anticancer marketing claim would be "an egregious stretch" and that the high risk of stroke seen with Evista canceled any anticancer benefits.[73]

Nonetheless, Lilly armed one thousand of its drug reps with an off-label Evista sales plan "maximizing" the breast cancer data, which included scripted answers if doctors asked about the "relatively small number of cases" behind the claims. Reps were told to hide a disclosure page that said, "The effectiveness of [Evista] in reducing the risk of breast cancer has not yet been established," and "All of the authors were either employees or paid consultants of Eli Lilly at the time this article was written." Reps were also armed with an "Evista Best Practices'" videotape that didn't just promote Evista for breast cancer and osteoporosis; it promoted it for cardiovascular disease, too![74]

Of course, marketing a drug for non-FDA-approved uses is illegal, and Lilly was charged with a violation of the Food, Drug, and Cosmetic Act by the Department of Justice in 2005 and ordered to pay a $36 million settlement. (Lilly made $260 million from Evista in just one quarter during the same year.)[75] Lilly's "Hail Mary" cancer promotion also caused problems with the drug company AstraZeneca, which makes the mother of all anti–breast cancer drugs, Tamoxifen®. AstraZeneca sought an injunction against Lilly's Evista marketing, and the case was settled, though details were not released.[76]

Meanwhile, Evista enjoyed personal promotion from former FDA deputy commissioner for medical and scientific affairs Scott Gottlieb, MD. Soon after Gottlieb left his post with the Bush administration, he penned a sour-grapes op-ed in the *Wall Street Journal* about Evista's legal troubles titled "Stop the War on Drugs." Because Evista eventually *did* get approved to prevent some types of breast cancer, Gottlieb felt the drug had initially received a bum rap and that the approval transformed Lilly's original misdemeanor into an actual "public service."[77] Penalizing Lilly's off-label promotion of Evista may have proved "fatal" for patients, Gottlieb charged.[78]

But there was another "fatal" side to Evista. Despite being approved to reduce some cancers ("risk of invasive breast cancer in postmenopausal women with osteoporosis and in postmenopausal women at high risk for invasive breast cancer"[79]), Evista ads and prescribing information warned about links to cardiovascular disease, liver problems, and "death due to stroke."[80] Evista doesn't even "completely prevent breast cancer," the FDA warned. "Breast examinations and mammograms should be done before starting Evista and regularly thereafter."[81]

Patient reviewers on Ask a Patient are as hard on Evista as they are on Fosamax and Boniva. Of 250 Evista users in 2010, more than one-half—130—

say they developed debilitating joint pain or muscle cramps similar to symptoms experienced by people on bisphosphonates. They also list insomnia, diminished memory, hair loss, and eye problems while on Evista (SERMS are linked to cataracts), and some say they lost rather than gained bone density.[82]

Of course, the search for bone drugs was fueled by the demise of hormone replacement therapy (HRT) in 2002, which, even though it caused cancer and heart attacks, it had prevented osteoporosis. Wyeth itself, who made the blockbuster HRT drugs Premarin® and Prempro® and was bought by Pfizer in 2009, was also developing a SERM called bazedoxifene, but it had similar coronary side effects to Evista.[83]

There are other drugs that help prevent osteoporosis in women while still exposing them to dangerous side effects. Amgen's Prolia®, made from genetically engineered hamster cells, received FDA approval as a treatment for "postmenopausal women with osteoporosis at high risk of fractures" in June 2010, two months earlier than expected.[84] Injected, immune-suppressing drugs like Prolia, called monoclonal antibodies (moAbs), which include Avastin®, Humira®, and Enbrel®, are so lucrative—Avastin treatment costs $100,000 a year per patient, according to most sources—they are regarded as Pharma's next big profit center. And as soon as Prolia was approved, Amgen pressed one thousand drug representatives into service to sell it.[85] Analysts predicted that Prolia would net $1 billion a year in sales.[86]

Since Prolia costs $825 per injection, with two injections required a year, Amgen also rolled out a ProliaPlus® program to "remind patients and providers about when the patient's next dose is due, thus helping to support patient adherence," reported *Medical Marketing and Media*.[87] Patient noncompliance and "prescription abandonment" at the pharmacy (when patients learn how much a drug costs and refuse to pay for it) represent huge losses to Pharma. Some Pharma adherence programs even send visiting nurses to patients' homes.

Amgen also spun Prolia in medical journals, but its attempts to seed an article (by authors with seventeen financial links to Amgen) in the *NEJM* before Prolia was even approved backfired.[88] "We should be tired of studies that compare the new, very expensive drugs with placebo, when we really need to see studies comparing them with conventional, often much less expensive treatment," wrote Stephen L. Blythe, DO. Prolia is "another expensive drug that nobody will be able to use."[89]

Athanassios Kyrgidis, MD, DDS, questioned the published Prolia research itself in an *NEJM* letter. Why were women "who had taken oral bisphosphonates" allowed to participate in the study when bisphosphonates are known to stay in the body? he asked. The Prolia researchers didn't seem to have "controlled for this variable," wrote Kyrgidis, suggesting that Prolia effects could be mixed with those from bisphosphonates.[90]

When Prolia came before an FDA advisory committee before its approval, there were more raised eyebrows. In preclinical trials, monkeys used in experiments developed tooth and jaw abscesses, and two died of protozoal infections, said briefing documents.[91] Ten people were hospitalized with serious skin infections during Prolia clinical trials, and human subjects developed cervical, ovarian, pancreatic, gastric, and thyroid cancers. In fact, breast cancer was called "the most common adverse event that led to discontinuation" of Prolia.[92] Cancer is an adverse event?

Even FDA researchers were perturbed. "Three subjects required hospitalization for pneumonia after a single dose [of Prolia]," noted then FDA clinical reviewer Adrienne Rothstein, MD, at the hearings. "Serious adverse events related to infection occurred in 3 percent" of subjects on Prolia, continued Rothstein, with none seen with those on a placebo or a bisphosphonate. "The incidence of serious infections" in Prolia subjects was higher in four different "primary trials in four different populations," Rothstein pointed out.[93] Side effects like the ones listed by Rothstein are common with moAbs because they suppress the body's immune system. Most of the moAbs the FDA has approved carry black-box warnings about superinfections, tuberculosis, and cancers—some of which are rare and unusual.[94]

Sometimes the FDA will approve a dangerous drug because there's a lack of medications to treat a serious condition or because the drug's benefits outweigh its dangers. But the bone-drug field is already pretty full, and Prolia actually performed *worse* than did the placebo in some trials.[95] How can a drug be worse than nothing at all? In bone-drug trials, subjects are routinely given vitamin D and calcium because they help bone strength, and it would be unethical to withhold them. So the groups receiving a "placebo" instead of

Prolia actually got vitamin D and calcium—which are perhaps the "conventional, often much less expensive treatment[s]" Blythe refers to in his journal letter.[96]

Could the very affordable calcium and vitamin D—less than ten dollars a bottle—work better than a prescription bone drug? Some studies imply that this is the case. In a *British Medical Journal* study of 68,500 patients, calcium and vitamin D "significantly reduced the risk of fracture," whereas bisphosphonates were "of borderline significance."[97] And vitamin D, given to 156 postmenopausal women receiving cancer treatments at Hospital del Mar in Barcelona, also prevented bone loss, researchers announced in 2011.[98] In these cases, nurses don't have to be sent to peoples' homes to remind them to take their vitamins.

But even though Prolia is expensive, dangerous, minimally effective, and part of a crowded drug field, the FDA waved it through. Among its warnings was one becoming all too familiar to women: "Prolia causes significant suppression of bone turnover and this suppression may contribute to the occurrence of osteonecrosis of the jaw, a severe bone disease that affects the jaw, atypical fractures, and delayed fracture healing."[99] Yes, Prolia had the same drawbacks as bisphosphonates! Would sales reps have to hide those warning pages, too?

WANTED: OLD BONES AND YOUNG

At the same time Pharma was cooking up the osteopenia crisis to sell bone drugs, Agribiz (the agribusiness industry) was creating the "Calcium Crisis" to sell fluid milk. And just as Pharma has the FDA to do its bidding, Agribiz has the US Department of Agriculture (USDA).

By the 1990s, the National Dairy Promotion and Research Board and the National Fluid Milk Processor Promotion Board partnered with the USDA to push milk drinking, which had been falling since the 1970s, especially among teens and tweens. The promotions even included partnerships with fast-food restaurants like Wendy's and McDonald's, who would seem unlikely comrades for a government agency sworn to protect the public health.[100]

At the heart of the milk campaign, which began with the catchphrase "Milk: It Does a Body Good" and segued into the celebrity "Got Milk?" "milk mustache" ads was the same claim that Merck, Roche, GSK, P&G, and Sanofi-Aventis were cashing in on: that bones would snap without, in this case, milk. "One in five victims of osteoporosis is male," said milk ads featuring top model Tyra Banks and targeting teens. "Don't worry. Calcium can help prevent it."[101]

"Shake it, don't break it. Want strong bones?" said another ad with musician Marc Anthony.[102] "Drinking enough lowfat milk now can help prevent osteoporosis later." By 2002, milk posters with "strong bones" claims, showing sports and music celebrities—many of whom were African American or Latino—were being disseminated to thirty-two thousand US public middle and high schools by the Milk Processor Education Program, an arm of the dairy industry.[103] But there was a credibility problem with the bone campaign beyond the conflict of interest inherent in public schools helping private industry sell milk (and the fact that Latinos and African Americans are the groups *least* likely to get osteoporosis).

Researchers say that fractures are not caused by "milk deficiencies" but by lack of exercise, diets that leech calcium, falls, and even prescription drugs. If milk deficiencies caused fractures, why do poorer countries where milk is not consumed often have lower fracture rates than industrialized countries? asks T. Colin Campbell, PhD, in *The China Study*.[104]

"There is growing evidence that consumption of a Western diet is a risk factor for osteoporosis through excess acid supply," says an article in the *Proceedings of the Nutrition Society*,[105] a theory also advanced by heart expert Dean Ornish, MD, then of the Preventive Medicine Research Institute.[106]

"Elderly women with a high dietary ratio of animal to vegetable protein intake have more rapid femoral neck bone loss and a greater risk of hip fracture than do those with a low ratio," says an article in the *American Journal of Clinical Nutrition*.[107]

And what about the Western "diet" of drugs? Popular asthma drugs, steroids, digestive drugs like Nexium® and Prilosec®, and antidepressants also can cause "drug-induced osteoporosis," says an article in the *American Journal of Medicine*.[108] And studies in the *Archives of Internal Medicine* found that patients on antidepressants like Prozac®, Zoloft®, and Paxil® had 6 percent lower bone density in their spines and 4 percent lower bone density in their hips than those not on antidepressants, reports *US News & World Report*.[109]

Psychoactive pills like antidepressants, antipsychotics, sleeping and anxiety pills, and sedatives can also cause fractures, write Joe and Teresa Graedon, authors of the *People's Pharmacy*, by increasing falls through memory and coordination impairment. "Avoiding drugs that increase the likelihood of falling may be just as important as taking drugs that can make bones stronger," write the Graedons.[110] In fact, according to a *British Medical Journal* article, the "strongest single risk factor for fracture is falling and not osteoporosis."[111] Meanwhile in 2011, with the patent on Fosamax long since expired and other bisphosphonate patents on their way to expiration, the FDA held hearings about possible new warnings for the drug class. Two advisory committees convened to consider whether the labels on bisphosphonates should be altered to reflect "adverse events" like atypical fractures, osteonecrosis of the jaw, and esophageal cancer—though members said the proof of the latter is lacking.[112] The hearings included testimonies from women on bisphosphonates whose bones fractured for no apparent reason. Among the subjects were a teacher who was reaching for something in the classroom, a woman who was just riding on the subway, and a woman who simply picked up the morning newspaper.[113] These were the same kinds of random fracture events that Pharma used to *sell* bisphosphonates, except that the bisphosphonates seemed to cause them.

After hearing the evidence of fractures and ONJ, committee members agreed that the FDA should limit how long people remain on bisphosphonates. They did not discuss limiting how long bisphosphonates should remain on the market.

Part 2

BIG FOOD

Chapter 7

WE'RE DRINKING WHAT?
THE RISE AND FALL OF MONSANTO'S
BOVINE GROWTH HORMONE

T he year was 1993. In between watching *Roseanne*, *Murphy Brown*, and *Cheers* on TV, Americans were captivated by a sci-fi thriller at the movie theaters about out-of-control technology called *Jurassic Park*. Little did they know, another science fiction–like technology—a cross between cow DNA and *E. coli* bacteria—was heading for their dinner tables.

In fact, even as the nation first debated genetically modified (GM) crops like the Flavr Savr® tomato, approved in 1994, and GM crops in the works like Roundup® Ready Soybeans, Bt-corn, and Golden Rice, milk made from cows treated with rBGH (recombinant bovine growth hormone) were already on store shelves. Unlabeled.

The Monsanto Company's genetically engineered rBGH, Posilac® (created from inserting the DNA sequence for a cow's natural growth hormone into the DNA of *E. coli*, making the cow produce more milk), was considered a technology, not a food. That meant it sailed through FDA approvals before the public could ask about its long-term effects, why it wasn't labeled, why more milk was needed when there was already a surplus, and what kind of mad scientist would cross a cow with bacteria.[1]

Selling milk looks easy and even fun when you see the "Got Milk?" celebrity "milk mustache" ads. In fact, it is neither. Despite almost twenty years of the mustache ads, milk sales continue to fall at a fast clip.[2] Why? According to the milk groups responsible for the marketing, the National Dairy Promotion and Research Program and the National Fluid Milk Processor Promotion Program, there are several reasons.[3] Calcium-fortified juices and vitamin-enhanced beverages have "undermined" milk's healthy image and are more available than milk "in many eating establishments."[4] The percentage of African Americans in the US population who are not big milk drinkers is rising, and the percentage of children under six who do drink a lot of milk (or did) is falling.[5] And the public's "preference" for milk itself may be changing.[6]

The marketers' reports could add that there are many groups that shun milk, from teens, young adults, dieters, athletes, health-food eaters, and certain ethnic minorities, to the lactose intolerant, people with allergies, alcohol drinkers, smokers, animal advocates, environmentalists, and kids themselves. (Which is why they invented chocolate milk.) Even health professionals denounce milk for its cholesterol, fat, calories, and allergens. Benjamin Spock, MD, the famous baby boom–era pediatrician, recommended no milk for children after age two to reduce their risks of heart disease, obesity, high blood pressure, diabetes, and diet-related cancers.[7]

In fact, there is so much undrunk and unmarketable milk that the government, by law, buys it up and dumps it in the school lunch programs and other federal food plans to create command consumers.[8] But despite federal price supports and guaranteed consumers, farmers also "manage" the milk surplus by simply killing, or as farmers call it, "culling," cows, like the fifty thousand destroyed *per week* during the 2009 milk glut, says the Associated Press.[9] Yet we need a drug that produces more milk?

Milk marketers have tried everything to reverse falling sales. Before the "Got Milk?" ads, they conducted a "Milk: It Does a Body Good" campaign in the late 1990s, which targeted young women with the message that milk would prevent osteoporosis in later life. The problem was, teens, tweens, and young women worry about getting osteoporosis when they get old just about as much as they worry about skin cancer from sunbathing and lung cancer from smoking. Who's gonna get old?

Then, taking a cue from the cartoon character Joe Camel, used by R. J. Reynolds to market Camel cigarettes until the American Medical Association objected, milk marketers redesigned milk bottles into hand-friendly, "fun" bottles called the Chug.[10] They didn't look like something your mother told you to drink. The whimsical, decanter-like bottles looked more like something you had to sneak. But they didn't work—for the same reason you can't hide a pill in a dog or cat's favorite food.

Next, milk marketers tried positioning milk as a cure for premenstrual syndrome, commonly called PMS. "We're talkin' *half the population*," you can imagine one marketing ace exclaiming to the other. Television ads showed bumbling boyfriends and husbands rushing to the store for milk to detoxify their stricken women. But the milk-as-Midol® campaign lasted about as long as an actual trip to the store. The study itself, on which the campaign was based, credited calcium, not milk, with helping PMS. And calcium is found in many sources besides milk, including the "calcium-fortified juices" that milk marketers battle against, and even the antacid TUMS®.[11]

Then milk marketers landed on the idea of milk as a diet food. Is there anything that *can't* be sold when it promises that it will help someone lose weight?

"Studies suggest that the nutrients in milk can play an important role in weight loss," said milk ads that kicked off the Great American Weight Loss Challenge in 2006. "So if you're trying to lose weight or maintain a healthy weight, try drinking 24 ounces of low-fat or fat-free milk every 24 hours as part of your reduced-calorie diet."[12] The marketing campaign was especially targeted to the Hispanic community, which is known both for its high obesity rates and its low milk consumption.[13] There was even a related school program called "Healthiest Student Bodies," which recognized twenty-five schools around the country for providing "an environment that encourages healthy choices for students."[14]

The milk-as-a-diet-food campaign had many other names: "Milk Your Diet," "Body by Milk," "Think about Your Drink," "Why Milk?" "24oz/24hours, 3-a-Day" (servings, that is), and, of course, "Got Milk?" Hey, one of these slogans has to work!

But the suggestions for "milking your diet" sounded more like a meal plan for a recovering anorexic than a diet to lose muffin tops, love handles, and saddlebags.[15] Ideas included: "Grab a carton of milk at the drive-through instead of a soda." "Sip on a cappuccino or latté instead of black coffee." "Enjoy a banana and glass of milk for a mid-morning snack." "Add milk to risotto and rice dishes for a creamier texture." "Order a milk-based soup like corn

chowder, potato leek, or cream of broccoli soup as a first course at dinner."
And even "Make a 'mocktail' in a goblet with milk and sugar-free hazelnut
syrup" and "Milk your dessert with puddings or custards"![16]

To lose weight with these suggestions, you'd have to eliminate almost
all other food—which may have been the point. But if burning and reducing
calories are doing the "heavy lifting," wrote a commentator on a nutrition
website, and causing the real weight loss, why not call it the "the apple diet"?
"Cut calories, burn calories, eat an apple before every meal."[17]

In fact, soon after the diet plan was unveiled, a study in the *American Journal of Clinical Nutrition* of twenty thousand men who increased their intake of
low-fat dairy foods found they did not lose weight.[18] "The hypothesis that has
been floating around is that increasing dairy can promote weight loss, and in
this study, I did not find that," said Swapnil Rajpathak, MD, then assistant
professor in the Department of Epidemiology and Population Health at the
Albert Einstein College of Medicine.[19]

Worse, the research behind the weight-loss claims was largely conducted
by Michael Zemel, PhD, then director of the Nutrition Institute at the University of Tennessee, who had "patented" the claim that calcium or dairy
products could help against obesity. The patent was owned by the university
and licensed to Dairy Management Inc., reported *USA Today*.[20] Zemel's coauthor, Sharon Miller, PhD, was later ensnared in a conflict-of-interest mishap
in the *Journal of the American Medical Association (JAMA)*.[21]

Alerted by food activists to the spurious science supporting milk and
weight loss, the Federal Trade Commission's (FTC) Bureau of Consumer Protection directed milk marketers to stop the weight-loss campaign "until further
research provides stronger, more conclusive evidence of an association between
dairy consumption and weight loss."[22] Susan Ruland, then spokesperson for
the chastened National Fluid Milk Processor Promotion Board, objected.
"There's a strong body of scientific evidence that demonstrates a connection
between dairy and weight loss," she said, although she promised that future
ads would comply.[23] After the FTC clampdown, marketing materials claimed
that low-fat dairy products *do not necessarily add weight* and may have "certain
nutrients that can help consumers meet dietary requirements"—pretty much
the definition of "food."[24] Soon the marketing read, "Soft drinks and other

sweetened beverages are now the leading source of calories in a teen's diet and these nutrient-void beverages are increasingly taking the place of milk."[25]

Meanwhile, milk marketers were citing research to the medical and scientific press about milk's value in "breast cancer, hypertension, and rickets" and in osteoporosis.[26] "The Fluid Milk Board continues to spotlight the high incidence of high blood pressure among African Americans and to promote milk and milk products as a dietary solution as part of the DASH [Dietary Approaches to Stop Hypertension] diet," said a yearly report to Congress. The milk-marketing program also addresses misconceptions about lactose intolerance and shows why "it should not be a barrier to including milk in the diet," says the report.[27] (Typically, when marketers use the word *barrier*, they mean profit barrier.)

The phony science was not limited to milk. In 2008, *JAMA* was forced to print a correction stating that authors of an article arguing for a higher recommended dietary allowance of protein were, in fact, industry flaks. Sharon L. Miller (Michael Zemel's patent coauthor, see above) was "formerly employed by the National Cattlemen's Beef Association," and author Robert R. Wolfe, PhD, received money from the Egg Nutrition Center, the National Dairy Council, the National Pork Board, and the Beef Checkoff through the National Cattlemen's Beef Association, said the clarification.[28] (In fact, Miller's former e-mail address was smiller@beef.org, which could have been the *JAMA* editors' first tip-off.) Apparently, Pharma is not the only industry playing fast and loose with the truth when it comes to journal submissions. And, like Pharma's many false and/or purchased science papers planted in journals, Miller and Wolfe's article was retracted.

A quick search of the literature reveals other "science" papers penned by the duo. The dairy industry funded a paper by Miller about milk and weight, as well as an entire "dietary protein" supplement for the *American Society for Nutritional Sciences*, which was edited by both Miller and Wolfe.[29] Other works by Wolfe have been funded by the National Cattlemen's Beef Association, the Egg Nutrition Center, the National Dairy Council, and the National Pork Board.[30] As director of the Center for Translational Research in Aging and Longevity at the University of Arkansas, Wolfe often addresses the national red-meat deficiency in the elderly. His article, funded by the National Cattlemen's Beef Association, "Seniors Need More Protein Rich Food to Decrease Muscle Loss, Improve Quality of Life," was even featured on Medical News Today, a prominent health website.[31]

Wolfe's nutritional research has taken some ghastly turns. He presided over the infusion with endotoxin of eighteen pigs—"until the pulmonary arterial pressure reached a pressure similar to that found in trauma victims"—to reach the conclusion (after killing the pigs and removing their lungs) "that the common practice of providing calories in the form of polyunsaturated [non-red meat] fatty acids to critically ill patients carries the risk of being detrimental to lung function."[32] Yes, the animals died from a saturated-fat deficiency!

Much of milk marketing is celebrity-driven. In fact, almost every A-, B-, and C-list celebrity who has ever made the news has posed in these ubiquitous "milk mustache" ads that appear in *Sports Illustrated for Kids*, *Spin*, *Electronic Gaming*, *CosmoGirl*, *Blender*, *Seventeen* and elsewhere.[33] In fact, milk marketers have cast such a wide celebrity net, they may have come to regret using some models like soccer star David Beckham, whose popularity nosedived when he came to play in the United States; *American Idol* singer Carrie Underwood, who turned vegan after posing for milk ads; and the New York Yankees' Alex Rodriguez, who admitted to using performance-enhancing drugs.

To unload surplus milk and grow young milk drinkers, the National Fluid Milk Processor Promotion Board ships posters of mustache-wearing actors, sports figures, musicians, and models to sixty thousand US elementary schools and forty-five thousand middle and high schools.[34] During the "Healthiest Student Bodies" promotion, students were told if they visited the website www.bodybymilk.com, they could win an iPod®, a Fender® guitar, or their schools could qualify for sports gear, classroom supplies, and musical instruments.[35] (Drink milk, and solve the school board's budgetary crisis!)

There was also in-class selling, using the type of peer-to-peer pressure that has worked so well for Pharma with paid doctors. Students at three California high schools got a chance to create their own "Got Milk?" campaigns aimed at their peers in a seven-week advertising and marketing class.[36] Winners got $2,000, an all-expense-paid trip to San Francisco to present their ideas to milk officials and to the milk campaign's main ad agency (Goodby,

Silverstein & Partners), and the chance to have their campaign used in future milk marketing. The cost of an ad campaign guaranteed to sell milk to teens because it was created and produced by them? Priceless.

In case any young people missed the fact that drinking milk is cool and fun, milk marketers also rolled out White Gold and the Calcium Twins, a spoofy musical group that rocked out on YouTube® and social-networking sites about milk's benefits for hair, teeth, nails, and biceps. In the same vein, the "Got Milk?" site included an animated cartoon called the "Moo Factory," which depicted cows, chickens, ducks, and pigs (and a horse working out on a treadmill), while milk cartons moved by on a conveyor belt. A helium balloon pops up continually, saying, "Tell Your Friends."[37] "Do you think drinking calcium fortified beverages like soy drinks and orange juice will meet your bones' requirements?" asks the site. "Not really, says research that concluded 75 percent of calcium added to popular beverages gets left at the bottom of the carton." Then a disclaimer pops up and confesses that milk's actual benefits for "bones, PMS, sleep, teeth, hair, muscles [and] nails" have been "purposefully exaggerated so as not to bore you."[38] The glib derision toward consumers, animals, and the truth gets even worse. "No animals were harmed in the making of this site," says the Moo Factory as you leave it. "In fact the animals aren't even real. If you think we could get a real pig to wear curlers, you're bonkers," says the site.

In fact, milk-industry huckstering in public schools is so brazen and offensive to some that it led to the firing of a Chicago-area middle-school art teacher in 2007. Forty-five-year-old David Warwak was fired from Fox River Grove Middle School, where he had taught for eight years, for "turning his classroom into a forum on veganism," said the District 3 School Board.[39] In addition to creating art projects with anti-milk messages, he asked the cafeteria manager to remove the milk posters and gave him a copy of John Robbins's *Food Revolution*. "It turned into a PETA [People for the Ethical Treatment of Animals] advertisement and it was against the school lunch program," said Tim Mahaffy, then principal of Fox River Grove Middle School, of Warwak's food activism.[40]

Warwak made the artistic statements that led to his firing with Peeps®, the yellow, marshmallow candy shaped like a baby chick and tradition-

Glamour (2006); also available at www.whymilk.com.

ally given out at Easter. First, he distributed them to students and faculty as "pets," telling them to take the Peeps home and protect them. But after people become "attached" to the Peeps, he consigned them to fates suffered by many real animals, like being hunted, caged in zoos, and reduced to sandwich meat, which angered authorities.[41]

Warwak's philosophical point, that you "can't teach kids to appreciate art till you get them to think about life," was lauded, at least partially, in a *Chicago Tribune* editorial.[42] And T. Colin Campbell, MD, the well-known former Cornell University professor and coauthor of the 2005 *The China Study*, flew all the way to Chicago to testify at Warwak's hearing. "The consumption of dairy, especially at the younger ages, is a problem," Campbell testified to the assembled school officials, citing a "threefold higher risk of colon cancer," the risk of four other kinds of cancer, and the risk of osteoporosis. The USDA dietary committee responsible for milk health claims is riddled with conflicts of interest, Campbell further testified. "Six of the eleven members of the committee, including the chair, had an association with the dairy industry."[43]

At the hearing, Warwak, a fisherman-turned-vegan, served as his own attorney. He also got the chance to direct questions at the principal, Tim Mahaffy, who fired him.

> *Warwak:* Would you say the school lunch goes against humane education?
> *Mahaffy:* I disagree. I don't see the connection.
> *Warwak:* The humane education says be nice to all things; the school lunch says, well, not animals?
> *Robert E. Riley (Counsel for District 3):* Objection. Arguing with the witness.
> *Warwak:* Does the school promote meat and dairy one-sided or do they allow other viewpoints on it?
> *Mahaffy:* The school is committed to following both the State and federal guidelines for serving school lunches.[44]

MORE MILK FOR PEOPLE TO NOT DRINK

If milk consumption is going down, the government is stuck buying the surplus, and cows are actually slaughtered en masse to keep the price of milk up, why would the United States want to produce *more* milk? Why does "Big Ag" develop genetically modified crops that grow twice as fast and feed antibiotics to livestock to grow faster? The answer is simple: profits.

Monsanto's rBGH was designed to let dairy operations get more money out of a cow "unit." Cows injected with the drug, called somatotropin, a synthetic version of bovine growth hormone, are hyperstimulated to produce 10 percent more milk—seven to fourteen additional pounds daily. The greater cow "efficiency" not only makes dairy farmers more money; it lets them feed the world and reduce their carbon output, say pro-rBGH sources.

"As farmers, we have an obligation to feed the world's growing population," says Bill Rowekamp, a Minnesota dairy farmer and member of a pro-rBGH advocacy group called American Farmers for the Advancement and Conservation of Technology, or AFACT.[45] "Also, using (rBGH) is a boon to the environment. For every million cows that are supplemented with the hormone, that's the equivalent, in terms of a carbon footprint, of taking 100,000 cars off the road."[46] An op-ed in the *Washington Times* agrees. "Fewer cows means less methane produced by bovine intestinal tracts, and manure production is cut by about 3.6 million tons" per year, it says. "At the same time, more than 5.5 million gallons of gasoline and diesel fuel (enough to power 8,800 homes) are saved, greenhouse gas emissions are lowered by 30,000 metric tons."[47]

The use of rBGH also enables dairy farmers to stay competitive, said Pennsylvania dairy farmer Tom Krall, then of AFACT. "For efficiency and for the benefit of the cow, there's not a better product made. We see no negative side effects whatsoever."[48]

But other farmers are more skeptical of rBGH, even when it first appeared. Neither the public nor dairy farmers will necessarily see cost benefits, David Campbell, then of the University of California Sustainable Agriculture Research and Education Program, told the eco-agriculture magazine *Acres U.S.A.* in 1994. More production coupled with decreasing consumption would "hurt prices for farmers," he said, and "additional government purchases of excess milk due to bST-induced [rBGH] will cost taxpayers as well as dairy producers."[49]

The Reverend Norm White, who served as a pastor to rural communities, also objected to the "logic" of rBGH in a column in *Acres U.S.A.* in 1994. "Will not increased production per cow result in greater over-production of milk, resulting in even lower prices for milk to the farmer, thereby forcing more dairy women and men out of dairy farming?"[50] White even set his objections to music, to the tune of *Old Man River*:

> Old milk river, that hormone river;
> It just keeps growing, it keeps on flowing along.
> Tote that syringe, grab that tail,
> Jab the old cow, 'til she fills the pail.[51]

Like the legalization of patenting life forms, which began with the Onco-Mouse® (a rodent genetically modified to carry an "oncogene," making it more susceptible to cancer and thereby suitable for cancer research), rBGH got the government go-ahead with little debate or public awareness. One reason for its easy path, said rBGH critics, was that former Monsanto vice president and chief lobbyist Michael R. Taylor had moved to the FDA by the time rBGH was under consideration and was responsible for its labeling guidelines.[52]

And speaking of labeling, the FDA said that milk from rBGH-treated cows and, by extension, cream, cheese, yogurt, buttermilk, ice cream, baked goods, and meat would not need labeling. (The FDA says the same thing about genetically modified crops and clone-produced food.) And, despite Taylor's zigzags between government and industry (which made him "the quint essential revolving door," according to Marion Nestle, New York University professor of nutrition), President Obama named him FDA Deputy Commissioner for Foods in 2009.[53]

But Taylor was not the only fox guarding the henhouse at the FDA during rBGH approval. "Concerned employees" at the FDA's Center for Veterinary Medicine sent an anonymous letter to the General Accounting Office (GAO) accusing Margaret Miller, PhD, then deputy director of the FDA's Office of New Animal Drugs and a former employee of Monsanto, of writing FDA opinions on rBGH labeling at the same time she was publishing rBGH papers with Monsanto scientists.[54] Susan Sechen, PhD, then with the Office of New Animal Drugs, was also linked to Monsanto, according to published reports, though the GAO cleared all three officials.[55]

Look at photos of the gigantic udders of rBGH-treated dairy cows, and it's easy to see the humane and health objections that led to the ban of rBGH in Canada, Australia, Japan, New Zealand, and the European Union's twenty-five countries.[56] The hyper-hormonal stimulation that rBGH causes throws cows into a negative energy balance, say farmers, pulling calcium out of their systems to produce milk and leaving them unable to eat enough to maintain their bodies.

After Michigan dairy farmer Steve Schulte's rBGH-treated cow died of an internal hemorrhage, he surmised, "She may have had a bit of a problem internally and all that extra production, it just burst something in there."[57] John Shumway, then a dairy farmer in Lowville, New York, said he had to sell 34 of his 200 cows because of rBGH-caused mastitis.[58] Charles Knight, then a dairy farmer from Florida, reported similar problems.[59]

Cows treated with rBGH need so much energy to maintain their "cracked-up" metabolisms that the era of cow cannibalism was ushered in, charges John Stauber, coauthor of *Mad Cow U.S.A.* "It was discovered in the early '90s that the cheapest source of fat and protein supplements for dairy cows in Wisconsin was dairy cows. In other words, [the cheapest feed source was] the meat unfit for human consumption—the stuff that doesn't make it onto the dinner plate—being rendered and fed back to dairy cows."[60] Of course, turning cows into cannibals is credited as the cause of mad cow disease.

According to a Canadian Veterinary Medical Association expert panel, rBGH raises "a number of legitimate animal welfare concerns . . . [including] an increased risk of clinical mastitis and lameness, and a reduction in the lifespan of treated cows."[61] Isn't getting more milk out of an animal by shortening its life an agricultural version of killing people to save the village?

"Those animals have to eat more," says Michael Pollan, author of *The Omnivore's Dilemma* and *In Defense of Food*, about rBGH cows. "And they have to be replaced more often, so the number of cows and resources used may be quite the same. The cows only go through a couple of lactations before they're sent off to the hamburger plant. So I don't know if it is in fact a more efficient use of resources."[62]

"Farmers work hard to prevent mastitis in their dairy cows and must, at times, use antibiotics to get rid of it. I don't believe that a 50 percent increase in mastitis is tolerable," argued Reverend Norm White in *Acres U.S.A.*[63]

"Many of us are concerned that increased use of antibiotics to fight mastitis (caused by rBGH) might well result in unwholesome meat. I surely wouldn't want to eat from the hypodermic pockmarked section of the cow."[64]

Then there are the questions that pertain to all food produced with growth drugs: What are their effects on human organs? Does a substance that triples the size of cow mammary glands have no effect on humans? Certainly the hormone in rBGH connected to growth, called insulin-like growth factor-1, or IGF-1, has an effect, say researchers.

Insulin-like growth factor-1 "is necessary for proper growth in children, but studies of men and women more than forty years old raise the possibility that it contributes to the growth of tumors," said an article about the work of Edward Giovannucci, MD, then an assistant professor at Harvard's School of Public Health, who has studied IGF-1. "Once cancer cells begin to form, IGF-1 will promote their growth as well as that of normal cells," says Giovannucci.[65] In fact, Harvard researchers have found that men with elevated IGF-1 have more than four times the risk of prostate cancer, and premenopausal women with elevated IGF-1 have seven times the risk of breast cancer.[66] Even without rBGH, IGF-1 contained in milk can encourage cancer, according to the European Commission and Harvard's Nurses' Health Study.[67] Would the additional IGF-1 from rBGH pose greater risks? "If we were to repeat such a study now, with people drinking milk with rBGH, it might be a bigger problem," says Michelle D. Holmes, MD, then the Nurses' Health Study lead researcher.[68]

The FDA had hoped to head off such concerns with an article in *Science* that found that rBGH is "biologically inactive in humans," since it is not "orally active in rats."[69] But Canadian scientists reviewing the same research, which came from Monsanto, found that 20 to 30 percent of the rats in the studies showed IGF-1 antibodies, implying that IGF-1 *was* indeed in their bloodstreams. Male rats also developed cysts on their thyroid glands and abnormalities in their prostates from the rBGH, reported the *New York Times*.[70] Could the prostate and breast cancers that seem epidemic since rBGH was legalized be linked? Even if people don't drink the milk, most cheap beef includes animals treated with rBGH cows.

Jon Scheid, then at the FDA's Center for Veterinary Medicine, admitted to the Associated Press that the FDA had never examined the raw data on the rat studies and had relied entirely on Monsanto's summary, essentially rubber-stamping it. "We do not have the data from that study," he said.[71]

In 1998, then Vermont senators Patrick Leahy and James Jefferds asked Donna Shalala, then secretary of the Health and Human Services Department, to formally investigate the FDA's swift 1993 approval of rBGH.[72] But Shalala was hardly impartial about rBGH.[73] "I'm telling you, this stuff is safe," she said in news reports. "My own kids grew up on milk from cows who were treated with it." Shalala also posed in milk ads and helped the dairy industry's "Calcium Crisis" campaign.[74] Even the FDA's claim in the *Science* article that rBGH didn't survive pasteurization was contradicted by a different journal article, reported the *Capital Times*.[75] It was based on a study that "erroneously heated milk for 30 minutes at the 15-second pasteurization temperature," and was conducted on calves, not humans, said the *Times*.[76] In fact, questions about the fate of IGF-1 in the human body led the American Public Health Association, the Oregon Physicians for Social Responsibility, the American Nurses Association, Breast Cancer Action, and 260 US hospitals to oppose rBGH.[77]

Insulin-like growth factor-1 is a "strong mitogen for mammary epithelium [producer of breast cancer]," said Gary Steinman, MD, in a letter to the *Journal of Reproductive Medicine*. And, Steinman continued, it is so prominent in rBGH-produced milk that it's suggested as a marker to detect illegal rBGH-produced milk in the European Union.[78] So much for surviving pasteurization!

But Trent Loos, then a columnist for the weekly agriculture newspaper *Feedstuffs*, dissented. "IGF-1 is [a] naturally occurring human hormone commonly measured in our saliva," he wrote on a pro-rBGH website. "Every person who has ever been diagnosed with cancer has also had saliva. Does that mean that saliva causes cancer? NO. Furthermore, if parents are worried about the impact of milk consumption on their kids, are they keeping the kids locked away from the sun? Malignant melanoma [is] the most serious form of skin cancer."[79]

LABEL ROULETTE

Even dairy farmers who embraced rBGH admitted that it added to milk surpluses at the price of animal welfare and posed no advantage for the consumer.

But for small, family, and organic-oriented dairy farmers who did not want to use the product, the playing field was especially asymmetrical because most US milk is pooled—the rBGH-produced milk mixed in with the non-rBGH-produced milk, before being sent to processors and distributers and made into other dairy products. Still, co-op or small dairies that *could* segregate or trace their milk began biting back. Swiss Valley Farms, ice cream makers Ben & Jerry's, Tillamook County Creamery Association (the nation's second-largest maker of chunk cheese), Shamrock Farms, Prairie Farms Dairy, and Darigold began claiming on their labels that they did not knowingly accept milk from rBGH-treated cows.[80]

"By not using rBGH, we protect the health of our cows, their milk and our customers," Dean Foods–owned Alta Dena Dairy proclaimed on its website.[81] "Since 1857, Borden has taken a lot of pride in providing customers with premium, great tasting dairy products. That's why we work exclusively with farmers that supply 100 percent of our milk from cows that haven't been treated with artificial hormones," said the dairy known for "Elsie the Cow." "We treat our cows with love not rBGH," said milk cartons from Kleinpeter Dairy in Louisiana.[82] "Many people believe that rBGH causes premature puberty in children. We want you to know that Kleinpeter Dairy is concerned about your children's healthy growth and wellbeing. Let our family comfort yours in this regard because our kids drink Kleinpeter milk, too!"

Of course "absence labels," labels that say a product does *not* contain an ingredient, can redefine a product landscape by implying that unless you see that a product is free from a certain item, it isn't. So Monsanto aggressively retaliated against the presumptuous dairies. It sued Swiss Valley Farms and Oakhurst Dairy, sent high-pressure letters to Tillamook County Creamery Association co-op members, and asked both the FTC and FDA to intervene to stop the "misleading" anti-rBGH marketing messages.[83] The messages were creating an "artificial demand" for rBGH-free milk, said Monsanto lawyers.[84] Monsanto may be the world's biggest seed company but those Ma-and-Pa dairies weren't playing fair!

Monsanto also used its "grassroots" pro-rBGH group AFACT and cultivated government officials to fight anti-rBGH sentiment.[85] In 2007, Pennsylvania's then agriculture secretary, Dennis Wolff, a former dairy farmer himself, announced a crackdown in his state on rBGH "absence labeling." A label that says "hormone free" is misleading because cows naturally produce hormones, said Wolff, and such labeling "confuses" consumers. But a label that says, "contains no artificial hormones," should not be allowed either, because no "test" could prove the claim, he said.[86]

While the FDA allowed rBGH absence labels, it mandated language that watered down the messages, like "There was no significant difference between milk from treated and untreated cows," and "There is currently no way to differentiate analytically between naturally occurring bST [fBGH] and recombinant bST in milk." "No test can distinguish between milk from treated and untreated cows."[87]

"If the same logic were applied to other products, a company advertising 'no artificial sweeteners' would have to add, 'the FDA says artificial sweeteners are safe,' and organic producers would have to add that pesticides used on food and crops are safe," wrote Benjamin Yale, then attorney for Pure Milk and Ice Cream Co., in *Acres U.S.A.*[88] The Waco, Texas–based dairy was one of the first companies to get a warning letter from Monsanto. Besides, added Yale, "a lot of people don't want rBST [rBGH] for reasons that have nothing to do with safety, but because they worry about the product's impact on family farms, or even on cows."[89]

Still, by 2010 Monsanto had essentially lost the battle for the public's heart—and stomachs—when it came to rBGH. Over one hundred top dairies were partially or completely rBGH-free, including household names like Dean Foods, Yoplait,® Dannon®, and Land O'Lakes®.[90] Most major grocery chains like Safeway, Walmart, Kroger, Costco, as well as many chains like Starbucks and Chipotle Mexican Grill, dropped rBGH—and entire public school systems went rBGH free.[91]

THE COWS BEHIND THE MUSTACHE

Thanks to "Got Milk?" ads, the Moo Factory, White Gold and the Calcium Twins, Chug bottles, and Elsie the Cow, milk has retained the image of a fun, almost zany product that no one could dislike. After all, giving milk doesn't kill an animal, so where's the harm? But a series of dairy exposés in the 2000s revealed that rBGH was just one part of extreme conditions US dairy cows had to endure to keep the nation in cheap milk. An undercover video from the

Westland/Hallmark Meat Company, a slaughterhouse in Chino, California, showed what "spent" dairy cows looked like.

The Humane Society of the United States (HSUS) video of "cull" cows bound for the National School Lunch Program showed the final conclusion of efficiencies on the dairy farm: cows in metabolic collapse, unable to walk or move, "waterboarded," and pushed with forklifts to the killing floor, their sad carcasses fetching only $400 each for the dairymen who sell the spent animals.[92] The dark side of dairy that few see—some refer to it as the "dark side of the moo"—forced government hearings, especially because government meat suppliers were involved.

"Why don't you have a system that uncovers this inhumane treatment of animals?" former Herb Kohl (D-WI) asked the new agriculture secretary, Ed Schafer, who had assumed his post just days earlier.[93] (His predecessor, Mike Johanns, assumed office just days before the first US mad cow was discovered.) Records revealed that Westland/Hallmark was not new to authorities but a repeat offender—cited by the USDA in 2005 for "too much electric prodding causing animals to get more excited while being driven towards [the kill] box." Westland/Hallmark was also cited by humane groups as early as 1996 for prodding cows that couldn't walk "repeatedly in the face" and allowing other cows to trample over them.[94]

When Ken Peterson, then assistant administrator of the USDA's Food Safety and Inspection Service told the press that the cows they saw were probably being moved "out of the slaughter chain" and not *into* the slaughter chain, or that they had had accidents, Miriam Falco, then of *CNN Medical News*, was skeptical. "You're saying that those [downers] (cattle unable to walk) never would have passed inspection anyway. But we see video of them going into the facility. So at what point does your inspection pick up on this?" she asked.[95]

And after Secretary Schafer vowed that the USDA would conduct its own investigation since the video amounted to only allegations, Bill Tomson, then of *Dow Jones News Wire*, said, "Do you actually expect to go down there and ask them if they were doing anything illegal, and people to say, well, yes, we were?"[96] Andy Dworkin, then of the *Oregonian*, also remarked on the farce of a federal inspection after the fact. How can inspectors observe slaughter activity and "be discreet" when "all the workers know who they are?" he asked.[97]

"It seems like maybe the folks had outsmarted the inspection system," observed Steve Cornet, then with *Beef Today*. "Is this a system that's . . . easily circumvented?"[98] The *Los Angeles Times* came out and said what the press and public were thinking. "The U.S. Department of Agriculture has 7,800 pairs of eyes scrutinizing 6,200 slaughterhouses and food processors across the nation. But in the end, it took an undercover operation by an animal rights group to reveal that beef from ill and abused cattle had entered the human food supply."[99]

Even cattlemen from the beef industry couldn't believe the living results of the happy "Got Milk?" campaign. "We just don't see that out here in beef country," said Steve Hilker, then a cattle hauler from Cimarron, Kansas, at congressional hearings after the Westland/Hallmark school lunch scandal. "Around here, a 'downer' cow in the feed yard is one that's got a leg issue—that's had something happen to them, like stepping on a rock or in a crack, something like that."[100] The then president of the Cattle Producers of Washington, Ted Wishon, also pointed out that the video showed dairy, not beef, cattle.[101]

As it turned out, Westland/Hallmark wasn't the only dairy from hell. Animals just as sick and weak from Willet Dairy, New York's largest dairy, were shown on *Nightline* two years later being treated cruelly.[102] Like Westland/Hallmark, Willet was not a first-time offender. "Our investigation found that you hold animals under conditions which are so inadequate that diseased and/or medicated animals bearing potentially harmful drug residues in edible tissues are likely to enter the food supply," reads a letter from the FDA to Dennis H. Eldred, the then owner of Willet Dairy, in 2005.[103] Willet also administered rBGH freely to the dairy's cows, according to employees.[104]

Five months later, undercover footage from Conklin Dairy Farm in Plain City, Ohio, revealed animal abuse so appalling, guards had to be stationed outside the farm because of the irate public after the footage aired. Then Sheriff Rocky Nelson in Union County said, "If there was a way this could be a felony charge, I would push for that."[105] Actors Jamie Lee Curtis, Christopher Guest, and Alex Baldwin wrote letters and blogs of protest.[106] Four months later, television personality Bob Barker narrated another undercover video from Buckeye Veal Farm in Apple Creek, Ohio, that showed what, for many, is the darkest side of the dairy industry: the gentle, newborn male calves, taken from their mothers at birth and chained by the neck until their date with the slaughterhouse.[107] Musician Willie Nelson spoke out against the confinement and tethering of veal calves in 2008. "As a cowboy, I must stand up for cows," he said.[108]

Do the sick and dying dairy cows in these undercover videos look that way because they were given rBGH? Or do dairy operators want to give rBGH to animals that look that way? The answer doesn't matter. The load that "animal units" carry on today's dairy farms to keep milk cheap is clearly criminal.

Meanwhile, in 2008, Monsanto sold rBGH (Posilac) to Elanco, the animal-drug division of drug company Eli Lilly.[109] "POSILAC safely increases productivity of dairy cows thereby allowing family farm owners to more easily provide for their family and employees, reinvest in their farms, and conserve resources like land, water and energy," says the press release. Key word: *family*. "Over the past 14 years, more than a half billion units of POSILAC have been successfully and safely used by tens of thousands of dairy producers on millions of cows to produce wholesome, nutritious, safe and affordable milk and dairy products."[110]

Dave Warwak, the vegan former middle-school art teacher, has not been able to find a new teaching job and is facing foreclosure on his home. Meanwhile, the "Got Milk?" campaign is buzzing along. In fact, in 2011 marketers brought back the milk-as-a-treatment-for-PMS campaign.

Chapter 8
"EGGSPOSÉS" AND TEFLON CHICKEN DONS

Surrounded by the sound of hundreds of dead insects crunching under our feet and the odor of feces and decaying flesh . . . I cringed as we passed mountains of cages filled with hens, some of who were crawling with insects and others caked with congealed blood. As I examined piles of these once living, feeling creatures, I saw one open her eye. I lifted her out of the mound of dead hens. She was motionless and could barely lift her head. She had been stripped of every natural instinct, tortured daily for maximum output until she had met her capacity and now she was the egg industry's trash.

—John Eudaly, investigator at Ohio Fresh Eggs,
"Jody's Story," *Outrage*, Spring 2005

As I made my way down one of the many long aisles, one hen immediately caught my attention. Her condition was horrifying. I looked into her cage to see her neck caught in the wiring of her small prison. The skin from her neck had been pierced by a sharp metal wire sticking down into the cage. To make the situation worse, her crowded cage mates were jostling against her. The more they moved, the more her neck ripped apart. Her skin was torn so badly that veins and muscles were exposed and visible all along the back of her neck. She could not reach food in the position and was barely breathing. I knew I could not leave her in that state. I opened the cage to offer her aid and free her neck from the sharp wire impaling her skin. Once she was loose, she simply collapsed on the cage floor. Her six cage mates trampled her weak and battered body I carefully lifted her out of the cage and carried her in my arms, feeling her heartbeat close to mine.

—Investigator at Ohio Fresh Eggs,
"From an Investigator's Log," *Outrage*, Spring 2005

Before the animal rights movement began, the egg was a kind of droll and comic product—the punch line to phrases like "laid an egg" and "egg on my face," and a shaming missile hurled at public figures who were "egged" like they were "pied." Just as absurd was the chicken itself, the source of everyone's favorite synonym for cowardice (Bwock, bwock! Bend elbow, flap "wing.") and for gender stereotypes ("mother hen" and "hen party"). A silly, overprotective bird that lays eggs and can barely fly? What's not to ridicule?

Even within the animal rights movement, eggs have had a hard time. Since the production of eggs doesn't require an animal to die—as with the production of milk or dairy products—how could egg production be cruel? It doesn't help that people eat eggs all the time without actually buying the eggs themselves since eggs are a hidden ingredient in so many foods.

But by 2000, two things changed. Thanks to animal rights groups exposing conditions on egg and dairy farms, a "vegetarian" diet—abstaining from meat but eating dairy products and eggs—was no longer regarded as cruelty-free. Contrary to images of a pastured "Elsie the Cow," dairy cows were now seen as doing *double* factory farm duty—first as milk machines and then being culled for cheap hamburger. (We won't even talk about how the milk-fed male calves become veal—making milk a vote for veal.) Nor are egg-laying hens exactly put out to pasture. They are gassed, suffocated, or otherwise "depopulated"—and some are probably fed to Elsie.

Then there was nanotechnology. Once cell-phone images of factory farming, shot by undercover activists/employees, went viral and bypassed indifferent news editors and politicians (animal lobbyists say all they see are the bottoms of politicians' shoes with their feet up on the desks), some food consumers began to vote with their forks. In fact, cyber-exposés can so demonize a brand or a food product that in 2011, Big Ag in Iowa, Florida, Minnesota, and New York introduced legislation that would criminalize filming at an animal-related business without an owner's express consent—even by legitimate employees or from public property. The Animal Facility Interference laws are successors to the Food Defamation laws introduced by Big Ag in the late 1990s. Talk-show host Oprah Winfrey was tried under the defamation laws for speaking against hamburgers during the mad-cow scares—and she was acquitted.

It's pretty clear why Big Ag wants to extinguish these undercover videos. By 2007, the eating public had been treated to (1) workers manually ripping off chickens' heads at a Tyson Foods plant, (2) chickens shackled by their necks instead of by their feet, and employees urinating on conveyers at two other Tyson facilities, (3) chickens not dead but "flapping wildly after their throats were slit on a processing line," at a Perdue plant, and (4) employees using birds' blood to write graffiti at a Pilgrim's Pride chicken plant—a KFC supplier.[1] (According to a video, the Pilgrim's Pride employees also spat tobacco juice into birds' mouths and exploded their bodies as dry-ice "bombs.")

But it's also clear that the answer to the ethical and hygienic black hole of US poultry production is not truth embargos. "I could've been arrested for trespassing," wrote then *New York Times* columnist Mark Bittman after attempting to view modern factory farms. "Extreme versions of ag-gag [Animal Facility Interference laws] would make it illegal for me to write about it, or at least publish pictures."[2]

By 2008, celebrities like Pamela Anderson and Rev. Al Sharpton were campaigning against Kentucky Fried Chicken ("Kentucky Fried Cruelty") on the basis of its cruel and inhumane videos like those from Pilgrim's Pride. (KFC was also criticized for its pink "Buckets for a Cure" by breast cancer activists who claimed that fried chicken causes obesity, which is linked to cancer. 3) In the United Kingdom, gourmet chefs like Jamie Oliver and Hugh Fearnley-Whittingstall launched "Chicken Out" and "Jamie's Fowl Dinners"— television campaigns that highlighted modern poultry horrors.[4] "A chicken is a living thing, an animal with a life cycle, and we shouldn't expect it should cost less than a pint of beer in a pub," said Oliver. "It only costs a bit more to give a chicken a natural life and a reasonably pleasant death."[5] Even *Gourmet* magazine reported on cruelty in the chicken industry in 2007.[6]

THE INCREDIBLE-BECAUSE-IT'S-EVEN-EDIBLE EGG

The chicken egg has the highest cholesterol of any other foodstuff—packing approximately 275 mg of cholesterol (more than one day's worth). Without being propped up by ad campaigns like "The Incredible Edible Egg," how do you sell what is essentially a stroke in a shell? Thirty-three and a half million Americans are already at risk for cholesterol-related heart problems, according to *Health Day*, and many are on statins.[7] Why would they want to increase their odds for a stroke by eating eggs or egg products?

In 2008, the American Heart Association's journal *Circulation* reported that just one egg a day increased the risk of heart failure in a group of doctors studied.[8] And in 2010, the *Canadian Journal of Cardiology* lamented the "widespread misconception . . . that consumption of dietary cholesterol and egg yolks is harmless." The article further cautioned that "stopping the consumption of egg yolks after a stroke or myocardial infarction [heart attack] would be like quitting smoking after a diagnosis of lung cancer: a necessary action, but late."[9] Damage to the ticker isn't the only health risk from eating eggs. According to studies in the journals *Nutrition* and *Diabetes Care*, eating eggs is "positively associated" with the risk of diabetes.[10]

Eggs also have a link to ovarian cancer, says an article in *Cancer Epidemiology, Biomarkers & Prevention*, and the culprit is not necessarily cholesterol.[11] "It seems possible that eating eggs regularly is causally linked to the occurrence of a proportion of cancers of the ovary, perhaps as many as 40 percent, among women who eat at least 1 egg a week," wrote the authors. In one study the article cites, three eggs per week increased ovarian-cancer mortality threefold, compared with less than one egg per week.

Why aren't eggs tarred like cigarettes (pun intended) in light of their health risks? Because of counterinformation distributed by Big Ag and the egg industry to both the medical and consumer press. For example, a 2010 egg industry–sponsored supplement in *Canadian Family Physician* found that "consumption of up to seven eggs per week is congruent with a healthy diet," and questioned the cholesterol/cardiovascular disease link.[12] The tobacco industry still doesn't accept the cigarette/lung cancer connection, either.

A blurb in *Akin's Healthy Edge*® magazine says, "In the past, eggs have been condemned as unhealthy because their yolks contain cholesterol. But studies from around the world show that the cholesterol found naturally in food isn't actually harmful, according to research presented at the Experimental Biology 2011 conference in Washington, DC. Unlike our government, health agencies in Europe and Canada don't recommend limits for dietary cholesterol."[13]

In 2010, US egg farmers in conjunction with Scholastic rolled out the "Good Egg Project" in schools to increase egg demand—similar to dairyindustry projects in schools to increase milk demand.[14] The "Back-to-Breakfast Teacher Challenge" gave teachers the chance to win $5,000 by explaining in an essay how the Good Egg Project grant "could be used to offer protein breakfasts in their schools."[15]

Diabetes, cancer, and stroke are not the only health risks associated with eggs. Thanks to their modern production methods—thirty thousand or more caged hens stacked on top of each other over their own manure—their *germ* content is as suspect as their nutritional content. The FDA reports that egg operations are so festooned with salmonella and other bacteria that during inspections, it found a hatchery injecting antibiotics directly into the eggs of laying hens, presumably to take the offensive with germ control.[16] Wouldn't eggs from an antibiotic-treated hen *also* have antibiotic residues? Good question. The *Journal of Agricultural and Food Chemistry* reports that "detectable residues were observed in eggs derived from enrofloxacin-treated hens" as well as "yolks from hens treated with enrofloxacin."[17]

Because antibiotics are so integral to factory farming to keep the overcrowding from causing disease and death, representatives from the egg, chicken, turkey, dairy, pork, and cattle industries stormed Capitol Hill in 2009 when the FDA threatened to limit their use.[18] By 2010, salmonella contamination in eggs had become such a thorny issue that President Obama, Agriculture Secretary Tom Vilsack, and Health and Human Services Secretary Kathleen Sebelius personally announced new testing and refrigeration standards to be instituted. But the testing wasn't implemented soon enough to obviate the largest egg recall in US history in 2010, which happened just months later—and caused more than sixteen hundred illnesses.[19]

Of course there's another side to the yuck factor of animals packed cheek to jowl in high-density food production that's not lost on the public: cruelty. By 2006, thanks to online exposés, outspoken food consumers, and even chefs, eighty US college food services, the US House of Representatives, Whole Foods Market, Wolfgang Puck restaurants, and socially aware businesses like Google and AOL announced they were refusing eggs from caged chickens. Egg sales dropped from 2.02 billion dozen in 2002 to 1.84 billion dozen.[20]

California's Proposition 2, which outlawed caged egg production by 2015, passed with more votes than were cast for President Obama in 2008. And the entire European Union resolved to phase out caged eggs by 2012.

Unfortunately, the public found out that crowding was just the beginning of the egg-farm experience for birds. To keep the caged birds from their natural instinct to peck each other, young birds are debeaked—their beaks are partially or totally removed with a hot knife or laser while they are fully conscious. Debeaking results in "intense pain, shock and bleeding," says veterinarian Nedim C. Buyukmihci, emeritus professor of veterinary medicine at the University of California. "Some chicks may die outright in the process," says Buyukmihci, who has specialized in farmed animals and chickens, "and there is loss of weight because the chicks are too [full of pain] or disfigured to eat properly, sometimes because the tongue is injured or severed during the process."[21]

The beak is a sensory organ necessary not just for grasping food but also for "preening, drinking, manipulating objects in the environment, nest building and defense," says veterinarian Debra Teachout. "As a practicing veterinarian, if I were treating a pet chicken of the same age [as egg-farm chicks] that required a similar surgical procedure on its beak for therapeutic reasons, and I did not use anesthetics followed by pain modulation, it would be considered malpractice."[22]

United Egg Producers (UEP), the trade group that represents 85 percent of US egg producers and 180 egg farms, admits to the cruelty in its own 2006 husbandry guidelines. Debeaking causes "acute pain, perhaps constant pain and stress," and other "welfare disadvantages," like bleeding and dehydration. But, like confining birds to "battery cages"—wire cages with less than sixty-seven square inches allotted to each hen—it is done to discourage hens' "more aggressive tendencies," says UEP.[23]

But experts outside Big Ag say caging *increases* aggression. "Laying hens confined to battery cages are not able to lay their eggs in the privacy of an enclosed nest box," says University of California–trained animal behaviorist Sara Shields, PhD. "Without a secluded, protected space in which to lay her egg, a hen is exposed to potential vent pecking and cannibalism by cage-mates."[24]

When rural communities whose air and water are polluted by factory farms object to their proliferation, Big Ag spins how many jobs in agriculture it is providing. But egg operations typically assign about one employee to 250,000 hens, which are housed in as few as sixteen barns. The only "care" the caretakers actually provide, besides giving feed, is removing dead hens, moving out "spent" hens to be euthanized, and installing newly arrived hens from the hatchery. Nor can you hardly blame any of the workers for not wanting to be in one of these barns longer than necessary. Concentrations of hydrogen sulfide, carbon monoxide, and ammonia are so high that people faint and sustain burned lungs. (Although, unlike the birds, they can leave.) Still, UEP guidelines assert that ammonia fumes can exceed 50 ppm but "should not adversely affect bird health."[25]

And then there is forced molting—denying hens food, which has the effect of jump-starting an additional laying cycle, perhaps the result of an atavistic species response to famine. According to 2006 UEP guidelines, such starving of hens is cost-effective for egg producers and "results in the need to add 40 to 50 percent fewer new hens each year."[26] This "results in significantly fewer spent hens that have to be handled, transported and slaughtered," assert the guidelines. "Without molting a flock's life is usually terminated at about 75 to 80 weeks of age. Under the right economic conditions, the useful life of a flock may be extended to 110 weeks or longer through the judicious use of induced molting."[27] *Good news, ladies. You get to stay in your cages and breathe those toxic fumes for thirty more weeks.*

To forestall public outrage against debeaking and forced molting and to slow the move away from battery cage–produced eggs, UEP developed an "Animal Care Certified" logo to assure consumers that its members' eggs were produced humanely. But in 2005, the Better Business Bureau ruled that the label was misleading, and the Federal Trade Commission (FTC) demanded that the label read not "Care Certified" but "United Egg Producers Certified."[28] United Egg Producers was also fined $100,000 and was made to sign an agreement with attorneys general in sixteen states to settle the false advertising claims.[29]

United Egg Producers' guidelines took a further hit in 2006 when People for the Ethical Treatment of Animals (PETA) exposed Mepkin Abbey Eggs, a UEP-certified, fifty-nine-year-old egg operation in Moncks Corner, South Carolina, that was caging, debeaking, and force-molting its hens like other UEP egg producers—spiritual credentials notwithstanding. In a statement to the media, the monks at the abbey called their egg operation "hard and honorable work" of which they were "proud," and they accused PETA of making it difficult to live a "quiet life of prayer, work and sacred reading."[30]

Scott Morris, then a columnist with *Decatur Daily*, managed to find humor in the idea of men of the cloth starving hens. "While fasting can serve as an impetus for a deep spiritual experience, it apparently has the added benefit of causing hens to lay more eggs," he wrote. "But the abbey chickens were allegedly forced to observe this religious practice rather than participating of their own free will. While this may cross some ethical line in the land of religious freedom, it doesn't actually kill the chicken. And you know the ancient Chinese proverb: 'That which does not kill the chicken, makes the chicken stronger.'"[31] Ha ha.

As bills outlawing caged egg production outright inched toward state ballots in 2008, and as entire hotel and restaurant chains were jettisoning battery cage–produced eggs, the egg industry rolled out spin doctors. "Modern chicken houses are heated, cooled and monitored in every possible area," said Nancy Reimers, a veterinarian then working for the UEP-supported Californians for Safe Food, which was created to defeat Proposition 2.[32] "Non-caged birds have more contact with their own droppings and are therefore at a higher risk of infecting their eggs," she said.[33] Moreover, it is in the egg farmers' own best interests to treat birds well since stressed "chickens quit laying eggs."[34]

"We'll supply the market with whatever consumers want," Mitch Head, then spokesman for UEP, told the *Columbus Dispatch* as the free-range egg movement took hold, "and 98 percent of consumers want caged eggs."[35]

Battery cages protect chickens from the threat of avian flu, submitted Jim Chakeres, then executive vice president of the Ohio Poultry Association, since birds have less "direct contact with wild migratory waterfowl or backyard poultry flocks."[36]

BRAVING THE BARNS

When the Ohio-based animal rights group Mercy for Animals (MFA), founded by twenty-something "farm kid" Nathan Runkle, announced it was moving its headquarters to Chicago in 2005, it sounded like a joke to Chicago animal activists. Animal activism was at such low ebb in Chicago that the answer to "How many animal rights activists does it take to change a lightbulb?" was probably seven: three to hand out soggy leaflets in the rain outside a fur store, two to argue about whether to protest carriage horses or captive whales at the Shedd Aquarium the next weekend, one to solicit donations in a can while holding his skateboard, and one to change the lightbulb.

Sure, by 2005, animal activists had become younger and hipper than the "little old ladies in tennis shoes feeding squirrels," who tended to populate the movement in the 1980s. But there was still no organization, no funding, no member unity, no respect from society, and—most importantly—no interest from news media. In fact, it was a good day when, in a city of three million people, eight activists converged at the same time and place for a demonstration. (And an even a better day when someone actually remembered to bring the signs and leaflets.) But after a couple of years, MFA—and specifically its undercover investigations at factory farm operations—did what even the established national animal rights groups PETA and the Humane Society of the United States (HSUS) hadn't always been able to do: it earned the trust and coverage of news outlets like the Associated Press, CNN, and *Nightline*.

There are several reasons why it's hard to get an animal-abuse story covered by mainstream news outlets. Exposés of big food producers or suppliers risk offending not only viewers and advertisers but also local and state regulators on whose watch they occurred. Since such exposés are usually undercover and come from one source, with hard-to-verify facts, the stories are inherently risky to report because the facts could be wrong. There is also compassion and outrage fatigue. One animal abuse story enrages people, but one a week can inure people to suffering.

To win the trust of news organizations, MFA video would include location markers and paycheck stubs from undercover employees. And to counter charges that employees allowed the abuse and/or that management didn't know about it, employees usually pointed out cruelty to bosses on camera (and the bosses would usually tell employees not to worry about it). Since MFA began undercover operations at factory farms, its documentation has been so accurate that it has aided prosecuting attorneys in discovery.

By 2007, MFA investigations were leading network and cable newscasts and were often provoking quick reactions. An undercover operation at the House of Raeford turkey slaughterhouse in Raeford, North Carolina, convinced the Denny's® restaurant chain, a Raeford customer, to suspend its supplier within hours.[37] The next year, video from Gemperle Enterprises egg farm in Turlock, California, inspired its customer Trader Joe's to do the same thing.[38]

"There are multiple shots of moribund chickens with ailments ranging from broken limbs to abscessed cloacae to illness so severe the birds are unable to open their eyes or stand," said Santa Rosa veterinarian Christi Camlbor after viewing the Gemperle video. "The presence of animals in such poor conditions without any apparent method to detect them or provide them with an instant death is extremely concerning."[39]

In addition to neglect, sadistic killing games were a regular part of work at Gemperle, according to an anonymous MFA employee. "Think I can kill it in just one hit?" he records a coworker asking him; the coworker holding a six-foot piece of PVC pipe and spying a stray chicken.[40] The Gemperle video shows what amounts to the entire life cycle of the modern caged laying hen from the stuffing of newly arrived pullets (young birds) from the hatchery into file drawer–sized cages to begin their laying life, to retrieving the birds for the "kill cart's" gas chamber when their usefulness is passed.[41]

Seventy to 85 percent of egg-farm hens are euthanized, admits the egg industry, often in unsavory ways, like the thirty thousand hens that were fed live into a wood chipper at Ward Egg Ranch in San Diego County, California, in 2003.[42] Temple Grandin, PhD, the celebrity animal scientist, confirms the cruelty in a paper she presented at the National Institute of Animal Agriculture. "Some egg producers got rid of old hens by suffocating them in plastic bags or dumpsters. When the egg producers asked me if I wanted cheap eggs I replied, 'Would you want to buy a shirt if it was $5 cheaper and made by child slaves?' Hens are not human but research clearly shows that they feel pain and can suffer."[43]

Gemperle Enterprises owner Ernie Gemperle, who died in 2008, was commended by the Boy Scouts of America–Greater Yosemite Council for transforming "a small family farm model to the current computer driven egg-producing company."[44] The Stanislaus County Board of Supervisors inducted him into the Agriculture Hall of Fame.[45] But when Sacramento's KCRA-3 TV camera crews asked him about a video showing the gassing of chickens, he defended the practice, saying "that's how you dispose of chickens."[46] Big Ag and the egg industry declined to comment on the Gemperle operation in light of the fact that the company was also UEP-certified.[47]

"It's been very difficult to get anyone involved in the egg industry to watch the video and comment," disclosed then reporter Dan Noyes with ABC-7. "Not the state Department of Food and Agriculture, the poultry experts at UC Davis, and not even the county extension agents who work with the farms. We had to go all the way to the University of Maryland to speak with an expert in the Avian and Animal Sciences Department."[48]

Ernie Gemperle, for his part, maintained in the agricultural business weekly *Feedstuffs* that an entry-level employee said he was "directed by the activist" to perform acts of abuse while being filmed.[49] And Gemperle isn't the only operator to blame undercover activists for instigating or tolerating cruelty for the sake of the cameras. In 2005, Tyson Foods said that an undercover employee "violated Tyson's animal-welfare policy by allowing some conscious birds to go into the scald tank for the sole purpose of videotaping what he should have been preventing."[50] Tyson's remark brings to mind what the *Los Angeles Times* said about cruelty at Westland/Hallmark Meat Packing. "The U.S. Department of Agriculture has 7,800 pairs of eyes scrutinizing 6,200 slaughterhouses and food processors across the nation. But in the end, it took an undercover operation by an animal rights group to reveal [animal abuse]"?[51]

Months later, an MFA undercover employee at Norco Ranch in Menifee, California, *did* point out abuse to management, according to his diary. "I found a live hen with her body trapped under her cage's front wall and draped over the egg belt with eggs backing up against her head," wrote the employee. "I picked up the hen and took her to a worker, saying, 'She's not dead.' The worker immediately grabbed the hen by the head and spun her in circles for several seconds before throwing her on the concrete floor, where she gasped, twitched her legs, and convulsed for nearly two minutes."[52]

Still, it wasn't an egg-farm video that vaulted an undercover investigation to the top of AOL News in September 2009 with the headline "Are Your Eggs Unethical?" It was footage from a hatchery. While the grinding up of live newborn male chicks in the egg industry (called *maceration*) is known as an accepted practice (they are worthless to the industry, like male dairy calves), few people had actually seen the procedure until MFA posted a video filmed by an undercover employee at Hy-Line Hatchery in Spencer, Iowa. The footage released to news stations showed an undulating mass of fuzzy, yellow balls bouncing and peeping even as they are fed into the blades of the macerator like so much litter.[53]

In the high-tech business of creating cheap eggs, there is no time to waste letting a chick peck its way out of its shell. The hatchery's "separator" machine efficiently disconnects newborns from their shells at the price of the few that fall to the ground or get caught in the machine and are "washed" along with equipment.

When the MFA employee asked a worker about the damp, panting newborns on the floor, half-born and half-dead, the worker says, "Some of them get on the floor and get wet and then they're no good. And those that were dumped down there were probably just dead ones that were stuck in the trays. That end of the machine is for washing the trays . . . if they're stuck in there, they get washed out and that's how come they're in there."[54]

Unlike gory videos of sick hens in battery cages—which the egg industry calls aberrant—UEP confirms the slicing up of newborn males; at the Hy-Line facility alone, 150,000 are killed in a single day.[55] "There is, unfortunately, no way to breed eggs that only produce female hens," UEP spokesman Mitch Head told the Associated Press. (That means there is no way to make eggs truly "cruelty-free" if they come from a major hatchery.) "If someone has a need for 200 million male chicks, we're happy to provide them to anyone who wants them. But we can find no market, no need."[56]

What happens to the pulverized baby males, described by the MFA employee as "bloody slush coming out of the bottom of the grinder"? The plant manager says in his diary that they are "used in dog food and fertilizer."[57]

"The vast majority of Americans care deeply about farmed animal welfare issues, yet, they're kept in the dark about the egg industry's painful disposal of male chicks," said MFA's Nathan Runkle in a statement. "Not only do grocery stores and consumers have an obligation to acknowledge the truth about eggs, there are many easy and delicious egg alternatives. If egg producers threw mutilated and ground up puppies or kittens, they'd be prosecuted for cruelty to animals."[58]

Mercy for Animals created an egg-carton label that says, "Warning: Male Chicks Are Ground-Up Alive by the Egg Industry" and depicts a chick atop grinding blades. The labels were sent to big grocery chains like Walmart, Kroger, and Safeway. There are no reports of stores using them.

TEFLON CHICKEN DONS

The "broken windows" theory of law enforcement says that neglect and lack of a moral code in a community produces more neglect and further lack of moral code. In agriculture, the broken windows theory means that neglect of animals extends to neglect of workers, the environment, farm neighbors, consumers, and even the food products themselves.

Many people may remember the 2003 testimony of the late Virgil Butler, a whistle-blower at Tyson's Grannis, Arkansas, chicken plant, who said that birds regularly miss the blade intended to kill them and are scalded alive in the defeathering tank.[59] Though the fact that birds enter the feather-picking machinery without having been killed appears to be true, USDA inspectors condemn this occurrence, say chicken-industry spokesmen. Birds processed while still alive are blemishes against these plants' performance standards, and managers have an incentive to prevent them. Two percent of US chickens meet such a death (it's so common that they're called "red birds" in the industry), according to the National Chicken Council. This means that 180 million birds are boiled alive a year.[60]

But Tyson has been under the ethical microscope for other issues, as well as for how it treats birds. In fact, its corporate operations are a good example of the broken windows theory, agricultural-style. Tyson was charged with bribing then Agriculture Secretary Mike Espy with gifts to influence legislation during the Clinton administration—leading to Espy's disgraced resignation in 1993. Tyson paid $6 million to settle the accusations, and two convicted Tyson executives faced prison time, though they were pardoned by President Clinton in 2000.[61]

In 2001, Tyson was served with a federal indictment charging that the company paid smugglers to transport illegal workers from Mexico across the Rio Grande, after which they were supplied with phony social security cards and brazenly paid with corporate checks.[62] "This is a company with a bad history," Rev. Jim Lewis, then an Episcopal minister in Arkansas, told the *New York Times*. "They cheat these workers out of pay and benefits, and then try to keep them quiet by threatening to send them back to Mexico."[63]

In 2003, Tyson pleaded guilty to violating the Clean Water Act with effluvia from its Sedalia, Missouri, facility and agreed to pay $7.5 million.[64] But before its probation ended, Tyson was charged by the state of Oklahoma with polluting the Illinois River watershed.[65] Poultry polluters eject as much phosphorous into the watershed as a city of *ten million people*, said State Attorney General Drew Edmondson after bringing the changes. Phosphorus causes overgrowth of algae and other aquatic plants which chokes off oxygen vital to other marine life, especially animals.

In 2004, an internal Tyson memo revealed that the wives of two veterinarians stationed at Tyson plants in Mexico had been receiving about $2,700 a month "for years," reported the *New York Times*. When Tyson executives discovered the bribes, the payments were simply switched to the veterinarians themselves.[66] "Doctors will submit one invoice which will include the special payments formally [*sic*] being made to their spouses along with there [*sic*] normal consulting services fee," said a Tyson's audit department memo.[67] (Apparently employees were absent the day both ethics and spelling were taught.) In 2006, Tyson cooperated with the Justice Department and the Securities and Exchange Commission in an investigation of the apparent bribery, but no one was ever named or charged in the investigation.[68] In fact, Greg Lee, then Tyson's chief administrative officer who received the e-mail about the veterinarians, received $1 million and a $3.6 million consulting contract when he retired.[69]

Greg Huett, president of Tyson International during the improper payments, became a director at Yuhe International, China's largest producer of day-old broiler chicks, says the *Times*.[70] Tyson is increasingly gravitating to China with its lenient agriculture climate and opened Jiangsu Tyson Foods near Shanghai in 2008 with a planned production of one million birds a week.[71] Richard Bond, then Tyson's president and chief executive, says the company intends to become "the first producer to deliver brand name, high quality fresh chicken to consumers in the eastern China market."[72] Some say it's a matter of time before most US fast-food chains serve chicken from China.[73]

And then there's the safety of Tyson food itself. Tyson used the advertising slogan "Raised without Antibiotics," on chicken products because the ionophores it uses in chicken production are not a medicine used in humans, though they are a type of antibiotic. But in 2007, the Department of Agriculture disallowed the Tyson claim inducing Tyson to adopt the fallback slogan "Raised without antibiotics that impact antibiotic resistance in humans."[74] But the next year, the USDA found more serious antibiotic fowl play: Tyson was also using the human antibiotic gentamicin, linked to liver toxicity and destruction of the balance system in humans, behind the public's back.[75] Tyson spokesman Gary Mickelson admitted that eggs were vaccinated with gentamicin before the birth of a chicken, but he rejected "any statement suggesting our products are anything less than safe and wholesome," reported the Associated Press.[76]

But long before Tyson became a candidate for the Worst Corporate Citizen award, a gigantic egg farm in Turner, Maine, was in the running. In 1977, neighbors who lived near Austin "Jack" DeCoster's huge egg operation began complaining about the lesser mealworm beetles (also known as guarno or litter beetles because of their affinity for manure) that infested their homes, and they sued the egg farm for millions.[77] By 1982, one person had died, thirty-six were sickened in New Hampshire, and four hundred were sickened in Massachusetts from eggs traced to DeCoster owned farms.[78] Five years later, in 1987, nine people had died, and five hundred were sickened in New York from eggs traced to DeCoster-owned farms. The state of New York banned the sale of DeCoster eggs the following year.[79] But, like Tyson, court systems often smiled on DeCoster, and he was allowed to ship eggs from Maryland to other states in 1992, despite the ten preceding deaths.[80]

By 1996, DeCoster had racked up twenty health and safety violations—including polluting groundwater with one hundred thousand rotting carcasses of birds he let perish in a fire, improper asbestos removal, and worker abuses like housing egg workers in cockroach-infested firetrap trailers and hiring children as young as nine as egg workers.[81] "The conditions in this migrant farm site are as dangerous and oppressive as any sweatshop we have seen," said Labor Secretary Robert Reich when he visited DeCoster's Turner facility in 1996. "I thought I was going to faint and I was only there a few minutes," said Cesar Britos, then an attorney representing egg workers, when he tried to enter an egg barn.[82]

But despite a decades-long rap sheet, DeCoster expanded his egg empire into Iowa, Ohio, and Maryland with the help of Boston public-relations guru George Regan; he even added hogs to the mix.[83] And despite a state-of-Iowa ban against DeCoster starting or expanding his farms—he was a "habitual violator" of environmental laws, said the attorney general—he opened new farms with colleagues' help, according to the Associated Press.[84]

So, in keeping with the broken windows theory, it came as no surprise when a 2009 MFA undercover investigation at the DeCoster-owned Quality Egg of New England and Maine Contract Farming in Turner yielded disturbing findings.[85] "A hen's head and wing were trapped under the cage's front wall. One of her legs was stretched out and would not move or bend. She had a gash on her right side, leaving the skin split open and mostly yellow inside. A gash on her left side was red from fresh blood with a layer of dust partially covering the wound," wrote the investigator. "Another live hen, also trapped under her cage's front wall, had the side of her face on a moving egg belt. I saw that the side of her face, including her eye, was encrusted in what appeared to be egg yolk and dust."[86]

Video showed birds with oozing beaks, too weak to use their limbs and unable to hold up their heads, being kept alive for one more egg-laying cycle. Workers are seen twisting birds by their necks to "kill" them but then casting them aside to flap on the floor in coordinated movements experts say are not mere reflexes. The prolonged death sequelae are difficult to watch.[87]

Conditions at Quality Egg were so appalling that state agriculture officials secured a search warrant after viewing the video and raided the 1,700-acre Quality Egg of New England and Maine Contract Farming with the help of state police—which was thought to be a law-enforcement first. For eight hours, law enforcement and agriculture officials collected dead and living hens and other evidence from the seven-hundred-foot-long barns reeking of ammonia. But the barns didn't sicken only the hens. They were so noxious that law-enforcement officials got sick. Four department workers had to be treated by doctors for burned lungs—at the exact place that Labor Secretary Robert Reich condemned as a sweatshop thirteen years earlier.[88] The live hens that had been rescued from the barns had to be euthanized, announced then state veterinarian Don Hoenig, who said officials found conditions on the egg farm "deplorable, horrifying and upsetting."[89]

Consumers in Maine were shocked by the raid and the images. "Seeing how awful these hens look. there [*sic*] hair falling out, and green stuff coming out of there [*sic*] eyes and nose. Are the eggs safe even to eat? I wouldn't think so," read a post on the *Sun Journal* website.[90]

But Quality Egg's customers denied that they were associated with the company, and it was hard to find stores that would admit to receiving any of the twenty-one million eggs Quality shipped each week. The chains Shaw's and Hannaford both denied doing business with Quality, even though the *Sun Journal* found eggs from the raided farm, stamped "1183" or "1203," at their stores.[91] And Eggland's Best, which maintained three dedicated barns on the Quality Egg grounds, according to the undercover MFA employee, also denied doing business with Quality Egg—even though an Eggland's Best truck can be seen in the video of the raid![92] "Eggland's Best eggs are different," says a magazine ad. "As soon as you open a carton of EBs, you see that the red EB stamp on every egg—the sign that you're getting the very best in freshness and quality."[93]

Bob Leclerc, then Quality Egg's compliance manager, was far from contrite after the raid. The apparent violations were "isolated incidents committed by a couple of employees," he said, and "none of these incidents were ever brought to the attention of management before."[94] Actually, video shows that the incidents were brought to the attention of management, including the owner's son, Jay DeCoster, all of whom had said to disregard it. Moreover, Quality Egg adheres to—any guesses?—*United Egg Producers' guidelines*, which ensures humane practices. Quality Egg also planned to conduct its own investigation, said Leclerc (perhaps to discover it has three million hens caged so tightly that they can't move).[95]

Jack DeCoster was rarely seen in public, even when reporters staked him out. He was often called the Teflon Chicken Don because, despite decades of charges against him, he has rarely been convicted. Yet on June 6, 2010, fourteen months after the Quality Egg raid, DeCoster made a rare personal appearance at the Androscoggin County District Attorney's Office in Auburn, Maine.

Accompanied by a lawyer, DeCoster pleaded guilty to failure to provide adequate shelter and sustenance for ten hens. He received a fine of $25,000 and agreed to making a donation of $100,000 to the Maine Department of Agriculture to inspect and monitor state egg farms against future animal abuse.[96] The settlement also requires Maine Contract Farming to give state investigators regular access to its facilities, to improve staff training, and to retain a veterinarian to treat the birds, reported the *Sun Journal*. The $25,000 includes $2,500 in fines and $967.41 in restitution for each hen abused.[97]

"From a financial perspective, it's the largest settlement I've seen," said MFA's Nathan Runkle, who was present at DeCoster's cruelty conviction—his first—along with then Assistant District Attorney (ADA) Andrew Robinson and Christine Fraser, then a Maine Department of Agriculture veterinarian. "We've had companies agree to a $100,000 settlement before, this had the added fines and restitution," said Runkle.[98]

"In a time of limited budgets, our staff size has been limited," said Fraser. "But this $100,000, I hope this helps give us more hours to do more inspections. If we are out there more often, we'll be able to stop things before they get this bad."[99]

"These chickens are better off now because of this agreement," said ADA Andrew Robinson, who spearheaded the settlement.[100]

But the heat was not over for DeCoster or his suppliers. Two months later, the whole country would recognize his name because his egg farms were at the center of the biggest egg recall in US history. Half a *billion* salmonella-contaminated eggs were recalled in August of 2010—380 million from the DeCoster-owned Wright County Egg in Iowa, and 170 million from the DeCoster-linked Hillandale Farms, also in Iowa.[101] And two months later, 288,000 more eggs were recalled from the Jackson, Mississippi–based CalMaine, an operation connected to DeCoster-linked Ohio Fresh Eggs.[102]

The maze of egg producers, distributors, feed producers, and hatcheries implicated in the salmonella recalls was daunting. "But when you check all these entities, they ultimately all come back to Jack DeCoster," said ADA Andrew Robinson after the salmonella outbreak, who had, just months earlier, helped facilitate DeCoster's cruelty conviction.[103] "It appears there may be some business benefit to having multiple entities responsible for different aspects of the egg farms," Robinson said.

Still, in September 2010, Jack DeCoster got a letter from the House Committee on Energy and Commerce—a pretty nice letter for someone whose operations were linked to 1,600 cases of salmonella. "When you testify before the Committee," wrote former Rep. Bart Stupak (D-MI), serving as chair, "we ask that you come prepared to explain why your facilities tested potentially positive for Salmonella Enteritidis contamination on so many occasions, what steps you took to address the contamination identified in these test results, and whether you shared these results with FDA or other federal or state food safety officials."[104] Lawmakers were a mite peeved, the letter admitted, that DeCoster had ignored their earlier letter, which requested information. It was also pointed out that DeCoster "did not inform the Committee of the potentially positive Salmonella Enteritidis test results." The committee humbly asked that DeCoster "explain" his omissions.[105]

On September 22, 2010, DeCoster made his second public appearance in decades, this time with his son Peter. He told the House Committee on Energy and Commerce's Subcommittee on Oversight and Investigations that he was sorry for making people sick, but that the company had grown too big

DID MICE HOLES CAUSE SALMONELLA?

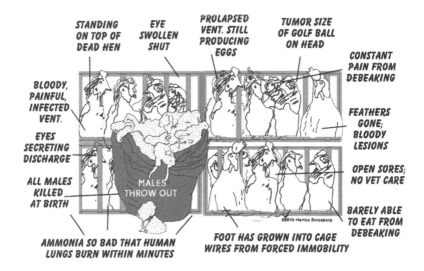

STANDING ON TOP OF DEAD HEN

EYE SWOLLEN SHUT

PROLAPSED VENT. STILL PRODUCING EGGS

TUMOR SIZE OF GOLF BALL ON HEAD

CONSTANT PAIN FROM DEBEAKING

BLOODY, PAINFUL, INFECTED VENT.

EYES SECRETING DISCHARGE

ALL MALES KILLED AT BIRTH

MALES THROW OUT

FEATHERS GONE; BLOODY LESIONS

OPEN SORES; NO VET CARE

BARELY ABLE TO EAT FROM DEBEAKING

AMMONIA SO BAD THAT HUMAN LUNGS BURN WITHIN MINUTES

FOOT HAS GROWN INTO CAGE WIRES FROM FORCED IMMOBILITY

©2010 Martha Rosenberg

too quickly.[106] And despite DeCoster's rap sheet and conviction three months earlier on animal cruelty; despite the law-enforcement officials sickened in his barns; and despite the 2010 fire at his Harpster, Ohio, facility that required 225 firefighters and killed 250,000 hens, there were . . . no hard feelings on the part of lawmakers!

Some government officials even leapt to DeCoster's defense. Kevin Buskins, then a spokesman for Iowa's Department of Natural Resources, which shares oversight of egg operations with the state agriculture department, said, "One of the things I've always said about DeCoster is that when there's a problem at his facilities, he acts fast," and that the state had brought no enforcement actions against him.[107] Even then FDA commissioner Margaret Hamburg indirectly defended DeCoster by reminding people that it is *their job* to cook out salmonella germs. The important thing, she said, is to not eat your eggs with "runny egg yolks for mopping up with toast."[108]

That's right, chirped Krista Beetle, then of the UEP's Egg Safety Center, appreciating the free government boost. "All the responsibility cannot be placed on the farmer," she said in *USA Today*. "Somewhere along the line consumers have to be responsible for what they put in their bodies."[109]

Meanwhile, FDA inspectors finally got around to investigating the DeCoster egg farms and found some "clues" to the source of the salmonella outbreak.[110] According to the *Los Angeles Times* they found

- barns with dozens of holes chewed by rodents that mice, insects, and wild birds used to enter and live inside the barns;
- flies on and around the egg belts and hen feeders;
- manure built up in four- to eight-foot-tall piles in pits below the hen houses, in such quantities that it pushed pit doors open, allowing rodents and other wild animals access to hen houses;
- dozens of hens, which had escaped their cages, roaming freely, tracking
- manure from the pit to other caged parts of the barns; and
- hen houses with significant structural damage and improper air ventilation systems.

What government inspectors *didn't* find, apparently, were thousands of hens in battery cages, their beaks cut off, their sores untreated, the living packed with the dead—all to make a cheap egg.

Chapter 9
THE DRUGSTORE IN YOUR MEAT

Most people have heard of the drug companies Pfizer, Eli Lilly, and Merck. But they may not have heard of the animal-drug companies, like Fort Dodge, Elanco, or Intervet, or the drugs these companies make.

Animal Pharma, the animal-drug divisions within drug companies, tends to operate under the public's radar—not only because the people who eat food grown with its products are not its customers but also because the additives, hormones, growth promoters, antiparasite and fungal drugs, and vaccines it uses would make people lose their appetites.

But Animal Pharma is a huge revenue engine that sells drugs by the ton, often with no prescription or veterinarian's approval necessary, and it provides a never-ending supply of compliant patients. Unlike "people" Pharma, Animal Pharma requires little advertising or marketing against competing drugs, schmoozing of doctors, and sales calls, and it seldom experiences the safety scandals that plague drugs for people and reach Capitol Hill.

Just as Pfizer is the world's biggest drug company, Pfizer's Animal Health became the world's biggest animal-drug company in 2009 when it acquired Wyeth and its Fort Dodge Animal Health subsidiary, surging it to five thousand employees, including seven hundred scientists and veterinarians, in more than sixty countries.[1] Pfizer's Animal Health made over $1 billion in one quarter in 2011.[2]

But in 2010, Merck acquired Schering-Plough and created Intervet/Schering-Plough, which was even bigger than the Pfzer/Wyeth combo—with sales of $2.94 billion.[3] The following year, Eli Lilly announced it would buy Johnson & Johnson's animal unit.[4] "Lilly is hoping Elanco, the world's fourth-biggest animal health business, will remain a bright spot in coming years as many of the Indianapolis-based drugmaker's top prescription drugs face plunging sales due to generic competition," reports Reuters.[5]

One reason for Animal Pharma's growth is that contemporary, intensive factory farming is predicated on maximum output from each animal "unit" in confined spaces. For example, chickens were once slaughtered at fourteen weeks old, when they weighed about two pounds, but by 2001 they were slaughtered at seven weeks, when they weighed between four and six pounds.[6] The continued efficiencies require high use of growth-producing drugs, and drugs to treat and prevent diseases caused by crowding, stress, and immobility.

Few consumers could name one animal drug used to produce the food they are eating since the names don't appear on labels (and would kill sales if they did.) And even though the organic-food movement and mad-cow scares have made people think about what their "meat eats"—look at the grass-fed-beef movement—they *still* don't ask what drugs the animal ingested. For example, who wants to eat an animal treated with the antibiotic tilmicosin? The drug label, intended for the farmer, says, "Not for human use. Injection of this drug in humans has been associated with fatalities."[7] Tilmicosin's label even has an emergency phone number printed right on the bottle, as well as a note telling physicians what to do in case the farmer accidentally injects himself. (It says, "The cardiovascular system is the target of toxicity and should be monitored closely. Cardiovascular toxicity may be due to calcium channel blockade."[8]) Yet tilmicosin is widely used in food animals and even shows up in the milk of treated dairy cows, reports central Ohio's WBNS-10 TV news.[9] In fact, according to a 2010 Office of Inspector General (OIG) report, 90 percent of veterinary drug residue violations are found in dairy cows and calves.[10]

Of course, Animal Pharma says the drugs are given for animal "health," but it is "health" measured in weeks, dollars, and the ability of the animal to get on the truck. Long-term drug effects are both unknown and irrelevant. "When a pig nearly ready to be slaughtered grows ill, workers sometimes shoot it up with as many drugs as necessary to get it to the slaughterhouse under its own power," writes Jeff Tietz about the hog industry in *Rolling Stone*.[11] As long as the pig remains ambulatory, it can be legally killed and sold as meat.

And it's not like people can actually *taste* this toxic stew of drugs, heavy metals, antibiotics, and even antibiotic-resistant bacteria in food. The many millions of pounds of contaminated beef recalled by Hudson Foods in 1997, Cargill and American Foods Group beef in 2007, Topps Meat Company and Nebraska Beef in 2008, and JBS Swift beef in 2009 probably tasted fine.[12]

But isn't meat tested for drug traces? Dream on. A 2010 OIG report found that Food Safety and Inspection Service (FSIS) supervision of cattle was a farce—with some drug residues missed, others not tested for, and clearly contaminated meat left in the food supply.[13] Among the drugs found in beef released to the public were penicillin; the antibiotics florfenicol, sulfamethazine, and sulfadimethoxine; the anti-parasite drug ivermectin, the nonsteroidal anti-inflammatory drug flunixin; and heavy metals.[14] The report goes on to say that "between July 12, 2007, and March 11, 2008, FSIS found that four carcasses were adulterated with violative levels of veterinary drugs and that the plants involved had released the meat into the food supply." Although the drugs involved could result in stomach, nerve, or skin problems for consumers, FSIS requested no recall.[15] Four plants had an astounding 211 drug residue violations, but repeat violators—"individuals who have a history of picking up dairy cows with drugs in their system and dropping them off at the plant"—are widely tolerated by the inspection service, says the report.[16]

Food Safety and Inspection Service records have also found gentamicin in dairy cows sold for food. Gentamicin is an antibiotic so dangerous that there is no published tolerance in edible animal tissue. One dairy farm caught selling gentamicin-contaminated animals for public consumption—Willet Dairy in Locke, New York—was featured on *Nightline* in 2010 for animal abuse.[17] Gentamicin is known for harming kidneys and ear/balance systems in humans and for remaining in livestock for eighteen months or more.[18] Of twenty-three pesticides known to be "high risk," FSIS tests for only one, says the OIG report, and some dangerous compounds like pesticide dioxin, lindane, and fire retardants called PBDEs (polybrominated diphenyl ethers) have no "established action levels" to test for.[19] Unlike bacterial pathogens like *E. coli*, drug and metal residues aren't neutralized by cooking, and some actually break down into more harmful compounds when heated![20]

Bob veal—the meat from calves under three days old that weigh only seventy to one hundred pounds—represents the biggest drug-residue risk to the food supply. "Farmers are prohibited from selling milk for human consumption from cows that have been medicated with antibiotics (as well as other drugs) until the withdrawal period is over; so instead of just disposing of this tainted milk, producers feed it to their calves. When the calves are slaughtered, the drug residue from the feed or milk remains in their meat, which is then sold to consumers."[21] In fact, both the Wright Place dairy in Clinton, Maine, and Corner View Dairies in Lyons, New York, were accused of such bob-veal violations in 2010. The Wright Place sold a bob-veal calf with the antibiotic neomycin in its kidneys, which came from the "unapproved use of Custom Calf White Plus NT Medicated Dairy Herd and Beef Calf Milk Replacer," says an FDA warning letter.[22] Corner View Dairies sold a bob-veal calf with penicillin in its kidneys.[23] Meat from bob calves is put into "value added" veal products like veal sausages and breaded veal patties.

During the same month, according to FDA records, Land Dairy in Mayo, Florida, sold a dairy cow "for food" with sulfamethazine in its liver; Martin Feed Lot in Harrisburg, Illinois, sold a beef heifer for food with flunixin in its liver; and Elma Dairy in Rochester, Washington, sold a dairy cow for food with desfuroylceftiofur, a metabolite from a cephalosporin antibiotic, in its kidneys.[24]

Feedlots were also accused of chemistry experiments at the expense of public health. Darr Feedlots in Cozad, Nebraska, put the non-approved antibiotics chlortetracycline and monensin in cattle feed, say FDA letters, and Templeton Feed & Grain in California mislabeled *sulfamethazine* as *sulfathiazole* in its Pig Starter & Grow Medicated Feed. Templeton also mislabeled the withdrawal information on the pig starter product. It was supposed to read, "Warning: withdraw 15 days prior to slaughter" but instead read "7 days."[25]

RESISTING ANTIBIOTIC RESISTANCE

One of the late Sen. Ted Kennedy's (D-MA) last legislative fights was about the overuse of livestock antibiotics. "It seems scarcely believable that these precious medications could be fed by the ton to chickens and pigs," he wrote in a bill called the Preservation of Antibiotics for Medical Treatment Act of 2007 (PAMTA), which, as of 2011, still had not passed.[26] "These precious drugs aren't even used to treat sick animals. They are used to fatten pigs and speed the growth of chickens. The result of this rampant overuse is clear: meat contaminated with drug-resistant bacteria sits on supermarket shelves all over America," said Kennedy.[27] In fact, ground beef with drug-resistant bacteria was recalled the summer after the bill was introduced.[28]

Over 70 percent of antibiotics go to livestock, not to people, says the bill, and they are the same drugs needed for urinary tract, intestinal, respiratory, ear, and skin infections in humans.[29] They are also crucial drugs in treating tuberculosis and sexually transmitted diseases.

Over 83 percent of grower-finisher swine farms, cattle feedlots, and sheep farms use antibiotics for animals that are not sick, says the bill, and 48 percent of national streams are tainted with antibiotics as a result.[30] The state of North Carolina alone uses more antibiotics for livestock than the entire United States uses for humans.[31] "These statistics tell the tale of an industry that is rampantly misusing antibiotics in an attempt to cover up filthy, unsanitary living conditions among animals," says Rep. Louise Slaughter (D-NY), who cosponsored the bill, and who has degrees in microbiology and public health.[32]

Anyone who has rented an apartment that has been sprayed—unsuccessfully—for bugs has firsthand experience with the principle of antibiotic resistance. Organisms can become impervious to what is supposed to kill them and can even become bigger and stronger. Mosquitoes also become resistant to insecticides—and, as the joke goes, when you slap them, they slap you back. In fact, antibiotic resistance might be the ultimate biological demonstration of the maxim "That which doesn't kill you makes you stronger."

Livestock use is not the only antibiotic-resistance culprit. Antibiotics are overused by hospitals, clinics, schools, public facilities, and households, and are unnecessarily put in dish and laundry detergent, soap, and even toothpaste by the chemical industry. In fact, antibiotics are overused and misused anytime they're used preventatively, for *potential* infections instead of for existing bacterial infections. Doctors and patients who "treat" colds and viruses with antibiotics also encourage antibiotic resistance because these conditions are not caused by bacteria. And people who stop taking antibiotics (when conditions *are* bacterial) before the medication is gone because they feel better *also* contribute to antibiotic resistance. The few bacteria that survive the antibiotic "bath" are stronger for the challenge and go on to cause more trouble, as in, "That which doesn't kill you . . . ."

Overuse of antibiotics may have yet another deleterious effect. Children who received antibiotics within their first six months of life were more likely to develop allergies and asthma, say researchers at Henry Ford Hospital.[33] What role might livestock antibiotics play? Even if you don't eat meat, don't drink tap water, and avoid antibiotics, you could be affected by livestock antibiotics. Researchers are now discovering crops that can harbor antibiotics, siphoning them right up from the soil.[34] Scientists at the University of Minnesota found antibiotic residues in corn, green onions, and cabbage after growing on soil fertilized with livestock manure for just six weeks.[35] Corn, lettuce, and potatoes also picked up the drugs.

"Around 90 percent of these drugs that are administered to animals end up being excreted either as urine or manure," said Holly Dolliver, PhD, a then professor of crop and soil sciences at the University of Wisconsin–River Falls, who worked on the research.[36]

Antibiotic-resistant organisms like the dreaded MRSA (methicillinresistant *Staphylococcus aureus*) are also increasing in the soil, said David Graham, PhD, then with the School of Civil Engineering and Geosciences at Newcastle University. His team found that 78 percent of resistance genes from four classes of antibiotics showed increasing levels of resistance since 1940.[37]

In fact, 45 percent of Midwest hog farms had MRSA germs present, according to research published by University of Iowa researchers in 2009, and *64 percent* of the workers were MRSA carriers.[38] Kim Howland became a MRSA carrier from working at an Oklahoma hog farm and gave the infection to her husband, she told *CBS News*. Pigs were regularly given antibiotics like Tylan®, Keflex®, and Baytril® at the facility, she said. "That's their fix for everything."[39]

And when CBS's Katie Couric asked Dave Kronlage, then an Iowa pig farmer, on the same show, how he prevents the routine antibiotics he gives his pigs from causing resistance, he said, "We don't always use the same antibiotics." Did this make anyone feel better?[40]

Methicillin-resistant *Staphylococcus aureus* infections, which kill twenty thousand people a year, are not confined to the hospital or to hog farms.[41] Researchers at the 2009 American Association for the Advancement of Science annual meeting reported that MRSA is plentiful on Florida swimming beaches, though they did not speculate on the sources of MRSA of which raw sewage could be one.[42]

Public health officials also worry about vancomycin-resistant enterococci (VRE) infections, linked to livestock antibiotics like avoparcin, which Europe banned in the 1990s. Avoparcin is not used in the United States, but VRE germs have still been identified in thirty-three states and in commercial chicken feed, reported the *Hartford Advocate* a few years ago. Few people fully recover from VRE infections, said the *Advocate*, since "once a patient is colonized with VRE—and survives—he is colonized for life."[43]

And resistant germs like MRSA and VRE get around! Johns Hopkins researchers report that they can be transported by farm trucks, farm workers, houseflies, and the air itself.[44] Even following a poultry truck in traffic can fill a car with resistant germs, say researchers, who found that the surface of an unopened soft-drink can in a car had been contaminated.[45]

The breadth and danger of antibiotic resistance is "not appreciated until it's your mother, or your son, or [you're] trying to fight off an infection that will not go away because the last mechanism to fight it has been usurped by someone putting it into a pig or a chicken," says Kellogg Schwab, PhD, then director of the Johns Hopkins Center for Water and Health.[46] Antibiotics are the ultimate wonder drug for farm operations for two reasons: they make animals absorb and process nutrients more efficiently, thereby growing bigger and faster with less feed, and they control disease in packed conditions in which animals are often surrounded by their own waste.

Big Ag does not hide its addiction to antibiotics. If the drugs could be used only for illness and not as growth promoters, it would cost the pork industry "$6 per pig the first year" more than it spends now and "$1.1 billion over ten years," says Jennifer Greiner, DVM, director of science and technology for the National Pork Producers Council.[47]

"A production complex raising 5 million turkey hens a year and feeding [the antibiotic] virginiamycin at 22 ppm could expect to produce an additional 670,000 kg of live weight and 35,000 kg more breast meat while saving 1,990 tons of feed," says a poultry journal, showing the powerful incentives in raw numbers.[48]

Since seventy thousand people in the United States die of resistant infections each year—more than the forty-five thousand a year who die from breast cancer—and groups like the American Medical Association and American Public Health Association endorse PAMTA, the bill seems like a no-brainer.[49] All the bill proposes is to phase out nontherapeutic use of "medically important antibiotics" in livestock and strengthen standards for new livestock antibiotics. Farms would still be able to treat animals that are actually sick. But to Animal Pharma and factory farmers, it's also a no-brainer. The bill would take away their profits, and that is something they will fight tooth and nail.

In fact, PAMTA, and the role of antibiotics in contemporary farming,

might be the only issue that actually divides medical professionals along species lines: doctor groups, concerned about patient infections, and veterinary
groups that focus on large animals, which often work closely with Big Ag. "At
the heart of this discussion is the premise that the use of antibiotics in animal agriculture directly contributes to bacterial resistance in humans," says
the American Veterinary Medical Association (AVMA), in an embarrassingly
"flat earth" position for medical professionals.[50] A livestock antibiotic ban in
Denmark "has not shown any clear declines in antibiotic resistance patterns in
humans," says the AVMA, which urges members to fight PAMTA.[51]

Actually, the AVMA is wrong. *CBS News*, *Food Safety News*, and the *Pew
Campaign on Human Health and Industrial Farming* have reported that antibiotic
resistance in Denmark is declined—and Sweden, Norway, the Netherlands, and
Australia also report reduced resistance with phased-out livestock antibiotics.[52]

The AVMA, which represents 86 percent of US veterinarians, often sides
with industry *against* animal welfare on such issues as supporting confinement and caged farming, pregnant-mare farms to produce the drug hormone
Premarin®, and the production of foie gras, during which ducks and geese
are force-fed to swell their livers. Why? Would doctors support child labor,
forced labor, or the death penalty?

Elanco, the animal division of Eli Lilly, also blasted antibiotic restriction,
using Europe as a case in point. "Bans implemented by the EU did achieve
their objective of reducing the incidence of resistance on indicator bacteria
in raw food products of animal origin," says an online brochure.[53] "However,
there has been no measurable improvement in antibiotic resistance in human
patients or hospitals."[54] Moreover, "monitoring antibiotic resistance in raw
meat products is not an appropriate measure to represent the bacteria that
reach the consumer," adds the brochure, "because cooking destroys these bacteria, and dead bacteria cannot transmit antibiotic resistance." Who minds
germs in their food if the bacteria are dead? Elanco also asserts that livestock
antibiotics keep occurrences of "food poisoning" down, as if food-poisoning
bacteria are not connected to farm conditions either.[55]

Michael Darre, PhD, then an extension poultry specialist at the University of Connecticut, agreed that the issue is not antibiotic overuse but how
well consumers decontaminate their food. "It's consumer education as much

as the processor," he says. "If you don't follow up at home, all that good work beforehand is useless."[56]

The National Pork Producers Council opposed PAMTA and says it actually feels like it is under attack. "We don't believe we are the main cause of antibiotic resistance," Dave Warner, the then council's communications director, told *Johns Hopkins Magazine*. Doctors who prescribe too many antibiotics are more culpable, said Warner. "There are only 67,000 pork producers [in the United States]. How many doctors are out there? And how many people?"[57] (But how many people are on antibiotics for life?)

The chicken industry also says it feels picked on. "We believe our use is responsible and limited," said Richard Lobb, then public relations director for the National Chicken Council, to the *Hartford Advocate*. "All this is approved by the FDA. Any trace of the drug is gone by the time the bird is processed. We feel our industry, pork and others are being blamed for antibiotic resistance problems. The route of transmission of antibiotic-resistant pathogens is a rather long and tenuous one."[58]

The Animal Health Institute (AHI) is the lobbying group for Animal Pharma, representing Abbott, Bayer Healthcare, Boehringer Ingelheim Vetmedica, Elanco/Lilly, Merck, Novartis, Pfizer, and others. Yet, despite its professional membership, it has a "flat earth" mentality when it comes to antibiotic overuse. "There is no scientific evidence that antibiotics used in food animals have any significant impact on the effectiveness of antibiotics in people," deadpans an AHI brochure created to oppose PAMTA.[59] "People would be more likely to die from a bee sting than for their antibiotic treatment to fail because of . . . resistant bacteria in meat or poultry."[60]

When it comes to protecting the livestock antibiotic gravy train, Animal Pharma really has *two* threats: PAMTA and retaining farmers' allegiance to antibiotics. Most farmers accept on faith that antibiotics work since they and their fellow operators can't remember a time when the drugs weren't used. But who really knows? Maybe antibiotics "have nothing to do with it," like Mae West used to say about goodness.

A 2007 article by Johns Hopkins University researchers using data on seven million Perdue chickens found that farmers actually *lose money* on antibiotics used for growth when the cost of the antibiotics are factored in.[61] Are farm antibiotics destined to become an ag version of Vytorin (see chapter 1)—an expensive ruse?

"The use of GPAs [growth-promoting antibiotics] in poultry production is associated with economic losses to the producers," write the Johns Hopkins researchers. "These data are of considerable importance in the ongoing national debate concerning the continued use of antibiotics for growth promotion of food animals. Based on the industry study and the resulting economic impact, the use of GPAs in U.S. poultry production should be reconsidered."[62]

The Johns Hopkins researchers were assailed in the ag press for averaging figures that are supposed to vary, for using the wrong valuation for an individual chicken, and for reaching flawed conclusions.[63] One of the paper's authors, Ellen Silbergeld, PhD, was assailed and was said to have a "political agenda" for citing dangers of arsenic products in poultry production, in a different paper.[64]

Of course, in 2011 Pfizer announced it would stop selling arsenic-treated chicken feed after the FDA found inorganic arsenic, a carcinogen, "at higher levels in the livers of chickens treated" than in untreated chickens—a finding that vindicated Silbergeld's agenda.[65] Who knew they were eating arsenic? Pfizer's arsenic feed product was used to control parasites, promote weight gain and feed efficiency, and improve "pigmentation," said the FDA.[66] Another arsenic-based feed additive, Histostat®, or nitarsone, is still on the market, reports the *New York Times*.[67]

Animal Pharma also has to deal with farmers like turkey producer Duane Koch, who then said he kicked the antibiotic habit over fourteen years ago.[68] Space for livestock, rather than confinement, is "our natural growth promotants," he told *CBS News'* Katie Couric. "By giving them more space, we can get weights that are really close to what they're getting, you know, with the growth promotants."[69] You mean exercise benefits animals as well as humans?

SEE YA ON THE HILL

You'd think in a battle with the government, scientists, doctors, and consumers on one side, and Animal Pharma on the other, the former would win. After all, livestock antibiotics clearly harm humans, animals, the environment, and even the economy through increased health costs and hospitalizations. But you'd be wrong. As long as people regard government service as a prelude to cushy, private-sector jobs, and as long as the private sector hires government workers for the colleagues they can squeeze, food safety and democratic representation is pretty much a joke. How many girls in Texas were slated to receive Gardasil® because then Governor Rick Perry's former chief of staff, Mike Toomey, decided to go to work for Merck, which makes the vaccine? Toomey was no doubt hired for the friends in high places he could squeeze—and did.[70]

Government/Pharma lobbying has a distinguished tradition, from Louisiana representative-turned-lobbyist Billy Tauzin, who presided over the Pharmaceutical Research and Manufacturers of America (PhRMA) until 2010, to former Centers for Disease Control and Prevention director Julie Gerberding, MD, who presided over flu epidemics before turning up as head of Merck vaccines in 2009.

Animal Pharma has always fought the FDA's efforts to restrict livestock antibiotics. Bayer Corporation, for example, fought the FDA's directive to remove the antibiotic Baytril® from poultry water for five years, though the FDA finally prevailed.[71] So, when the FDA announced in 2008 that it was issuing an order to ban one type of antibiotic, cephalosporins, in livestock, it was no surprise that Big Ag and Animal Pharma stormed Capitol Hill. The FDA's original announcement was clear. "We are issuing this order based on evidence that extralabel use of these drugs [cephalosporin antibiotics] in food-producing animals will likely cause an adverse event in humans and, as such, presents a risk to the public health," said the FDA in July.[72] (Notice the order doesn't say "could" or "might" but rather "will" and "presents.")

Cephalosporins are crucial drugs for treating salmonella infections in children, and FDA surveillance data clearly showed human and animal resistance developing to them.[73] Over one million human salmonella infections occur in the United States per year, resulting in sixteen thousand hospitalizations and nearly six hundred deaths.[74]

But by the time hearings were held two months later—after FDA phones presumably rang from dear, former colleagues—the hearing about the cephalosporin order of prohibition had somehow become a hearing to review the

advances in animal health within the livestock industry.[75] *Ban, advances*: same idea, right? Considering the name change, attendees might have walked right past the room, if it weren't for the assemblage of representatives from the egg, chicken, turkey, milk, pork, and cattle industries and the AHI yelling, "Unfair!"

"To raise turkeys without antibiotics would increase the incidence of illness in turkey flocks," whined Michael Rybolt, PhD, then director of scientific and regulatory affairs, National Turkey Federation, at the FDA hearings. He pointed out that this practice would also increase the carbon footprint of turkey operations. Not being able to cram turkeys together "would result in a decrease in density or an increase in the amount of land needed," said Rybolt, as well as more crop rotation and an "additional 175,500 tons of feed."[76] And if you think our farms produce a lot of waste now, Rybolt continued, calling a 227-acre turkey farm "small," take turkeys off antibiotics, and "the decrease in feed conversion" will result "in an increase in manure!"[77] Take that, environmentalists!

All dairy cows and "22 to 70 percent of calves" receive antibiotics on dairy farms, admitted Robert D. Byrne, PhD, then vice president of scientific and regulatory affairs of the National Milk Producers Federation at the hearings. But the animals get only FDA-approved drugs, (we hope), and the antibiotics are used only to "reduce the level of potentially harmful bacteria which result in infections and sickness," assuaged Byrne.[78]

There is also a drug "withdrawal time" to make sure milk isn't contaminated, and milk is "screened" before it is accepted into a processing plant, said Byrne.[79] But milk is tested for only six of twenty antibiotics, says the *New York Times*, and when the FDA proposed testing for *more* drugs in 2011—788 dairy cows had residues at slaughter in 2008—the dairy industry got so furious, it used the *d*-word.[80] Agri-Mark, a Northeast cooperative, sent a letter to its members instructing them to *dump* milk if it had been tested by the FDA, "to ensure that all of our milk sales, cheese, butter and other products are in no danger of recall." Do they know something we don't know?

And John J. Wilson, then a senior vice president for Dairy Farmers of America, said that the idea of testing for more antibiotics was "very damaging to innocent dairy farmers," and that "there was little reason to think that the slaughterhouse findings would be replicated in tests of the milk supply."[81]

One month after the hearings, with presentations from the egg, chicken, turkey, dairy, pork, and cattle industries and the AHI, Big Ag brought in its heavy artillery: the American Veterinary Medical Association. The AVMA sent a rambling, almost incoherent eighteen-page letter with sixty-two footnotes, telling the FDA that cephalosporin-resistant human pathogens aren't increasing, and even if they are, they're not affecting human health, and even if they're affecting human health, how do you know they originated from the livestock drugs, and even if they are from the livestock drugs, the FDA has no legal authority to ban cephalosporin.[82] Got that?

The letter, alternately maudlin and accusatory, even says that banning cephalosporin is a "food security issue," playing on terrorism fears, which affects "the number of animals available for the food supply." It also says a cephalosporin ban would impede veterinarians' ability "to relieve the pain and suffering of animals," as if cephalosporins are pain killers, other drugs aren't available, and antibiotics are given for animals' welfare instead of revenue welfare![83] Nowhere in the arguments about terrorism, the food supply, the FDA overstepping its legal boundaries, and the alleged pain and suffering of animals does the AVMA mention the reason for Big Ag's collective temper tantrum: it would lose money if cephalosporin were banned.

But less than one month after the letter was sent, on November 25, 2008, the FDA quietly revoked the cephalosporin order, and it still had not revived the order three years later. Why? The letter was from W. Ron DeHaven, DVM, the government's former top veterinarian, who headed the USDA's Animal and Plant Health Inspection Service, overseeing 8,300 employees. He was now the AVMA's executive vice president. Good hire, AVMA!

One year after the buried cephalosporin prohibition order, there were still a few hopeful moments for pure food advocates. The newly appointed FDA commissioner, Margaret A. Hamburg, MD, and Deputy Commissioner Joshua Sharfstein, MD, were not industry insiders. Hamburg was the former New York City health commissioner, and Sharfstein, a pediatrician, was a former food safety staffer for Rep. Henry Waxman (D-CA). Sharfstein even signaled the FDA's support of PAMTA at a House Rules Committee meeting, infuriating Rep. Leonard Boswell (D-IA), former chairman of the House agriculture subcommittee.[84] But by 2011, Sharfstein had left the FDA, and Hamburg was writing paeans to industry in the *Wall Street Journal* and vowing to eliminate conflict-of-interest laws to let more Pharma-linked doctors onto advisory committees that recommend drugs approvals.[85] How could there be "more"? asked critics, when Pharma links were already the FDA committees' norm?

OTHER WEAPONS OF GROWTH

Just as few people wonder what drugs were ingested by the animals they eat, few people think about the fact that Europe won't eat the same meat that Americans eat every day. The European export market has been shut to US meat since 1989 because of the hormones used in production. Hormones like oestradiol-17 (an estrogen), testosterone, progesterone and zeranol, trenbolone acetate and melengestrol acetate are banned in Europe's domestic and imported meats by the European Commission (EC). Melengestrol acetate, a synthetic progestin put in feed, is thirty times as active as natural progesterone, says the EC. Trenbolone acetate, a synthetic androgen used as an ear implant, is several times more active than testosterone.[86] The European Commission not only refuses US hormone-grown beef but it also doesn't hold back on its reasons for doing so: "There is an association between steroid hormones and certain cancers and an indication that meat consumption is possibly associated with increased risks of breast cancer and prostate cancer," says the Scientific Committee on Veterinary Measures. "The highest rates of breast cancer are observed in North America, where hormone-treated meat consumption is highest in the world," it says, adding that the same statistics apply to prostate cancer.[87]

In fact, Kwang Hwa, Korea, has only seven new cases of breast cancer per one hundred thousand people whereas non-Hispanic Caucasians in Los Angeles have 103 new cases per one hundred thousand people, says the EC report.[88] The breast-cancer rate also increases among immigrant groups who move to the United States, the report adds, suggesting that the differences are environmental and not genetic. Hormonal growth producers and residues from other drugs, like antibiotics, in the meat may even be responsible for the United States' increasing rates of allergy diseases and precocious puberty, the report suggests, which is in accordance with the research from Henry Ford Hospital.[89]

But the hormones Europe boycotts are not the only US growth promoters with unsavory side effects that other countries won't use. Another growth producer, called ractopamine, is used in 45 percent of US pigs, in 30 percent of ration-fed cattle, and in turkeys, yet few pharmacologists, food researchers, or consumer advocates are even aware of it.[90] Ractopamine, an asthma-like drug called a beta agonist, was recruited for livestock use over ten years ago after its ability to increase muscle by "repartitioning" nutrients and slowing protein degradation was noticed by researchers developing an asthma drug with laboratory mice.[91]

However, unlike many veterinary drugs that are withdrawn near to slaughter, ractopamine is begun at slaughter and never withdrawn.[92] It is given to cattle for their last twenty-eight to forty-two days, to pigs for their last twenty-eight days, and to turkeys for their last seven to fourteen days. Ractopamine, marketed as Paylean® for pigs, as Optaflexx® for cattle, and as Topmax® for turkeys, is banned in livestock production in Europe, China, and Taiwan. In China, the Sichuan Pork Trade Chamber of Commerce reported that more than seventeen hundred people have been "poisoned" from eating Paylean-fed pigs since 1998.[93] And in 2007 China seized US pork for its ractopamine residues.[94]

Taiwan experienced actual riots over ractopamine in 2007, similar to South Korean riots the following year over mad-cow risks from US beef—and similarly underreported. A rumor that Taiwan's ractopamine ban would be lifted inspired as many as 3,500 pig farmers, some carrying pigs, to mass at the Department of Health and Council of Agriculture in Taipei City in 2007, led by "legislators across party lines," reported *Taiwan News*.[95] Chanting, "Get out, USA pork" and "We refuse to eat pork that contains poisonous ractopamine," protesters threw rotten eggs, some of which contained dead chicken fetuses, at police, military soldiers, and reporters. Riots persisted for two hours, with protesters hurling pig dung at government buildings, until Hou Sheng-Mou, the department's minister of health, appeared and assured the crowd that ractopamine was still a banned substance in Taiwan. He was forced to sign a letter promising that his claim was true and to touch a piglet, for unclear reasons, before the crowds would disperse.[96]

But the crowds did not go home. The demonstration moved to the Council of Agriculture and the American Institute in Taiwan, where institute spokesman Thomas Hodges, speaking in fluent Mandarin, defended ractopamine's safety but agreed to pass a petition on to US officials. Farmers told reporters that "the use of ractopamine in pigs will serve only to harm consumers and the local swine industry, because ractopamine residue will most likely stay in the internal organs of livestock, thus local consumers would fall victim to health problems if the ban is lifted," reported *Taiwan News*.[97]

Reports of ractopamine's lack of safety are not hard to find. In 2009, the European Food Safety Authority (EFSA) termed ractopamine a cardiac stimulator capable of causing undue stress and health risks in animals.[98] "The use of highly active beta-agonists as growth promoters is not appropriate because of the potential hazard for human and animal health," said the journal *Talanta* unequivocally in 2010.[99] And a report from Ottawa's Bureau of Veterinary Drugs says that rats fed ractopamine developed a constellation of birth defects like cleft palate, protruding tongue, short limbs, missing digits, open eyelids, and enlarged heart.[100] Like tilmicosin's packaging, the ractopamine label is not reassuring, especially for a drug that is not withdrawn at slaughter. "Not for use in humans," it says. "Individuals with cardiovascular disease should exercise special caution to avoid exposure. Use protective clothing, impervious gloves, protective eye wear, and a NIOSH [National Institute for Occupational Safety and Health]-approved dust mask."[101]

Three years after Paylean's 1999 approval, when it was already in wide use, transparency questions arose. The FDA accused Elanco, Eli Lilly's animal subsidiary, of withholding information about ractopamine's "safety and effectiveness" and "adverse animal drug experiences" in a fourteen-page warning letter in 2002.[102] Elanco, said the FDA, failed to report furious farmers phoning the company about "dying animals," "downer pigs," animals "down and shaking," "hyperactivity," and "vomiting after eating feed with Paylean." The company was also accused of suppressing clinical trial information.[103]

But thanks to probable lobbying, the FDA proceeded to approve ractopamine for use in cattle the following year, 2003, and for use in turkeys in 2009. In fact, one-third of all meetings on the Food Safety and Inspection Service's posted public calendar during several months in 2009 were either with Elanco representatives or about ractopamine.[104] And, in 2010, the FDA enlarged the feeding approvals for Optaflexx 45 in cattle.[105]

The downers reported by pork farmers that Elanco failed to relay to the FDA did not stay a secret for long. Soon the ag community was talking about it. "Simply, the pig will go down and not be able to get back up," said Gary Bowman, an Ohio State Extension veterinarian with the College of Veterinary Medicine, about the effects of ractopamine as early as 2002.[106] "The pig has so much muscle that it's too stiff and not able to move." Ractopamine-treated pigs also have "gait problems" and spend "more time lying and less time walking," cautioned a 2003 *Journal of Animal Science* article. They have "elevated heart rates" and are "more difficult to handle," which puts them at greater risk for "rough handling and increased stress during transportation."[107]

Even ractopamine's federal registration warns: "Caution: Pigs fed PAYLEAN are at an increased risk for exhibiting the downer pig syndrome (also referred to as 'slows,' 'subs,' or 'suspects'). Pig handling methods to reduce the incidence of downer pigs should be thoroughly evaluated prior to initiating use of PAYLEAN."[108]

Temple Grandin, PhD, the well-known animal expert, has also discussed hard-to-handle and "downer" pigs affected by ractopamine, and poses other welfare questions about beta-agonists, including associated hoof problems.[109]

Elsewhere, veterinary journals note increased "aggressiveness," animal "well-being" questions, and potential hazards "for human and animal health."[110] Certainly if ractopamine were a drug for humans, it would have forced hearings on Capitol Hill soon after its approval and probably would have been withdrawn from the market.

As it did with antibiotics and the now discredited recombinant bovine growth hormone (rBGH), Big Ag has presented ractopamine as a drug that

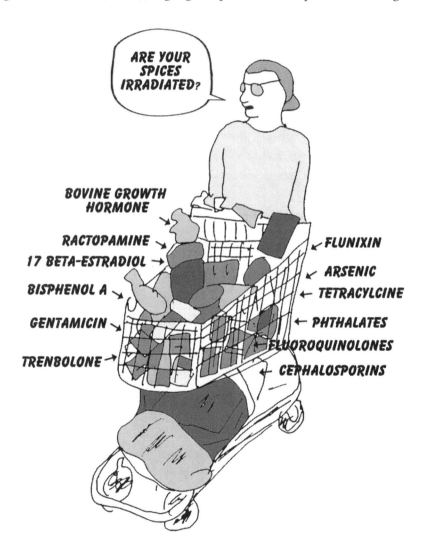

reduces the carbon footprint. It is said to increase "average daily weight gain, [improve] feed efficiency, [save] on feed, and [decrease] the number of days to market when higher doses are administered," and have "positive environmental benefits for livestock producers in terms of decreased nitrogen and phosphorus excretions, and reduced amount of total animal waste," as reported in one journal article.[111] But like antibiotics and rBGH, the Agribiz profits come at the price of human and animal health.

How can drugs designed to make animals gain weight fast not have an impact on national obesity? How can a drug present at slaughter not be in the meat? And how can an asthma drug that causes hyperactivity in animals, as reported by farmers, not contribute to hyperkinetic behavioral and ADHD problems in children when it's used in a large portion of US pigs, cows, and turkeys?

The sad fact is that even though fewer people are aware of Fort Dodge, Elanco, or Intervet than they are of Pfizer, Eli Lilly, or Merck, more people may actually be taking their drugs.

Chapter 10

FARMER JONES

DO YOU KNOW WHO
YOUR EMPLOYEES ARE?
NOT *THOSE* EMPLOYEES!

D id people just discover where meat comes from? Trent Loos, a sixth-generation farmer and agricultural activist thinks so.

"Most Americans have just now realized or considered the fact that an animal dies to make their hamburger," he wrote in a column in *Feedstuffs*, a weekly agricultural industry magazine. "I believe it is a thought many well-fed Americans have never had before."[1] With his cowboy hat and handlebar mustache, Loos is a one-man army against sentimentalizing food animals, especially in the era of frequent farm "cruelty" exposés. He is known for following Robert F. Kennedy Jr., the outspoken environmentalist, "all over the country," saying "menacing things," says Kennedy, after Kennedy's anti-factory-farming speeches.[2]

Trent Loos organized a Loos Tales FoodLink Chuck Wagon float in Chicago's McDonald's Thanksgiving Parade in 2008 to highlight "the modern food production system and the progress made over the past century as a result of the application of science and technology."[3] And Loos and his wife even went undercover at a conference hosted by the animal rights group Farm Sanctuary in Chicago in 2004.[4]

In combating animal rights, Loos has taken extreme positions, like defending horse slaughter; approving of rBGH in milk; deeming nitro-samines, the carcinogens in processed meat, healthful; and defending convicted dog abuser Michael Vick. Vick, the Atlanta Falcons quarterback and dog-fighting enthusiast who served prison time for cruelty to animals, was "charged with the crime of letting a dog be a dog" and "not treating his dog like a kid," said Loos.[5]

But Loos is not the only pushback voice against the sentimentalizing of animals. The Center for Consumer Freedom, "a nonprofit organization devoted to promoting personal responsibility and protecting consumer choices," also criticizes animal activists, though it also lobbies against legislative restrictions against alcohol, junk food, and cigarettes.[6] "Congress could require U.S. farmers to supply every pig, chicken, duck, and cow with private rooms, daily rubdowns, video iPods®, and organic meals catered by Wolfgang Puck," said David Martosko, then the center's director of research, at congressional hearings about humane slaughter in 2007. "But even this wouldn't satisfy activists who actually believe farm animals have the 'right' not to be eaten."[7]

Another pushback group was the Animal Agriculture Alliance, whose then executive vice president, Kay Johnson, told ag journalists, "improvements in animal welfare should be based on reason, science and experience, not on the opinions of activists who have absolutely no vested interest in farm animals," as if not having a vested financial stake in the use of animals weren't exactly what legitimizes an ethical stance.[8]

Angry farmers also protested a speech by food reformer Michael Pollan, author of The Omnivore's Dilemma and In Defense of Food at the University of Wisconsin in Madison in 2009. The land grant, ag-based university, in the middle of the nation's dairy land, had also given a free copy of In Defense of Food to all incoming freshmen as part of its Go Big Read reading program. In Defense of Food, which won a James Beard Award, was discussed in French classes and in political science classes and was included in an exhibit on the history of food at the university.[9]

But the glorification of Pollan, known for saying "Eat food. Not too much. Mostly plants," and for telling people not to buy foods they've seen advertised on television, is a perfect example of biting the hand that feeds you, say Pollan critics. Especially in America's heartland.[10]

Farmers, who were bused in by Madison-based feed company Vita Plus, wore matching green T-shirts that said "In Defense of Farming: Eat Food.

Be Healthy. Thank Farmers." They told local reporters that students get all their facts from writers like Pollan and have never visited a farm for firsthand knowledge of food production.[11]

Pollan doesn't just bash meat and processed food as not healthful; he bashes their carbon footprints, too, said Loos. He reported that Pollan said, "Meat is the biggest food issue in terms of climate change" at an Ohio university after his University of Wisconsin appearance. "If you are a meat eater, removing meat from your diet would cut your carbon footprint by 25 percent," recounts Loos.[12]

In addition to being wrong, Pollan is also an elitist who is not in touch with the American pocketbook, say his critics. "You're currently standing in the state with the highest rate of unemployment in the country, and a lot of the ways that you propose we consume and produce food—whether that's more local, organic, mostly plants—will inevitably result in higher food prices," one Madison student pointed out to Pollan. "How do you justify a group of people who can afford these luxuries driving food policy and food production practices for those who can't?"[13]

In a 2007 editorial in *Feedstuffs* about animal activists, representatives from the Center for Consumer Freedom and the Animal Agriculture Alliance as well as the farmers at Pollan's speech complained that there are too few pro-ag voices like Loos.[14] "Why are they winning? It's simple. They have their game together, while animal agriculture and its allies have a fragmented, hopelessly under-funded, ineffective, reactive approach," the editors wrote. We need to "get to consumers before the activists do—before, not after, it's on the ballot or passed as law or posted on a despicable web site."[15] Nineteen months after the *Feedstuffs* editorial, California's Prop 2 passed, a law that prohibited the confinement of farm animals in a manner that does not allow them to turn around freely, lie down, stand up, and fully extend their limbs— proving *Feedstuffs* editors' point.

Pro-ag politicians were so shocked at the velocity of farm animal–reform propositions that when Michigan passed a similar "stall bill" in 2009, then Ohio state representative Mike Simpson actually called Agribiz, arguably the third-biggest industry in the nation, a financial underdog. "Agribusiness would never be able to put up the kind of money for a successful ballot campaign like [the Humane Society of the United States] can," he said, referring to the Humane Society of the United States, which backs animal-welfare referendums.[16]

There is no question that animal rights activists, with the help of concealed miniaturized cameras and the web, have forced farm-animal treatment onto the national front page, with a parade of cruel, upsetting, and gruesome exposés. To capture the farm vérité, often all they have to do is get hired at a factory farm or slaughterhouse, which is apparently not too hard to do.

The influence that animal rights activists are having on the nation's farms can be measured in the pages of *Feedstuffs*. In the late 1990s, articles in the eighty-plus-year-old magazine were dedicated to grain prices and animal diseases, and words like *humane* and *ethics* or the names of groups like HSUS and PETA were nowhere to be found. Ten years later, *Feedstuffs* resembles an academic or political-issues journal, covering the pros and cons of farm-animal treatment in depth. On *Feedstuffs*'s first inner page is a Washington, DC, update, touching on new or developing animal-welfare legislation. In its middle section is a "threatened-industry-of-the-week," which is in the news because of a health scare or recall, and *Feedstuffs*'s national news pages tend to cover cruel undercover videos, new since last week.

Many farmers and ag professionals are miffed that the days of "it's-none-of-your-business" farming are over. Once upon a time, consumers cared only about the price and wholesomeness of food and didn't worry about—or investigate—its origins and "disassembly." Now consumers increasingly want to know how an animal lived, died, and even what it ate in between—and they think it is their business. Some of the newly engaged consumers are motivated by health, wanting to avoid hormones in milk, antibiotics in beef, arsenic in chicken, and who knows what in seafood. But most are motivated by what Loos would call sentimentalizing animals—not wanting them to suffer and die.

Food producers, on the other hand, are not used to being told how to farm—welfare laws are seldom applied to their animals—or to having consumers, the press, animal rights activists, and their customers looking over their shoulder and breathing down their neck.

Like the old ads for Tareyton cigarettes used to ask, "What do you want, good grammar or good taste?" (the ads depicted smokers with black eyes and the caption "Us Tareyton smokers would rather fight than switch"), many food producers ask, What do you want, good prices or animal welfare? Or, as the Center for Consumer Freedom's David Martosko asks accusingly, "private rooms and daily rubdowns" or economical food?[17]

It doesn't help that US food producers are also trying to compete with cheaper imported food—much of which is produced in a way that would *really* upset the activists—and seriously pinching pennies. Finding employees to work the dirty, dangerous, demoralizing, and low-paying jobs in agriculture has never been easy. But it is actually becoming more difficult, what with looming federal initiatives that would force agriculture employers to verify the legal-immigration status of all workers.

A Texas AgriLife Research study of 5,005 dairy farms in 2010 found that 41 percent of employees were foreign workers and estimated that the US economy would suffer an $11 billion loss if that workforce were cut in half. Those workers also contribute to jobs in "grain production, animal health services and the transportation of milk products," says the report.[18] But employees who don't present immigration problems and seem eager to work could be packing cameras!

Nor is it easy to aggregate animal industries into a united front since they have no common philosophy or purpose except using animals for profit (and the enmity of activists). Some groups have *tried* to unify disparate trades attacked by animal activists, from dog breeders to sport hunters, to fur farmers to animal researchers, but their efforts seldom take off because the connections seem based on the proverb "The enemy of my enemy is my friend."

Besides, why would the vealer want to import the foie gras producer's woes when he has enough problems of his own? Why would animal researchers want to incur the wrath of antifur activists? A *Feedstuffs* editorial even tells meat producers not to feel obliged to defend all agricultural practices, if they are "defensible," because it "makes no sense and causes you to lose credibility."[19] And, let's face it. There are many farm practices—tail docking, horn burning, debeaking, branding, castration, euthanasia, and, of course, slaughter itself—that cannot be shown without doing more harm than good.

The Alliance for the Future of Agriculture in Nebraska even produced videos to address the image and transparency problems. "Many people have justifiable questions about how livestock producers raise animals and why producers use certain production practices," said *Feedstuffs* about these videos.[20]

And what about *consumer* hypocrisy? Many consumers want their meat killed *nicely* but killed nevertheless—out of sight, out of earshot by someone else, so they don't have to feel guilty (as Trent Loos says). Wanting someone else to kill your meat so it arrives pristine and packaged at the Safeway is no different, philosophically, from wanting the homeless removed from your community (*nicely*, by someone else) or the sick and elderly cared for (*nicely*, by someone else). We won't even talk about delegating the waging of war.

To avoid being tarred with other animal users' brushes, and/or tarring themselves by mistake, many animal industries try to avoid drawing ethical lines altogether. One example is seen in the debate over the production of foie gras, a delicacy that requires geese and ducks to be force-fed to bloat their livers, often until they can barely walk and their throats are bloody or punctured. You might think the American Veterinary Medical Association (AVMA) would be a leading voice for animal welfare, but an AVMA delegate actually defended foie gras production during 2005 hearings. Walter K. McCarthy, DVM, said that he was afraid that outlawing foie gras, as many countries have done, would lead to resolutions against veal calves and other "production agriculture."[21] Aren't veterinarians supposed to relieve animal

suffering? "We cannot condemn an accepted agricultural practice on . . . emotion," said McCarthy, adding that the death rate of ducks and geese in foie gras production "is much less than at most agricultural facilities."[22]

McCarthy is hardly the only foie gras defender to employ the "You think *that's* bad" argument (which is dispelled by "two wrongs don't make a right.") Chefs have also used the "slippery slope" arguments in defending foie gras. When the late celebrity Chicago chef Charlie Trotter renounced foie gras on his menu, then rival chef Rick Tramonto of Tru restaurant regaled him for alleged hypocrisy. "Look how much veal this country goes through with all the Italian restaurants and the scallopinis [sic]," he said. "It's killing those babies, right?"[23]

Paul Kahan, then chef at Chicago's Blackbird restaurant, joined in the fray. "There are so many things people eat every day that are raised in an inhumane way," he said. "The way chickens are raised, if people saw it . . . commodity pork, I could just go on."[24] What about rabbit and squab? added celebrity chef Grant Achatz.[25]

Of course, cruel animal production also brings up "freedom of choice" arguments. "Why should someone tell us what we can or can't serve, buy or produce that the FDA puts its stamp on daily?" asked then chef Michael Tsonton of Copperblue restaurant in Chicago.[26] "We live in a free-market society and if people are truly offended they won't buy it," agreed David Richards, then owner of Sweets & Savories.[27]

In fact, Chicago chefs were so afraid of a slippery ethical slope that could graduate from banning foie gras to other dishes; they created a group called Chicago Chefs for Choice to fight a very short-lived Chicago ban on foie gras. Then *Chicago Tribune* restaurant critic Phil Vettel ridiculed the ban and wrote, "Has City Council finally quacked?" Will undercover "quack-easies" spring up—to deflect the cruelty issues?[28] Even former Chicago mayor Richard Daley ridiculed the ban, citing it as an example of putting animals before people.

Restaurateurs held Foie Gras Fest fundraisers and all–foie gras menus. Sweets & Savories began to feature a Kobe beef burger topped with foie gras pâté and seared foie gras accompanied by pumpkin flan to push the envelope.[29] Graham Elliot Bowles, then chef at Avenues in the Peninsula Hotel, offered a foie gras tasting menu with a foie gras custard, mousse, brioche, vinaigrette, lollipop, and milkshake for $238 per diner. A fourth course was a terrine of foie gras, snow frozen and whirred into a powder and served with kangaroo, lime, eucalyptus, and melon.[30] But some chefs *were* willing to accept a slippery slope of ethically problematic menu items. In 2007, Wolfgang Puck renounced foie gras as well as veal and pork from crated animals, eggs from caged hens, and nonsustainable seafood in one fell swoop at his ninety-four restaurants and forty-three catering venues.[31]

Because of the "You think *that's* bad" argument, animal users and trade groups often circle the wagons when gory undercover videos surface—of which some are foie gras operations. When a 2004 undercover video at Agriprocessors' kosher slaughterhouse surfaced, showing cows that did not die from having their throats cut but got up and thrashed, some rabbis condemned the gory scenes. But they later reversed their condemnation and formed a united front with those who had always defended it.[32]

In another video, a sow was shown being hung from the top of a frontloader by a Creston, Ohio, hog farmer as a method of "euthanasia"—inspiring an HBO movie titled *Death on a Factory Farm.* The National Pork Producers Council said the video "shows practices at a hog farm that are not condoned and, in fact, are abhorred by responsible pork producers."[33] But the Ohio Pork Producers Council actually donated $10,000 to the farmer's legal defense![34] And Iowa veterinarian Paul Armbrecht testified at the trial that hanging was an acceptable method of euthanasia. This testimony led to the acquittal of the farmer, Ken Wiles.[35]

It is so embarrassing to food producers to have their cruel practices exposed on video that their defensiveness is often over the top. "That's not our farm," they claim, "and even if it is, those are not abusive practices, and even if they are abusive practices, the employees were put up to it by the activists, and even if they weren't put up to it, there were only a few bad apples, and we've fired them, and even if there were a few bad apples, why did the activists tolerate the abuse and not report it to us, and even if they did report the abuse to us, these people have a vegetarian agenda and want everyone to give up meat!"

Owners of Gemperle Farms, a California egg farm whose conditions were videotaped by undercover animal activists (see chapter 8), denied the scenes were from their farm *and* defended the gassing of birds seen in the video.[36]

Kirt Espenson, then owner of the ten-thousand-calf E-6 Cattle Company in Hart, Texas, from which disturbing video surfaced, said animals were denied medical care for their sores and painful conditions so that people who ended up eating the animals wouldn't get drug residues. (He defended the widescale death of other animals, saying they were sick from the cold weather and had to be eliminated, as if cold weather were an untreatable disease.)[37]

When the animal group Compassion Over Killing publicized cruel videos it said were filmed at Michael Foods, the sixth-largest commercial US egg producer, in 2009, the company's defenses included the following explanations:[38]

1. Not all the footage can be identified as from the Michael's LeSueur, Minnesota, facility, as is claimed on the video.

2. Footage was shot by a thirty-four-year-old male who was hired after misrepresenting his past employment.

3. Dead hens are not left to accumulate in their cages for days but are removed during daily cage inspections, and "we believe that this person let dead birds accumulate," to convey excessive mortality and negligence.

4. Hens are not "routinely" caught in the wires of their cages but on rare occasions, and, during daily inspections, any birds found caught are immediately freed.

5. Egg operations fully comply with the United Egg Producers' (UEP) guidelines, whose audit of Michael Foods passed in 2008.

6. Michael passed a US Department of Agriculture audit after the video, with the highest possible score, and there was no evidence of dead hens remaining in cages.

7. The video was intended to promote Compassion Over Killing's mission to eliminate animal-based protein production and to support vegetarianism.[39]

Feedstuffs wrote a similar lame explanation in response to *Food, Inc.* (2008), a controversial film that shows cruel food practices, in which both Michael Pollan and *Fast Food Nation* author Eric Schlosser appear. According to *Feedstuffs*, "Most people work away from home" and require such convenience foods, and Americans demand "competitively priced, inexpensive food." Nor can the ag practices in the film be called "corporate greed," said the paper, because "many consumers are also shareholders in food companies and expect gains on their investments."[40]

But even when videotaped abuse is uncontestable, and there is no context in which it is not cruel, farmers are usually exonerated. Ken Wiles, responsible for the sow hanging, and Gary Conklin, whose Ohio farmed needed police guards to hold off protestors after videotapes exposed cruelty, were both found not guilty.[41] An editorial on the website Farm and Dairy about the Conklin investigation also accuses the undercover employee of allowing the abuse to continue and suggests another employee who was arrested in connection with the abuse was "paid" by the animal rights group and was "a supporter."[42]

Customers of exposed farms and slaughterhouses are also known to excuse practices, like Atlantic Veal and Lamb of New York, which said that video filmed at its supplier, Buckeye Veal Farm in Apple Creek, Ohio, showing chained calves covered with feces was "acceptable practice."[43] Atlantic Veal and Lamb is known as the company that shipped veal with backbone pieces thought to carry mad cow disease risk to Japan and single-handedly torpedoed a year's worth of US trade negotiations with Japan to open the country to exports after a mad-cow scare.[44] In a denial similar to that of the Gemperles, Gaylord Barkman, services and sales director for Buckeye Veal, said that "only a small amount of footage is from our farms," and that "in one of the barns shown on the video, 85 percent of the calves already are in group housing."[45] The Giant Eagle grocery chain, a customer of Atlantic Veal and Lamb, said Atlantic had assured it that Buckeye's current practices were "within industry guidelines," and it had no plans of discontinuing the sale of veal, reported the Associated Press.[46]

But there are also voices of moderation in the ag world, like Dan Murphy, then a reporter from *Meat & Poultry* magazine. "When any industry is forced to be reactive and continually defend its business model, the chances of moving the needle on public acceptance or understanding is minimal," he said in a speech to trade officials.[47] "What needs to happen is that all industry stakeholders, from livestock producers to meatpackers to animal protein processors, need to get ahead of the activists' laundry list of demands surrounding animal welfare and voluntarily incorporate humane handling, sustainable production and environmentally conscious programs on farms, ranches and processing plants," said Murphy. "Not in response to politically motivated demands from change agents, but as a product of sound science and sincere investment in the welfare of the food animals that comprise such an essential segment of our food supply."[48]

An editorial in *Feedstuffs* strikes a similar chord. In "How to Lose the Argument on Animal Welfare," D. A. Daley cites "using economics" to justify practices on the farm as one of ten reasons why animal producers lose the debate with animal activists.[49] People who raise animals for a living tend to think "of course we treat them well or we won't make money," says Daley, but the argument does not help "efforts with the public" because "you can have extreme conditions that are not good for animals that can be profitable."[50] Temple Grandin, PhD, the well-known animal expert who serves as a kind of Ralph Nader of the slaughterhouse, agrees with Murphy in a 2009 *Feedstuffs* article. She tells food producers that they have done a "lousy, lousy, lousy job" at fixing the "bad stuff" and making sure the public knows they have fixed it. She says food producers' operations need to be clean enough to show "to your wedding guests."[51] Photos and videos showing the outside of barns and plants are nice, says Grandin, but they don't show the inside, "where the hens and pigs are." Grandin suggests that meat producers actually stream the insides of their feedlot, barns, and plants on the web.[52] Yes, like the animal activists!

Grandin has especially harsh words for "uncaring producers," who somehow get "named to committees to establish welfare guidelines." She also castigates pork producers who need "to control growth promotants that lead to fatigued pigs, which lie down and don't want to move," likely referring to ractopamine.[53] One plant, she notes in the *Feedstuffs* article, charged producers $25 for every nonambulatory pig that had to be moved with a Bobcat, and its problems quickly ended—perhaps because the growth drugs were curtailed.[54] Grandin is the author of *Animals Make Us Human* and *Animals in Translation* and is a professor of animal science at Colorado State University. She is known for interpreting how the world looks to animals because of an alternative perspective that derives from having autism.

UNDERCOVER LIKE ME

Animal rights activists are not the only ones going behind the scenes into the murky world of US meat production. Former *New York Times* reporter Charlie LeDuff worked undercover for one month on the hog killing floor of the Smithfield plant in Tar Heel, North Carolina, the world's largest slaughterhouse, hired under his own name, to write the 2000 article "At a Slaughterhouse, Some Things Never Die: Who Kills, Who Cuts, Who Bosses Can Depend on Race." He describes African American women "assigned to the chitterlings room, where they would scrape feces and worms from intestines," workers throwing "a piece of shoulder at a friend across the conveyor" just to get his attention, and prisoners who preferred their cells to work release at the plant.[55]

In 2004, former *Chicago Tribune* reporter Andrew Martin continued the pork charm offensive and reported that "dozens of dead piglets are dumped in piles or encased in pools of manure beneath the floor, having drowned there after falling through a hole," as he visited the HKY Farm in Bloomfield, Nebraska.[56] "Dead hogs remain in their cages, discarded and stiff in walkways or rotting in pens as other pigs gnaw at their carcasses. Many of the 1,800 or so pigs that are alive are emaciated, crippled or covered with open sores, having been poked by jagged iron bars from broken cages or fallen through slats that separate them from the manure pits below."[57]

Then, as if the nation needed more behind-the-scenes descriptions of its pork cutlets, *Rolling Stone* magazine also ran an exposé about Smithfield hog operations titled "Boss Hog" in 2006, with a photo of a mountain of dead, pink pigs looking eerily like children. The liquid in the infamous "holding ponds" of manure is not brown, says author Jeff Tietz.[58] "The interactions between the bacteria and blood and afterbirths and stillborn piglets and urine and excrement and chemicals and drugs turn the lagoons pink," he writes. "Even light rains can cause lagoons to overflow; major floods have transformed entire counties into pig-shit bayous. To alleviate swelling lagoons, workers sometimes pump the shit out of them and spray the waste on surrounding fields, which results in what the industry daintily refers to as 'overapplication.' This can turn hundreds of acres—thousands of football fields—into shallow mud puddles of pig shit. Tree branches drip with pig shit."[59]

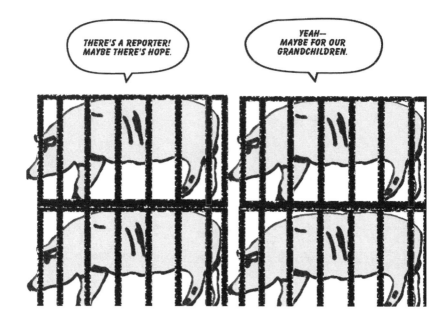

Meanwhile, former National Public Radio contributor Daniel Zwerdling gave graphic coverage of chicken slaughter for the now defunct *Gourmet* magazine—a subject almost unprecedented in a food magazine.[60] And who can forget Eric Schlosser's *Fast Food Nation*, which camped out on the *New York Times* Best Seller list for two years? But, except for LeDuff, few reporters have rolled up their sleeves, donned their work gloves and steel tips, and gone to work day after day in the front lines of animal production. (Though it is said that Upton Sinclair, author of *The Jungle* [1906], did.)

How hard is it to get hired at a slaughterhouse or on a factory farm? Can you start this afternoon? There is not a long line to fill jobs whose descriptions are "Remove dead animals from 98-degree ammonia-infused pens wearing face mask, $8 an hour possible, depending on experience," or "Determine sex of newborn chicks and grind up unwanted males for dog food: $6 dollars an hour; chance for advancement."

"Aaron," an undercover investigator for Mercy for Animals, was hired to maintain the egg conveyor belts in eleven barns at Norco Ranch in Menifee, California. The job paid $8.50 an hour, twelve hours a day, six days a week, with no overtime. But Aaron says he still earned considerably more than his non-English-speaking coworkers, who were in charge of removing manure (toxic, with pink fly-poison pellets) and "depopulating" unwanted hens in carbon dioxide chambers on wheels.[61]

At Norco, two employees work seven barns, each holding thirty thousand hens; and another employee is responsible for six barns, Aaron said in an interview. The barns are infested with mice and maggots, and the distress calls of the packed birds are deafening. No veterinary care is given to hens who suffer from lesions plastering their eyes shut, trauma around their vents (a bird's posterior vaginal and urinary opening) from egg laying, and other painful conditions, according to Aaron.[62] "I told one woman who had worked at Norco for twenty-seven years that the birds had prolapsed egg vents, which were bleeding and painful," Aaron said. "You mean their insides are coming out?" she asked. Her question implied she was unaware of the condition, though it was rampant in the hens, recounts Aaron. "You should kill them . . . but first ask the supervisor," she replied. The supervisor said to kill them if "it wasn't too many."[63]

"Sam," another undercover employee, was hired as a "live hanger" at the House of Raeford turkey slaughterhouse in Raeford, North Carolina. "The alarm rings at 3:45 a.m. I reach for the ibuprofen. Without it my hands are too sore and swollen to even close . . . much less hold a turkey's legs." This is how Sam describes the start of his day in a diary entry. "Wearing a pair of rubber gloves, cotton gloves and taping them doesn't help when you're banging into shackles all day. The flesh is still raw and exposed. I dress with the video cam that's become part of my daily outfit carefully hidden and fortify myself with enough food to get through the work day. When we arrive at House of Raeford the trucks full of live turkeys are already waiting to be unloaded; it's not even 5:30 a.m."[64]

Modern turkeys are drugged and bred to grow so quickly that their legs cannot support their own weight, and many arrived with legs broken or dislocated, according to an interview with Sam.[65] When you try to remove them from their crates, their legs twist completely around, limp and offering no resistance. The turkeys must have been in a lot of pain, reflected Sam, but they don't cry out. In fact, the only sound as they are hung, he says, is the "trucks being washed out to go back and get a new load."[66] "There were 100 turkeys and chickens dead upon arrival today, many missing feathers with open wounds and with large sores on their feet," Sam wrote in his Raeford diary. "I saw a chicken with an abscess on her left leg about the size of a tennis ball and another chicken whose right leg was mashed to the point of bloody pulp and [she was still] hanged by both legs to go down the line.[67]

"Mike," also an undercover employee, was hired as a barn technician at Country View/Hatfield Quality Meats in Fannettsburg, Pennsylvania, where he was able to witness the euthanasia of unwanted pigs and piglets.[68] "The gas cart was filled to the brim with pigs today, a total of 39, including 9 large pigs that were at weaning age. They were left in the cart all day to trample each other, before being gassed all at once," he wrote in a diary on the Mercy for Animals website. "32 starve-outs, 16 runts, 10 ruptures, 9 poor quality, 3 deformed and 2 joint infections" were killed in five days.[69] The captive bolt pistol at slaughterhouses and factory farms is supposed to render an animal unconscious. But at Country View/Hatfield Quality Meats, it often didn't work, as Mike reports. "My supervisor told me she was dubbing my coworker 'Two-Shot' in light of the fact he rarely kills the sow with one bolt," he wrote. One such pig "just stood there looking stunned as blood trickled from her forehead. She then got her bearings and tried to turn and run."[70] Veterinarians who viewed Mike's Country View video did not hold back their professional denunciation. "There are dead piglets in the farrowing crates, and one moribund piglet is captured on video in her last minutes of life," said Illinois veterinarian Debra Teachout. "She is in trembling and in lateral recumbency, respirations are shallow and gasping, eye is swollen and shut. There is a large lesion on her face, and suggests that she is dying of sepsis. This piglet should never have been allowed to get to this point without medical intervention."[71]

"The pig seizuring in the stall unattended is nightmarish, as is the sloppy use of the captive bolt," said Bernard Rollin, PhD, then distinguished professor of animal science at Colorado State University and Pew Commission member.[72] "The gas 'euthanasia' using CO2 is widespread in the industry. It is horrendous, as the animals suffocate and experience major fear and distress."[73] At the time of the video, Country View/Hatfield Quality Meats was a supplier to Walmart, IGA, Shaw's, Stop & Shop, Sam's Club, Costco, Giant, and other well-known food chains.[74]

"Steve," another undercover employee, was hired as a mechanic at Willet

Dairy in Locke, New York, which was featured on *Nightline* for instances of animal cruelty. Video that Steve filmed at the seven-thousand-animal dairy shows calves being pulled away from their mothers to make veal, the mothers pathetically rushing after their young and vocalizing as they are dragged away.[75] After finding a severely ill calf at eight-thirty in the morning, the worker responsible for newborns tells Steve she was "cold" and would soon be dead. But "at 4:30 p.m. the dying calf was still in the same place, her throat barely expanding and contracting in slow breaths," writes Steve.[76] "Her eyes were completely gray. I sat down beside her and stroked her hair. She did not respond, but when I got up to walk away, she let out a weak bleat, so I returned and continued to pet her." The next day, the calf had frozen to death and had been "dragged into a corner," he wrote.[77] "Two other calves cuddled next to each other, shivering from the cold. A mother hovered over the pen, helplessly watching and moaning in distress."[78]

"Pete," another undercover employee, was hired to work at Wiles hog farm in Creston, Ohio, the six-thousand-sow-farrowing operation depicted in the 2009 HBO movie *Death on a Factory Farm*. Pete even appears in promotions for the movie, a twenty-something guy wearing blue jeans, a camouflage cap, and sunglasses. In an interview, Pete says that the farm owner, Ken Wiles, actually allowed pigs to starve to death.[79] "I'd watch them get thinner every day until they died," he says, noting that Wayne County municipal judge Stuart Miller threw out the starvation charges in the original indictment and refused to allow most of the video into evidence. He said "he didn't want to watch it."[80] There were other farm practices that made as little sense. "There were two different 'vaccines' with different names and different colored labels we were supposed to give the pigs to prevent diseases," said Pete in an interview.[81] "I asked when we should be giving one versus the other and Ken Wiles said it didn't matter as long as the animals got one or the other. But when I looked, one was nothing but sterile dilutant." A dilutant, also called a diluent, is liquid filler to make fluids flow more easily and has no medicine in it. "Shock poles [devices similar to cattle prods] were used on pigs even when there was nowhere for them to go or when they were so piled together they couldn't stand up anyway," says Pete. "They were even used when they would cause the animal to charge you. It made no sense at all."[82]

Some abuse that undercover employees document can be explained by ignorance; cost margins at volume operations that make it cheaper to kill animals than treat their illnesses; and the frustration of degrading, low-paying jobs that seem to be made more difficult by the animals themselves. ("You'll learn to hate them," the mechanic training Steve at Willet told him of the cows.[83])

But other operations seem to harbor employees who actually enjoy hurting animals. At Willet Diary, an employee believed to have worked there for nineteen years brags to Steve, on camera, about braining a bull with a two-by-four and then kicking its genitals, "stomping" another animal by jumping off a gate and onto its head repeatedly, and brutalizing a tied-up calf so badly the manager asked why it was so bruised. He seems proud of his deeds. "What do you think that wrench did to her?" the worker asks Steve, on camera, recounting another incident of cruelty in which a wrench was the weapon. "Cracked her right over the [expletive] skull."

"With her head in a headlock?" asks Steve.

"Yep. Dropped her right down. [*yells*] Stupid bitch!"[84]

At Country View/Hatfield Quality Meats, the hog farm, a worker tells undercover employee Mike that he "prays" to run over animals on the highway and was looking forward to bolting a prolapsed sow because "I just feel like killing something." Another worker at the facility swung a ruptured pig into the gas cart, telling it with glee to "die, %#@&," employing a racial epithet.[85]

And the disturbing violence of Billy Joe Gregg, an employee at Conklin Dairy Farm, earned him eighteen months in jail, though his sentence was suspended to less than half that because of time served.[86] (Protesters outside the courtroom demanded a more severe sentence, and a *New York Magazine* blog said of Gregg's short sentence, "Where are the zealots espousing eye-for-eye justice when you need them?"[87])

Revelations of cruelty on US farms often have immediate, "viral" results. Customers of the operation sometimes suspend their business, consumers may boycott products, and politicians have even introduced legislation to stop exposed cruel practices. Yet prosecuting attorneys usually refuse to bring charges against perpetrators because the harmed parties are not just animals—they're food animals.

David Phillips, for example, then the Union County prosecuting attorney, said no charges would be filed against Conklin Dairy owner Gary Conklin because "in context, Mr. Conklin's actions were entirely appropriate."[88] Phillips actually blamed the undercover employee for allowing the abuse to continue.[89] When given the Willet dairy video (which aired on *Nightline*), Cayuga County assistant district attorney Diane Adsit allegedly threw up her hands and said, "Who cares?" and that she had "human" cases to work on, says Daniel Hauff, director of investigations with Mercy for Animals.[90]

Prosecuting attorneys even say they will launch "their own" investigations, as if the farm operations would not have been subsequently cleaned up after exposing videos. In fact, after a raid at Quality Egg/Maine Contract Farming actually sickened law enforcement officials who entered barns, compliance manager Bob Leclerc invited the press to inspect his barns precisely *because* they had been cleaned up and the sick birds had no doubt been "depopulated." "These don't look like the bald, sick birds Mercy for Animals found," wrote Scott Taylor, then of the *Sun Journal*.[91] Similarly, Michael Foods passed a USDA inspection soon after grotesque video from its egg barns was posted on the web. No dead hens were found intermingled with lives ones when government inspectors were onsite.[92] Imagine that.

UNDERCOVER INVESTIGATORS OR TRESPASSERS?

Trent Loos, the agricultural activist, and undercover employees like Aaron, Mike, Sam, Steve, and Pete have more in common than being willing to go undercover as they fight their animal-related causes. They believe that a horse is no different from a muskrat or a chicken or a dog, which is to say they are not "speciesists." Speciesism says that an animal's value come from its appeal or usefulness to humans. They also believe that people who eat animals should stop pretending they grow on trees and take a good, long look at how they're slaughtered.

But whereas animal activists think the undercover scenes they make possible on the web will cure people of wanting to eat meat, Loos thinks it will cure them of their guilt and denial. Animals receive "better treatment than the children who lived in those thousands of high-rise dumps we passed on our train ride from O'Hare," Loos and his wife Kelli told the *High Plains Journal* after going undercover at the humane group Farm Sanctuary's conference in Chicago.[93] Don't criticize farmers with your mouths full, Loos is known to admonish.[94]

Rural and farm people may be more comfortable with the way meat gets to the table than are urbanites, but the protracted suffering of animals at so many farm operations reduces no one's guilt. Nor is it easy to believe the "bad apple" theory after fifteen years of such videos at countless major operations.

It was no surprise, then, that in 2011 Iowa introduced legislation, written in cooperation with the Iowa Poultry Association, to criminalize the undercover videos.[95] The bill proposed to make it a crime to "produce, distribute or possess photos and video taken without permission at an agricultural facility," which, of course, would chill news media who would accept and distribute such materials.[96] The Iowa bill, quickly imitated by Florida, Minnesota, and other states, would also criminalize lying on an application to work at an agriculture facility "with an intent to commit an act not authorized by the owner."[97]

The first offense for producing the criminalized images, said the Iowa Animal Facility Interference bill, would be an aggravated misdemeanor, graduating to possible felony charges for the second misdemeanor. And "interferers" could also be charged with animal-facility fraud, crop-operation tampering, crop-operation interference, and crop-operation fraud, said an editorial in *Food Safety News*.[98]

If an employee is willing to lie on an application, he might go further and stage fake videos, destroy equipment, or carry diseases onto farms, said Kevin Vinchattle, chief executive of the Iowa Poultry Association, which helped write the bill.[99]

"People are scared to death that they might be found in a compromising position," said Craig Lang, a dairy farmer and then president of the Iowa Farm Bureau.[100] The Interference bills, quickly dubbed the "Ag-Gag" bill by critics, would "make producers feel more comfortable," said John P. Kibbie, then a state senator from Emmetsburg and president of the Iowa State Senate.[101]

Of course, the Animal Facility Interference bills are anti-free-speech laws, which would chill whistle-blowers in addition to reporters. And the bills were lambasted by CNN, the *New York Times*, and *Time* magazine, as well as by First Amendment advocates, food safety advocates, animal and consumer activists, and public health professionals. Republican strategist Mary Matalin and the late actress Cloris Leachman expressed outrage and indignation.[102] The bills were defeated—at least for the 2011 legislative session—but many expect them to return.

Meanwhile, Big Ag is also facing more employment pressure than the threats of workers packing miniature cameras. Its companies will soon likely be required to use the electronic system known as E-Verify to ascertain the legal immigration status of workers.[103] Former Rep. Lamar Smith (R-TX), the bill's backer, said that by preventing illegal immigrants from taking jobs while unemployment is rampant, the measure "could open up millions of jobs for unemployed Americans and legal workers."[104] But Mike Carlton, then director of labor relations for the Florida Fruit and Vegetables Association, was less optimistic about the jobs the bill will create for US citizens. Of 344 US citizens hired to fill citrus-fruit pickers' jobs, he says, 336 quit before two months.[105] Only eight US citizens would or could do the farm work.

Meanwhile, Trent Loos is continuing his campaign against animal rights, animal rights activists are continuing their undercover campaigns, and farmers increasingly don't know *who* they can hire for six dollars an hour.

Chapter 11
SLAUGHTER TRANSPARENCY AND ITS DOWNSIDES

A BBC reporter visits an Illinois farm for an article about Midwest agriculture and spies a pig with a wooden leg.

"Is there a story connected to that pig?" asks the reporter.

"Oh, that animal! He is amazing," says the farmer. "When we had a barn fire, he opened the doors and saved the animals. When we had a tornado, he lifted up the debris and saved my own daughter. When we had a flood, he swam into the house and saved my son. When I was in a tractor accident, he went and got my wife and saved me."

"That is amazing," agrees the reporter. "But what about his wooden leg?"

"Well, a pig like that, you don't eat all at once," says the farmer.

Almost everyone in industrialized and Western countries is uncomfortable with slaughter, which is why many of us make jokes about it. Since the United States moved from an agrarian society to an urban one, many complain that kids think chicken nuggets grow on trees and that we have lost our awareness and respect for the fact than an animal died to make lunch.

Because meat is daintily wrapped in cellophane at the grocery store, we are able to pretend no violence, sacrifice, or pain was involved (not even the pain experienced by the workers). And because meat is cheap, we can—and do—eat it so frequently it ruins our health and the environments in which it is raised (if we ever visit them, which most urban dwellers don't).

Many people realize that even though they may eat meat all day and every day, they would not be able to kill an animal themselves. This guilt and awareness of how cushy their dietary situations are can produce a perverse respect for hunters, like Sarah Palin, former governor of Alaska, who have the "honesty" to acknowledge where meat comes from. On her TLC live-action show, *Sarah Palin's Alaska*, Palin bludgeoned a gigantic halibut to death and then displayed its still-beating heart triumphantly for the at-home television audience.[1] She also guns down a docile, unresisting female caribou with six shots, two rifles, and help from her dad. She delights in the fact that liberals "get all wee-wee'd up" about her animal realpolitik, like when she held her baby shower at a shooting range or let her teenage daughter gut salmon.

Even though catch-and-release fishing has replaced a lot of catch-and-eat fishing, and camera safaris have replaced big-game hunting, practically every US presidential contender still feels compelled to don blaze orange outerwear and kill a few for the "Gipper" of public opinion. It's almost like a candidate can't achieve sufficient "guy-dom" (or, in the case of Hillary Rodham Clinton, "gal-dom") to be elected to high office without a hunting résumé.

Both former president Bill Clinton and Massachusetts senator John Kerry embarked on self-conscious duck hunting trips while running for office, that had "photo opportunity" written all over them. Hillary Clinton sucked up to the gun lobby about her love of the shooting sports to the point that a 2008 presidential candidate, rival Barack Obama, referred to her as "Annie Oakley."[2] Of course, she later became Secretary of State Annie Oakley.

New Mexico governor and Democratic presidential candidate Bill Richardson bragged about the exotic long-horned African antelope he killed on media tycoon Ted Turner's Armendaris Ranch in New Mexico.[3] A photo shows him kneeling beside the animal, its muzzle sunk into the sand. But presidential candidate and former Massachusetts governor Mitt Romney's characterization of himself as a lifelong hunter on the basis of a few hunting trips in which he shot small animals was ridiculed by the gun press during the 2008 election campaigns.[4]

And Arkansas governor Mike Huckabee's attempt to snare the good-ol' boy vote during the 2008 elections when he was a Republican presidential candidate was probably the most awkward of all. Huckabee did everything right for his cammo close-up. He scheduled the pheasant hunt the day after Christmas, when there is usually no news. He intoned the usual Department of Natural Resources catechism about hunting actually being stewardship:

"It's the hunters who actually keep the wildlife alive." He even wore a cap that said "EAT, SLEEP, HUNT"—a good visual for TV cameras.[5] But even though the press dutifully trailed Huckabee into Iowa wing-shooting country—"underdressed," according to some reporters—he got no bounce out of the event. It might have even cost him approval points—although that might have had something to do with the rumors swirling at the time about Hucka-bee's son, David, who allegedly *hung a dog* while he was a counselor at the Boy Scout's Camp Pioneer in Hatfield, Arkansas. Huckabee had made a "conscious attempt to keep the state police from investigating his son and seemed to be obstructing justice," a former FBI chief in Little Rock told *Newsweek*.[6]

But the dip in approval points was probably due to the way Huckabee, also a Baptist preacher, joked about the bird he shot having his opponent's name written on its rear end. "See, that's what happens if you get in my way," he chortled to the press. "Each of these three birds made a sacrifice for the campaign."[7] A bird may be just a bird, but how could a pastor find death—even that of an animal—*funny*? Was that the household attitude in which his son grew up?

The 2008 campaign seemed to pivot on wooing gun owners. Huckabee, the late former Arizona senator John McCain, and former Tennessee senator Fred Thompson started out with a leg up over New York City mayor Rudy Giuliani, who was on the wrong side of gun control. But then McCain found himself in the doghouse with the gun lobby for wanting to close the "gun show loophole," which allows firearm sales with no background checks at gun shows.[8]

Of course, you can't talk about politicians and hunting without mention-ing former vice president Dick Cheney. But even though the nation remem-bers how, in 2006, he shot his companion, seventy-eight-year-old attorney Harry Whittington, in the face instead of shooting a quail, Cheney's true love is put-and-take hunting, or canned hunting, which confers as much "guy-dom" as hitting women and children.

In 2003, Cheney's hunting party killed 417 pheasants at the Rolling Rock Club in Ligonier Township, Pennsylvania; Cheney personally killed seventy pheasants and an undisclosed number of ducks.[9] Three years later, Cheney headed to Clove Valley Rod & Gun Club in a caravan of fifteen sport utility vehicles—with an ambulance—at a local-taxpayer cost of $32,000.

This was not Cheney's first visit to the four-thousand-acre club, which costs $150,000 a year to join and features a male-only clubhouse.[10]

Gun-club staff would not divulge whether the veep was shooting pheasants, ducks, or the "Hungarian partridges," the club advertises, but a *New York Daily News* photographer snapped a photo of a Confederate flag displayed in a Clove Valley Rod & Gun Club garage.[11] There was something about the Cheney trip to offend everyone! Cheney spokeswoman at the time Megan Mitchell said neither Cheney nor his staff saw the flag, but civil rights leader Rev. Al Sharpton demanded that Cheney "leave immediately, denounce the club and apologize for going to a club that represents lynching, hate and murder to black people."[12] Feminists and animal lovers no doubt agreed.

There was also a hunting backstory to former South Carolina governor Mark Sanford's Buenos Aires/Father's Day meltdown. Many remember that the guv went AWOL from his gubernatorial duties to "hike the Appalachian Trail" in 2009, only to confess later that he had been in the arms of his consort, María Belén Chapur, in Argentina. But how many are aware that part of the "official delegation" included dove hunting in Cordoba, paid for by cabinet member and commerce secretary Joe Taylor, a Sanford appointee?[13] News reports don't give the name of the delegation's lodge, but the website of one Cordoba lodge advertises that "it is normal to shoot between 1,000 to 1,500 shells per hunter per day," and that "hunters regularly use two guns and a reloaded to prevent barrel overheating" thanks to "no bag limits or seasons." Photos show *mountains* of deceased birds in front of grinning he-men.[14]

"Both of my boys became members of the Club 1000 for shooting more than 1,000 birds in a single day—a proud papa moment," wrote John Horton of Austin, Texas, on the Miles & Miles lodge site.[15]

While there are some people who think no hunting is wrong and others who think no hunting is right, most people agree that hunting when the meat is not eaten and when the animal has no means of escape is not ethical. Many lost respect for the late Troy Lee Gentry of the country-and-western band Montgomery Gentry for killing a pet bear named Cubby on videotape trying to appear the tough guy. Gentry pleaded guilty to "falsifying a hunting tag" in the 2006 incident, which some called a bear-snuff film.[16] "Your career is over unless you take drastic measures to save it, and by taking drastic measures, I mean you need to fight a wild bear," wrote one fan on a website. "No guns, no bows, no cages, no 'Cubbies' this time. Just you and a big, angry, wild bear."[17]

Many also lost respect for pop star Madonna when she held canned hunts at Ashcombe House, her historic Wiltshire mansion, stocked with battery-cage-raised pheasants from France that guests were invited to blow away.[18] "City bankers and brokers pay up to £10,000 a day to shoot on Madonna's Ashcombe House estate," reported the *Sunday Times*. Guests included actor Brad Pitt and former football player and actor Vinnie Jones.

"You have more respect for things you eat when you go through, or see, the process of killing them," Madonna told BBC Radio One in 2001. "When you're shooting, you are standing in the forest for really long periods of time, so you end up looking at the leaves and the sky and the trees and you have a lot of time to meditate," she rhapsodized.[19]

Has anyone told Madge that you can look at the trees and sky unarmed?

A DIFFERENT KIND OF "CHUTE"

Of course, hunting or killing your own meat can seem downright ethical when compared to the way animals live on factory farms today. That's a point on which hunters, their admirers, their critics, and animal lovers all agree. That's why some chefs, foodies, and even students are taking the knife into their own hands, to try to circumvent the horrors of factory farming—and sometimes their own hypocrisy—with varying degrees of success.

Then college student Jake Lahne enrolled in a meat-production course at the University of Illinois, a strong agricultural school, to achieve "a real understanding of where meat comes from."[20] But during his flirtation with do-your-own slaughtering, he found that "animals do not want to die. They can feel pain and fear, and, just like us, will struggle to breathe for even one single more second." He even warns future DIY slaughterers, "If you're about to run 250 volts through a pig, do not look it in the eyes. It is not going to absolve you."[21]

Christine Muhlke, then a *New York Times* food writer, planned to report on one of the first uses of a van-like "mobile slaughterhouse," which serves customers who live far away from slaughterhouses or who have a hard time transporting animals. But even though she describes herself as a "meat hipster who serves pickled pigs' tongues," the frenetic "wild thrashing" of the slaughtered animal in the box horrified her.[22]

And then there was *New York Times* city critic Ariel Kaminer, who decided to take the life of a Bourbon Red turkey with rich brown feathers "flecked with white" at an Islamic slaughterhouse in Queens. "Stepping out of the slaughterhouse and squinting at the light, I didn't feel brave. I didn't feel idealistic. I felt crummy," she found.[23]

Slaughter transparency got so popular, the BBC announced that it would show the deaths of piglets, lambs, and veal calves as part of a TV series titled "Kill It, Cook It, Eat It."[24] But the National Farmers' Union objected. "We don't have a problem with people being shown how their meat is produced. We think it is important that the public do know what's involved so they can eat meat with a clear conscience," said then spokesperson Anthony Gibson. But showing baby instead of adult animals killed "is a gratuitous play on the emotional heart strings of the public."[25]

Reporters are seldom allowed in slaughterhouses for the same reason the public isn't. It is horrifying, terrifying, and ruins one's taste for meat. A contractor who worked for one day in a veal slaughterhouse reported that his mustache had absorbed so much of the smell, he couldn't wash it out and had to shave off the entire mustache.[26] A chemist who worked as a slaughterhouse-maintenance employee as a teenager described seeing "rats as big as cats" while he hosed down the blood.[27] Even film directors making documentaries about how meat is produced are not allowed in slaughterhouses.

Still, stories get out—and they do ruin your appetite. After the 2000 report from the *New York Times* about the Smithfield pork slaughterhouse in Tar Heel, North Carolina, the *Washington Post* published a story revealing that slaughterhouse lines move so fast, "killing" an animal is a detail lost in pursuit of economics. Ramon Moreno, a "second legger" whose job was to cut hocks off of carcasses at a rate of 309 per hour at the Iowa Beef Packers (IBP) plant in Wallula, Washington, told the *Post* that the animals are far from dead. They "blink. They make noises. The head moves, the eyes are wide and looking around," even as he dismembered them.[28]

Then Virgil Butler (see chapter 8), a chicken slaughterer at the Tyson

Foods plant in Grannis, Arkansas, broke his silence and testified, "I was responsible for trying to slit the throats of the chickens the machine missed on the nights I worked the killing room. Our line runs 182 shackles per minute. It is physically impossible to catch them all. Therefore, they are scalded alive. When this happens, the chickens flop, scream, kick, and their eyeballs pop out of their heads."[29]

After whistle-blowing employees spoke out about the effects of fastmoving assembly lines on animals, so did US Department of Agriculture (USDA) meat inspectors. Lester Friedlander, DVM, a federal meat inspector for ten years who trained other USDA veterinarians, told the press, "My plant in Pennsylvania processed 1,800 cows a day, 220 per hour," and that stopping the line cost about $5,000 a minute, so veterinarians are pressured "to look the other way" when violations happen.[30]

The federal government has made several efforts to clean up the daily horror movies going on at the nation's slaughterhouses. Before Upton Sinclair's 1906 book *The Jungle*, which described workers falling into meat vats and being processed as meat, there were no rules or laws governing safety, hygiene, and welfare at US slaughterhouses. But the muckraking book upset and disgusted the nation so quickly that it led to both the Meat Inspection Act and the Pure Food and Drug Act of 1906, as well as to the establishment of the Bureau of Chemistry, which was to become the Food and Drug Administration.

Yet it took a similarly upsetting 1957 film of hog slaughter, created by Arthur P. Redman and shown to Congress, for the nation to come up with the idea of stunning animals before their deaths.[31] "We are morally compelled, here in this hour, to try to imagine—to try to feel in our own nerves—the totality of the suffering of 100 million tortured animals," said Sen. Hubert Humphrey, then a Minnesota Democrat and later vice president under President Lyndon B. Johnson. "The issue before us today is pain, agony and cruelty— and what a moral man must do about it in view of his own conscience."[32]

Humphrey is remembered today as a civil rights leader and voice during the Vietnam War, but he spearheaded the drafting and passage of the 1958 Humane Methods of Slaughter Act, which requires animals to be made insensitive to pain before being "shackled, hoisted, thrown, cast or cut." President

Dwight D. Eisenhower signed the act and remarked that "if I depended on my mail, I would think humane slaughter is the only thing anyone is interested in."[33] Guess who opposed the act? The United States Department of Agriculture.

Humphrey wanted humane slaughter to be the law of the land, but a compromise was forced in 1958, making it only a condition of doing business with the federal government. In 1978, the year Humphrey died, Sen. Bob Dole (R-KS) strengthened the law to make it mandatory for the nation, except for religious slaughter. Senator Dole was also instrumental in passing the 1985 Improved Standards for Laboratory Animals Act.

Whether or not an animal is properly stunned and insensible to pain is easy to determine, writes Temple Grandin, PhD, the University of Colorado animal expert whose guidelines "Animal Welfare and Humane Slaughter" are widely observed in the nation's slaughterhouses.

> At no time, either during or after stunning should the animal vocalize (squeal, moo or bellow). Vocalization is a sign that a sensible animal may be feeling pain. It is easy to evaluate insensibility after an animal is hanging vertically on the bleed rail; it should hang straight down and have a straight back, and the head should be limp and floppy. If the stunned animal has kicking reflexes, the head should flop like a limp rag. If the animal makes any attempt to raise its head, it may still be sensible. An animal showing a righting reflex must be immediately re-stunned. There should also be no rhythmic breathing and no eye reflexes in response to touch. Blinking is another sign of an animal that has not been properly stunned and thus may still be sensible.[34]

There are several ways to stun an animal, writes Grandin, but they all carry the risk of being done wrong, such as volts to an animal's head applied improperly; fatigued operators "missing" animals; and equipment malfunctioning, like unmaintained captive blot pistols.[35] The speed of the assembly line is also important because if it moves too fast, the stunner will miss animals, but if the line moves too slowly, animals can regain consciousness in time for painful bleed-out, which the stunning is intended to prevent.

If ethics weren't reason enough for meat processors to practice humane slaughter, the meat of animals that are sensible and struggling at slaughter is also less marketable. Poultry that go into the scalding tank fully alive, known in the industry as "red birds" because it happens so often, are "disfigured and missing body parts because they've struggled so much in the tank," as Tyson's Virgil Butler testified.[36] Pigs that experience stress and panic at slaughter develop pale, soft, and exudative meat (PSE) that is of "poor quality and is generally unacceptable to the consumer."[37]

"Kosher" is widely interpreted as meaning pure, and many think kosher slaughter is better or more humane than traditional methods. But ritual slaughter is capable of causing great suffering, says Grandin.[38] "Some plants use cruel methods of restraint, such as suspending a conscious animal by a chain wrapped around one hind-limb. In more progressive plants, the animal is placed in a restrainer that holds it in a comfortable, upright position," she writes.[39] "Most large cattle slaughter plants are using more comfortable methods of restraint, but there are still some plant managers who have no regard for animal welfare," continues Grandin about kosher slaughter. "They persist in hanging large cattle and veal calves upside down by one hind-leg. There is no religious justification for use of this cruel method of restraint. The plants that suspend cattle/calves by one hind-leg do so in order to avoid paying the cost of installing a humane restraint device. Humane restraint devices can often pay for themselves by improving employee safety."[40]

In both kosher (sanctioned by Jewish law) and halal (sanctioned by Islamic law) slaughter, cattle, sheep, goats, and other animals have their throats cut while fully conscious. Because they are not stunned or otherwise rendered insensate, their consciousness can be "prolonged for over 60 seconds," even though the laws, Grandin notes, were devised to minimize cruelty. Almost half of cattle that are hoisted and shackled bellow loudly, according to one study, and "in some cases, those vocalizations can be heard outside the building," writes Grandin.[41]

Ritual slaughter is illegal in New Zealand, Switzerland, and the Scandinavian and Baltic countries.[42] In 2011, the Dutch parliament voted to approve a ban on kosher and halal slaughter pending Senate approval. There are over one million Muslims and fifty-two thousand Jews in the Netherlands, and both groups take the proposed ban as a direct attack.[43] "This is not about animal rights," said Joe M. Regenstein, then a professor of food science who ran a kosher and halal food program at Cornell University. "It's an invitation to Jews and Muslims to leave."[44] But animal advocates say the opposite: "Ritual slaughter isn't about religious freedom at all but about cruelty to animals."[45] Former actress, sex symbol, and animal rights advocate Brigitte Bardot is a strong critic of ritual slaughter and the holiday Eid al-Adha, during which Muslims ritually slaughter sheep and other animals, often in public. "1,000 sheep were slaughtered last month only 300 yards from my house," she lamented to the *Washington Post*, asking when the French government would enforce its stunning laws, which are similar to those in the United States.[46]

In the United States, the sale of kosher meat has escalated through the perception that it is somehow comparable to organic meat. And, even though some Jews and Muslims might be bitter enemies, meat is one thing they agree on: Muslims "often substitute kosher foods when their own ritually produced and certified halal foods are not available," reports the *Sioux City Journal*.[47]

MEAT PRODUCED BY THE "HONOR SYSTEM"

Being a federal Food Safety and Inspection Service (FSIS) inspector must be the worst job on earth. You are responsible for a plant's compliance with the Humane Methods of Slaughter Act and are probably treated to grotesque, sad, and haunting images that stay with you for life.[48] But only 20 percent of your time can be devoted to humane slaughter, because you're also responsible for the plant's compliance with the Federal Meat Inspection Act (or Poultry Products Inspection Act or the Egg Products Inspection Act), which has to do with the wholesomeness of the meat. Plant managers and employees resent you because any action you take costs them money. And there are few actions you can take—ever since the inspection system Hazard Analysis and Critical Control Points (HACCP) was implemented in 2000. Instead of visually examining carcasses, as meat inspectors used to do, under HACCP, federal inspectors simply ratify that companies are following their own self-created systems—which is to say that it is essentially a system of "Trust us." Even the FSIS district office may not back up inspectors.

The HACCP system was developed by former Monsanto lobbyist Michael Taylor, who is considered an inveterate industry cheerleader.[49] While working at the FDA, he has facilitated the approval of unlabeled genetically engineered (GE) crops and recombinant bovine growth hormone (rBGH), both made by Monsanto, and he has even lobbied against the Delaney Clause, which prohibits cancer-causing chemicals in food.[50] Many think HACCP is also a gift to industry. Food activists call HACCP a "politically-based policy masquerading as a science-based measure" that privatizes the meat inspection process for large plants while regulating smaller plants out of business.[51] It allows contaminated meat to leave the plant with "smaller downstream processors . . . left accountable for problems caused by the original slaughterhouses," writes Nicole Johnson.[52] Many inspectors and meat producers agree.[53]

Soon after HACCP was implemented, a study by the Government Accountability Project and Public Citizen found that 62 percent of inspectors surveyed allowed contamination like feces, vomit, and metal shards in food under HACCP on a *daily or weekly basis*, which had never happened before.[54] Almost 20 percent of inspectors said they'd been instructed not to document violations. In fact, a full 80 percent of 451 inspectors surveyed said that HACCP attenuated their ability to enforce the law and the public's right to know about food safety.[55] No wonder HACCP has been dubbed "Have a Cup of Coffee and Pray."[56]

Dean Wyatt, an FSIS supervisory public health veterinarian from Williston, Vermont, who testified at congressional hearings in 2010 about humane slaughter problems, sounds like the poster boy for the harms of HACCP.[57] At Seaboard Farms, a hog slaughterhouse in Guymon, Oklahoma, and at Bushway Packing, a slaughterhouse in Vermont, his attempts to cite humane slaughter violations were consistently undermined by industry and his own FSIS bosses. "I observed conscious pigs on the conveyor belt; some were moving and one was blinking and breathing regularly," he recounted about Seaboard Farms, where he worked in 2007. "As I stopped by the leg shackle station, a plant employee pointed at the blinking pig, indicating that he knew the pig was conscious, yet the pig was shackled and its neck was slit while it was awake."[58]

Soon afterward, Wyatt testified, he "found pigs already shackled on the slaughter line that were awake and kicking rapidly. They were being stuck with a knife and I verbally ordered the plant to stop operations," he told Congress. "I went to the USDA office to obtain official USDA reject tags to place on the stunning chambers. When I returned to the area, pigs were still being processed despite my suspension order."[59] "After tagging the machinery," continued Wyatt in his testimony, "I wrote an NR [noncompliance report] detailing my findings, which included an admission from a stunning foreman that there were many pigs being shackled and stuck who were conscious." In fact, "workers were trying to use a captive bolt stun gun on the pigs as they moved swiftly upside down along the 'bleed line'—an indication that the Seaboard workers were aware that the animals were conscious." But rather than backing Wyatt up, the FSIS District Office said that Wyatt "was not close enough to have seen" what he reported and granted Seaboard's appeal violation.[60] Wyatt witnessed pigs being unloaded from a truck so aggressively, they were being trampled and crushed, and he suspended inspections, ordering all activity ceased. But a plant manager "willfully" ignored his orders and told him "it was 'normal' for pigs to pile up and that I [Wyatt] needed to use common sense," he said.[61] Again, the FSIS District Office allowed the plant to resume operations in defiance of its own officer.

Emboldened by its friends in high places, the plant installed "rubber partitions and truck panels that prevented FSIS personnel from viewing what was happening inside the trucks and during the off-loading," testified Wyatt.[62] Both Wyatt and public health veterinarian Deena Gregory reported that they witnessed a Seaboard employee hit an "animal hard in the face and nose 8–12 times," but David Ganzel, DVM, then the district veterinary medical specialist, deemed the acts not "egregious," and hence not a violation, said Wyatt.[63] Soon Seaboard employees snickered when Wyatt walked past.

At Bushway Packing, the overt disrespect for government authority and humane slaughter laws continued. There, Wyatt witnessed a cow "shot once near her eye, again in her nose, and was still standing, fully conscious, and obviously suffering." Stunning an animal with a rifle is legal, but FSIS regulations require that one bullet should cause immediate unconsciousness, explained Wyatt. But when the inspector tried to suspend the plant for the egregious humane slaughter violation, "I was told by FSIS management to only document the event on a weekly meeting letter and not to even write an

NR on the issue." The FSIS District Office also deleted and sanitized reports, for example, changing the word "threw" to "dropped" in a report detailing how a worker threw an animal, said Wyatt.[64] Veal calves arriving at Bushway "were destined to spend yet another 12–18 hours without food, when already they had been deprived of sustenance for perhaps days, since they were usually removed from their mothers immediately after birth," said Wyatt. "Sometimes calves are held overnight and it always broke my heart that employees would carry the bodies of these dead baby calves out of the pen because they died of dehydration and starvation. This should be considered inhumane handling."[65] Bushway Packing was shut down by the USDA in the fall of 2009.[66] An employee, Christopher Gaudette, received a sentence of one to three years, "all suspended except for a thirty day sentence," and "forfeited all future rights to participate in any animal husbandry or slaughterhouse activity involving live animals."[67] Bushway Packing had been certified as an "organic processor."

Dean Wyatt, DVM, died shortly after the hearings at the age of fifty-nine. He was a second-generation federal meat inspector whose father died in the "line of duty"—contracting a lethal pathogen at a turkey slaughter plant he inspected. "Public service is in my blood," Dean Wyatt told Congress.[68]

The animal rights group People for the Ethical Treatment of Animals

(PETA) is known for making headlines, which it certainly did in 2004 when it released undercover video from the nation's largest kosher slaughterhouse, Agriprocessors, in Postville, Iowa. The video shows cows very much alive after being "slaughtered" and having their throats cut, and it led to a USDA investigation that "reported many violations of animal cruelty laws at the plant," says the *New York Times*.[69] The undercover activists who shot the video were later identified as Hannah and Phillip Schein, a married couple who keep kosher themselves.[70] The huge Agriprocessors operation supplied kosher meat to the nation (and other countries, including Israel), as well as nonkosher beef, veal, lamb, turkey, and chicken products marketed as Iowa Best Beef, Aaron's Best, and Rubashkin's, all sold at major grocery chains. Most kosher beef is not from dedicated plants like Agriprocessors but from firms that send rabbis into nonkosher slaughterhouses, says the Jewish paper the *Forward*. Kosher meat companies like Empire Kosher and Hebrew National couldn't hold a candle to Agriprocessors's range and type of products, says the newspaper.[71]

When the grisly video surfaced, a coalition of rabbis and kosher certifying agencies in the United States was quick to defend the images. "After the animal has been rendered insensible, it is entirely possible that it may still display certain reflexive actions, including those shown in images portrayed in the video," they wrote on a kosher-certification website.

> These reflexive actions should not be mistaken for signs of consciousness or pain, and they do not affect the kosher status of the slaughtered animal's meat. There may be exceptional circumstances when, due to the closing of jugular veins or a carotid artery after the shechita cut, or due to the noncomplete severance of an artery or vein, the animal may rise up on its legs and walk around. Cases when animals show such signs of life after the slaughter process are extremely rare, and even such an event would not invalidate the shechita if the trachea and esophagus were severed in the shechita cut.[72]

Israel's then Chief Rabbinate also defended the images. "To those unfamiliar with the slaughter industry—kosher or non-kosher—scenes showing postshechita movement of several animals, such as are shown on the video, can be very disturbing. But it must be realized that during the six or seven weeks during which the video was taken, approximately 18,000 animals were slaughtered by the plant in question. With such numbers, it is inevitable that aberrations do sometimes occur," a press statement said. "It is also import- ant to understand that such occurrences are not unique to the AgriProcessors plant, but happen in every abattoir, whether kosher or non-kosher."[73]

But soon Agriprocessors would have more charges to defend. A year and a half after the video, the *Forward* paid a visit to Postville and reopened public scrutiny. "The animals slaughtered here at the nation's largest kosher meat packing plant have been the object of nationwide sympathy since an animal rights group released videos from the kill floor in December 2004," wrote the paper. "But a tour of the mobile homes and cramped apartments just outside town, where AgriProcessors' immigrant workers live, quickly shifts a visitor's attention to a more striking concern: the impoverished humans who do the factory's dirty work."[74] In fact, the *Forward* found hundreds of semiindentured immigrant employees working ten- to twelve-hour shifts, six days a week, for $6.25 to $7 a hour, unable to quit, complain, or even leave Postville, since the miniscule farm town has no public transportation.

Agriprocessors had six Occupational Safety and Health Administration (OSHA) violations in one year, and Equal Employment Opportunity Com- mission (EEOC) complaints that supervisors extorted bribes from workers. Employees were untrained and unprotected from dangerous equipment, reported the *Forward*. Two workers required amputations in *one month*, and one was still working at the plant with a hand missing when the *Forward* vis- ited, "hoping to collect enough to pay off his debts back home."[75] Of course, slaughterhouse jobs are the nation's most dangerous and low paying, but labor leaders, industrial experts, and a Human Rights Watch reporter said they expected kosher slaughterhouses would reflect the fact of their religious affil- iation. Wrong. Working conditions are not a factor considered in the kosher certification process, says the largest certifying agency, the Orthodox Union.[76] While the *Forward* exposé drew mail from readers who reconsidered their consumption of Agriprocessors meat or any kosher meat, it also drew an angry letter from Sholom Rubashkin, Agriprocessors's then plant manager and son of owner Aaron Rubashkin. "PETA has apparently joined forces with the peo- ple who came to Postville to organize a union at Agriprocessors plant," he wrote, implying that the worker charges were driven by unionizers.[77]

Almost two years later, Rubashkin might have thought that PETA and union organizers had joined forces with the federal government. On May 14, 2008, hundreds of officers from US Immigration and Customs Enforcement (ICE) swooped down on Agriprocessors with helicopters in the largest single-site raid in US history, arresting half of the eight-hundred-person workforce. Two hundred and ninety Guatemalans, ninety-three Mexicans, two Israelis, and four Ukrainians were marched off to a waiting phalanx of buses and vans and a makeshift detention center.[78]

Initial charges against Agriprocessors's employees included harboring illegal aliens, use of child labor, document fraud, identity theft, physical and sexual abuse of workers, unsafe working conditions, wage and hour violations, and shorting workers' pay.[79] According to the search warrant, one thousand discrepancies between worker names and social security numbers occurred in three years. There was even a methamphetamine production plant existing within the slaughterhouse, *sanctioned by management*.[80] Even Barack Obama, then an Illinois senator, weighed in on Agriprocessors. "They have kids in there wielding buzz saws and cleavers. It's ridiculous," he said during a campaign stop in Davenport, Iowa.[81]

The Jewish community had mixed feelings about the raid. Twenty-five orthodox rabbis who visited Agriprocessors three months later said they found nothing amiss. "At this point I don't see any reason why someone should not buy things from Agriprocessors," said Rabbi Daniel Moscowitz, then regional director of Chabad Lubavitch of Illinois and president of the Chicago Rabbinical Council. "They run a very impressive operation."[82]

But an op-ed in the *New York Times* by Rabbi Shmuel Herzfeld, then of Ohev Sholom, the National Synagogue, questioned whether a product produced from "abusive practices" could even be considered kosher.[83] And Rabbi Neal Gold, then of Temple Shir Tikva in Wayland, Massachusetts, said of the worker abuse, "We should be outraged. We should be appalled. And we should be humiliated."[84]

Labor leaders lamented what seemed to be a lose-lose situation. "There are no clear winners here. The workers have been freed from jobs which they willingly embraced; they are about to be thrown out of their adopted community," wrote Jon Coppelman, then of *Workers' Comp Insider*. "Jewish consumers

have lost their primary source of kosher meats. The town of Postville has lost
its primary employer and will soon see the evisceration of its tax base."[85]

Three hundred workers served federal prison sentences of five months for
identity theft, and human resources managers and floor supervisors were convicted of felony charges of harboring illegal immigrants. Agriprocessors itself
filed for bankruptcy.[86] While thousands of child-labor charges were initially filed
against Agriprocessors's owner, Aaron Rubashkin; his son Sholom; and others,
the charges were dropped as prosecutors unspooled elaborate financial wrongdoing at the plant, which they pursued instead.[87] In 2008, Sholom Rubashkin was
convicted of eighty-six counts of federal-bank fraud in connection with loans to
the company, including fabricating fake collateral for loans, ordering employees
to create false invoices, and laundering millions through a secret bank account
in the name of Torah Education, reported the *New York Times*.[88] Sentencing documents also suggest the Postville mayor, Robert Penrod, received or extorted
money from Agriprocessors to discourage unionizing at the plant.[89]

But when prosecutors asked for a life sentence for the young Rubashkin,
citing his lawlessness and lack of remorse, more than one dozen former US
attorneys cried to the judge: Unfair! "We cannot fathom how truly sound and
sensible sentencing rules could call for a life sentence—or anything close to
it—for Mr. Rubashkin, a 51-year-old, first-time, nonviolent offender," said
a letter signed by former attorney generals Janet Reno, William Barr, Richard Thornburgh, Edwin Meese III, Ramsey Clark, and Nicholas Katzenbach.
(Nonviolent, except for running a slaughterhouse where animals lost their
lives and people lost their hands.)[90]

But the story has a happy ending . . . for the meat industry. Within
months of the raid, and long before any Rubashkin trials, Agriprocessors had
replaced most of the lost "knockers, stickers, bleeders, tail rippers, flankers,
gutters, sawers, [and] plate boners," industry names for specialized slaughterhouse workers. Recruitment firms hired by Agriprocessors canvassed homeless shelters, bus stations, chapel services, and other slaughterhouses, and ran
ads in Spanish-language newspapers and on Mexican radio stations in the
Rio Grande Valley to replenish the workforce. (One recruitment firm, Labor
Ready, says it recalled 150 workers days after placing them, over Agriprocessors's "safety conditions.")[91]

Agriprocessors soon discovered, just as the meatpackers JBS Swift, Tyson Foods, and Gold'n Plump already had, that Somalis were ideal slaughterhouse workers because of their legal status in the United States as refugees fleeing civil war and their willingness to accept low wages.[92] Palauans from the Palau Islands in the Pacific, near Guam, are also legal workers in the United States, and Agriprocessors had hired one hundred of the new workers six months after the raid.[93] Some note that Somalis, Sudanese, and Pacific Islanders are replacing Hispanic slaughterhouse workers, just like the Hispanic workers replaced Eastern European workers one decade ago, as meat processors pursue the lowest possible wage.

In fact, the replenished workforce at Agriprocessors was buzzing along so nicely after the raid that some saw a Steinbeck novel in the "stew of humanity" that included "Muslims from Sudan packing chickens in a Jewish kosher plant."[94] "Postville's groove—the characteristic that makes it special—is that disadvantaged people, through dint of hard labor, can still come here and build a better life for their children," said Maryn Olson, then a community leader helping former Agriprocessors workers.[95] "It's not about what you have or where you came from. Work is the great equalizer, and everyone who's willing to work hard has a chance to get ahead in Postville."[96]

Photographers shot pictures of the Somalis, Sudanese, Palauans, and Guatemalans (some still wearing arrest bracelets on their legs) as if they were in Iowa to exchange cultural traditions or folk art instead of to slit animals' throats for six dollars an hour to keep America in cheap meat.[97] Meanwhile, Agriprocessors got a new owner named Hershey Friedman after its 2009 bankruptcy. The Canadian businessman immediately rehired "hundreds" of original employees, including a Rubashkin son, son-in-law, and grandson.[98] The kosher slaughterhouse was renamed Agri-Star.

Chapter 12

MAD COW DISEASE— FORGOTTEN BUT NOT NECESSARILY GONE

There is good news and there is bad news about mad cow disease in the United States. The good news is that it seems to be gone from the food supply for now and US beef exports are limping back. The bad news is, if it comes back, government denial, ineptitude, and supplication to Big Ag (like protecting the identities of afflicted ranches or food outlets) put everyone at risk.

Mad cow disease is a fatal transmissible spongiform encephalopathy (TSE), known as bovine spongiform encephalopathy (BSE) in cows and as chronic wasting disease (CWD) in deer and elk. In humans, it is a terminal neurological brain disease called variant Creutzfeldt-Jakob disease (vCJD), and it shares some features with Alzheimer's disease, though it is rarer.

Many people remember England's bout with mad cow disease in the 1990s, when thousands of cows contracted the disease and millions more were destroyed because they were at risk. But fewer remember the United States' experience with mad cow disease, during which three mad cows were confirmed, and in some cases eaten, and untested cows eluded inspection, leading to worldwide boycotts of US beef.

There are many scare stories about mad cow disease: that flies and mosquitoes can transmit it; that milk and cosmetics carry it; that household pets, pigs, and fish can get it; that animals used in mad-cow research are in the food supply; and, of course, that people diagnosed with Alzheimer's disease really have vCJD. But the actual facts about BSE and vCJD are frightening enough that they need no urban legends to embellish them.

Scrapie, a degenerative disease in sheep and goats; BSE; vCJD in humans; and CWD in elk and deer are all believed to be transmitted by prions, invisible infectious particles that are not viruses or bacteria but proteins. Though prions are not technically "alive" because they lack a nucleus, they manage to reproduce and are almost impossible to "kill." Prions are essentially indestructible. They are not inactivated by cooking, heat, autoclaves, ammonia, bleach, hydrogen peroxide, alcohol, phenol, lye, formaldehyde, or radiation, and they remain in the soil, contaminating it for years. Alcohol actually makes prions more transmissible by binding them to metal like surgical instruments. A scientific paper says that after a prion-contaminated electrode was treated with "benzene, 70 percent ethanol, and formaldehyde vapor," it still transmitted CJD to two patients.[1] Needless to say, surgeons and morticians approach vCJD cases with trepidation.

But surgery is not the only way prions are transmitted to the public. Researchers at the University of Wisconsin–Madison report that prions also survive wastewater decontamination and can "end up in discharged treated water or in fertilizers made from the wastes."[2] In fact, authorities stopped a 2006 mad-cow study at the National Animal Disease Laboratory in Ames, Iowa, when the facility's own lab workers said that improperly treated infectious wastes were being released into the city's water-treatment plant, which empties into the Skunk River.[3] Residents near a Division of Wildlife facility in Fort Collins, Colorado, that also researches prions had similar worries since the facility is located near the city's raw water-treatment plant and houses infected animals.[4]

Officials with the US Department of Agriculture (USDA), which runs the Ames facility charged with confirming national cases of mad cow, don't even sound like they "get it." They said the "heat treatment" that was used to destroy prions at the facility is "an approved method that deactivates the protein that causes the disease," reported the *Des Moines Register*. Lab workers, on the other hand, disagreed and said bleaching then cooking was safer and was the method used by "other labs."[5] It sounds like the lab workers also don't get it.

Earlier in the year, at the Ames facility, before the Skunk River fears, plumbers fixing a pipe in the lab caused a sewage backup that included discarded animals and flooded the yard. But "workers bleached the area, and the workers said the water did not get near the storm sewer," says the *Register*.[6]

Many people have forgotten the infighting, misinformation, and bumbling idiocy that marked the federal response to the first US mad cows between 2004 and 2007. Ag officials openly disagreed with each other, contradicted themselves, and didn't even seem to understand mad cow disease's transmissibility. But there was a darker side to the comedy of errors: the government's willingness to put the well-being of US beef markets over the well-being of food consumers.

On December 23, 2003, as the nation headed into Christmas, the USDA announced that a Holstein cow, imported from Canada and slaughtered in Moses Lake, Washington, on December 9 for human food, tested positive for mad cow disease. Ann Veneman, then USDA secretary, along with other USDA officials, said it was discovered because it was a "downer" (unable to walk), indicating that the mad cow–testing program worked since it screened downers as the main source of mad-cow risk. But three workers who saw the animal said it walked just fine.[7] What followed, believe it or not, were congressional hearings, a federal criminal investigation, and a General Accounting Office (GAO) investigation largely over *whether or not the animal walked to slaughter*. Because if the animal looked fine and walked under its own steam to slaughter, the entire federal mad cow–testing program was misconceived and was letting millions of similar animals into the food supply. But if the slaughterhouse workers were lying, as the government hoped, and the animal was prodded or fork-lifted to slaughter, we might have a farming system that values money over living things and chews them up and spits them out, but at least the mad-cow alert system works.[8]

In testimony before Congress, then USDA inspector general Phyllis K. Fong blamed "procedural errors" for the conflicting data about whether or not the animal walked, and said an employee "who alleged that the BSE-positive cow was ambulatory and healthy when it arrived at the facility described a different animal from the one that arrived in the same trailer and later tested BSE-positive."[9]

Unfortunately, that was not the only government discrepancy. There were two very different versions of what happened to the meat from the Washington State mad cow. The government said, "By December 27, 2003, FDA had located all potentially-infectious product rendered from the BSE-positive cow in Washington State. This product was disposed of in a landfill in accordance with Federal, State and local regulations."[10]

But the *Los Angeles Times* reported that despite "a voluntary recall aimed at recovering all 10,000 pounds of beef slaughtered at the plant the day the Washington state cow was killed, some meat, which could have contained the Washington cow, was sold to restaurants in several Northern California counties."[11] And eaten, it turns out.

"In an interview, Alameda County health officer Dr. Anthony Iton recalled that in early January 2004, almost a month after the initial discovery, state health officials informed him that five restaurants in the Oakland area had received soup bones from the lot of tainted beef," says the *Times*. "It immediately dispatched inspectors to the restaurants. But it was too late; soup made from the bones had been eaten. He was particularly disturbed to learn that none of the restaurant owners had received written notice of the recall and that federal inspectors did not visit them until 10 days after the recall."[12]

There was a third affront to food consumers besides letting the mad cow into the food supply and lying about it: the California Department of Health Services officials *protected the identities* of stores or restaurants that purchased the meat, reported the *San Francisco Chronicle*. "Alameda and Santa Clara counties have been informed by the state that 11 local restaurants and a market purchased soup bones from the suspect lot, but they have also declined to identify which establishments purchased them," said the *Chronicle*. "The U.S. Department of Agriculture insists the recall is precautionary and the meat poses no health risk.[13]

There was yet a *fourth* affront to consumers when then USDA spokesman Matthew Baun told them that *the recall information was a trade secret*, and they had to call restaurants themselves to find out if any food they ate was at risk. It is "up to consumers to check with their grocers, butchers or restaurants to find out if any of the recalled meat may have landed on their tables," said Baun. "We are prohibited from releasing information that companies would consider proprietary. If you are concerned whether you may have purchased the product, you can call your retail store. They would know. . . . The only way to know for sure is to contact stores."[14]

And there were more risks than those found in the meat at restaurants and stores whose identities were protected in Alameda and Santa Clara Counties. Eleven head of cattle thought to have eaten the same feed as the Washington cow were also never found. Nor did authorities ever find out the "source of the feed thought to have sickened the Holstein" says the Associated Press.[15]

State and federal governments may have saved some domestic beef outlets by protecting their identities, but they couldn't salvage US beef's world export markets. Within twenty-four hours of the USDA's mad-cow announcement, Mexico, Russia, Brazil, South Africa, Hong Kong, Japan, Singapore, Taiwan, Malaysia, South Korea, and ninety other countries banned US beef.[16] (The only reason the European Union didn't ban it was because it had *already* banned it for its high use of growth hormones.[17]) Ninety-eight percent of the United States' three-billion-dollar overseas beef market evaporated almost overnight.

Some US beef producers tried to retain their export business by pledging to their foreign-trading partners to conduct their *own* mad-cow testing, but the US government sought an injunction against them. The government said wider testing did not guarantee food safety and could result in false positives that could scare consumers.[18] (The government came to eat its words when, instead of false positives, *false negatives* pertaining to mad cow appeared.)

One week after the Washington State mad cow was discovered, the USDA announced a ban on downers in the food supply and a new requirement to remove specified risk materials (SRM) from cattle to be eaten by humans.[19] Specified risk materials included the brain, skull, eyes, spinal cord, tonsils, spleen, lymph tissue, and most of the vertebral column and small intestine, said the government. "Science indicates that in animals with BSE, these materials harbor the infectious agent before the animal shows any clinical signs of disease."[20]

Feeding cows to cows, widely believed to have caused mad cow disease, was already banned, though beef producers were allowed to use up their existing "cannibal" feeds. The new bans also restricted "advanced meat recovery" and "air-injection stunning," two procedures that also increase SRM in final products. Food-safety and consumer-advocate groups were not appeased. What about milk replacer? they asked—the *blood* that is fed to weaning calves instead of their mothers' milk? After all, blood certainly carries prions.[21] What about chicken feed, which is up to 30 percent meat and bonemeal, according to the FDA, and is fed to cows as chicken "litter" with feces and feathers swept up from barn floors? (At least their recycling efforts are admirable.) Both "foodstuffs" were still allowed under the SRM ban.

And what about all the other places in a cow (or deer) where prions could be residing besides the SRM? Studies in scientific journals have found prions in the muscles and flesh of infected animals and in their kidneys, pancreases, livers, blood, and saliva.[22] A study in *PLoS Pathogens* found that prions likely accumulate in animal's *fat*, too.[23] Articles in the journal *Science* warned that "humans consuming or handling meat from CWD-infected deer are at risk to prion exposure" and that even casual contact with infected animals could put people at risk.[24]

"All parts of the carcass contain the CWD agent," Ed Hoover, then a Colorado State University distinguished professor in the Department of Microbiology, Immunology, and Pathology warned deer hunters about prions.[25]

Another risk, according to Michael Hansen, PhD, senior scientist with Consumers Union, which publishes *Consumer Reports*, came from the fact that the government allowed feed that was labeled "Do not feed to cattle and other ruminants" to be given to other animals on the farm.[26]

> "Effectively, FDA is saying that it will cost renderers and the feed industry too much to dispose of all SRMs. All SRMs couldn't just be deposited in a land fill, because the potential infectivity of these tissues can survive in the soil; a study demonstrated that scrapie-infected hamster brain buried for three years still contained detectable infectivity," he writes. "But rather than burden the industry with disposal costs, FDA will allow them to dispose of this material in animal feed. This FDA view is clearly bending to the economic concerns of the feed industry at the expense of public health."[27]

Slaughterhouses are not even capturing the tissues determined to be SRM, admits the government in a Food Safety and Inspection Service (FSIS) report issued in 2008. "FSIS cannot effectively demonstrate that its verification of establishment controls and written procedures for the removal, segregation, and disposition of SRMs is adequate to detect noncompliance," says the report. "Inspectors did not always detect or consistently document noncompliances with SRM control requirements."[28]

One example of slaughterhouse "noncompliance" is reuse of sawing equipment for at-risk cows. Cows over thirty months of age are considered to be at risk of mad cow, whereas cows under thirty months are considered risk-free. "The establishment did not break down and clean the equipment" between the two animal groups, says the government report about one facility. Worse, the supervisory public health veterinarian said the reuse was okay, "because there were no 'visible SRMs' on the equipment."[29] Visible?

You don't have to be a scientist to see what a hygienic farce this is. First of all, you can't "see" the prions, so equipment would need to be broken down and cleaned all the time. But prions are indestructible, so they can't be "cleaned" away, anyway! But, according to the report, *even FSIS Headquarters officials* "believed the sanitizer spray was sufficient to address the problem"— suggesting that the inmates are guarding the asylum when it comes to mad-cow prevention.[30] Even the arbitrary designation of calves under thirty months as risk-free is contested in the scientific literature.[31]

The National Joint Council of Food Inspection Locals, the union that represents meat and poultry inspectors in federally regulated slaughterhouses, was even more blunt about the risks than the FSIS report. In a letter to the USDA in 2004, the union said that SRM was "being allowed into the production chain."[32] Heads and carcasses of cattle over thirty months old sailed through slaughter and processing lines, said the whistle-blowing inspectors. "We couldn't determine that every part out of there was from a cow under 30 months," said Stan Painter, the union's then chairman, to MSNBC. "There was no way to determine which one was which."[33]

Inspectors were "told not to intervene" when kidneys from older animals were sent down the line to be packed for the Mexican market, which prohibits cows over thirty months, the union charged.[34] Lester Friedlander, DVM, a former USDA meat inspector, corroborates the union allegations. Friedlander says a USDA official told him in 1991 not to say anything if he ever discovered a case of mad cow disease, and that he knew of cows that had tested positive at private laboratories but were ruled negative by the USDA.[35] Friedlander told United Press International that the USDA attempted to force him out after he alleged, on national TV, that meat from downer cows supplied the school-lunch programs, a charge that later proved true and led to the biggest meat recall in US history.[36]

BE CAREFUL WHAT YOU EAT AND WHAT YOU *EAT* EATS

Even without mad cow disease, the 2000s were cruel to the US meat industry.

- Just as most people had forgotten about the heart attack in 1988 suffered by actor James Garner, the face of the "Real Food for Real People" beef campaign, the chairman and CEO of McDonald's Corporation, Jim Cantalupo, suffered a fatal heart attack at a company event in 2004.
- Charlie Bell, Cantalupo's replacement as McDonald's CEO, was diagnosed with colon cancer two weeks after taking office.
- *Fast Food Nation* and *The Omnivore's Dilemma*, books unfriendly to the meat industry, stayed on bestseller lists for years.
- Video of abused downer cows sparked the largest meat recall in US history, tarring the National School Lunch Program in 2008.
- Both Oprah Winfrey and Bill Clinton flirted with meat-free diets.
- Martha Stewart, the doyenne of taste and nutrition, broadcast a vegetarian Thanksgiving show in 2009.
- More than one-half of Americans cut back on meat because of the 2008 recession.[37]
- The National Association of State Departments of Agriculture tried to increase Supplemental Nutrition Assistance Program (SNAP) meat allowances to get rid of "the oversupply."[38]
- A world outbreak of swine flu in 2009 was linked, said some news sources, to factory pig farms. (The meat industry beseeched the press to call the disease the H1N1 flu.)[39]
- More than twenty-four workers in pork slaughterhouses in charge of pulverizing pork brains developed a debilitating nerve condition—that didn't go away.[40]
- Red meat was regularly linked to cancer and heart disease, and scientific organizations told the public to limit its intake.[41]
- Warnings about nitrites and nitrates in processed meat linked the preservatives to cancers of the colon, esophagus, liver, lung, and pancreas, and even to Alzheimer's disease.[42]
- Ninety-five percent of registered dietitians said that people in the

United States were getting too *much* protein in their diets, not too little![43]

Even the government, which has the dual role of supporting the meat industry and protecting the public's health, got into the act of meat bashing. After years of warning consumers about the dangers of *undercooked* meat and bacteria lurking on cutting boards and utensils, it began warning consumers about *overcooked* meat. "Heterocyclic amines" and "polycyclic aromatic hydrocarbons," said the government, from dripping fat and *grilled* meat, were highly linked to breast, colon, stomach, and prostate cancers.[44]

By 2012, the best thing any nutritionist would say about red meat was that it could "be part of" or "contribute to" a healthy diet. So can sawdust. So can street tar. So can cigarettes. Still, no bad news about red meat took as swift and devastating a toll on US beef as mad cow disease. Two of the top-three importing nations did not immediately reopen their doors to beef after the US mad-cow scare—Japan, worth $1.5 billion a year, and South Korea, worth $800 million a year. Beef trade with Canada, which had represented $2 billion to the United States, was also shut.[45]

In fact, Mike Johanns, the new agriculture secretary who followed Ann Veneman, was summoned to Washington, DC, to explain the trade mess to senators even though he was not even in office when the Washington State cow was found. Meat producers and members of the Senate Agriculture Committee were especially miffed about the reclosing of the Canadian border because *more* mad cows had surfaced, just as the border was due for reopening. Whereas the Washington cow was born before a ban on feeding cows to cows, subsequent mad cows in Canada were born *after* the ban and therefore implied leaks in the safety system.[46]

But even as Secretary Johanns, the former governor of Nebraska, appealed, hat in hand, to the intransigent Asian trade partners to resume trade, the unthinkable happened: the United States found a *second* mad cow. Unlike the first cow, which was born in Canada, the second was homegrown on a Texas ranch (the identity of which was protected by the government). The twelve-year-old cow was born and raised on the Texas ranch and never traveled off the premises, said the Associated Press.[47]

And that was just the beginning. The Texas-born cow, discovered eleven months after the Washington cow, had been tested twice by US authorities (unbeknownst to the public) and found to be okay, as in "false negative." But Phyllis Fong, the inspector general also involved with the first mad cow, ordered the more precise "Western blot" test to be conducted in the United Kingdom, because she had doubts—and she had done so over Johann's head and behind his back. When tests came back in June of 2005, seven months after suspicions, the cow indeed was found to have mad cow disease.[48]

It's hard to know who was madder about the second mad cow—beef producers, trading partners, Congress, or Johanns himself, whose authority had been undermined. "From my standpoint, I believe I was put there to operate the department and was very disappointed," Johanns said to reporters about Fong's unilateralism.[49]

Consumers had a right to be angry, too, had they even known. During the seven-month delay while the Texas cow was considered safe, they were possibly eating its herd mates or offspring. And the government's eventual investigation of 413 suspicious cows connected to the Texas cow revealed that *85 percent—350 cows*—probably went into the human food supply, reported the *Dallas Morning News*.[50]

Asked why the United States' best technology was missing mad cows—a bigger issue than Fong's unilateralism—Johanns conceded to reporters that prion distribution in a brain could make "it possible for one sample to test negative while another sample might test positive," reported the *Houston Chronicle*. He also conceded that "the protocol we developed just a few years ago to conduct the tests, including the type of antibody used, might not be the best option today."[51]

Amazingly, suspicions of a second mad cow, so soon after the first one, did not further damage relations with Japan as the United States was trying to woo it back. "We entered negotiations with Japan with them knowing full well we were in the surveillance program, that we may find others and still they went forward with the agreement," said John Lawrence, a livestock economist with the Iowa State University Extension to the Associated Press. The suspect cow would not have been a candidate for a Japan export anyway, he said.[52] But in January of 2005, something else happened that *did* further damage relations with Japan: one month after Japan agreed to start importing US beef again, younger cattle, a shipment to Japan was discovered to contain SRM—banned backbone material—and Japan reimposed the trade ban. Japanese officials no doubt felt like Charlie Brown trying to kick the football as Lucy pulled it away yet again, but so did US beef producers. "Japan has been jerking us around with another stalling tactic," said Sen. Conrad Burns (R-MT). "It's time they open the market."[53] Meanwhile, Japan had replaced US beef with beef from Australia, New Zealand, and South America, and probably had no pressing need to reopen US trade, especially if it was going to get SRM "presents."[54]

To smooth over what was rapidly becoming an international incident, the USDA conducted a self-policing "export verification audit" and came up with twelve recommended improvements for trade relations, like requiring a second signature on export certificates, additional training of inspection export personnel, and delisting and investigating the company that shipped the SRM.[55] (The Department of Agriculture relisted Atlantic Veal and Lamb, the company that shipped the veal with backbone still attached, as a legal exporter after one year.[56])

But in a phone conversation with Johanns, Japan's then agriculture min-

ister, Shoichi Nakagawa, told the ag secretary that some of the US audit findings did not reassure Japan at all—like investigators' inability to verify SRM procedures and the United States' lax controls of downer cows.[57] Legally, the downers could be slaughtered for food in the United States, only if they were known to have suffered an acute injury after passing a previous inspection.

No kidding! In the USDA's export verification report, nine meatpackers and slaughterhouses were found to be in noncompliance with SRM policies, and elsewhere it was reported that the gigantic Swift & Co. plant in Grand Island, Nebraska, was banned from shipping beef to Japan altogether.[58]

Just as worrying, the report found that twenty-nine downers at two *unidentified* slaughterhouses (we wouldn't want them to go out of business) went into the human food supply, and twenty were *not tested* for mad cow disease.[59] The reason they were not tested was even more appalling: government inspectors "stated they did not believe that they had the authority" to go into the pens where the animals were held and get samples, says the report.[60] Was that the final result of HACCP's demotion of inspectors?

In answers to written questions from Japanese ag officials, Johanns said the twenty-nine cattle were healthy until they arrived at the slaughterhouses, "where they suddenly became unable to walk because of injury or other factors," reported Eiji Hirose of *Yomiuri Shimbun/Daily Yomiuri*. Johanns did not give any "clear evidence for his conclusion," wrote Hirose, and his overall comments appeared "to show the U.S. government does not take the issue seriously enough."[61]

Nevertheless, four months later Japan announced it would resume US beef imports pending inspection of US slaughterhouses by its own agriculture officials who wanted to witness firsthand the removal of spinal cords and other SRM.[62] Teams of Japanese officials inspected thirty-five US slaughterhouses, but some slaughterhouses declined a visit. "There are a lot of guys who don't want to go through the hassle of these inspections," explained Deven Scott, then executive vice president of the North American Meat Processors Association.[63]

CLUSTER BOMBS

Needless to say, the only thing more harmful to the US beef industry and US trade than *rumors* of mad cows is rumors of humans with vCJD (the human form of mad cow disease.) And the only thing worse than *humans* with vCJD is *clusters* of humans with vCJD.

Not all cases of Creutzfeldt-Jakob disease (CJD) come from eating infected meat. Most cases, according to government sources, originate spontaneously and are called sporadic CJD, or originate genetically and are called hereditary CJD. Variant CJD tends to occur in younger patients and has a different clinical course, but a diagnosis can only be made from a brain biopsy, usually after death. Also, neither sporadic nor hereditary CJD, which are both randomly sprinkled in the population, would occur in clusters the way variant Creutzfeldt-Jakob disease (vCJD) from eating meat could or would.[64]

In fact, three months after the Washington cow surfaced, the Centers for Disease Control and Prevention (CDC) and the New Jersey Department of Health and Senior Services agreed to investigate a potential "cluster" of nine to thirteen or more possible vCJD cases in southern New Jersey.[65] The cases were unified by ties to the Garden State Racetrack in Cherry Hill and possibly infected beef eaten there, said Janet Skarbek, a New Jersey activist who believes the cases are from mad cow disease.[66] But two months later, the CDC's *Morbidity and Mortality Weekly Report* declared that five of the racetrack-related cases were sporadic CJD, not variant CJD; six were "probable" CJD but not variant (brain tissue wasn't available); three were *not* CJD; and three were still under investigation.[67] Fourteen CJD deaths among racetrack attendees in a little over nine years "would not be considered unusual," soothed the CDC, stressing that sporadic CJD and variant CJD are different diseases.

But of course, the CDC release also conveys the problem with vCJD— and mad cow in cows for that matter: the disease can't be diagnosed without an autopsy or brain biopsy.[68] And even with brain samples, tests can produce false negatives, as seen with the second mad cow in Texas. No wonder people are cynical when they are reassured that a CJD case in their area is sporadic and *not from the meat* while the patient is still alive.

Since there is a "small, but definite, risk that the surgeon or others who handle the brain tissue may become accidentally infected by self-inoculation," says the National Institute of Neurological Disorders and Stroke, it's not always easy to have CJD tests even conducted.[69] In fact, the difficulty in getting a true diagnosis of variant or sporadic CJD, even at top government centers, is evidenced in the case of Patrick Hicks, who died of apparent CJD in California in 2004 at the age of forty-nine.[70]

Ron Bailey, then a neurologist at Riverside Medical Center in Riverside, California, who treated Hicks, said that "clinically, the case did look like it was variant CJD—no question about that." However, the National Prion Disease Pathology Surveillance Center (NPDPSC) in Cleveland ruled Hick's condition as *sporadic* CJD after receiving a brain sample. It was when Bailey asked the Prion Center to perform a more accurate, genetic test that the troubles began. Bailey was told there was no frozen brain sample from Hicks, an omission in defiance of the center's own protocols, which require a frozen sample.[71] A different Prion Center employee told Bailey the entire brain had been "fixed in formalin," by a party other than the center, which would make genetic analysis or other tests impossible.[72]

Pursuing the matter and, no doubt, wondering how the center could "diagnose" Hicks's brain at all with imperfect specimens, Bailey was told by an employee that the center had actually used 1-800-Autopsy (not a joke) of Los Angeles to collect the brain sample, reports United Press International.[73] A spokesperson at 1-800-Autopsy confirmed to Bailey that the company had sent Hicks's sample but said his and all samples are never frozen because "we don't have the capability to freeze it."[74] (The required refrigeration equipment was too expensive, said the employee.) Worse, the government knew that 1-800-Autopsy did not have the ability to freeze brain tissue, according to center protocols, when it ordered the sample, said the employee.[75] When Bailey asked the Prion Center why would it would use a supplier unable to follow its own protocols, he got no answer.[76]

The Prion Center was not the only entity that could not or would not pursue vCJD cases, Bailey found out. The Riverside County coroner's office refused to conduct an autopsy on Hicks even after the Prion Center phoned them, says Bailey, which led to the use of 1-800-Autopsy's services.[77] "If you have a condition that is this rare with the potential to be the first variant CJD case in the state, it raises questions in my mind why they would be so reluctant to do an autopsy on him," observed Bailey.[78]

After the New Jersey cluster that wasn't, other suspected vCJD clusters surfaced. Nine people were diagnosed with a "rare brain disease" in Idaho in 2005. Three tested positive for "an infectious disease of the nervous system," with tests outstanding, two cases proved negative, and four people were buried without autopsies, reported the *Herald Journal*.[79] One woman told the *Journal* that funeral homes refused to handle her husband's body if he had an autopsy because the risks would be greater, so she had to forfeit one.[80]

Then, in 2007, a "rare degenerative brain disorder" was suspected in the deaths of four people in northeastern Indiana, all within five months of each other.[81] Even though statistically the Fort Wayne area would have one CJD death a year, health officials said the four deaths "appear to be from classic [sporadic] CJD and not related to mad cow disease," reported the Associated Press.[82]

Two years later, Tennessee health officials investigated a confirmed and suspected CJD case, which relatives of victims feared was from beef, saying the "odds of two cases within the same county diagnosed at about the same time are astronomical."[83] But Jiri Safar, MD, a top prion researcher, told the *Knoxville News Sentinel* the chances of the deaths being linked to mad cow disease were "extremely remote or nil."[84]

And there were other reassurances before the facts were in. When a CJD patient was admitted to an Amarillo, Texas, hospital in 2008, making cattle futures at the Chicago Mercantile Exchange sink, Ted McCollum, then a beef-cattle specialist with the Amarillo office of Texas AgriLife Extension, called the case sporadic before tests were concluded and on the same day health officials said they didn't know.[85] And in Kansas, the doctor of a fifty-three-year-old man who died of CJD said it was "not the mad cow version" before tests and despite the man's history of being a slaughterhouse worker and elk hunter.[86] Hospital health officials have also termed CJD patients "sporadic" and not "variant" before they can possibly know in instances where surgical instruments might have spread the disease.

Texas got more scares in 2010 when two "mysterious" cases of CJD surfaced in McLennan County.[87] It was "a statistical anomaly considering that only one in 1 million people worldwide is affected by the condition in any given year," said the *Waco Tribune-Herald*. Nevertheless, Hammad Akram, MD, then the health district's epidemiologist, said the two cases were not linked.[88]

A quick visit to the Texas Department of State Health Services website shows a map that is not reassuring. Cases of CJD in Texas have been rising dramatically since 2006, though the cases have not been ruled as vCJD. The map shows two areas that have had thirteen to twenty-one cases in the last decade, indicating what could possibly be clusters.[89] And, after former Buffalo mayor James D. Griffin passed away from CJD in 2009, Laszlo Mechtler, MD, then of the Dent Neurologic Institute, who helped treat Griffin, cited a "cluster" of three confirmed cases in western New York but said he did not feel it was from mad cow and people shouldn't worry.[90]

There used to be a joke among newspaper people that headlines will never say "Plane Landed Safely Today." But federal and state governments are so eager to prevent the panic, social upheaval, and overnight collapse of agricultural markets that a vCJD outbreak or cluster would bring that headlines became similarly positive when suspected cases were cleared. "Elmore County Man Tests Negative for CJD," read an Associated Press headline during the Idaho scare. The news reduced "to seven the possible CJD cases in Idaho this year."[91]

But the beef industry has two agricultural parachutes if a mad-cow outbreak or cluster does occur: Variant CJD has such a long incubation period, it would be impossible to prove the food source biologically or legally. And federal and state governments will probably shield the identity of implicated businesses, as they have done before.

TRACE-BACKS AND FALLBACKS

The seven-month delay between when a Texas cow was suspected of having mad cow disease and when it was confirmed to have it is just the beginning of questions about government handling policies of the second US mad cow.

The twelve-year-old "cream-colored Brahma cross" from an unidentified Texas operation was sold by a farmer (whose identity was protected) at a livestock sale and purchased by an order buyer who sent the cow to the slaughterhouse four days later, according to the government final report.[92] But when the truck arrived at H&B Packing in Waco, the animal was already dead, reported the *Star-Telegram*, and so she was transported instead to Champion Pet Food, which was across town.[93] Even though there were reports that the cow was unable to walk at the livestock sale where she was nonetheless sold for meat, the farmer who owned her told government investigators that "the cow had always been excitable and had fallen while she was being loaded to go to the market, but that this was not unusual behavior for her"[94] (Notice how animals never have poor health, they have "accidents". . . .) The farmer was "relatively sure" he had not kept any offspring from the cow, which could have been eaten by the public, but "there were essentially no records maintained on the index farm," reported the government.[95] So, who really knows?

The important thing, from the perspective of similar cow operations, was that, despite selling for food an animal that couldn't walk, maintaining no records, and having murky ownership of the farm itself, according to investigators, the farm was cleared to resume selling meat within one month.[96] Why should a meat operation suffer just because it risked the lives of people who ate its product?

On March 13, 2006, a deep-red, crossbred beef cow estimated to be ten years old from an Alabama operation became the third US mad cow.[97] As with the Texas cow, several tests had to be conducted at government centers before the Alabama cow was found to be positive for the disease.[98] And like the Texas cow, it was a downer and "had at her side a 2- to 3-week old red Charolais cross female calf" at the time of her death.[99] The identity of the Alabama operation was also protected. Despite investigations at thirty-seven farms, "investigators were unable to locate the herd of origin," says the government report about the Alabama cow.[100]

Of course, Americans were to see a lot more downer cows, unable to walk to slaughter and possibly harboring mad cow disease, when a Humane Society of the United States (HSUS) video surfaced in 2008 from Westland/Hallmark Meat Company in Chino, California. Meat from the dying cows, which were forced to their feet with cruel methods, was going to the National School Lunch Program just as the federal meat inspector Lester Friedlander had said.

The violation of FSIS regulations, which prohibit downers in the food supply and the abuse of defenseless, sick animals, was so flagrant and linked to government programs, it forced hearings on Capitol Hill.[101] One hundred and forty-three million pounds of beef were recalled in the largest meat recall in history.[102] Still, something unexpected came out of the Westland/Hallmark–School Lunch scandal: When then agriculture secretary Edward Schafer, who had replaced Mike Johanns by 2008, tried to tell the public the same thing that USDA spokesman Matthew Baun had said four years earlier—that the identity of stores selling risky meat was proprietary and none of the public's business, people said, *"You're protecting WHO?"*

The Bush administration was forced to reverse its position on shield laws. "People want to know if they need to be on the lookout for recalled meat and poultry from their local store," conceded Schafer, and health departments obligingly published long rosters of establishments that had received the meat.[103]

The Westland/Hallmark beef recall had another effect besides roiling public appetites and cattle markets: it reopened the beef industry's original export travail. As the United States and South Korea prepared to sign the free-trade agreement, KORUS FTA, South Korean citizens who had seen the Westland/Hallmark video staged demonstrations in Seoul and in twenty-two other South Korean cities. "We Don't Like the FDA," "Mad Cow, You Eat It!" and "Send Mad Cow to the Presidential Office!" they chanted at candlelight vigils, some protestors dressed in cow costumes. Some called the demonstrations a "naembi phenomenon," named after a type of Korean copper-alloy pot that heats up and cools down very quickly.[104]

The KORUS FTA agreement, drafted one year earlier but not yet signed, would boost two-way trade between the nations to $98 billion a year, from $78 billion, under the condition that South Korea lift almost all restrictions on US beef, including the age requirement of butchered cattle.[105] KORUS FTA was considered the most significant event in South Korea–US relations since the 1953 military accord and was punctuated by a visit from newly elected South Korean president Lee Myung-bak to Camp David, where no South Korean president had ever been invited. Lee was considered a pro-American conservative, unlike his predecessor Roh Moo-hyun, who was elected on an anti-American platform.[106]

Boosting South Koreans' fears was a professor of medicine at Hallym University in Chuncheon, who reported that South Koreans were genetically more vulnerable to vCJD, a claim other scientists refuted.[107] Because South Korean cuisine "includes cow bones and intestines that are believed to have a higher concentration of prions," wrote Cho Jin-seo in *Korea Times*, South Koreans felt they were at greater risk.[108] There were also Internet rumors about mad cow-tainted cosmetics, diapers, sanitary napkins, and noodles.

South Koreans also worried about the wording of the pact. They interpreted the KORUS FTA prohibition of "the use of the entire carcass of cattle not inspected and passed for human consumption, unless the cattle are less than 30 months of age, or the brains and spinal cords have been removed" to mean that uninspected cattle less than thirty months old or cattle older than thirty months but stripped of SRM were fair game.[109] Until the Washington State mad cow in 2003, South Korea was among the top three importers of US beef.[110] It had eased the ban in 2006 only to find banned backbone material—an eerie parallel to the Japan incident—and rebanned the meat.[111] It must have been déjà vu to beef producers.

Adding to the embarrassment of the nightly vigils in South Korea, during Lee's visit to Camp David, a possible US vCJD case surfaced. It was a "perfect storm" case—the woman was twenty-two years old—vCJD cases tend to be younger people—and she had never traveled to countries known to have mad cow disease.[112] Richard Raymond, MD, then USDA undersecretary for food safety, was forced to assure the South Korean and American public that it wasn't vCJD, citing the same "preliminary results" and happy talk officials had used for five years to forestall panic.[113] "An official release once all testing is completed and confirmed is expected soon," he promised, no doubt hoping it would come after the South Koreans signed the agreement.

And there was something else about the pact the South Koreans distrusted: there was a provision in it that said South Korea couldn't halt beef imports if mad cow disease broke out again in the United States, unless the World Organization for Animal Health actually downgraded the United States' safety rating.[114] This loophole about future mad-cow cases didn't seem right to South Koreans. Did the United States have doubts?

Chapter 13

BRAVE NEW FOOD
SO SAFE IT'S NOT EVEN LABELED

Almost every issue that food activists care about—unlabeled ingredients and drug traces; crowded, polluted farms; Agribiz cornering the food supply; and animal suffering—is magnified when cloned and genetically modified (GM) or genetically engineered (GE) animals are added into the equation.

Afraid there are antibiotics or antibiotic-resistant germs in your food? With cloned and GE animal products, you're actually eating altered genes! Worried about what crowded, manure- and drug-polluted farms do to workers, animals, the environment, and people who eat the products? Cloned and GM animals permit even greater production "efficiencies," say biotech farmers—that's why it's done. Concerned over ag giants and chemical companies squeezing family farmers and poor nations out of existence through patents and robber-baron laws? Every mouthful of a cloned or GM animal is "owned" by a corporation. Horrified to see dairy cows forklifted to slaughter because they are too weak to walk? Cloned and GM animals, like dairy cows on recombinant bovine growth hormone (rBGH), are designed to get more money's worth out of each animal "unit," at the price of higher culls and mortality.

Of course, genetically engineered or modified crops are nothing new. Roundup® Ready Soybeans, Bt-corn, and Golden Rice are presumably in any food without an "absence" label that says they are free of GMO (genetically modified organisms). And genetically engineered animals are used in areas other than food. A transgenic goat, a species with a gene or genes transferred from another species, now exists with a human gene and has been patented by GTC Biotherapeutics to produce a blood-clotting drug. And goats given a *spider* gene produce material to be spun into textile fibers, largely under the public's radar.[1]

Though most people have barely noticed GM animals created to make human drugs and other products (sometimes called "pharm animals"), animal rights groups have condemned them. Creating new animals for a dedicated human use "is a mechanistic use of animals that seems to perpetuate the notion of their being merely tools for human use rather than sentient creatures," says the Humane Society of the United States.[2]

Food produced from genetic engineering has received mixed reviews in the United States. While copious foods are made with unlabeled GM crops and eaten daily, the public largely rejected milk made with rBGH ten years after its quick FDA approval. That's why consumers, chemical and biotech companies, the food industry, and many importing and exporting nations are watching the saga of the US-created AquAdvantage® Salmon (AAS) closely: its approval or rejection is likely to set the precedent for future GM foods.

The AAS, created by Boston-based AquaBounty Technologies, is a GE salmon created to grow twice as fast as wild Atlantic salmon, participants at three days of FDA hearings in 2010 about the proposed salmon were told. Instead of reaching its full size in three years, it is ready for dinner plates in just eighteen months, cutting production costs in half. The GE salmon was created by inserting the coding sequence from a Chinook salmon growthhormone gene under the control of an "antifreeze protein promoter and terminator" from ocean pout into wild Atlantic salmon.[3] Got that? It was quickly dubbed a Frankenfish by critics.

Ninety-five to 99 percent of AAS are sterile, says AquaBounty, so they are unlikely to breed and threaten wild-salmon stocks if they escape. (If they did breed, though, it could be a disaster since they eat five times more food than wild salmon and have less fear of predators.) But 1 to 5 percent of the fifteen million eggs AquaBounty plans to grow still amounts to 750,000 fertile fish, says a *Food Safety News* editorial. Worries are also fueled by the fact that Canadian researchers have determined that GM Atlantic salmon can pass their genes on to wild salmon.[4]

To prevent such risks, AquaBounty plans to grow the eggs at a facility on Prince Edward Island in Canada, where escapees could not survive.[5] "Water from the facility, including effluent from all floor drains, fish tanks and egg incubators, eventually discharges" into a tidal river that flows into the Gulf of Lawrence, says the AquAdvantage FDA briefing package. Because water temperatures in the winter months are very low and the water has a high salinity, "it is highly unlikely that early life stages of any Atlantic salmon at the facility would be able to survive if they were able to escape."[6]

AquaBounty also has safety plans for the adult salmon, which it plans to grow out and slaughter in the country of Panama because that environment is also hostile to survival. "In the lower reaches of the watershed, the water temperature is in the range of 26 to 28 degrees C, at or near the upper incipient lethal level for Atlantic salmon," says the FDA report. "As a result, it is extremely unlikely that AquAdvantage Salmon would ever be able to survive and migrate to the Pacific Ocean."[7]

Because the gene changes that created the AAS are a "transformational (i.e., genetic) event" that imparts traits to the fish as if a drug had been administered, the FDA has ruled the fish a new *animal drug*, not a *food*.[8] That means its approval falls under the jurisdiction of the FDA's Center for Veterinary Medicine. It also means the advisory committee experts who considered its application were mostly veterinarians, not medical doctors.[9] Not too comforting.

Both promoters and critics of the AAS object to the "animal drug" classification, saying it shows how unprepared the government is to regulate GM animals. Critics also asked why the third day of 2010 hearings addressed how the salmon should be labeled, as if approval was a done deal and the hearings were a sham. But Deputy Commissioner Joshua Sharfstein assured participants that approval was not a fait accompli and that the label hearings were simply to give the agency a jump on the work ahead, if the salmon were approved.[10] Still, the roster of scientists who spoke against the fish on that day of the hearings was not heard by the Veterinary Medicine Advisory Committee (VMAC) considering the actual fish's application. Instead, critics spoke in front of Center for Food Safety and Applied Nutrition staff, which was like a tree falling in the forest with no one to hear it. Statements by high level scientists were not heard by the committee considering the AAS's actual approval; only those who would label it.

Government and industry speakers began their pro-AAS remarks by agreeing with critics that aquaculture is a lamentable stew of effluvium, toxic drugs, algae blooms, sea lice, disease, and fish mortality. There are many ways aquafarmed fish can escape from their holding areas, they said, from storms and hurricanes to sharks and seals cutting holes in containing nets. Government and industry speakers also agree with critics that wild fish stocks, including the endangered Atlantic salmon itself, are being destroyed by modern fishing methods in which miles of nets and airplanes are used to scope schools of fish that are unable to escape. Some government and industry speakers even condemned the common practice of catching and feeding dwindling reserves of wild fish to aquaculture fish which is as environmentally blasphemous as clear-cutting rain forests to graze cattle.

But the agreement stopped there. Speaker after speaker presented the AAS production plan as the *un-aquaculture* that would spare wild fish reserves while avoiding traditional risks. The proposed salmon would provide high-quality food and "feed the world," help the US trade deficit, and boost US food industries, speakers said.[11]

The beauty of AAS production, said Yonathan Zohar, PhD, then from the Center of Marine Biotechnology at the University of Maryland, is that it's a *land-based system*. It is away from coastal waters—to discourage escapes—and closer to domestic population centers to reduce the "carbon footprint."[12] (Does the reduced carbon footprint take into consideration travel from the egg hatchery in *Canada* to the grow-out facility in *Panama* or the fish's five-time-sas-normal appetite?)

The carbon footprint will be further reduced, said Zohar, by greater densities of fish than those found in traditional aquaculture—up to "80 to 100 per cubic meter," which photos reveal means bumper-to-bumper fish.[13] Will such densities require greater veterinary drugs to keep disease from breaking out? Zohar did not say. Is it ethical for a swimming animal to spend eighteen months practically standing on its tail? Zohar did not hide his zeal for what he called the "promise" of aquaculture or his contempt for Greenpeace and other groups that are against growing "fish in cages."[14]

Ron Stotish, then the CEO of AquaBounty, echoed to the advisory committee that the land-based AAS production system offers "better biosecurity" than traditional aquaculture. It also offers a "reduction of the transportation costs associated with moving large quantities of salmon, for instance, from the south of Chile or from the north of Europe to consumption centers here in the United States," he said. Both Norway and Chile had outbreaks of infectious salmon anemia virus (ISAV) that all but wiped out those nations' salmon industries, Stotish noted.[15]

At first, the hearings went swimmingly for AquaBounty. "This technology is holding incredibly great promise specifically for the world's food supply," said Bernadette Dunham, DVM, then director of the FDA's Center for Veterinary Medicine, as she opened the hearings—not that she had formed a opinion.[16] Other staffers, like Eric Silberhorn, a member of the FDA's Animal Biotechnology Interdisciplinary Group, seemed to itemize AquaBounty's safety systems right out of AquaBounty's own playbook. But when FDA food scientists Kathleen Jones and Kevin Greenlees, also of the Animal Biotechnology Interdisciplinary Group, presented AquaBounty's allergy studies at the hearings, the Veterinary Medicine Advisory Committee pounced.[17]

How can safety be determined for the levels of allergens when you haven't determined a number that would not be safe, asked the committee. It's as if "you selected a particular allergen in goat meat and another allergen that was in sheep meat and you compared the two and you found a significant difference but both of them were at irrelevantly low numbers," said Louisiana State University's David F. Senior, who chaired the committee. "Who cares?" Other members berated the low numbers of fish used in studies, the inclusion of irrelevant fish in studies which "diluted out the power of the study," and the generally bad science.[18]

And if studies with numbers as low as six or seven fish weren't bad enough, there were even errors in them, accused the committee. In table 15 of the allergy study data there are six "controls," observed James D. McKean, then with the Department of Veterinary Diagnostic and Production Animal Medicine at Iowa State University. And, "in Table 16, there are 7. And I am still unclear as to where that extra sample came from?"[19]

"Nothing reliable can be gained from this study," said Craig Altier, DVM, then with the College of Veterinary Medicine at Cornell University about other data presented, calling the work a "real mess." This "is an important thing to study and the experiment was a bust, why hasn't it been done again?"[20] The mistakes are "my fault," apologized Greenlees.[21]

"I am not a statistician but we work with one of the best statisticians around and unfortunately she was not able to be here today," said Jones apologetically. The studies were absolutely "above board," she added—though no one had suggested otherwise.[22] "You've reached the limit of my statistical knowledge," said Larisa Rudenko, from the Animal Biotechnology Interdisciplinary Group, also apologetically.[23]

It was a low moment in government/industry/consumer relations. Not only did the "science" make both the government and AquaBounty look inept; the government representatives were actually reciting AquaBounty errors—verbatim! Could anyone in the government or AquaBounty count? Could anyone design a valid study? Should such people be in charge of launching a new GM species on the world?

A quick peek into the government's and AquaBounty's briefing materials raised more questions about allergies.[24] The briefing packet says the FDA could not determine if the AAS would cause more allergies than other fish because excessive culling of "abnormal" salmon and other "technical flaws" in AquaBounty's study so "skewed" data as to "limit its interpretation that we cannot rely on its results"![25]

Why are there so many "abnormal" salmon in a fish product facing approval? Why, if the science is so flawed, is the salmon even under consideration?

The briefing report also found high incidences of "jaw erosion" and "focal inflammation" (infection) in AAS, which it called findings "of low magnitude and not likely to be debilitating to fish in a production setting." (What about the people who eat them?)[26] And it identified low glucose levels and a possible "increase in the level of IGF-1 [insulin-like growth factor-1] in the AquAdvantage salmon compared to sponsor control fish."[27]

As we saw in chapter 7, IGF-1 is linked to cancer and early puberty, whose presence in rBGH-created milk made the product so controversial. Government scientists have said that IGF-1 is destroyed by digestion or pasteurization, but other scientists disagree.[28] Could IGF-1 in the fast-growing AquAdvantage Salmon affect human hormones or accelerate human tumors? Alison Van

Eenennaam, PhD, then with the Department of Animal Science at University of California–Davis, who served on the Veterinary Medicine Advisory Committee, told participants at the label hearings, where she was a speaker, that the IGF figures are much ado about nothing. Even though IGF-1 was 10 percent higher in AAS, there was no "scientific basis for selecting that 10 percent," she said, and the difference is not "an a priori safety concern." Van Eenennaam also said that the IGF "will presumably be digested in the gut."[29]

Van Eenennaam did not hide her support for the AAS, declaring that it "poses no additional risk" than normal fish and criticizing the *New York Times* for bringing up IGF/cancer links.[30] She also expressed derision for pure and safe food culture, making jokes about the proliferation of peanut-allergy labels and high prices at Whole Foods Market.[31] Nor was it clear why an advisorycommittee member from the previous day, who supposedly had not made up her mind, would speak on behalf of AAS at the label hearings. Who made that decision?

Even though the AAS is a high-tech genetic product, its production plan includes low-tech logistics, like shipping eggs from Canada to Panama in "hard plaster coolers" and the operation of facilities outside the United States.[32] How often (if ever) would the FDA inspect the Panama site? advisory-committee members wanted to know. What are the safeguards against human error, employee theft, and natural disasters to keep fish from escaping? And what is AquaBounty's final worldwide marketing plan? Answers to such "after-the-sale" questions were as reassuring as, well, the allergy and IGF studies.

One example of the "low-tech" issues is AquaBounty's policy for handling dead fish in Panama. According to AquaBounty's Environmental Assessment report,

> the small number of dead eggs and morbid or dead animals removed during daily surveillance and maintenance of the grow-out facility in Panama will be buried on-site. Each burial pit will be excavated to an initial depth of 1.0 m (0.5–0.75 m diameter). As dead fish are deposited, they will be covered with caustic lime, followed by another layer of dead fish and caustic lime, and so on, until the burial pit is ~0.5 m deep, at which point it will sealed with plastic and covered with soil. Successive pits will be located at a minimum distance of 0.5–1.0 m from those used previously; the aggregate

collection of such pits will be located on high ground that is not within the 100-year flood plain. . . . In the event that disposal capacity at the site is inadequate to handle the immediate or aggregate waste volume, alternative means of disposal will be sought.[33]

Why are so many fish expected to die that second burial-site plans may be necessary? And why would people want to eat fish stock so unhealthy it is likely to die?

Still, for any food consumers old enough to remember the 1993 movie *Jurassic Park*, in which cloned dinosaurs run amok, a bigger worry than deceased and mutated fish leaking into the water supply, or even cancer and precocious puberty from IGF, is losing genetic and physical control over the new species. The Great Lakes states have spent millions trying to "call back" the voracious Asian carp, and it's not even a GM fish!

In fact, the *Jurassic Park* factor is probably why the government and AquaBounty avoid using loaded terms like "genetic drift" and "mutate," and instead use the euphemism "durability" in briefing materials and presentations.[34] And there are durability questions. An unexpected and unwanted "rearrangement" in AquAdvantage salmon in which the original inserted genetic material has moved from "the far upstream promoter regions" to a "downstream location relative to the growth hormone coding region" is mentioned in the FDA briefing packet.[35]

When the advisory committee asked Jeff Jones, a veterinarian presenter at the hearings, if such unforeseen genetic "rearrangements" could pose dangers like the AAS growing or mutating out of control, the answer *seemed* to be reassuring. The genetic "piece" that had "moved downstream" is not "a complete promoter by itself so that that piece by itself could not drive expression of a gene," he said.[36]

SEEMS SAFE, BUT WHO KNOWS?

Coming five months after the Deepwater Horizon oil spill, which occurred in spite of similar, redundant safety systems, the public did not seem reassured by the AquAdvantage salmon hearings. Two weeks later, it was apparent that lawmakers felt the same way.

Eleven senators and twenty-four congresspeople wrote a letter to FDA commissioner Margaret Hamburg, asking her to "halt proceedings" because the "potential human health and environmental impacts have not been fully or openly reviewed," and the FDA has "no adequate process to review a GE animal intended as a human food."[37]

And that was just the beginning. A few months later, then Alaska senators Mark Begich and Lisa Murkowsk introduced legislation to ban genetically engineered salmon and also presented companion legislation requiring GE fish to be labeled, if the legislation somehow got approved. "Frankenfish threatens our wild stocks, their habitat, our food safety, and would bring economic harm to Alaska's wild salmon fishermen," said Senator Begich.[38] "The FDA has not studied the environmental effects, let alone the economic impacts on the salmon and seafood markets that would result from approval," said Senator Murkowsk.[39] Does it need to be mentioned that Alaska has a big salmon industry?

Next, California legislators drafted a mandatory labeling bill for GE salmon that passed the California Assembly Health Committee in May. "Knowing whether our salmon is genetically engineered is important for a host of reasons, including risks to our native salmon species, and allowing consumers to make dietary choices consistent with concerns they may have for the environment, food safety, and religiously or ethically based dietary restrictions," said then Assemblyman Jared Huffman.[40]

The following month, AAS opponents, led by then Alaska representatives Lynn Woolsey and Don Young, achieved a rare victory. By voice vote, with few lawmakers expecting the vote and few representatives even present, they passed a House amendment that actually banned the FDA from spending any funds on genetically engineered salmon approvals—making it illegal for further review to continue.[41] Nice knowing ya, AquAdvantage salmon!

Approving the AAS for food could have "grave, unintended consequences on human health," said then Rep. Sam Farr (D-CA), who supported the bill. "Preliminary studies show that the compounds in genetically engineered salmon may be linked to cancer and severe drug allergies."[42] "Because genetically engineered salmon are more sexually aggressive and resistant to environmental toxins, their escape would pose a catastrophic threat to wild salmon populations," added Representative Woolsey (D-CA).[43]

But the contretemps was not over! Two months later, thirty-eight agriculture and biotech groups including the American Meat Institute and the Biotechnology Industry Organization (BIO) wrote then office holders Speaker of the House John Boehner, Senate Minority Leader Mitch McConnell, Senator Majority Leader Harry Reid, and House Minority Leader Nancy Pelosi that the maneuver, if it became law, "would disrupt the FDA's Congressional mandate to base its assessments of human and animal drugs, devices, vaccines, and process applications on the best-available science."[44]

Even Alison "Peanut Allergy" Van Eenennaam took part in the counteroffensive. She coauthored a sour-grapes, "no good deed goes unpunished" article in the journal *Nature Biotechnology*, apparently timed to appear at the same time the food groups wrote their letter to congressional leaders.[45] What is the hold-up with AquAdvantage Salmon, Van Eenennaam asks in the article, titled "Transgenic Salmon: A Final Leap to the Grocery Shelf?"[46] The FDA released an "unprecedented" 171-page briefing package about the fish, and AquaBounty released an 84-page Environmental Assessment. What else could opponents and skeptics want to know?[47] Van Eenennaam was especially irked by critics' charges that AAS has fewer of the desirable fish oils than real salmon, because promoting it as an abundant source of the good oils was part of the sales plan. According to Michael Hansen, PhD, senior scientist with Consumers Union, "in terms of the ratio of omega-3 to omega-6 fatty acids, GE salmon fare worse than wild fish and slightly worse than farmed salmon."[48]

Why don't these critics realize that a GM animal is no different than any selectively bred animal? asked Van Eenennaam, as if creating a new species were the same as controlling for color in toy poodles. She even issues a warning: protracted safety concerns about GM animals could "jeopardize future access to improved genetic lines resulting from new technological developments (e.g., disease-resistant GM animals), with negative consequences on food security and other broadly supported societal goals, including improved human and animal health."[49]

Translation: reject AquAdvantage Salmon today and be afflicted with disease and starvation tomorrow!

PIMPING FOOD

Of course, the AquAdvantage Salmon is not the only GM food animal in the works. Scientists at the Roslin Institute at the University of Edinburgh in Scotland, where Dolly the cloned sheep was created, have spent years creating chickens that can be used as "biofactories" to make eggs with interferon and other disease-fighting substances.[50] "Once you've made the transgenic birds, then it's very easy," enthused scientist Helen Sang, PhD. "You can breed up hundreds of birds from one cockerel [young male]—because they can be bred with hundreds of hens and you can collect an egg a day and have hundreds of chicks in no time.[51]

Other researchers are working on food that would contain omega-3, like the AAS was hoped to have. Scientists at Harvard Medical School, the University of Missouri, and the University of Pittsburgh Medical Center have concocted "white piglets with muscle tissue larded with omega-3 fatty acids," reports the *New York Times*.[52] All they had to do was modify a roundworm enzyme that converts omega-6 to omega-3, inject the gene into mouse embryos to create mice that make their own omega-3, and transfer the genetic material into pigs. "People can continue to eat their junk food," said Alexander Leaf, MD, at Harvard at the time. "You won't have to change your diet, but you will be getting what you need."[53] Aren't animals great?

We may not be eating GM animals yet (although an FDA presenter at the AAS hearings says there are reports that "transgenic shrimp" are already mixed into US imports[54]), but we are certainly eating food from cloned animals, say many reports.

The FDA ruled in 2008 that products from clones and their offspring were safe to eat but asked producers to "voluntarily keep milk and meat from clones out of the food and feed supplies until we finish assessing their safety."[55] Key words: *asked* and *voluntarily*. The FDA also said it didn't "expect food from clones to enter the food supply in any great amounts any time soon, as these animals will be used for breeding" (though "soon" was not defined, and nothing was said about clone offspring).[56] The FDA also said that clone-derived food *would not be labeled* because it is "no different from food derived from conventionally bred animals." That's what is said about rBGH-produced milk.

But a 2010 demonstration in England over possible unlabeled and illegal food from clones in that country revealed that clones may also be on the American dinner plate, with Americans being the last to know. Reporting on a cloned British herd (attributed to cloned embryos shipped by then Wisconsin dairy farmer Mark Rueth), the BBC said that cloned products have been in the US food supply for two years.[57] Who knew?

Jim McLaren, then president of Scotland's National Farmers Union, concurred and told the press, "If you go to the US or Canada you will almost certainly be consuming meat and dairy products from cloned animals at every turn."[58]

Margaret Wittenberg, then global vice-president of Whole Foods Market, agreed. United States customers are "oblivious" to cloned products in the food supply, she verified to the BBC. "You don't hear about it in the media. And when you do tell people about it they look at you and say 'you're kidding! They're not doing that are they? Why would they?'" Whole Foods says it bans the sale of cloned products.[59]

When then Agriculture Secretary Tom Vilsack was asked point-blank, during a 2010 trade mission in Canada, if "cloned cows or their offspring have made it into the North American food supply," he put no fears to rest.[60] "I can't say today that I can answer your question in an affirmative or negative way. I don't know. What I do know is that we know all the research, all of the review of this is suggested that this is safe."[61] Thanks for that.

Meanwhile, Cyagra, a Pennsylvania-based clone company that Wisconsin dairy farmer Mark Rueth says convinced him to start cloning, boasts about selling clone products to US butchers (who presumably sell to customers) and about its employees regularly dining on cloned products.[62]

Since the first cloned mammal, Dolly the sheep, was created, cattle, horses, goats, pigs, and mice have been cloned, as well as dogs and cats, a mouflon sheep, a mule, and a racing camel. In fact, cloning doesn't even make headlines anymore, compared with GM animals that we might actually eat, like the AquAdvantage Salmon, chickens with interferon in their eggs, and pigs interlarded with omega-3. But the FDA's 968-page report on cloning in 2008 and a European Food Safety Authority report, designed to assuage consumer fears, do the opposite. They raise questions about the health of cloned animals and their offspring, the safety of their and their offspring's milk and meat, and even the soundness of the cloning process itself.[63]

While cloning may sound exciting and adventurous, it's riddled with inexactitude, mishaps, and genetic surprises. To clone an animal, "scientists start with a piece of ear skin and mince it up in a lab. Then they induce the cells to divide in a culture dish until they forget they are skin cells and regain their ability to express all of their genes," wrote Karen Kaplan in the *Los Angeles Times*. "Meanwhile, the nucleus is removed from a donor egg and placed next to a skin cell. Both are zapped with a tiny electric shock, and if all goes well the egg grows into a genetic copy of the original animal."[64] So far, so good—except that many clones lack the ability to be the perfect replica they are supposed to be because they can't "reprogram the somatic nucleus of the donor to the state of a fertilized zygote," says the FDA report.

The reprogramming problem, called epigenetic dysregulation, means many cloned cattle and sheep—up to 90 percent—die or are born with deformities like enlarged umbilical cords, respiratory distress, heart and intestine problems, and Large Offspring Syndrome (LOS), the latter often killing the clone and its "mother," the surrogate animal that had been implanted with the embryo.[65]

"The newborns tend to be large for their breeds, and often have abnormal or poorly developed lungs, hearts, or other affected internal organs (liver and kidney), which makes it difficult for them to breathe or maintain normal circulation and metabolism," says the FDA report. "LOS newborns may appear to be edematous (fluid filled), and if they are to survive, often require significant veterinary intervention. Problems have also been noted in muscle and skeletal development of animals with LOS. These animals also often have difficulty regulating body temperature."[66]

In addition to requiring surgery, oxygen, and transfusions at birth, the clones can eat insatiably and not necessarily gain weight, says the report.[67] Of forty clone pigs, twenty-seven died during the "perinatal period from a variety of health problems including diarrhoea, meningitis and heart functional abnormalities," says one study, and only twelve made it to adulthood.[68] In five years of cloning in three countries, 42 percent of cattle clones died between delivery and 150 days of life, reports the Scientific Committee/Scientific Panel of the European Food Safety Authority.[69] Included in the deaths were "depressed and weak" calves that couldn't get up and animals with enlarged umbilical cords, respiratory problems, and contracted flexor tendons.

No wonder the FDA admits that "incomplete or inappropriate epigenetic reprogramming appears to be one of the primary underlying causes for the relatively low success rate of cloning, and the source of potential subtle hazards for the consumption of food from animal clones."[70]

In fact, so many animals die to make one surviving clone, the European Group on Ethics in Science and New Technologies (EGE) concluded in 2008 that "considering the current level of suffering and health problems of surrogate dams and animal clones, the EGE has doubts as to whether cloning animals for food supply is ethically justified."[71]

The FDA report was written in collaboration with Cyagra (yes, the Cyagra that says it is already selling the meat to US butchers) and Austin, Texas-based ViaGen, another clone company. Maybe that's why there's an answer for every objection that could be raised about cloned animals' health.

"Residual epigenetic reprogramming errors that could persist" in clones—also known as genetic roulette? They "reset" over time, says the report![72] Got elevated levels of "growth indicators" in clones compared to normal calves?

They can be explained by the "clones' stage of life or stress level," says the FDA. Clones with elevated glucose? "Not considered to be clinically relevant," says the FDA, and it is "most likely a short-lived response to stress." A four-and-a-half month-old clone Jersey calf with early mammary development? "This age is young for mammary development but the phenomenon sometimes occurs in conventional heifers if they are overfed," says the report.[73] Like low glucose, high IGF-1, jaw erosion, and focal inflammation in AquAdvantage Salmon, all the ominous symptoms are *just a coincidence*.

And speaking of coincidences, rats fed cloned meat and milk exhibited greater "frequency of vocalization" during studies—a behavior linked to emotion. But the changes were probably "incidental and unrelated to treatment," says the report.[74] How about the actual meat and milk from clones? Meat and milk differed in one study and had "alterations in fatty acid composition and delta-9 desaturase [an enzyme that synthesizes fat] activity," says the report. These changes imply that "*lipid metabolism may be altered*," in cloned cattle.[75] Like the high-tech AAS shipped in plastic coolers and buried onsite under lime, there are also disturbing low-tech issues regarding clone production. For example, even though clone experts can inject a nucleus into an egg, they can't analyze whether milk from a clone source has hazards! "Determining whether animal clones are producing a hazardous substance in their milk although theoretically possible, is highly impractical," says the report. "Milk from cows, sheep, and goats are mixtures that are estimated to be composed of more than 100,000 molecules," and cloners say they will rely on federal nutrition labeling requirements to catch problems.[76] Clone scientists will also rely on federal *slaughterhouse inspections*, says the report, to catch clones in the food supply.[77] "It is not likely that clones of this age group would be consumed for food, although there may be some circumstances in which culled clones might be sent into the food supply. There were no consistent analyte [component] or physical observations indicating a food safety concern."[78]

Take the case of Calf No. 100 that "presented with both umbilical abscess and a high WBC [white blood cell count, suggesting infection]. In the unlikely event that this animal was sent to slaughter with a large abscess, it would be detected on inspection," says the FDA report. "The carcass would be

condemned if there was evidence of systemic involvement. The abscess would otherwise be cut out and the carcass processed normally."[79]

Obviously the FDA, Cyagra, and ViaGen haven't read the reports about the Alabama, Texas, and Washington State mad cows.

Still, Scott Gottlieb, MD, who served as FDA deputy commissioner for medical and scientific affairs from 2005 to 2007, thinks clones are so safe that we should eat the *leftover cloned lab animals*, too. "The process of making genetically engineered animals for drug production also can sometimes produce large numbers of surrogate dams or non-genetically engineered offspring that have no drug producing qualities," he writes in a brochure for BIO, the world's largest biotechnology organization. (BIO was one of the companies who signed the complaint letter to congressional leaders about the AquAdvantage stall.)[80] "These animals are nonetheless difficult and expensive to continue to maintain, and therefore are ideally suited for placement in the food supply chain. In fact, some observations suggest that using genetically engineered animals to develop drugs is only cost efficient when these surrogate dams and (or) non-genetically engineered offspring can be safely harvested for human consumption."[81]

Engineering animals with "environmental benefits" will reduce the carbon footprint, says Gottlieb, like the AAS whose shortened production time means "supply can be increased without proportionately increasing the use of coastal waters." He also cites the Enviro-Pig®, which excretes 75 percent less phosphorus and could, he says, use 33 percent less land.[82]

Cows can even be engineered to resist human-made problems, says Gottlieb, like cattle engineered to have no prions that would host mad cow disease and dairy cows engineered to resist mastitis, so common with rBGH, by secreting lysostaphin in their milk.[83] But others see an unfolding sciencefiction nightmare, driven by industry. Cloned food is a "huge experiment conducted on the public like rBGH in which a cow gene was inserted into E. coli" in unlabeled milk, says Shiv Chopra, a veterinarian, microbiologist, and human rights activist.[84]

Slow Food Italia and Coldiretti, Italy's two largest farming interests, say that despite the "most accurate legal systems" and "scientific information," it is "impossible to make long term safety predictions" about cloned foods, as the mad-cow outbreaks have demonstrated. Genetic uniformity from cloning could also represent danger in the case of unpredicted illnesses, say the Italian food companies in posted remarks on the European Food Safety Authority (EFSA) website.[85]

The Liaison Centre for the Meat Processing Industry in the European Union (CLITRAVI) says that safety and health questions pertaining to cloned foods are made more serious by the United States' refusal to label cloned products. "Given the fact that it would be impossible to determine the provenance of meat from such sources we believe that the US should be asked to delay any marketing until such time that most, if not all animal health and welfare problems have been solved," says the organization on the EFSA website.[86]

The US-based nonprofit science group Union of Concerned Scientists heartily agrees. "The choice of whether to purchase such foods should be in the hands of individual consumers, not the government or the industry," says the 250,000-member group. "Consumers will have such a choice only if the foods are labeled."[87]

Even though the FDA refuses to label cloned products, it couldn't save the similarly unlabeled rBGH milk when enough people got angry. Brave New Food is not just an experiment on humans and nature, it turns animals into "products" like TVs or bicycles, notes an anonymous poster on the EFSA site. It steals their "dignity" and desecrates their essential natures that took "thousands of years to grow."[88] In fact, in the genetic co-opting of the food supply, animals might be the biggest victims of all.

EPILOGUE

Since the first edition of this book, food and drug risks have only escalated thanks to deceptive marketing and high-level conflicts of interest. For example, President Joe Biden's pick[1] for FDA commissioner in 2021, Robert Califf, MD,[2] sported *at least 43 financial links* to the drug industry, according to an opinion piece he wrote in the *Journal of the American Medical Association* (*JAMA*)[3] yet he was still confirmed by the Senate[4] to regulate the industry that funded him. Could the vote represent the fact that there are two pharmaceutical lobbyists for every member of Congress in Washington, DC?[5]

When it comes to pharmaceutical corruption in the last few years, exhibit A is the opioid crisis which caused more than 500,000 deaths in the US from prescription and illicit opioids between 1999 and 2020.[6]

In 2020, Purdue Pharma, who made the notorious opioid OxyContin [oxycodone], agreed to pay roughly $8.3 billion in fines because it "knowingly and intentionally conspired and agreed with others to aid and abet" doctors dispensing medication "without a legitimate medical purpose."[7] The company had already paid $600 million in fines for downplaying opioid risks in 2007.[8] According to the *Washington Post*, "the medical community and government agencies failed to take effective action, even when it became apparent that these pills were fueling addiction and overdoses and were getting diverted to the streets."[9]

The Sackler family, who owned the now bankrupt Purdue Pharma, agreed to pay $4.5 billion in opioid related settlements.[10] Some of the many scientific and artistic institutions funded by the wealthy, philanthropic family have since erased the Sackler name.[11]

In 2022, three US opioid wholesalers—AmerisourceBergen, Cardinal Health, and McKesson—and Johnson & Johnson who made generic opioid—

agreed to pay nearly $26 billion to settle opioid-related lawsuits.[12] There was plenty of guilt to go around.

And it wasn't just drug makers and sellers who were implicated in the opioid crisis. Medical associations and academies were also found to have had their hands in the cookie jar.

Research published in 2015 in the non-profit Annual Reviews revealed that:[13]

> Between 1996 and 2002, Purdue Pharma funded more than 20,000 pain-related educational programs through direct sponsorship or financial grants and launched a multifaceted campaign to encourage long-term use of OPRs [opioid pain relievers] for chronic non-cancer pain. As part of this campaign, Purdue provided financial support to the American Pain Society, the American Academy of Pain Medicine, the Federation of State Medical Boards, the Joint Commission, pain patient groups, and other organizations. In turn, these groups all advocated for more aggressive identification and treatment of pain, especially use of OPRs.

IN THE LAST DECADE DRUG PRICES HAVE SOARED

Before and during the opioid crisis, prescription drug prices also skyrocketed, leading to Congressional hearings.[14] "What the Committee has learned should be troubling to lawmakers, taxpayers, and any American who has ever struggled to afford their prescriptions," said New York Rep. Carolyn B. Maloney, Chairwoman of the Committee on Oversight and Reform to committee members after drug price investigations in 2021. "Drug companies have raised prices relentlessly for decades while manipulating the patent system and other laws to delay competition from lower-priced generics. These companies have specifically targeted the US market for higher prices, even while cutting prices in other countries, because weaknesses in our health care system have allowed them to get away with outrageous prices and anticompetitive conduct."[15]

Some of the biggest cost increases were seen in the price of insulin which rose by 54 percent between 2014 to 2019[16] and the anti-parasitic drug Daraprim which was repriced from $13.50 to $750 in 2015[17] by Turing Pharmaceuticals founder Martin Shkreli.[18] Adding to dramatic price hikes, the drug giant Mylan raised the price of EpiPen, the emergency allergy injection that so many relied upon, to $600 from $100 with no warning.[19] Revelations[20] that the former president and CEO of EpiPen drugmaker Mylan, Heather Bresch, was the daughter of then North Carolina senator Joe Manchin intensified questions about government/Big Pharma conflicts of interest and faulty regulation.

Some of the most outrageous prices seen in the US were in drugs that could, for the first, time cure hepatitis C,[21] a liver-attacking virus that can lead to cancer, cirrhosis and the necessity of having a transplant.[22] Until then, drugs merely treated the condition but the new drug class actually cured the disease.

Gilead Science priced Sovaldi, one of the first such hepatitis C drugs, at a shocking $1,000 a pill or $84,000 for a course of treatment[23]—extortion pricing said some. Lawmakers worried that the opportunistic prices would sack entitlement programs and they did; in 2014 alone, Medicare and Medicaid spent over $5 billion on Sovaldi and Gilead's follow-up drug, Harvoni.[24]

In 2017, Harvoni ad campaigns on TV, in broadcast and on posters along train commuter lines unabashedly stressed screening, warning people that if they were born between 1945 and 1965, they could have hepatitis C, not even know it. Even if you have no symptoms you might silently be at risk and need these drugs said the Pharma messaging, often called "disease mongering" because it employs fear of diseases to grow customers and screening as a marketing tool to enlarge demand and the "patient pool."

The shift to scare tactics and a push for screening was not a coincidence. According to the pharmaceutical trade website Fierce Pharma, Gilead's hepatitis blockbusters at the time were "in freefall, and its pool of eligible patients has shrunk dramatically thanks to the success of its meds." If "all baby boomers got tested for the virus, though? That could help stem the tide—and it's exactly the move the company is recommending with its latest awareness push," continued the site.[25]

Some of the ads for hepatitis C drugs included the Centers for Disease Control and Prevention (CDC) logo which instantly increased credibility but also raised questions about Gilead donations to the CDC foundation and quid pro quos.[26] Few realize that the CDC foundation boasts many drugmaker donors like Abbott, AbbVie, Bayer, AstraZeneca, Merck, Pfizer, GlaxoSmith-Kline Biologics, Eli Lilly, Amgen, Genentech . . . and Gilead which raises questions about monetary conflicts of interest as did the Prescription Drug User Fee Act (PDUFA) enacted in 1992.[27] PDUFA allowed drugmakers to pay significant fees to the notoriously underfunded Food and Drug Administration (FDA), streamlining product reviews but possibly incentivizing approvals in the process, charged critics.

DO FASTER APPROVAL FOSTER GREATER SAFETY SIGNALS?

Price was only one problem with the new, higher priced drugs that debuted and with incentivized approvals. The lucrative hepatitis C drugs, for example, had been rushed to market so quickly, a serious side effect had been missed: the drugs' penchant for reactivating *pre-existing hepatitis B*![28] When the over-looked safety signal surfaced, the FDA had to add to the label a post hoc warning about the dangerous side effect but the drugs were already widely in use,[29] causing critics to wonder if patients had served as "guinea pigs." The missed safety signal was reminiscent of the "osteonecrosis of the jaw" side effect attributed to bone drugs that was discussed in the "Protecting Bones from Products That Protect Bones" chapter of the first edition of this book. It was *dentists* not drug makers or the FDA who caught the serious side effect with patients again serving as de facto lab animals.

In 2017, the New York Times reported additional, undisclosed risks with the hepatitis C drugs.[30] Of 250,000 patients treated with them, 524 experienced liver failure and 165 died, wrote the newspaper. "An additional 1,058 had severe liver injury, and in 761 the drugs appeared not to work."

Thomas J. Moore, a senior scientist at the Institute for Safe Medication Practices, echoed what many were thinking as the hepatitis drug risks unfolded: does the rush to bring a new drug treatment to market come at an unforeseen cost to patient safety? Were they approved too quickly?[31]

SELECTIVE SEROTONIN REUPTAKE INHIBITORS (SSRI) ANTIDEPRESSANTS DISCREDITED

In 2022, a group of University College London [UCL] scientists wrote in the journal *Molecular Psychiatry* that after reviewing decades of research, there is no evidence that serotonin levels or serotonin activity are responsible for depression—the theory on which selective serotonin reuptake inhibitors (SSRI) antidepressants were based and marketed.[32]

"The popularity of the 'chemical imbalance' [serotonin] theory of depression has coincided with a huge increase in the use of antidepressants. Prescriptions for antidepressants have risen dramatically since the 1990s," said the article's lead author, Professor Joanna Moncrieff, a professor of Psychiatry at UCL.[33] "Thousands of people suffer from side effects of antidepressants, including the severe withdrawal effects that can occur when people try to stop them, yet prescription rates continue to rise. We believe this situation has been driven partly by the false belief that depression is due to a chemical imbalance. It is high time to inform the public that this belief is not grounded in science."

Dr. Mark Horowitz, a training psychiatrist and clinical research fellow in Psychiatry at UCL and co-author of the article added,[34] "One interesting aspect in the studies we examined was how strong an effect adverse life events played in depression, suggesting low mood is a response to people's lives and cannot be boiled down to a simple chemical equation."

People experiencing depression should pursue better management of stress and trauma as well as exercise, mindfulness and psychotherapy wrote the authors.[35] Moreover, the role of poverty, stress, and loneliness in depression has been overlooked because of fidelity to the now discredited serotonin theory they suggest. The authors also note that SSRIs could actually produce "the opposite effect in the long term"—causing greater depression.

ANTIDEPRESSANTS ADDICTIVE AND NOT ALWAYS EFFECTIVE

The findings of the UCL scientists help to explain the enigma that has baffled many: even as antidepressant use has never been higher[36] suicides are also up, zooming and accounted for 14.5 deaths per 100,000 people in the US in 2019.[37] Are they even working? In the military, where antidepressants are heavily prescribed, suicides have never been higher.[38]

While the over-prescription of antidepressants, "selling" of depression and speciousness of the serotonin theory have been exposed for decades, other risks have emerged since the drugs were first marketed. For example, SSRIs are now correlated with bone loss and fracture risk[39] as well as the dreaded intestinal condition of Clostridium difficile.[40]

In 2018, the *New York Times*[41] exposed another danger of SSRI antidepressants: they can be very difficult to quit and truly addictive (though drug makers prefer to call the addiction effects a "discontinuation syndrome"). Some patients say they were not warmed by their doctors that they may be indefinitely parked on the drugs because of side effects like dizziness, nausea, headache and brain zaps they experience when they try to stop the drugs reported the *Times*. Brian, a 29-year-old Chicagoan who did not want his name used, told me in an interview that he has remained on a SSRI antidepressant for years despite his wish to quit. "Every time I try to stop, I get something that feels like an electrical current in my head and I can't do it," he said.

The *Times* article drew a huge backlash from psychiatrists.[42] "By amplifying the social media echo chamber, the article creates the unfortunate impression that most patients are forced to continue antidepressants out of fear of withdrawal rather than out of prevention of recurrence," wrote 39 psychiatrists, terming depression "chronic" and "undertreated." Will they read the 2022 research in *Molecular Psychiatry* that discredits the serotonin theory that sold so many antidepressants bogusly?

OTHER PROBLEMATICAL PRESCRIPTION DRUGS

Hepatitis C drugs and SSRI antidepressants are far from the only prescription drugs once presented as safe that have come under safety clouds in the last few years, often after wide usage.

- Long term use of proton pump inhibitors (PPIs), aggressively marketed for gastroesophageal reflux disease and other gastrointestinal disorders, is now linked to the "risk of fractures, pneumonia, Clostridium difficile diarrhea, hypomagnesemia, vitamin B12 deficiency, chronic kidney disease, and dementia," according to the Mayo Clinic Proceedings.[43]

- The seizure drug Topamax® was found to present a two- to five-fold increase in the risk of cleft lip or cleft palate in infants born to mothers who used the drug in early pregnancy. [44]

- In 2016, the FDA strengthened warnings about the link of fluoroquinolones (a class of antibiotics which includes Cipro and Levaquin) to "disabling and potentially permanent side effects with tendons, muscles, joints, nerves and the central nervous system."[45] Two years later the agency strengthened warnings about "mental health side effects and serious blood sugar disturbances" with the antibiotics drug class.[46]

- In 2019, the FDA held a Joint Meeting of the Pediatric and Drug Safety and Risk Management Advisory Committees to address growing reports of neuropsychiatric events linked to the asthma drug Singulair® in pediatric patients including suicides.[47] The next year a "black box warning," the highest warning, was added to the drug and the FDA said it should "only be used to treat patients with allergic rhinitis and asthma that do not tolerate or do not respond to alternative medications."[48]

- In 2020, the FDA requested the withdrawal of prescription and over-the-counter (OTC) ranitidine from the market, a heartburn drug sold as Zantac®, due to the presence of a contaminant known as N-Nitrosodimethylamine (NDMA).[49]

Meanwhile, a 2019 follow-up of subjects in the federal Women's Health Initiative found the "hormone replacement therapy" (HRT) depicted in the chapter, "Weapons of Hormonal Therapy," is *still* unsafe years after the original study revelations. "[B]reast cancer risk from menopause hormones may last decades," said the follow-up. The study found that women prescribed hormone replacement therapy had a 29 percent greater incidence of breast cancer *19 years after using the drugs* than those who never used the drugs, said the analysis.[50]

BIG FOOD GETS BIGGER

MILK SALES CONTINUE TO FALL AND MILK ALTERNATIVES RISE

The tanking milk sales and desperate try-anything marketing that was covered in the first edition of this book has bottomed out. "Got milk? You probably don't. Or you do, and it's just a splash in your coffee. Or you do, but it's not from a cow," wrote *Fast Company* as it reported that "Dean Foods, the largest U.S. milk producer" had filed for Chapter 11 bankruptcy protection in 2019.[51]

"Despite our best efforts to make our business more agile and cost-efficient, we continue to be impacted by a challenging operating environment marked by continuing declines in consumer milk consumption," said Eric Beringause, a newly installed CEO at Dean in 2019.[52]

Dean "has found itself unable to compete as plant-based and lactose-free dairy alternatives rise in popularity," agreed the *New York Times*.[53]

Not only was Dean Foods a casualty of the many non-dairy milks now available, the milk producer "increased its ownership percentage in leading brand of flaxseed-based milk alternatives, Good Karma," unabashedly joining the *other side* according to Food Table TV.[54] The turnabout parallels the meat giants like Tyson, Smithfield, Purdue, and Hormel who now offer plant-meat alternatives in their product lines—as in "if you can't beat 'em, join 'em."[55]

Nondairy milks available today include soy, rice, oat, coconut and almond milks as well as pea, hemp, flax, cashews, hazelnut, pistachio, walnut, peanut, macadamia, pecan, lupine, quinoa, garbanzo bean, sesame seed, tapioca starch, and even potato milks. While some are refrigerated, many are in the dry goods section of the grocery store which further propels sales because of their greater shelf life.

Why the sea change in milk drinking behavior? The new milks presented less of dairy milk's negatives like cholesterol, calories, antibiotics, and hormones and often offered nutritional or taste advantages.[56] Just as important were ethical reasons that vegan-oriented food consumers cited for abstaining from cow's milk: the dairy industry's shocking treatment of cows and calves, depicted in the food chapters of the first edition of this book.[57] Additionally, manure and fly saturated dairy operations exert such negative environmental effects, they have been called "rural crack houses."

THE FALL AND (UNDERREPORTED) RISE OF PINK SLIME

Many people have forgotten about the 2012 "pink slime" scandal in which beef scraped from animals' skeletal muscle at processing plants was extruded through tubes (looking like spaghetti or intestines) was being treated with ammonia to kill bacteria. Few knew that pink slime was in 70 percent of US ground meat, unlabeled. (A US Department of Agriculture microbiologist had claimed the product was not even ground beef at all but connective tissue.)[58]

A series of exposes by ABC News in 2012 about pink slime, officially known as "lean finely textured beef" (LFTB), provoked such national revulsion that the product's primary producer, Beef Products Inc. (BPI), lost contracts with 72 customers, closed three of its four plants, and laid off 700 workers, almost overnight. Cattle futures on the Chicago Mercantile Exchange hit a low.[59]

There were two shockers—first that ammonia was in human food, unlabeled, and secondly that bacteria were so entrenched in slaughterhouses, especially E. coli, that it was necessary. The public was especially outraged over the revelation that pink slime was in school lunches—that kids were unwittingly eating it. Once that news was out, 47 out of 50 states declined to purchase any of the product for the 2012–2013 school year. A quarter of a million people signed a change.org petition to ban the product in school lunches and the USDA quickly told schools that relied on the government for ground beef, they could choose beef without the pink slime.[60]

After such swift responses, you would think pink slime would have vanished from the food landscape but the opposite has occurred. In 2018 the Food Safety And Inspection Service (FSIS), part of the USDA, reclassified pink slime as "ground beef" and it now can legally constitute up to 15 percent of ground beef![61] It has not gone away—it has been assimilated,

Meanwhile, Beef Products Inc. (BPI), the main pink slime producer, sued ABC News for "false, misleading and defamatory statements" and "product and food disparagement" and in 2017 the suit was given a green light because BPI was ruled a "public figure."[62] BPI actually prevailed and reached a settlement with ABC out of court for the alleged disparagement which was rumored to be as high $177 million.[63]

RITUAL SLAUGHTER: MORE CRITICISM AND SUPPORT

Since the publication of the first edition of this book, ritual slaughter of animals—kosher, sanctioned by Jewish law and halal, sanctioned by Islamic law—has received more news coverage. Because the cattle, sheep, goats, and other animals are not stunned or rendered insensate during ritual slaughter, the suffering and agony can be prolonged and upsetting to watch.

In 2017, before Eid al-Adha, or the Islamic Feast of Sacrifice, Veysel Eroğlu, the Minister of Forestry and Water of Turkey, admonished Turks to slaughter their animals rapidly to prevent gruesome images of animals pathetically fighting for their lives.[64] Yet, as some countries have sought to limit or outlaw ritual slaughter, other voices charge "religious persecution" when such restrictions are considered. For example, a 2019 *New York Times* editorial [65] called bans on ritual slaughter possible "smoke screens for bigotry against Jews and Muslims." It warned that "those who really care about the welfare of animals should be wary of making common cause with right-wing nationalists whose hostile intent is to make life more difficult for religious minorities."

Some EU countries now require stunning before ritual slaughter and ritual slaughter is banned entirely in Slovenia.[66] Yet Poland overturned a 2013 ban on unstunned slaughter practices on the grounds of religious freedom. The following year, 2022, Belgian lawmakers legalized ritual slaughter in Belgium's capital, Brussels, after the country had banned kosher and halal slaughter in 2019.[67, 68] The Netherlands sought to tighten its ritual slaughter laws but after a backlash ruled that a veterinarian must be present during slaughter and if the animal doesn't lose consciousness in 40 seconds, it must be stunned.[69] Clearly there are strong sentiments on both sides. In 2020, nine out of ten Europeans polled wanted a ban on slaughtering animals that have not been stunned.[70] Animal lovers question if religious dictates should override secular law if a religious practice specified beating a child.

SLAUGHTER LINES GET FASTER

There is a natural antipathy between private meat companies and federal inspectors who can stop their slaughter line, production, and operations and intrude on their bottom line. In interviews, inspectors report being ignored, laughed at, and openly defied by meat operations and not supported by their own local and national offices. One FSIS inspector was so bullied at a slaughterhouse, a FSIS employee who knew her told me, she took her own life.

Private meat companies desire to "self-police" is especially playing out over new inspection systems, such as the New Swine Inspection System (NSIS)[71] and New Poultry Inspection System[72] (NPIS) which have the effect of speeding up the slaughter lines. For example, under the existing poultry system, the Hazard Analysis and Critical Control Point–Based Inspection Models Project or HIMP, the number of birds slaughtered a minute is 140 birds but under NPIS it is 175.[73] NPIS is a pilot system, requiring slaughterhouses to procure a waiver and is only in use at 53 chicken plants so far.[74]

Still, in March of 2022, 26 groups of poultry worker representatives, worker rights advocates, occupational safety experts, animal right advocates, consumer rights advocates, and public and community health organizations wrote the administrators at the FSIS and Office of Food Safety at the USDA objecting to the new faster kills speeds on the basis of worker safety, food safety, and animal welfare.[75]

The new Swine Inspection System (NSIS), called the Modernization of Swine Slaughter Inspection rule,[76] added to the Federal Register[77] in 2018, has also received blowback. More than 6,500 hog plant workers, members of the United Food and Commercial Workers International Union [UFCW] and its Locals filed a lawsuit to stop the new system in 2019 which also increases slaughter line speeds.[78]

Marc Perrone, then international president of the UFCW, said faster line speeds would mean more worker injuries and food that is less safe. "We urge the USDA to hear their voices and rewrite this rule so that the people who work in pork plants and the millions they serve can all be kept safe," he said.[79]

While the public may not know or care about the speed at which pigs and chickens for their meals are killed, the issue represents a growing face-off between meat producers and government about the future regulation of meat.

TEFLON EGG DON AND SON GO TO JAIL

The rap sheet of the "Teflon Egg Don" Austin (Jack) DeCoster began in 1977 when neighbors who lived near his huge, family-owned egg operation complained about litter beetles infesting their homes and sued the operation.[80] By 1982, eggs traced to DeCoster-owned farms had sickened hundreds with salmonella[81] and in 1987, hundreds more were sickened with salmonella and nine died.[82] The state of New York banned the sale of DeCoster eggs the following year.[83]

By 1996, DeCoster had racked up twenty health and safety violations[84] yet extended his egg empire to Iowa, Ohio, and Maryland, adding hogs to the mix.[85] When an undercover investigation by the animal welfare group Mercy For Animals was conducted at the DeCoster-owned Quality Egg of New England and Maine Contract Farming in Turner, Maine in 2009, the DeCoster rap sheet lengthened.[86]

Conditions at Quality Egg were so appalling that the lungs of four state agriculture officials were harmed by ammonia as they removed dead and dying hens from the reeking barns along with the law enforcement officials.[87]

Fourteen months after the Quality Egg raid, DeCoster pleaded guilty to failure to provide adequate shelter and sustenance for ten hens. He received a fine of $25,000 and agreed to make a donation of $100,000 to the Maine Department of Agriculture to inspect and monitor state egg farms against future animal abuse.[88]

Two months later, however, the DeCoster name was again in the news. DeCoster egg farms were at the center of the biggest egg recall in US history encompassing half a *billion* salmonella-contaminated eggs.[89] But the wheels of justice turned slowly for the humans and animals harmed by the egg operations . . . and mercifully for the Teflon Egg Don. In 2007, seven years after the massive recall,[90] DeCoster and his son Peter were ordered by a United States District Court judge in the Northern District of Iowa to spent three months in federal prison for selling the tainted eggs.[91] The judge did say, however, that DeCoster could serve his sentence in New Hampshire, close to his Maine residence, and scheduled son Peter DeCoster's sentence to allow him to attend his daughter's wedding.[92]

It has been said that agricultural crime is seldom or lightly prosecuted and the Teflon Egg Don's fate is a case in point.

IMMIGRATION RAIDS AT SLAUGHTERHOUSES CONTINUE

Immigration raids at US slaughterhouses have not stopped since the gigantic raid at Agriprocessor in Postville, Iowa in 2008 described in the first edition of this book. The raids continue to highlight Big Meat's abuse of workers and animals to produce cheap meat.

In 2018, US Immigration and Customs Enforcement (ICE) swooped down upon Southeastern Provision, a cattle slaughterhouse in Bean Station, Tennessee, detaining the workforce of 97 employees[93] and leaving only three workers. Thirty-two of the detainees were released the same day, but 54 were kept in detention and 10 were arrested for defying previous deportation orders.[94]

While early news reports focused on the immigration detentions, the back story was the raid was prompted by the slaughterhouse owners' alleged withdrawal of millions of dollars to avoid paying $2.5 million in payroll taxes.[95]

The raid was conducted in partnership with the IRS, reported Knox News.[96]

According to the Associated Press, the Tennessee Occupational Safety and Health Administration found 27 violations at the Southeastern Provision operation including the "lack of appropriate eye or face protection, inadequate safety training, hazardous chemicals inadequately labeled and toilet facilities not maintained."[97]

In 2019, the following year, Koch Foods, a giant chicken processor that supplies Burger King, Kroger, and Walmart[98] (not affiliated with the Koch brothers) experienced immigration raids at four plants in small Mississippi towns. Five days after the raids, however, Koch Foods was already holding "job fairs" and finding successful replacement workers.[99] Cynics have observed that on today's industrial farms, workers are as dispensable as animals.

Abused workers are not the only reason meat is cheap. According to David Robinson Simon, author of the book *Meatonomics*, if Big Meat did not offload its true costs onto society "a two-pound package of pork ribs would run $32."[100] What are some of the offloaded costs? Degraded water and air, reduced property values near factory farms, higher taxes through government subsidies and higher health care costs from meat-related conditions like heart diseases and obesity, writes Simon.

CONCLUSION

Since the first edition of this book, ongoing food and drug scandals prove that the regulatory agencies charged with protecting consumers still put industry first—that industry profits come before public health.

ACKNOWLEDGMENTS

I am grateful to the editors at Prometheus Books, to my agent, Barry Zucker, and to the many editors who have taught and guided me along the way, including Chad Rubel; Mark Karlin; Meg White; the late Alex Cockburn; Jeffrey St. Clair; Kim Petersen; Sunil K. Sharma; Angie Tibbs; Selwyn Manning; David McLellan; George McLellan; Rob Kall; John Roberts; Pascale Fusshoeller; John McEvoy; Daniel Ballarin, MD; Alan Gray; Judyth Piazza; Tom Williams; Don Hazen; Tana Ganeva; Tara Lohan; Liliana Segura; Adele Stan; Bev Conover; Craig Brown; Jon Queally; the late William Franklin McCoy, MD; the late Stephan Gregory; Diana Mathias; Maureen Zebian; Christine Lin; Stephanie Lam; Dan Wilson; Barry Sussman; the late Lydia Sargent; Robert Whitcomb; Lois Kazakoff; Nicholas Goldberg; Nick King; Marshall Froker; Colin McMahon; Sidney Wolfe, MD; Gregg Runburg; Karen Sorensen; Mark Law; Sherren Leigh; and Mary Helt Gavin of the Evanston RoundTable.

I am indebted to the research support of Samantha Martin, Dianna Stirpe, and Patrick Sugrue, the librarians at Northwestern University, University of Illinois at Chicago, Rush University, and the Evanston Public and Harold Washington Libraries, and to my brilliant pharmacology professors, whom I sometimes actually understood.

I also greatly appreciate the consumers, patients, clinicians, and researchers who've written me; the activists working in animal welfare and drug safety; and my steadfast friends at Quartet and the North Shore Club.

Finally, thank you to my family, and to John Hughes and John Keyser Tice, PhD, who still light my path.

NOTES

PART 1: BIG PHARMA

CHAPTER 1. WHEN THE MEDICATION IS READY, THE DISEASE (AND PATIENTS) WILL APPEAR— OR, WHEN TV MAKES YOU SICK

1. Coca-Cola advertisement, *Journal of the American Medical Association* (1956).

2. Ibid.

3. Aventyl® advertisement, *Hospital & Community Psychiatry* 19, no. 1 (1968).

4. These quotations are from two Aventyl advertisements in *Hospital & Community Psychiatry* 19, no. 4 (1968); and *Hospital & Community Psychiatry* 18, no. 12 (1967).

5. Triavil advertisement, *Journal of the American Medical Association* 211, no. 1 (1970): 102–104.

6. Triavil advertisement, *Journal of the American Medical Association*, (n.d.).

7. Tofrānil® advertisement, *Hospital & Community Psychiatry* 19, no. 7 (1968), http://www.bonkersinstitute.org/medshow/femgrad.html (accessed September 26, 2011).

8. Premarin advertisement, *Journal of the American Medical Association* (n.d.).

9. Mellaril advertisement, *Journal of the American Medical Association* 23, no. 7 (February 12, 1968): 62–64.

10. Valium advertisement, *Hospital & Community Psychiatry* 21, no. 5 (1970).

11. Dexedrine® advertisement, *Journal of the American Medical Association* 160, no. 10 (1956): 79.

12. Sinequan advertisement, *Journal of the American Medical Association* (n.d.).

13. Ibid.

14. Doriden advertisement, *Journal of the American Medical Association* 207, no. 10 (1969): 1942–44.

15. Valium advertisement, *Journal of the American Medical Association* 213, no. 6 (August 10, 1970).

16. Ibid.

17. Serpasil advertisement, *Psychosomatic Medicine* 18, no. 4 (1956).

18. Thorazine advertisement, *Mental Hospitals* 7, no. 7 (1956).

19. Thorazine advertisement, unknown journal (1959), http://www.bonkersinstitute.org/medicineshow.html (accessed September 26, 2011).

20. Miltown® advertisement, *Journal of the American Medical Association* 199, no. 9 (February 27, 1967): 224–26.

21. The information in this paragraph comes from three Thorazine advertisements in *Mental Hospitals* 7, no. 7 (1956): 2; *California Medicine* 86, no. 1 (1957); and *California Medicine* 88, no. 4 (1958).

22. Ritonic advertisement, *California Medicine* 90, no. 3 (1959): 15.

23. Quaalude advertisement, *Archives of General Psychiatry* 25, no. 5 (1971): 30–33.

24. Mellaril advertisement, *Journal of the American Medical Association* 15, no. 1 (January 4, 1971).

25. Matthew Arnold, "DTC Report: Flat Is the New Up," *Medical Marketing & Media*, March 15, 2010, http://www.mmm-online.com/dtc-report-flat-is-the-new-up/article/166958/; John W. Schoen, "How Much Is the War in Iraq Costing Us?" MSNBC, October 22, 2006.

26. From a comedy special on cable TV. (Note: Rock used the term "drug," not "DTC.")

27. Ted McDonough, "Pill Poppers. Doctors 'Just Say No' to Drug Company Hype and Freebies," *Salt Lake City Weekly*, June 16, 2005.

28. Ibid.

29. "Vioxx Linked to Thousands of Deaths," *MSNBC News*, October 6, 2004.

30. J. K. Wall and John Tuohy, "Woman Participating in Lilly Trial Hangs Self," *Indianapolis Star*, February 9, 2004; Food and Drug Administration, "Risk of Oral Birth Defects in Children Born to Mothers Taking Topiramate," press release, http://www.fda.gov/NewsEvents/Newsroom/PressAnnouncements/ucm245594.htm (accessed September 26, 2011).

31. "Early Communication about an Ongoing Safety Review of Tumor Necrosis Factor (TNF) Blockers (Marketed as Remicade, Enbrel, Humira, and Cimzia," Food and Drug Administration, http://www.fda.gov/Drugs/DrugSafety/PostmarketDrugSafetyInformationforPatientsandProviders/DrugSafetyInformationforHeathcareProfessionals/ucm174449.htm (accessed September 26, 2011); "Information for Healthcare Professionals: Cimzia (Certolizumab Pegol), Enbrel (Etanercept), Humira (Adalimumab), and Remicade (Infliximab)," Food and Drug Administration, http://www.fda.gov/Drugs/DrugSafety/PostmarketDrugSafetyInformationforPatientsandProviders/ucm124185.htm (accessed September 26, 2011).

32. J. Corren et al., "Safety and Tolerability of Omalizumab," *Clinical & Experimental Allergy* 39, no. 6 (June 2009): 788–97.

33. "Safety Review Update on Reports of Hepatosplenic T-Cell Lymphoma in Adolescents and Young Adults Receiving Tumor Necrosis Factor (TNF) Blockers, Azathioprine and/or Mercaptopurine," Food and Drug Administration, http://www.fda.gov/Safety/MedWatch/SafetyInformation/SafetyAlertsforHumanMedicalProducts/ucm251443.htm (accessed September 26, 2011).

34. Alice Goodman, "Excess Deaths Reported in Patients Receiving RA Drug, but Trial Continues," *Pain Medicine News* 9, no. 6 (June 2011), http://www.painmedicinenews.com/ViewArticle.aspx?d=Clinical+Pain+Medicine&d_id=82&i=June+2011&i_id=739&a_id=17324; Bill Gillette, "Psoriasis Drugs' Heart Risk Unclear," *Modern Medicine*, August 31, 2011, http://www.modernmedicine.com/modernmedicine/Dermatology/Psoriasis-drugs-heart-risk-unclear/ArticleStandard/Article/detail/737486 (accessed January 5, 2012); Caitriona Ryan et al., "Association between Biologic Therapies for Chronic Plaque Psoriasis and Cardiovascular Events. A Meta-Analysis of Randomized Controlled Trials," *Journal of the American Medical Association* 306, no. 8 (August 24, 2011): 864–71.

35. Ed Silverman, "New Psoriasis Drugs Show No Heart Risk, But . . . ," *Pharmalot*, August 24, 2011, http://www.pharmalot.com/2011/08/new-psoriasis-drugs-show-no-heart-risk-but/; Julie Steenhuysen, "No Major Heart Risk Seen in New Psoriasis Drugs," Reuters, August 23, 2011.

36. Mark Greif, "The Hard Sell," *New York Times*, December 30, 2007.

37. Liz Szabo, "Number of Americans Taking Antidepressants Doubles," *USA Today*, August 4, 2009.

38. Natalie Wood-Wright, "Prescriptions for Antidepressants Increasing among Individuals with No Psychiatric Diagnosis, EurekAlert! August 4, 2011, http://www.eurekalert.org/pub_releases/2011-08/jhub-pfa080411.php (accessed September 26, 2011).

39. Shirley S. Wang, "More Patients Took Antidepressants & Antipsychotics Together," *Wall Street Journal*, August 4, 2009.

40. SSRI Stories, http://ssristories.com; Jay C. Fournier et al., "Antidepressant Drug Effects and Depression Severity," *Journal of the American Medical Association* 303, no. 1 (January 6, 2010): 47–53.

41. Craig Lambert, "Worse Living through Chemistry. The Downsides of Prozac," *Harvard Magazine*, May–June 2000.

42. Martha Rosenberg, "Phillip Sinaikin, M.D., 'Psychiatryland' Author, Explains How Psychiatry Is Broken," *Huffington Post*, July 1, 2011, http://www.huffingtonpost.com/martha-rosenberg/phillip-sinaikin-psychiatryland_b_884863.html.

43. Steven Woloshin and Lisa M. Schwartz, "Think inside the Box," *New York Times*, July 4, 2011, http://nytimes.com/2011/07/05/opinion/05Woloshin.html.

44. Vladimir Maletic et al., "Neurobiology of Depression: Major Depressive Disorder as a Progressive Illness," Medscape, http://www.medscape.com/viewarticle/567400_5 (accessed September 26, 2011).

45. "Depression: Recognizing the Physical Symptoms," WebMD, http://www.webmd.com/depression/recognizing-depression-symptoms/physical-symptoms (accessed September 26, 2011); "Prozac Defence Stands in Manitoba Teen's Murder Case," *National Post*, December 7, 2011, http://news.nationalpost.com/2011/12/07/prozac-defence-stands-in-manitoba-teens-murder-case/ (accessed February 1, 2012).

46. "Depression: Recognizing the Physical Symptoms."

47. Ibid.

48. Ibid.

49. Craig Stoltz, "Behind the Screens—Who Are the Companies behind the Web Sites Competing to Provide You with Health Information? Can You Trust Them with . . . Your Life?" *Washington Post*, May 16, 2000.

50. "What Is Shift Work Disorder?" Wake-Up Squad, http://www.thewakeupsquad.com/ (accessed September 26, 2011).

51. "Some Facts about Shift Work Disorder," Wake-Up Squad, http://www.thewakeup squad.com/facts-about-swd.aspx?template=print (accessed September 26, 2011).

52. *The Flame*, University of Chicago student newspaper, May 4, 2010.

53. Vyvanse advertisement in *Men's Fitness*, September, 2010; Provigil advertisement, "Struggling to Fight the Fog?" distributed as a media insert.

54. "Truckin'," by the Grateful Dead, words by Robert Hunter, music by Garcia, Lesh, and Weir, http://artsites.ucsc.edu/GDead/agdl/truckin.html.

55. Drugs.com, "Halcion," http://www.drugs.com/monograph/halcion.html (accessed September 26, 2011).

56. Food and Drug Administration Center for Drug Evaluation and Research, Food and Drug Administration and National Transportation Safety Board Joint Public Meeting, Transportation Safety and Potentially Sedating or Impairing Medications, National Transportation Safety Board Headquarters, November 14, 2001.

57. Roni Caryn Rabin, "Awareness: On Drug Labels, Vital Facts May Be Missing," *New York Times*, October 29, 2009; Stephanie Saul, "F.D.A. Warns of Sleeping Pills' Strange Effects," *New York Times*, March 15, 2007.

58. Ed Silverman, "Abbott Uses Fear to Promote Sleeping Pills in India," *Pharmalot*, July 8, 2011, http://www.pharmalot.com/2011/07/abbott-uses-fear-to-promote-sleeping-pills -in-india/.

59. Saul, "F.D.A. Issues Warning on Sleeping Pills."

60. "Ambien in the Driver's Seat," editorial, *New York Times*, March 11, 2006; "Ambien: A Growing Drugged-Driving Problem," Car Connection, http://www.thecarconnection.com/ review/1008806_drivers-news-gas-prices-heading-up (accessed September 26, 2011).

61. Department of Health and Human Services, Food and Drug Administration, Senate Committee on Labor and Human Resources, Statement on Promotion of Unapproved Drugs and Medical Devices (William B. Schultz Deputy Commissioner for Policy), February 22, 1996; Chris Adams and Alison Young, "FDA Rules Becoming Irrelevant—Unapproved Drug Uses Now the Norm," *Saint Paul Pioneer Press*, November 4, 2003.

62. "Pfizer to Pay Record Fine for Bextra Fraud," United Press International, September 2, 2009; Chuck Bartels, "Ark. Announces $18.5M Settlement with Eli Lilly," Associated Press, February 16, 2010; Matthew Perrone, "AstraZeneca Paying $68.5M in Seroquel Settlement," Associated Press, March 10, 2011.

63. Martha Rosenberg, "Why Are Pfizer's Ghostwritten Hormone Therapy Articles Not Retracted?" *OpEdNews.com*, February 2, 2010, http://www.opednews.com/articles/Why-Are -Pfizer-s-Ghostwrit-by-Martha-Rosenberg-100202-181.html.

64. Bernadette Tansey, "Huge Penalty in Drug Fraud," *San Francisco Chronicle*, May 14, 2004; "Migraine, Cluster, Trigeminal Neuralgia, and Mood Disorders: Common Ground Anti-epileptic Drugs for the Treatment of Migraine," Medscape, http://www.medscape.org/view article/416383_6 (accessed September 26, 2011).

65. Stephanie Saul, "Gimme an Rx! Cheerleaders Pep Up Drug Sales," *New York Times*, November 28, 2005, http://www.nytimes.com/2005/11/28/business/28cheer.html?pagewanted =1&th&emc=th.

66. PR Newswire, "The Doctor Won't See You (Mr. Pharma Rep), Now," news release, ZS Associates, May 6, 2010.

67. Ted McDonough, "Pill Poppers: Doctors 'Just Say No' to Drug Company Hype and Freebies," *Salt Lake City Weekly*, June 15, 2006, http://www.cityweekly.net/utah/print-article -2510-print.html.

68. Martha Rosenberg, "Medical Conference Looks at Re-Balancing Pharmaceutical Industry Influence," *YubaNet*, May 20, 2010, http://yubanet.com/usa/Medical-Conference -Looks-at-Re-Balancing-Pharmaceutical-Industry-Influence.php#.TuzQ1EZjjZk.

69. Martha Rosenberg, "No Free Pens but Pharma Influence Still Felt at Psychiatric Meeting," *Scoop*, May 31, 2010, http://www.scoop.co.nz/stories/HL1005/S00245.htm.

70. Ibid.

71. Mike Mitka, "New 'Law' Attempts to Explain Strategies Drug Marketers Use to Sway Prescribing," *Journal of the American Medical Association* 305, no. 11 (May 16, 2011): 1083–1084, http://jama.ama-assn.org/content/305/11/1083.extract.

72. Ibid., italics mine.

73. Martha Rosenberg, "The Doctor Won't See You Now: New Training Helps Pre-scribers Cope with Pharma Over Promotion, Food Consumer, May 21, 2010, http://www.food consumer.org/newsite/Non-food/Healthcare/training_helps_prescribers_cope_with_pharma _2105101231.html (accessed February 1, 2012).

74. Ibid.

75. Ibid.

76. Ibid.

77. *Chicago Reader* (n.d.), *Daily Northwestern* (n.d.).

78. Steve Stanek, "Debate Persists over Drug Advertising's Side Effects," *Chicago Tribune*, March 9, 2004.

79. Amy Toscano, "Direct-to-Consumer Promotion: The Role of FDA," speech, Pharmed Out Conference, Georgetown University Medical Center, June 16, 2011.

80. Michael Sauers, regulatory review officer, Division of Drug Marketing, Advertising, and Communications, Department of Health and Human Services, to Michelle Sharp, Eli Lilly and Company, March 26, 2009.

81. Martha Rosenberg, "Doctors Learn How to Immunize Themselves against Big Pharma's Bribes and Misleading Marketing Using Pfizer Settlement Funds," *BuzzFlash*, May 20, 2010, http://blog.buzzflash.com/contributors/3214 (accessed January 2, 2012).

82. Ibid.

83. Toscano, "Direct-to-Consumer Promotion: The Role of FDA."

84. Wellbutrin XR advertisement, unidentified magazine, 2006.

85. Lunesta advertisement, *Parade*, November 4, 2007.

86. Actonel advertisement, *New York Times*, January 11, 2006.

87. Jack Neff, "FDA Ruling Gives Actonel Boost in Osteoporosis-Drug War," *Advertising Age*, April 17, 2007.

88. Marie McCullough, "An Unhealthy Dose of Hollywood Celebrities Making Health-Care Appeals Usually Make Money, Too—For Themselves and the Drug Companies That Hire Them," *Philadelphia Inquirer*, June 16, 2003.

89. National Institutes of Health, "NHLBI Stops Trial of Estrogen Plus Progestin Due to Increased Breast Cancer Risk, Lack of Overall Benefit," news release, National Heart, Lung, and Blood Institute, July 9, 2002, http://www.nhlbi.nih.gov/new//press/02-07-09.htm (accessed September 25, 2011).

90. Rich Thomaselli and Ira Teinowitz, "Ad Groups Unfazed by DTC-Drug Debacles. Industry Still Opposes Moratorium Despite Flap over Vytorin, Zyprexa," *Advertising Age*, February 4, 2008.

91. Shirley S. Wang, "Congress to Pfizer: Why Is Robert Jarvik the Lipitor Man?" *Wall Street Journal*, January 7, 2008, http://blogs.wsj.com/health/2008/01/07/congress-to-pfizer-why-is-robert-jarvik-the-lipitor-man/.

92. McCullough, "An Unhealthy Dose of Hollywood Celebrities Making Health-Care Appeals Usually Make Money, Too."

93. Maryann Napoli, "The Marketing of Osteoporosis," *American Journal of Nursing* 109, no. 4 (April 2009), http://www.womens-health.org/nz/uploads/The_Marketing_of_Osteoporosis.pdf.

94. Melissa Healy, "Sold on Drugs/Selling the Patient," *Los Angeles Times*, August 6, 2007.

95. Katherine Hobson, "Mental Health Group's State Chapters Get Millions from Pharma," *Wall Street Journal*, April 28, 2010.

96. Gardiner Harris, "Drug Makers Are Advocacy Group's Biggest Donors," *New York Times*, October 21, 2009.

97. Healy, "Sold on Drugs."

98. "Depression Is Real," public service announcements, http://www.dbsalliance.org/site/PageServer?pagename=advocacy_dir (accessed September 26, 2011).

99. Joel M. Kremer, "Treating to Target: The Changing Paradigm for Achieving Remission and Addressing the Challenges to Implementation," Medscape, disclosures, http://www.medscape.org/viewarticle/744769 (accessed October 12, 2011); Jane E. Brody, "Living Better with Rheumatoid Arthritis," *New York Times*, August 12, 2008.

100. Stephen B. Hanauer, "Clinical Perspectives in Crohn's Disease. Turning Traditional Treatment Strategies on Their Heads: Current Evidence for 'Step-Up' versus 'Top-Down,'" *Reviews in Gastroenterological Disorders* (impact factor: 1.28), suppl. 2 (February 2, 2007): 22.

101. Martha Rosenberg, "Rheumatoid Arthritis Drug Humira Linked to Psoriasis, Herpes, Possibly Cancer," *AlterNet*, September 18, 2008, http://www.alternet.org/health/98959?page=2.

102. J. A. Singh et al., "Adverse Effects of Biologics: A Network Meta-Analysis and Cochran Overview," Cochrane Database System Review 2 (February 16, 2011): CD008794.

103. Advertising supplement, *New York Times Magazine*, October 28, 2007.

104. Ibid.

105. Martha Rosenberg, "Sex Pill for Women: Big Pharma Trying to Profit from Low Sex Drive?" *AlterNet*, June 4, 2010, http://www.alternet.org/reproductivejustice/147112/sex_pill_for_women%3A_big_pharma_trying_to_profit_from_low_sex_drive/.

106. "Lisa Rinna on Sex, Brain, Body Connection," *CBS News*, May 19, 2010.

107. "Understanding Female Sexual Desire, The Brain-Body Connection," pt. 1, Discovery Channel, http://dsc.discovery.com/videos/cme-understanding-female-sexual-desire-part-1.html (accessed September 26, 2011).

108. Todd Neale, "Many Women with Sexual Dysfunction Simply Don't Care," MedPage Today, October 31, 2008, http://www.medpagetoday.com/OBGYN/GeneralOBGYN/11574 (accessed September 26, 2011).

109. Michelle Miller, "FDA Nixes 'Female Viagra' Flibanserin," *CBS Evening News*, June 18, 2010.

110. Boehringer Ingelheim, "Following Regulatory Feedback Boehringer Ingelheim Decides to Discontinue Flibanserin Development," press release, October 8, 2010, ingelheim.com/news/news_releases/press_releases/2010/08_october_2010_fliba.html (accessed September 26, 2011).

111. Neal Conan, "Prescription Drug Deaths Major Killer in the U.S.," National Public Radio, September 27, 2011.

CHAPTER 2. FRAGILE: HANDLE WITH RISPERDAL . . . AND SEROQUEL AND ZYPREXA AND GEODON

1. Martha Rosenberg, "Phillip Sinaikin, M.D., 'Psychiatryland' Author, Explains How Psychiatry Is Broken," *Huffington Post*, July 1, 2011, http://www.huffingtonpost.com/martha-rosenberg/phillip-sinaikin-psychiatryland_b_884863.html.

2. Jeanne Whalen, "Hurdles Multiply for Latest Drugs, *Wall Street Journal*, August 1, 2011.

3. Ibid.

4. Ibid.

5. Ibid.; Duff Wilson, "For $520 Million, AstraZeneca Will Settle Case over Marketing of a Drug," *New York Times*, April 26, 2010.

6. Gwen Olsen, "Drugging Our Children to Death," *Health News Digest*, June 29, 2009, http://healthnewsdigest.com/news/Guest_Columnist_710/Drugging_Our_Children_to_Death.shtml (accessed September 25, 2011).

7. "FOX 5 Investigates Singulair," Fox News, November 8, 2010.

8. Emily P. Walker, "Senators Question Use of Psych Drugs in Nursing Homes," MedPage Today, August 15, 2011, http://www.medpagetoday.com/Geriatrics/Dementia/28052.

9. Martha Rosenberg, "Meeting the Drug Industry," *CounterPunch*, June 4–6, 2010, http://www.counterpunch.org/2010/06/04/meeting-the-drug-industry/.

10. Martha Rosenberg, "No Free Pens but Pharma Influence Still Felt at Psychiatric Meeting," *AlterNet*, June 2, 2010, http://blogs.alternet.org/speakeasy/2010/06/02/no-free-pens-but-pharma-influence-still-felt-at-psychiatric-meeting/.

11. "Evaluating Antipsychotic Polypharmacy Regimens for Patients with Chronic Mental Illness," poster from Maimonides Medical Center in Brooklyn, American Psychiatric Association 2010 meeting, New Orleans.

12. Gardiner Harris, "Research Center Tied to Drug Company," *New York Times*, November 24, 2008.

13. Gardiner Harris and Benedict Carey, "Researchers Fail to Reveal Full Drug Pay," *New York Times*, June 8, 2008; "Private Money, Public Disclosure," *Science*, July 2009.

14. Xi Yu, "Three Professors Face Sanctions Following Harvard Medical School Inquiry Investigation by Medical School and Massachusetts General Hospital Punishes Psychiatrists Accused by Senator," *Harvard Crimson*, July 2, 2011.

15. Harris, "Research Center Tied to Drug Company."

16. Gardiner Harris, "Drug Maker Told Studies Would Aid It, Papers Say," *New York Times*, March 19, 2009.

17. Ibid.

18. Rob Waters and Julie Ziegler, "Harvard Teaching Hospital Reviewing J&J Ties to Psychiatry Unit," *Bloomberg*, November 25, 2008.

19. Martha Rosenberg, "Why You Should Care about the University of Miami NIH Scandal," *CounterPunch*, June 22, 2010; Bradley F. Marple and Matthew W. Ryan, "Facing Conflicts: The Battle between Medicine and Industry," ENT Today, April 2009, http://www.enttoday.org/details/article/497837/Facing_Conflicts_The_Battle_between_Medicine_and_Industry.html.

20. Ibid.

21. Jim Rosack, "New Data Show Declines in Antidepressant Prescribing," *Psychiatric News* 40, no. 17 (September 2, 2005): 1.

22. United States District Court, District of Massachusetts Civil Action No. 08 CA 11318 DPW, Second Amended Complaint for False Claims Act Violations 31 U.S.C. § 3729, ET SEQ., March 13, 2009.

23. Jim Edwards, "J&J and Risperdal: New Claims of Kickbacks and Fraudulent Marketing," *BNET*, December 17, 2008, http://www.cbsnews.com/8301-505123_162-42840276/j038j-and -risperdal-new-claims-of-kickbacks-and-fraudulent-marketing/ (accessed January 30, 2012).

24. United States District Court, District of Massachusetts Civil Action No. 08 CA 11318 DPW.

25. M. Alexander Otto, "Drugs Might Breed Violence," *News Tribune* (Tacoma, WA), May 28, 2007.

26. Michael Sernyak and Robert Rosenheck, "Experience of VA Psychiatrists with Pharmaceutical Detailing of Antipsychotic Medications," *Psychiatric Services* 58 (October 2007): 1292–96.

27. Margaret Cronin Fisk and Jef Feeley, "Lilly Paid Doctors to Prescribe Zyprexa," *Bloomberg*, September 8, 2009, http://www.bloomberg.com/apps/news?pid=newsarchive&sid =aHXOSlLoUMbM.

28. "$515 Million California Claims Drug Giant Bribed Docs to Prescribe," Associated Press, March 23, 2011.

29. Alex Berenson, "Lilly Settles Alaska Suit over Zyprexa," *New York Times*, March 26, 2008; Sanjay Gupta et al., "Atypical Antipsychotics and Glucose Dysregulation: A Series of 4 Cases," *Primary Care Companion, Journal of Clinical Psychiatry* 3, no. 2 (2001): 61–65, http:// www.ncbi.nlm.nih.gov/pmc/articles/PMC181163/.

30. Martha Rosenberg, "States Taking Pharma to Court for Risky Antipsychotic-Prescribing Spree," *AlterNet*, October 19, 2008, http://www.alternet.org/health/103543.

31. Benedict Carey, "Risks Found for Youths in New Antipsychotics," *New York Times*, September 15, 2008.

32. Ibid.

33. Peter Tyrer et al., "Risperidone, Haloperidol, and Placebo in the Treatment of Aggressive Challenging Behaviour in Patients with Intellectual Disability: A Randomised Controlled Trial," *Lancet* 371, no. 9606 (January 5, 2008): 57–63; Lon S. Schneider et al., "Effectiveness of Atypical Antipsychotic Drugs in Patients with Alzheimer's Disease," *New England Journal of Medicine* 355 (October 12, 2006): 1525–38.

34. Clive Ballard, "Quetiapine and Rivastigmine and Cognitive Decline in Alzheimer's Disease: Randomised Double Blind Placebo Controlled Trial," *British Medical Journal* 330 (February 18, 2005): 874.

35. Ed Silverman, "Antipsychotics, Nursing Homes & Increased Risks," *Pharmalot*, November 19, 2007, http://www.pharmalot.com/2007/11/antipsychotics-nursing-homes -expendable-patients/.

36. Ibid.

37. Stephanie Saul, "In Some States, Maker Oversees Use of Its Drug," *New York Times*, March 23, 2007.

38. Ibid.

39. Edwards, "J&J and Risperdal."

40. Emily Ramshaw, "Filing Alleges Drug Maker Defrauded Texas to Get on Medicaid List," *Dallas Morning News*, December 17, 2008.

41. Ibid.

42. United States District Court, District of Massachusetts Civil Action No. 08 CA 11318 DPW.

43. "Welcome to NAMI Arapahoe/Douglas Counties: A NAMI Colorado Affiliate," National Alliance on Mental Illness, http://www.nami.org/MSTemplate.cfm?MicrositeID=257.

44. Jim Edwards, "Pfizer Used Docs Accused of Misconduct to Prep Geodon Submission to FDA," *BNET*, September 22, 2009, http://www.cbsnews.com/8301-505123_162-42843001/pfizer-used-docs-accused-of-misconduct-to-prep-geodon-submission-to-fda/.

45. "Individualizing ADHD Pharmacotherapy in Patients with Disruptive Behavioral Disorders," Medscape, December 28, 2007, http://www.medscape.org/viewprogram/8468 (accessed September 25, 2011).

46. Daniel Carlat, "New York Times Covers Industry Funding of CME," *Carlat Psychiatry Blog*, October 21, 2009, http://carlatpsychiatry.blogspot.com/2009/10/new-york-times-covers-industry-funding.html (accessed September 25, 2011).

47. Jan Croonenberghs et al., "Risperidone in Children with Disruptive Behavior Disorders and Subaverage Intelligence: A 1-Year, Open-Label Study of 504 Patients," *Journal of the American Academy of Child & Adolescent Psychiatry* 44, no. 1 (January 2005): 64–72; Gardiner Harris, "Use of Antipsychotics in Children Is Criticized," *New York Times*, November 18, 2008.

48. Alex Berenson, "Drug Files Show Maker Promoted Unapproved Use," *New York Times*, December 18, 2006.

49. Ibid.

50. "Wyeth—Prempro: 'No Boundaries, No Limits to Your Selling Effort,'" *Pharmagossip*, July 26, 2006, http://pharmagossip.blogspot.com/2006/07/wyeth-prempro-no-boundaries-no-limits.html.

51. "Ad Stars, Pharm Exec Honors the Most Innovative Ads in 2004," *Pharmaceutical Executive*, http://pharmexec.findpharma.com/pharmexec/data/articlestandard//pharmexec/182006/323074/article.pdf.

52. Epica 2004, "Award Winners," AdForum.com, http://www.adforum.com/awards/showcase/6650180/2004 (accessed September 25, 2011).

53. "Best of Health Awards," Institute of Practitioners in Advertising, 2007, http://www.ipabestofhealthawards.co.uk/write/Documents/plugin-BOHSupplement_07.pdf (accessed September 25, 2011).

54. Jim Edwards, "AstraZeneca Allegedly Recruits Tigger and Eeyore to Sell Seroquel®," *BNET*, November 6, 2008.

55. Comment from Mary Kitchens to Paul Raeburn, "One Flew Over the Morning News," *Columbia (University) Journalism Review*, August 21, 2008, http://www.cjr.org/the_observatory/one_flew_over_the_morning_news.php?page=all.

56. Martha Rosenberg, "Pediatric Zyprexa Brochures Embarrass British Health Service," *OpEdNews.com*, November 19, 2010, http://www.opednews.com/articles/Pediatric-Zyprexa-Brochure-by-Martha-Rosenberg-091118-587.html.

57. Radha Chitale, "Keeping Jani Alive: The Perils of Childhood-Onset Schizophrenia," *ABC News*, July 1, 2009.

58. Gabriele Masi, "Children with Schizophrenia: Clinical Picture and Pharmacological Treatment," *CNS Drugs* 20, no. 10 (2006): 841–66.

59. Ibid.

60. Ibid.

61. "Conflicts of Interest for Practice Parameters Not Listed in Parameter," Practice Parameters, American Academy of Child & Adolescent Psychiatry, http://www.aacap.org/cs/root/member_information/practice_information/practice_parameters/conflicts_of_interest_for_practice_parameters_not_listed_in_parameter (accessed September 25, 2011).

62. Joan L. Luby et al., "Preschool Depression Homotypic Continuity and Course Over 24 Months," *Archives of General Psychiatry* 66, no. 8 (2009): 897–905.

63. Ibid.

64. "Father Convicted of 1st-Degree Murder in Death of Rebecca Riley," *Boston Globe*, March 26, 2010; Tim Carpenter, "Child's Death a Tragic Destiny," *Topeka Capital-Journal*, June 6, 2009.

65. Edecio Martinez, "After 7-Year-Old Gabriel Myers' Suicide, Fla. Bill Looks to Tighten Access to Psychiatric Drugs," *CBS News*, March 17, 2010.

66. Martha Rosenberg, "Big Pharma's Push to Drug Children. Dr. David Healy Interview," *Epoch Times*, January 16, 2008.

67. Luby et al., "Preschool Depression."

68. Andy C. Belden and Joan L. Luby, "Preschoolers' Depression Severity and Behaviors during Dyadic Interactions: The Mediating Role of Parental Support," *Journal of the American Academy of Child & Adolescent Psychiatry* 45, no. 2 (February 2006): 213–22; Jim Edwards, "Doc Who Urged Antipsychotics for 3-Year-Olds Funded by J&J, AZ and Shire," *BNET*, August 28, 2009, http://www.cbsnews.com/8301-505123_162-42842712/updated-doc-who-urged-antipsychotics-for-3-year-olds-funded-by-j038j-az-and-shire/.

69. Mani Pavuluri, as quoted at University of Illinois–Chicago, website, http://www.psych.uic.edu/brain-center/director.html (accessed February 2, 2012).

70. Tushita Mayanil et al., "Emerging Biosignature of Brain Function and Intervention in Pediatric Bipolar Disorder," *Minerva Pediatrica* 63, no. 3 (June 2011): 183–200; Mani Pavuluri, "Double-Blind Randomized Trial of Risperidone versus Divalproex in Pediatric Bipolar Disorder: fMRI Outcomes," *Psychiatry Research* 193, no. 1 (July 30, 2011): 28–37.

71. Alessandra M. Passarotti and Mani N. Pavuluri, "Brain Functional Domains Inform Therapeutic Interventions in Attention-Deficit/Hyperactivity Disorder and Pediatric Bipolar Disorder," *Expert Review of Neurotherapeutics* 11, no. 6 (June 2011): 897–914.

72. Mani Pavuluri et al., "An fMRI Study of the Neural Correlates of Incidental versus Directed Emotion Processing in Pediatric Bipolar Disorder," *Journal of the American Academy of Child & Adolescent Psychiatry* 48, no. 3 (March 2009): 308–19.

73. Ibid.

74. Mani Pavuluri et al., "Enhanced Working and Verbal Memory after Lamotrigine Treatment in Pediatric Bipolar Disorder," *Bipolar Disorder* 12, no. 2 (March 2010): 213–20.

75. "Over-Diagnosis of Bipolar Disorder and Disability Payments—A Link?" *Science Daily*, May 19, 2010.

76. Bill Berkro, "Prescription Drug Use by US Children on the Rise," Reuters, May 19, 2010.

77. Anna Wilde Mathews, "So Young and So Many Pills," *Wall Street Journal*, December 28, 2010.

78. "Children's Consumption of Chronic Medications Rising," Medco Health Solutions, May 5, 2010, http://www.disabled-world.com/medical/pharmaceutical/child-medications.php (accessed September 25, 2011).

79. Jodi A. Mindell, "Pharmacologic Management of Insomnia in Children and Adolescents: Consensus Statement," *Pediatrics* 117, no. 6 (June 2006): e1223–32.

80. Martha Rosenberg, "8-Year-Olds on Cholesterol Meds? Is Big Pharma Pumping Kids Full of Dangerous Drugs?" *AlterNet*, January 26, 2011, http://www.alternet.org/story/149685/8-year-olds_on_cholesterol_meds_is_big_pharma_pumping_kids_full_of_dangerous _drugs.

81. Julia Hippisley-Cox and Carol Coupland, "Unintended Effects of Statins in Men and Women in England and Wales: Population Based Cohort Study Using the QResearch Database," *British Medical Journal* 340 (May 2010): c2197.

82. Michael J. Breus, "Statins for Kids?" *Huffington Post*, August 5, 2008, http://www .huffingtonpost.com/dr-michael-j-breus/statins-for-kids_b_116379.htm (accessed September 25, 2011).

83. Darshak Sanghavi, "The Reflex to Treat Reflux," *Slate*, June 17, 2010, http://www .slate.com/id/2257038/pagenum/all/#p2 (accessed September 25, 2011).

84. Ibid.

85. Ibid.

86. Laurie Barclay, "Proton Pump Inhibitor Use Linked to *Clostridium difficile* Infection," Medscape, May 11, 2010, http://www.medscape.com/viewarticle/721579 (accessed September 25, 2011); "Avoiding Overuse of Proton Pump Inhibitors (PPIs)," *Worst Pills, Best Pills* newsletter, March, 2008.

87. Marilyn Mann, "Eli Lilly Pleads Guilty to Illegal Marketing of Zyprexa," US Securities and Exchange Commission, http://www.americanbar.org/newsletter/publications/aba _health_esource_home/Volume5_07_Mann.html (accessed September 25, 2011); "Pharmaceutical Giant AstraZeneca to Pay $520 Million for Off-Label Drug Marketing," United

States Department of Justice, Office of Public Affairs, April 27, 2010, http://www.justice.gov/opa/pr/2010/April/10-civ-487.html (accessed September 25, 2011); Cary O'Reilly and Tony Capaccio, "Pfizer Agrees to Record Criminal Fine in Fraud Probe," *Bloomberg*, September 2, 2009, http://www.bloomberg.com/apps/news?pid=newsarchive&sid=a4h7V5lc_xXM.

88. "Psychopharmacologic Drugs Advisory Committee Meeting (to discuss) NDA 20-639/S-045 and S-046: Seroquel (quetiapine fumarate) tablets NDA 20-825/S-032: Geodon (ziprasidone hydrochloride) capsules NDA 20-592/S-040 and S-041: Zyprexa (olanzapine) tablets," Food and Drug Administration Center for Drug Evaluation and Research, June 9, 2009, http://www.fda.gov/downloads/AdvisoryCommittees/CommitteesMeetingMaterials Drugs/PsychopharmacologicDrugsAdvisoryCommittee/UCM172869.pdf; "Psychopharmaco-logic Drugs Advisory Committee Meeting (to discuss) NDA 20-639/S-045 and S-046: Sero-quel (quetiapine fumarate) tablets NDA 20-825/S-032: Geodon (ziprasidone hydrochloride) capsules NDA 20-592/S-040 and S-041: Zyprexa (olanzapine) tablets," Food and Drug Administration Center for Drug Evaluation and Research, June 10, 2009, http://www.fda.gov/downloads/AdvisoryCommittees/CommitteesMeetingMaterials/Drugs/Psychopharmacologic DrugsAdvisoryCommittee/UCM172870.pdf.

89. Psychopharmacologic Drugs Advisory Committee Meeting transcript, Food and Drug Administration, Center for Drug Evaluation and Research, June 9, 2009, http://www .fda.gov/downloads/AdvisoryCommittees/CommitteesMeetingMaterials/Drugs/Psychopharma cologicDrugsAdvisoryCommittee/UCM172869.pdf (accessed September 25, 2011); "National Alliance on Mental Illness Montgomery County Heroes Dinner," GailGriffith.com, October 18, 2005, http://www.gailgriffith.com/news-archive.html.

90. Jim Rosack, "New Data Show Declines in Antidepressant Prescribing," *Psychiatric News* 40, no. 17 (September 2, 2005): 1,

91. Psychopharmacologic Drugs Advisory Committee Meeting, June 9–10, 2009.

92. Ibid.

93. Ibid.

94. Ibid.

95. Ibid.

96. Ibid.

97. Ibid.

98. Ibid.

99. Ibid.

100. Ibid.

101. Ibid.

102. Ibid.

103. Ibid.

104. Ibid

105. Ibid.

106. Martha Rosenberg, "Are Veterans Being Given Deadly Cocktails to Treat PTSD?" *AlterNet*, March 6, 2010, http://www.alternet.org/world/145892/are_veterans_being_given _deadly_cocktails_to_treat_ptsd?page=entire.

107. Kris Hundley, "Approval Process Lowers the Number of Kids on Atypical Prescriptions," *St. Petersburg Times*, March 29, 2009.

108. Ibid.

109. "FDA Panel OKs 3 Psychiatric Drugs for Kids," Associated Press, June 10, 2009.

110. Ibid.

111. John H. Krystal et al., "Adjunctive Risperidone Treatment for Antidepressant-Resistant Symptoms of Chronic Military Service-Related PTSD: A Randomized Trial," *Journal of the American Medical Association* 306, no. 5 (August 3, 2011): 493–502.

112. "VA Spent $717 Million for Useless Post-Traumatic Stress Drug," AllGov, August 25, 2011, http://www.allgov.com/Where_is_the_Money_Going/ViewNews/VA_Spent_717_ Million_Dollars_for_Useless_Post_Traumatic_Stress_Drug_110825 (accessed September 25, 2011).

113. Bob Brewin, "VA Awards New Contract for Debunked PTSD Drug," Nextgov, August 25, 2011, http://www.nextgov.com/nextgov/ng_20110825_1279.php (accessed September 25, 2011).

CHAPTER 3. WEAPONS OF HORMONAL THERAPY

1. Natasha Singer and Duff Wilson, "Menopause, as Brought to You by Big Pharma," *New York Times*, December 12, 2009; Sue Woodman, "The Women's Enron," *Nation*, August 15, 2002.

2. "Psychoneuropharmacological Women's Issues," Bonkers Institute, http://www .bonkersinstitute.org/medshow/fem.html (accessed September 25, 2011).

3. Tofrānil® advertisement, *Hospital & Community Psychiatry* 19, no. 7 (1968), http:// www.bonkersinstitute.org/medshow/femgrad.html.

4. Marplan advertisement, *Mental Hospitals* 11, no. 6 (1960), http://www.bonkers institute.org/medshow/femsymbol.html.

5. Benzedrine advertisements, *Psychosomatic Medicine* 8, no. 3 (1946), http://www .bonkersinstitute.org/medshow/fembenz.html (accessed September 25, 2011).

6. Sally A. Shumaker, "Estrogen plus Progestin and the Incidence of Dementia and Mild Cognitive Impairment in Postmenopausal Women," *Journal of the American Medical Association* 289, no. 20 (May 28, 2003): 2651–62; Susan M. Resnick, "Postmenopausal Hormone Therapy and Regional Brain Volumes, the WHIMS-MRI Study," *Neurology* 72 (January 13, 2009): 125–34.

7. National Heart, Lung, and Blood Institute, National Institutes of Health, "NHLBI

Stops Trial of Estrogen plus Progestin Due to Increased Breast Cancer Risk, Lack of Overall Benefit," news release, July 9, 2002, http://www.nhlbi.nih.gov/new//press/02-07-09.htm (accessed September 25, 2011).

8. Tom Rickey, "Proceedings of the National Academy of Sciences," EurekAlert! September 5, 2006, http://www.eurekalert.org/pub_releases/2006-09/uorm-hth090506.php; Bette Liu et al., "Gallbladder Disease and Use of Transdermal versus Oral Hormone Replacement Therapy in Postmenopausal Women: Prospective Cohort Study," *British Medical Journal* 337 (July 10, 2008): a386; Jody E. Steinauer, "Postmenopausal Hormone Therapy: Does It Cause Incontinence?" *Obstetrics & Gynecology* 106, pt. 1 (November 5, 2005): 940–45; Real F. Gómez et al., "Hormone Replacement Therapy, Body Mass Index and Asthma in Perimenopausal Women: A Cross Sectional Survey," *Thorax* 61, no. 1 (January 2006): 34–40; Elsje R. Koomen et al., "Estrogens, Oral Contraceptives and Hormonal Replacement Therapy Increase the Incidence of Cutaneous Melanoma: A Population-Based Case–Control Study," *Annals of Oncology* 20, no. 2 (February 2009): 358–64; Bette Liu et al., "Reproductive History, Hormonal Factors and the Incidence of Hip and Knee Replacement for Osteoarthritis in Middle-Aged Women," *Annals of the Rheumatic Diseases* 68, no. 7 (July 2009): 1165–70.

9. "Learn about Cancer," American Cancer Society, http://www.cancer.org/cancer/cancercauses/othercarcinogens/medicaltreatments/menopausal-hormone-replacement-therapy-and-cancer-risk (accessed September 25, 2011); Valerie Beral, "Ovarian Cancer and Hormone Replacement Therapy in the Million Women Study," *Lancet* 369, no. 9574 (May 19, 2007): 1703–10; James R. Cerhan et al., "Hormone Replacement Therapy and Risk of Non-Hodgkin Lymphoma and Chronic Lymphocytic Leukemia," *Cancer Epidemiology, Biomarkers & Prevention* 11, no. 11 (November 2002): 1466–71; Christopher G. Slatore, "Lung Cancer and Hormone Replacement Therapy," *Journal of Clinical Oncology* 28, no. 9 (March 20, 2010): 1540–46.

10. Mary B Laya et al., "Effect of Postmenopausal Hormonal Replacement Therapy on Mammographic Density and Parenchymal Pattern," *Radiology* 196, no. 2 (August 1995): 433–37.

11. Christopher Li et al., "Relationship between Menopausal Hormone Therapy and Risk of Ductal, Lobular, and Ductal-Lobular Breast Carcinomas," *Cancer Epidemiology, Biomarkers & Prevention* 17, no. 1 (January 2008): 43–50; Rowan T. Chlebowski et al., "Estrogen plus Progestin and Breast Cancer Detection by Means of Mammography and Breast Biopsy," *Archives of Internal Medicine* 168, no. 4 (February 25, 2008): 370–77; Michaela Kreuzer et al., "Hormonal Factors and Risk of Lung Cancer among Women?" *International Journal of Epidemiology* 32, no. 2 (April 2003): 263–71; Tracy Hampton, "Lung Cancer Mortality Higher in Women Who Used Combination Hormone Therapy," *Journal of the American Medical Association* 302, no. 6 (August 12, 2009): 615–16.

12. Serena Gordon, "Decline in HRT Use Linked to Drop in Breast Cancer," *HealthDay*, April 18, 2007; Singer and Wilson, "Menopause, as Brought to You by Big Pharma."

13. Gordon, "Decline in HRT Use Linked to Drop in Breast Cancer."

14. Theresa Agovino, "Wyeth Faces First Trial over Hormone Replacement Therapy," Law.com, July 26, 2006, http://www.law.com/jsp/law/LawArticleFriendly.jsp?id=115381833 3651&slreturn=1&hbxlogin=1 (accessed September 25, 2011).

15. Prithi Yelaja, "Drug Firms Are Faulted for Hormone Therapy Mess," *Toronto Star*, October 25, 2002.

16. Fawn Vrazo, "FDA Panel Notes Heart Benefits of Postmenopausal Estrogen Drug," *Philadelphia Inquirer*, June 16, 1990.

17. Ibid.

18. Lila Nachtigall et al., "Update on Vaginal Atrophy," Menopause Management, September–October 2005, http://www.menopausemgmt.com/issues/14-05/MM14-5_Vaginal Atrophy.pdf.

19. Duff Wilson, "Investigation Links Wyeth to Articles on Its Drug," *New York Times*, December 13, 2008.

20. C. B. Hammond and Lila Nachtigall, "Is Estrogen Replacement Therapy Necessary?" *Journal of Reproductive Medicine* 30, suppl. no. 10 (October 1985): 797–801.

21. Lila Nachtigall, "Enhancing Patient Compliance with Hormone Replacement Therapy at Menopause," *Obstetrics & Gynecology* 75, suppl. no. 4 (April 1990): 77S–80S.

22. Lila Nachtigall and L. B. Nachtigall, "Protecting Older Women from Their Growing Risk of Cardiac Disease," *Geriatrics* 45, no. 5 (May 1990): 24–29.

23. DesignWrite, Strategic Publications Development Meeting, memo, December 5, 2000, http://dida.library.ucsf.edu/pdf/aic37b10 (accessed September 25, 2011); Barbara E. Klein et al., "Are Sex Hormones Associated with Age-Related Maculopathy in Women? The Beaver Dam Eye Study," *Transactions of the American Ophthalmological Society* 92 (1994): 289–97.

24. COPE retraction guidelines, http://www.publicationethics.org/resources/guidelines (accessed Feburary 2, 2012).

25. William T. Creasman, "Is There an Association between Hormone Replacement Therapy and Breast Cancer?" *Journal of Women's Health* 7, no. 10 (December 1998): 1231–46.

26. DesignWrite, Strategic Publication Plan Tracking; DesignWrite, Premarin Publication Plan, 1997, http://dida.library.ucsf.edu/pdf/ohc37b10 (accessed September 25, 2011).

27. Howard M. Fillit, "The Role of Hormone Replacement Therapy in the Prevention of Alzheimer Disease," *Archives of Internal Medicine* 162, no. 17 (September 2002): 1934–42; Barbara Sherwin, "Mild Cognitive Impairment: Potential Pharmacological Treatment Options," *Journal of the American Geriatric Society* 48, no. 4 (April 2000): 431–41.

28. Lori Mosca, "The Role of Hormone Replacement Therapy in the Prevention of Postmenopausal Heart Disease," *Archive of Internal Medicine* 160, no. 15 (August 14–28, 2000): 2263–72; Charles E. Rackley, "New Clinical Markers Predictive of Cardiovascular Disease," *Cardiology in Review* 12 (2004): 151–57, http://dida.library.ucsf.edu/pdf/tec37b10; DesignWrite, Karen Mittleman to Charles Rackley, MD, letter, August 24, 2001, http://dida.library.ucsf.edu/pdf/hsb37b10 (accessed September 25, 2011).

29. Hilary Macht Felgran and Ann Hettinger, "The Wonder Drug That Wasn't," *Columbia (University) Journalism Review*, July–August 2002.

30. Coleman v. Wyeth Pharmaceuticals, Inc., Superior Court of Pennsylvania, argued July 21, 2009, 6 A.3d 502 (2010), Leagle, http://www.leagle.com/xmlResult.aspx?page=11&xmldoc=in%20paco%2020100830373.xml&docbase=cslwar3-2007-curr&SizeDisp=7 (accessed September 25, 2011).

31. "Description of Council on Hormone Education," University of Wisconsin, Office of Continuing Professional Development in Medicine and Public Health, December 17, 2008.

32. "Quality of Life, Menopausal Changes, and Hormone Therapy," Wisconsin School of Medicine and Public Health and DesignWrite, LLC, July 15, 2007.

33. John Fauber and Susanne Rust, "UW Course for Doctors Pushed Risky Therapy," *Milwaukee Journal Sentinel*, January 25, 2009.

34. Leon Speroff, "Putting Research into Practice," *Council on Hormone Education* 4, no. 2 (2004).

35. Leon Speroff, "Postmenopausal Hormone Therapy and the Risk of Breast Cancer: A Contrary Thought," *Menopause* 15, no. 2 (March–April 2008): 393–400.

36. James V. Fiorica, "Postmenopausal Hormone Therapy and Breast Health: A Review for Clinicians," University of Wisconsin Medical School, supplement to *Women's Health in Primary Care*, October 2001.

37. Gina Kolata, "Breast Cancer News Brings a Range of Reactions," *New York Times*, December 18, 2006.

38. Gina Kolata, "Reversing Trend, Big Drop Is Seen in Breast Cancer," *New York Times*, December 15, 2006.

39. Ibid.

40. Ibid.

41. Singer and Wilson, "Menopause, as Brought to You by Big Pharma."

42. Steve Shapiro et al., "Risk of Localized and Widespread Endometrial Cancer in Relation to Recent and Discontinued Use of Conjugated Estrogens," *New England Journal of Medicine* 313, no. 16 (October 17, 1985): 969–72.

43. Hershel Jick et al., "Replacement Estrogens and Endometrial Cancer," *New England Journal of Medicine* 300, no. 5 (February 1, 1979): 218–22.

44. Ibid.

45. Gordon, "Decline in HRT Use Linked to Drop in Breast Cancer."

46. "The Cancer Risk Rapidly Fell Once Women Stopped Hormone Use," Associated Press, October 1, 2009.

47. Kanaka D. Shetty, "Hormone Replacement Therapy and Cardiovascular Health in the United States," *Journal of Medical Care* 47, no. 5 (May 2009): 600–606.

48. "2009 Independent Medical Education Support," transparency report, Pfizer, January 1, 2009–December 31, 2009, http://www.pfizer.com/files/responsibility/grants_contributions/independent_medical_education_support_2009.pdf (accessed September 25, 2011).

49. Thomas Ginsberg, "Wyeth to Close N.Y. Plant by 2008," *Philadelphia Inquirer*, October 12, 2005.

50. Brenda Craig, "Confidential Letters Show Sales Staff Thought Hormone Drug Was Dangerous," Lawyers and Settlements.com, October 24, 2010, http://www.lawyersand settlements.com/articles/prempro/Premarin-prempro-hormone-replacement-therapy-15258 .html (accessed September 25, 2011).

51. "Verdict History Shows Juries Find Wyeth Downplayed Breast Cancer Risk for HRT," letter, Beasley Allen, *Legal News*, http://www.beasleyallen.com/media/2011/05/Payne -letter-RD.pdf (accessed September 25, 2011).

52. Jennifer Walker-Journey, "Wyeth Sales Rep Expresses Concern in Letter to Conduct Board," Beasley Allen, *HRT Legal*, May 27, 2011, http://www.hrt-legal.com/news/2011/05/27/ wyeth-sales-rep-expresses-concern-in-letter-to-conduct-board/ (accessed September 25, 2011).

53. Andrew DeMillo, "Jury Finds for Wyeth in Suit over Hormone Replacement Therapy," Associated Press, September 18, 2006; "Hormone Drug Could Cost Pharma Co. Big $," Associated Press, July 25, 2006.

54. Andrew DeMillo, "Lawyers Say Wyeth Drugs Promoted Cancer in Ark. Woman," Associated Press, September 12, 2006.

55. Linda Satter, "3rd Hormone-Drug Case Goes to Jury," Morris Law Firm, http://www .jamlawyers.com/news-articles/13.html (accessed September 25, 2011).

56. "Wyeth's Prempro Again on Trial in Ark.," *ABC Money*, January 23, 2007; "Wyeth Loses Suit Involving Its Hormone Drug," Associated Press, February 26, 2008.

57. "FDA Takes Action against Compounded Menopause Hormone Therapy Drug," Food and Drug Administration, January 9, 2008, http://www.fda.gov/NewsEvents/Newsroom/ PressAnnouncements/2008/ucm116832.htm (accessed September 25, 2011).

58. John Fauber and Susanne Rust, "UW Course for Doctors Pushed Risky Therapy," *University of Wisconsin–Milwaukee Journal Sentinel*, January 25, 2009.

59. "Menopause and Hormones," Food and Drug Administration, http://www.fda.gov/ forconsumers/byaudience/forwomen/ucm118624.htm (accessed February 2, 2012).

60. Shelley Salpeter, "Meta-Analysis: Cardiovascular Events Associated with Non-steroidal Anti-Inflammatory Drugs," *American Journal of Medicine* 119, no. 7 (July 2006): 552–59; Shelley Salpeter et al., "Mortality Associated with Hormone Replacement Therapy in Younger and Older Women: A Meta-Analysis," *Journal of General Internal Medicine* 19, no. 7 (July 2004): 791–804.

61. "Perspective on the WHI: Where Are We Now?" Workshop Abstracts, National Institute on Aging, September 28, 2004, http://www.nia.nih.gov/ResearchInformation/ ExtramuralPrograms/NeuroscienceOfAging/NNA_Conferences/WorkshopAbstracts.htm (accessed September 25, 2011).

62. United States District Court, Eastern District of Arkansas, Western Division, MDL No. 1507, No. 4:03CV01507, Transcript, January 26, 2007, In Re: Prempro Products Liability, http://dida.library.ucsf.edu/pdf/zmb37b10 (accessed September 25, 2011).

63. Kronos Longevity Research Institute, "Eight Study Centers Announced for 5-Year, $12 Million Research on Women, Menopause and Hormone Use," press release, April 20, 2004, http://www.keepstudy.org/news/pr_042004.cfm (accessed September 25, 2011).

64. S. Mitchell Harman, "KEEPS: The Kronos Early Estrogen Prevention Study," *Climacteric* 8, no. 1 (March 2005): 3–12; "EMPREss: Enhancing Menopause Management through Understanding the Physiology of Receptors of Estrogen: Multiperspective Case Consults, Case #2," disclosure, Medscape, http://www.medscape.org/viewarticle/706604 (accessed September 25, 2011); DesignWrite, Minutes of the Premarin Publication/Presentation Management Meeting, June 19, 2000, http://dida.library.ucsf.edu/pdf/smc37b10; "Management of Osteoporosis in Postmenopausal Women: 2010 Position Statement of the North American Menopause Society," *Menopause* 17, no. 1 (2010) 23–24, http://www.menopause.org/PSosteo10.pdf (accessed September 25, 2011); "Preventing Alzheimer's Disease and Cognitive Decline," National Institutes of Health, NIH State-of-the-Science Conference, disclosure, http://consensus.nih.gov/2010/alzabstracts.htm (accessed July 30, 2011); Kronos Longevity Research Institute, "Early Estrogen Prevention Study," KEEPS, http://www.keepstudy.org/publications/index.cfm (accessed August 29, 2011).

65. "Alzheimer's Disease: Therapeutic Potential of Estrogen," National Institutes of Health, Clinical Trials, NCT00066157, http://clinicaltrials.gov/ct2/show/NCT00066157?term=Institute+of+Aging+Sanjay+Asthana&rank=1 (accessed August 29, 2011).

66. The primate photos are from Clarkson's presentation at the National Institute on Aging's "WHI: Where Are We Now?" workshop, Workshop Abstracts, National Institute on Aging, http://www.nia.nih.gov/ResearchInformation/ExtramuralPrograms/NeuroscienceOfAging/NNA_Conferences/WorkshopAbstracts.htm (accessed July 2010).

67. Karen Richardson, "Wake Forest Researchers Add New Dimensions to the Raging Hormone Replacement Controversy," *Visions*, Wake Forest University Baptist Medical Center (Spring/Summer 2004).

68. Ibid.

69. "New Cause of Cognitive Decline in Aging Population Discovered in Nerve Cell Specializations," *Science Daily*, June 1, 2010; Sally J. Krajewski et al., "Ovarian Steroids Differentially Modulate the Gene Expression of Gonadotropin-Releasing Hormone Neuronal Subtypes in the Ovariectomized Cynomolgus Monkey," *Journal of Clinical Endocrinology & Metabolism* 88, no. 2 (February 2003): 655–62.

70. Susan E. Appt et al., "Destruction of Primordial Ovarian Follicles in Adult Cynomolgus Macaques after Exposure to 4-Vinylcyclohexene Diepoxide: A Nonhuman Primate Model of the Menopausal Transition," *Fertility & Sterility* 86, suppl. 4 (October 2006): 1210–16.

71. Carol A. Shively, Thomas B. Clarkson, and Jay R. Kaplan, "Social Deprivation and Coronary Artery Atherosclerosis in Female Cynomolgus Monkeys," *Atherosclerosis* 77, no. 1 (May 1989): 69–76.

72. Krajewski et al., "Ovarian Steroids Differentially Modulate the Gene Expression."

73. Marilynn Marchione, "Hormone Pills May Make Lung Cancer More Deadly," Associated Press, May 30, 2009.

74. James Simon, "A Fresh Look at Hormone Therapy," continuing medical education course, University of North Texas Health Science Center, http://www.hsc.unt.edu/education/pace/Documents/08-67_final_4.pdf (accessed September 25, 2011).

75. Lifei Liu et al., "Progesterone Increases Rat Neural Progenitor Cell Cycle Gene Expression and Proliferation via Extracellularly Regulated Kinase and Progesterone Receptor Membrane Components 1 and 2," 2009 American College of Neuropsychopharmacology annual meeting disclosures, *Endocrinology* 150, no. 7 (July 2009): 3186–96.

76. Martha Rosenberg, notes from workshop, "Mood, Memory, and Myths: What Really Happens at Menopause," American Psychiatric Association Annual Meeting, May 25, 2010.

77. Tara Parker-Pope, "Review Suggests Benefits in Estrogen," *New York Times*, December 13, 2010.

78. "Life Can Be Meaningful Beyond Menopause," *Manila Daily Tribune*, May 30, 2009, http://www.tribuneonline.org/life/20090530lif5.html.

79. Anita Slomski, "Once Again, Scientists Are Sharply Divided over Hormone Therapy for Menopausal Women," *Washington Post*, May 12, 2009; Eliot A. Brinton et al., "Can Menopausal Hormone Therapy Prevent Coronary Heart Disease?" *Trends in Endocrinology & Metabolism*, August 2008, http://protomag.com/assets/hormone-replacement-therapy (accessed September 25, 2011).

80. Cynthia Gorney, "The Estrogen Dilemma," *New York Times Magazine*, April 14, 2010, http://www.nytimes.com/2010/04/18/magazine/18estrogen-t.html; "Disclosure Information," JournalWATCH®, http://womens-health.jwatch.org/misc/board_disclosures.dtl#dSoares; Louann Brizendine, "Managing Menopause-Related Depression and Low Libido," *Journal of Family Practice* 16, no. 8 (August 2004), http://www.jfponline.com/Pages.asp?AID=3365 (accessed September 25, 2011).

81. Denise Grady, "Earlier Hormone Therapy Elevates Breast Cancer Risk, Study Says," *New York Times*, January 28, 2011.

82. Ibid.

83. Martha Rosenberg, "Big Pharma Shamelessly Shills Dangerous Bone Drugs You Don't Need," *AlterNet*, November 10, 2010.

84. Michael Clearfield, "The Role of Statin Therapy and Hormone Replacement Therapy: The Impact of Statin Therapy on CHD Risk Reduction in Women," Medscape, http://www.medscape.com/viewarticle/484038_4 (accessed August 12, 2011); "Pregabalin (Lyrica) for the Treatment of Hot Flashes," Massachusetts General Hospital, MGH Center for Women's Health, http://www.womensmentalhealth.org/posts/pregabalin-lyrica-for-the-treatment-of-hot-flashes/ (accessed August 12, 2011).

85. Phillip Gates, "Just What Is Menopause Insomnia and How Is It Treated?"

Submit Content Online, June 22, 2011, http://www.addnewarticles.com/health/just-what-is-menopause-insomnia-and-how-is-it-treated.html (accessed September 29, 2011).

86. Linda A. Johnson, "FDA Seeks Further Testing of Wyeth Drug," Associated Press, July 31, 2007.

87. Evelyn Pringle, "Suicide Prevention Drug Pushing Racket—Part II," *Natural News. com*, August 21, 2009, http://www.naturalnews.com/026895_suicide_drug_children.html (accessed September 29, 2011).

88. Cafepharma Boards, Cafepharma.com, June 25, 2008, http://www.cafepharma.com/boards/showthread.php?t=282105 (accessed September 29, 2011).

89. Ibid.

90. Ibid.

91. Daniel Carlat, "Dr. Drug Rep," *New York Times*, November 25, 2007.

92. Daniel Carlat, "Top 5 Reasons to Forget about Pristiq," *Carlat Psychiatry Blog*, March 1, 2008.

93. D. W. Stovall, "Aprela, a Single Tablet Formulation of Bazedoxifene and Conjugated Equine Estrogens (Premarin)," *Current Opinion in Investigative Drugs* 11, no. 4 (April 2010): 464–71.

94. "FDA Issues Non-Approvable Letter for Pfizer's Oporia," M2 Press Wire, September 16, 2005.

95. DesignWrite, Strategic Publications Development Meeting, Meeting Agenda, January 29, 2004, http://dida.library.ucsf.edu/pdf/lgb37b10 (accessed August 29, 2011); Michelle Warren, "A Comparative Review of the Risks and Benefits of Hormone Replacement Therapy Regimens," *American Journal of Obstetrics & Gynecology* 190, no. 4 (April 2004): 1141–6/.

CHAPTER 4. THE WAR AFTER THE WAR: HOW A SCANDAL-LINKED DRUG IS ADDING TO COMBAT TROOPS' WOUNDS

1. Steve Stecklow and Laura Johannes, "Test Case: Drug Makers Relied on Two Researchers Who Now Await Trial," *Wall Street Journal*, August 8, 1997, http://www.pbelow-consulting.com/pdf/test_case_WSJ_08-18-97.pdf (accessed April 2, 2011).

2. Richard Borison et al., "ICI 204,636, an Atypical Antipsychotic: Efficacy and Safety in a Multicenter, Placebo-Controlled Trial in Patients with Schizophrenia," *Journal of Clinical Psychopharmacology* 16, no. 2 (April 1996): 158–69, http://dida.library.ucsf.edu/pdf/rnv09b10 (accessed April 2, 2011); Alan F. Schatzberg and Charles B. Nemeroff, *Textbook of Psychopharmacology* (New York: American Psychiatric Publishing, 2009), p. 609.

3. S. Charles Schulz, Ruth Thomson, and Martin Brecher, "The Efficacy of Quetiapine vs. Haloperidol and Placebo: A Meta-Analytic Study of Efficacy," *Schizophrenia Research* 62, no. 1

(July 1, 2003): 1–12, http://www.schres-journal.com/article/S0920-9964(02)00522-4/abstract. For more information, see http://www.scribd.com/doc/50125923/Schulz-Poster-Presentation.

4. Maura Lerner and Janet Moore, "Once-Secret Drug-Company Records Put U on the Spot," *Star Tribune*, March 19, 2009.

5. Andy Mannix, "Charles Schulz under Scrutiny for Seroquel Study Suicide," *City Pages*, February 2, 2011, http://www.citypages.com/2011-02-02/news/charles-schulz-under-scrutiny-for-seroquel-study-suicide/2/ (accessed April 2, 2011).

6. Henry A. Nasrallah and Rajiv Tandon, "Efficacy, Safety, and Tolerability of Quetiapine in Patients with Schizophrenia," *Journal of Clinical Psychiatry* 63, suppl. 13 (2002): 12–20.

7. "Top 200 Drugs for 2009 by Sales," Drugs.com, http://www.drugs.com/top200.htm (accessed April 2, 2011).

8. "AstraZeneca in $68.5 Mln Settlement over Seroquel," Reuters, March 10, 2011.

9. Matthew Perrone, "Questions Loom over Drug Given to Sleepless Vets," Associated Press, August 30, 2010.

10. Andrew Tilghman, "Any Soldier Can Deploy on Anything," *Military Times*, March 17, 2010, http://militarytimes.com/news/2010/03/military_drugs_downrange_031710w/ (accessed April 2, 2011).

11. "AstraZeneca to Pay $68.5 Million in Seroquel Settlement," *Los Angeles Times*, March 10, 2011, http://latimesblogs.latimes.com/money_co/2011/03/astrazeneca-to-pay-685-million-in-seroquel-settlement.html (accessed April 2, 2011); "Pharmaceutical Giant Astra-Zeneca to Pay $520 Million for Off-Label Drug Marketing," Department of Justice, April 27, 2010, http://www.justice.gov/opa/pr/2010/April/10-civ-487.html (accessed June 2, 2011); Andrew Tilghman and Brendan McGarry, "Accidental Overdoses Alarm Military Officials," *Army Times*, June 6, 2010.

12. Letter to AstraZeneca, DA # 20–639, 22–047 Seroquel (quetiapine fumarate) Tablets, December 1, 2008, Food and Drug Administration, http://www.fda.gov/downloads/Drugs/GuidanceComplianceRegulatoryInformation/EnforcementActivitiesbyFDA/WarningLettersandNoticeofViolationLetterstoPharmaceuticalCompanies/ucm053948.pdf (accessed September 24, 2011).

13. Jim Edwards, "AstraZeneca's New Seroquel Ad Has 5 Pages of Legal Disclaimers," *BNET*, January 11, 2010.

14. "NIMH Study to Guide Treatment Choices for Schizophrenia" National Institute of Mental Health, 2005, http://www.nih.gov/news/pr/sep2005/nimh-19.htm (accessed April 2, 2011).

15. Seroquel/Quetiapine Fumarate approval package, Application # 20639 FDA, Food and Drug Administration, http://www.accessdata.fda.gov/drugsatfda_docs/nda/97/020639ap_Seroquel_admndocs.pdf.

16. L. K. Misra et al., "Quetiapine: A New Atypical Antipsychotic," *South Dakota Journal of Medicine* 51, no. 6 (June 1998): 189–93.

17. Gajwani Prashant, Leopoldo Pozuelo, and George E. Tesar, "QT Interval Prolongation Associated with Quetiapine (Seroquel) Overdose," *Psychosomatics* 41, no. 1 (January–February 2002): 63–65.

18. C. Griffiths and R. J. Flanagan, "Fatal Poisoning with Antipsychotic Drugs, England and Wales 1993–2002," *Journal of Psychopharmacology* 19, no. 6 (November 2005): 667–74.

19. Cathleen Hasulak, "Seroquel Strategic Plan 1997–2001," AstraZeneca Deposition Exhibit, April 1996, http://dida.library.ucsf.edu/pdf/yov09b10 (accessed May 28, 2011).

20. Christina Jewett and Sam Roe, "Drugmaker Paid Psychiatrist Nearly $500,000 to Promote Antipsychotic, Despite Doubts about Research," *Chicago Tribune*, November 11, 2009.

21. Jim Edwards, "AstraZeneca's Seroquel Research Director Confessed to Sex-for-Studies Affairs," *BNET*, March 12, 2009, http://www.bnet.com/blog/drug-business/astrazeneca-8217s -seroquel-research-director-confessed-to-sex-for-studies-affairs/906 (accessed May 28, 2011).

22. "FDA Approves AstraZeneca's SEROQUEL for Bipolar Depression Treatment," press release, October 20, 2006, http://www.lifesciencesworld.com/news/view/12152 (accessed May 28, 2011).

23. Miriam Hill, "Conflicts for FDA Committee Set to Weigh Risks of Seroquel," *Philadelphia Inquirer*, April 4, 2009.

24. Jim Edwards, "NAMI Board Member Was Paid Consultant on AZ's Seroquel, Documents Say," *BNET*, October 22, 2009.

25. AstraZeneca, "FDA Approves AstraZeneca's SEROQUEL."

26. Serious Mental Illness Statistics, National Institute of Mental Health, http://www .nimh.nih.gov/statistics/index.shtml (accessed May 28, 2011).

27. Information found at www.abilify.com (accessed February 2, 2012).

28. Bob Brewin, "Half the Afghanistan and Iraq Veterans Treated by VA Receive Mental Health Care," Nextgov.com, March 22, 2011, http://www.nextgov.com/nextgov/ ng_20110322_2917.php (accessed April 2, 2011).

29. Perrone, "Questions Loom."

30. Bob Brewin, "Military's Drug Policy Threatens Troops' Health, Doctors Say," Nextgov.com, January 18, 2011, http://www.nextgov.com/nextgov/ng_20110118_8944.php (accessed April 2, 2011).

31. David Olinger and Erin Emery, "Soldiering on in Pain," *Denver Post*, August 26, 2008, http://www.denverpost.com/search/ci_10302647 (accessed May 28, 2011).

32. Robert J. Birnbaum, Elspeth Ritchie, and Terence M. Keane, "The Returning Veteran: PTSD and Traumatic Brain Injury," Massachusetts General Hospital Psychiatry Academy, May 28, 2008, http://www.mghcme.com/events/details/?eventid=17 (accessed May 28, 2011).

33. Seroquel Clinical Trial, funded by AstraZeneca, Clinical Trial NCT00237393, http:// clinicaltrials.gov/ct2/show/NCT00237393 (accessed September 24, 2011); Seroquel Clinical Trial, funded by AstraZeneca, Clinical Trial NCT00292370, http://clinicaltrials.gov/ct2/show/ NCT00292370 (accessed September 24, 2011).

34. S. Robert et al., "Quetiapine Improves Sleep Disturbances in Combat Veterans with PTSD: Sleep Data from a Prospective, Open-Label Study," *Journal of Clinical Psychopharmacology* 4 (August 25, 2005): 387–88.

35. Charles Schulz et al., "Broadening the Horizon of Atypical Antipsychotic Applications," Medscape, June 15, 2004, http://www.medscape.org/viewprogram/3137 (accessed May 28, 2011).

36. "Sen. Grassley Requests Information on Continuing Medical Educational Grants from Pharmaceutical Companies," *Medical News Today*, February 27, 2008, http://www.medicalnewstoday.com/articles/98639.php (accessed May 28, 2011).

37. Charles Schulz et al., "Broadening the Horizon of Atypical Antipsychotic Applications," slide/lecture presentation, June 2004, http://www.medscape.org/viewprogram/3137 cois are on drop down disclosure menu. For more information, see http://www.medscape.org/viewarticle/479929_5.

38. Ibid.

39. "VA Spent $717 Million for Useless Post-Traumatic Stress Drug," AllGov, August 25, 2011, http://www.allgov.com/Where_is_the_Money_Going/ViewNews/VA_Spent_717_Million_Dollars_for_Useless_Post_Traumatic_Stress_Drug_110825 (accessed September 24, 2011).

40. Patrick J. McGrath, "Tranylcypromine versus Venlafaxine Plus Mirtazapine Following Three Failed Antidepressant Medication Trials for Depression: A STAR*D Report," *American Journal of Psychiatry* 163, no. 9 (September 2006): 1531–41; Mark B. Hamner, curriculum vitae, principal investigator, two-site collaboration with Dr. Lori Davis, "Alabama: A Randomized, Placebo-Controlled Trial of Adjunctive Quetiapine in PTSD Refractory to Paroxetine Monotherapy," http://www.charleston.va.gov/Documents/research/Hamner-CV.htm (accessed September 24, 2011).

41. Matthew Friedman, "Pharmacological Treatments of PTSD and Comorbid Disorder," slide one, "I received an honorarium from AstraZeneca in the past year," National Center for PTSD, October 1, 2009, http://www.ptsd.va.gov/professional/ptsd101/course-modules/pharmacotherapy.asp (accessed September 24, 2011).

42. Medical University of South Carolina College of Medicine, Pfizer Visiting Professorships in Neurology/Psychiatry, visiting professor Matthew Friedman, MD, April 12–15, 2011, http://www.pfizerfellowships.com/PreviousWinners.aspx?AwardID=2228 (accessed May 28, 2011).

43. Friedman, "Pharmacological Treatments of PTSD."

44. David Benedek et al., "Treatment of Patients with Acute Stress Disorder and Post-traumatic Stress Disorder," *Focus* 341 (Spring 2009): 204–213, http://focus.psychiatryonline.org/cgi/content/full/7/2/204 (accessed May 28, 2011).

45. Public Citizen Health Research Group, "Food and Drug Administration's Request for Comment on First Amendment Issues, Docket No. [02N-0209]," September 13, 2002,

http://www.fda.gov/ohrms/dockets/dailys/02/Sep02/091602/80027d27.pdf (accessed May 28, 2011).

46. James Dao and Dan Frosch, "Feeling Warehoused in Army's Trauma Care Units," *New York Times*, April 25, 2010.

47. Ibid.

48. Andrew Tilghman and Brendan McGarry, "Accidental Overdoses Alarm Military Officials," *Military Times*, June 6, 2010, http://www.militarytimes.com/forum/showthread.php?1586676-Accidental-overdoses-alarm-military-officials&s=d4e606f020fbbb6aa30cd0dcb ffcbdc1 (accessed May 28, 2011).

49. Ibid.

50. Dao and Frosch, "Feeling Warehoused."

51. Mary Galione-Nahas, telephone interview with the author, March 27, 2011.

52. Ibid.

53. Pauline Arrillaga, "Once Called 'Coward,' He Fights for PTSD Victims," Associated Press, April 19, 2010.

54. "VA Warns Doctors about Lariam," United Press International, June 25, 2004; Cilla McCain, *Murder in Baker Company* (Chicago: Chicago Review Press, 2010), pp. 92–94; Daniel Zwerdling, "Former Soldier Helps Others Fight Army for Help," National Public Radio, July 7, 2007.

55. Galione-Nahas, telephone interview.

56. Ibid.

57. Erica Lampe, telephone interview with the author, March 18, 2011.

58. Ibid.

59. Ibid.

60. Julie Oligschlaeger, telephone interview with the author, March 24, 2011.

61. Ibid.

62. Tom Vande Burgt and Diane Vande Burgt, interview with the author, Charleston, West Virginia, March 16, 2011.

63. Ibid.

64. Ibid.

65. Ibid.

66. Martha Rosenberg, notes from Lest We Forget meeting, Charleston, West Virginia, March 17, 2011.

67. Ibid.

68. Ibid.

69. Ibid.

70. Vande Burgt and Vande Burgt, interview.

71. Ibid.

72. Ibid.

73. Stan White and Shirley White, interview with the author, Charleston, West Virginia, March 18, 2011; Vande Burgt and Vande Burgt, interview; Rosenberg, notes from Lest We Forget meeting.

74. Rosenberg, notes from Lest We Forget meeting.

75. Ibid.

76. White and White, interview, March 18, 2011.

77. Ibid.

78. Ibid.

79. Stan White and Shirley White, interview with the author, Charleston, West Virginia, March 17–18, 2011.

80. Georgeann Underwood, interview with the author, Charleston, West Virginia, March 17, 2011.

81. Ibid.

82. Ibid.

83. Ibid.

84. White and White, interview, March 17–18, 2011.

85. "Healthcare Inspection Quality of Care of Two Deceased West Virginia Veterans," Department of Veterans Affairs, Office of Inspector General, Report No. 08-01377-185, August 14, 2008, http://www.va.gov/oig/54/reports/VAOIG-08-01377-185.pdf.

86. T. Christian Miller and Daniel Zwerdling, "Aftershock: The Blast That Shook Psycho Platoon," *Propublica*, March 22, 2011, http://www.propublica.org/article/aftershock-the-blast-that-shook-psycho-platoon/single (accessed May 28, 2011).

87. Office of the Chief of Public Affairs, "Health Promotion, Risk Reduction and Suicide Prevention Report," press release, www.Army.mil, July 28, 2010, http://www.army.mil/-news/2010/07/28/42934-army-health-promotion-risk-reduction-and-suicide-prevention-report/index.html (accessed May 28, 2011).

88. Armen Keteyian, "Suicide Epidemic among Veterans," *CBS News*, November 13, 2007.

89. Yochi J. Dreazen, "A Prescription for Tragedy," *National Journal*, October 2, 2010.

90. Ibid.

91. "Health Promotion, Risk Reduction and Suicide Prevention Report."

92. Birnbaum, Ritchie, and Keane, "The Returning Veteran."

93. "Health Promotion, Risk Reduction and Suicide Prevention Report."

94. Alex Brill, "Overspending on Multi-Source Drugs in Medicaid," American Enterprise Institute, March 28, 2011, http://www.aei.org/paper/100207 (accessed May 28, 2011).

95. "Information for Healthcare Professionals: Varenicline (Marketed as Chantix) and Bupropion (Marketed as Zyban®, Wellbutrin®, and Generics)," Food and Drug Administration, July 1, 2009, http://www.fda.gov/Drugs/DrugSafety/PostmarketDrugSafetyInformationforPatientsandProviders/DrugSafetyInformationforHeathcareProfessionals/ucm169986.htm

(accessed May 28, 2011); "Isotretinoin (Marketed as Accutane) Capsule Information FDA," Food and Drug Administration, October 22, 2010, http://www.fda.gov/Drugs/DrugSafety/ PostmarketDrugSafetyInformationforPatientsandProviders/ucm09//ucmo94305.htm (accessed May 28, 2011); "Early Communication about Ongoing Safety Review of Montelukast (Singulair)," Food and Drug Administration, March 3, 2008, http://www.fda.gov/Drugs/Drug Safety/PostmarketDrugSafetyInformationforPatientsandProviders/DrugSafetyInformationfor HeathcareProfessionals/ucm079523.htm (accessed May 28, 2011).

96. Matt Ford, "Army Curbs Prescriptions of Anti-Malaria Drug," *USA Today*, Associated Press, November 19, 2011.

97. McCain, *Murder in Baker Company*; "VA Warns Doctors about Lariam," United Press International, June 25, 2004.

98. "Health Promotion, Risk Reduction and Suicide Prevention Report."

99. "Army Vice Chief Peter Chiarelli Addresses Soldier Suicides, Drug Abuse," National Public Radio, July 29, 2010.

100. "Health Promotion, Risk Reduction and Suicide Prevention Report."

101. Ibid.

102. Gregg Zoroya, "Obama Approves Condolence Letters in Military Suicides," *USA Today*, July 7, 2011.

103. Bob Brewin, "Time to Take Another Look at Seroquel?" Nextgov.com, August 5, 2011.

104. Psychopharmacologic Drugs Advisory Committee materials, Food and Drug Administration, April 8, 2009, http://www.fda.gov/AdvisoryCommittees/CommitteesMeeting Materials/Drugs/PsychopharmacologicDrugsAdvisoryCommittee/ucm126199.htm (accessed January 6, 2012); Wayne Ray et al., "Atypical Antipsychotic Drugs and the Risk of Sudden Cardiac Death," *New England Journal of Medicine* 360, no. 3 (January 15, 2009): 225–35.

105. Ibid.

106. Ibid.

107. Duff Wilson, "Heart Warning Added to Label on Popular Antipsychotic Drug," *New York Times*, July 18, 2011.

108. Ibid.; Psychopharmacologic Drugs Advisory Committee materials, Food and Drug Administration, April 8, 2009.

109. Wilson, "Heart Warning Added to Label on Popular Antipsychotic Drug."

110. Janet Woodcock to Danielle Brian and Paul Thacker, April 15, 2011, Project on Government Oversight, http://pogoblog.typepad.com/pogo/2011/07/paging-dr-woodcockdr -janet-woodcockdo-you-have-any-clue-whats-happening-inside-the-fda.html.

111. Wilson, "Heart Warning Added to Label on Popular Antipsychotic Drug."

112. Ibid.

113. John H. Krystal et al., "Adjunctive Risperidone Treatment for Antidepressant-Resistant Symptoms of Chronic Military Service–Related PTSD," *Journal of the American Medical Association* 306, no. 2 (August 3, 2011): 493–502.

114. Matthew Perrone, "AstraZeneca Paying $68.5M in Seroquel Settlement," Associated Press, March 10, 2011.

115. Jim Edwards, "AstraZeneca's Marketing Strategy: Sue Us, Please!" *BNET*, August 5, 2010, http://www.bnet.com/blog/drug-business/astrazeneca-8217s-marketing-strategy-sue-us-please/5298.

116. Ibid.

117. Bob Brewin, "Military Continues Off-Label Drug Use, Despite Concerns," Nextgov .com, September 28, 2011.

118. Ibid.

CHAPTER 5. A SIDE EFFECT FROM WHICH THERE IS NO RECOVERY

1. Jef Feeley, "Pfizer Settles Neurontin Suit over Minister's Death," *Bloomberg Businessweek*, May 17, 2010.

2. Jahna Berry, "Expert: Police in Airport Death Could Have Done More," *Arizona Republic*, November 12, 2007.

3. J. K. Wall and John Tuohy, "Woman Participating in Lilly Trial Hangs Self," *Indianapolis Star*, February 9, 2004.

4. "State Department Official Resigns over 'D.C. Madam,'" *CNN News*, April 27, 2007.

5. "How Prozac, Depression, and Suicide Changed Lilly Chief Randall Tobias," *Indianapolis Monthly* 18, no. 7 (February 1995).

6. "Leaving a Legacy of Progress," *Indianapolis Star*, June 13, 2009.

7. Stephanie Saul, "F.A.A. Bans Antismoking Drug, Citing Side Effects," *New York Times*, May 22, 2008; "Girlfriend Believes Chantix Contributed to Texas Musician's Death," *ABC News*, September 19, 2007.

8. "The Mystery of Medications Linked to Suicide," MSNBC, May 7, 2008; Kate Miller, interview with the author, June 20, 2009.

9. Martha Rosenberg, "Neurontin Killed Our Husbands, We Believe," *Huffington Post*, June 21, 2011, http://www.huffingtonpost.com/martha-rosenberg/pfizer-neurontin-suicide_b _875603.html.

10. Ibid.

11. Ibid.

12. Ibid.

13. Ibid.

14. Ibid.

15. Ibid.

16. Ibid.

17. Ibid.

18. Miller, interview, June 20, 2009.

19. "FDA Requests Labeling Change for Leukotriene Modifiers," Note to Correspondents, Food and Drug Administration, http://www.fda.gov/NewsEvents/Newsroom/Press Announcements/ucm166293.htm (accessed September 26, 2011).

20. "FDA Launches a Multi-Pronged Strategy to Strengthen Safeguards for Children Treated with Antidepressant Medications," Food and Drug Administration, http://www.fda .gov/NewsEvents/Newsroom/PressAnnouncements/2004/ucm108363.htm (accessed September 26, 2011); Shankar Vedantam, "Antidepressants a Suicide Risk for Young Adults," *Washington Post*, December 14, 2006.

21. Michael Smith, "Teen Suicide Spike Linked to SSRI Black Box," MedPage Today, February 6, 2007, http://www.medpagetoday.com/Pediatrics/GeneralPediatrics/5005 (accessed September 26, 2011).

22. Ibid.; Alan F. Schatzberg and Charles B. Nemeroff, *Essentials of Clinical Psychopharmacology* (Washington, DC: American Psychiatric Association, 2001), p. xxiii; Craig Schneider, "Controversial Emory Researcher Leaving," *Atlanta Journal-Constitution*, October 30, 2009; Denise Gellene and Thomas H. Maugh II, "Doctor Accused in Congress' Probe," *Los Angeles Times*, October 4, 2008.

23. Michael Smith, "Teen Suicide Spike Linked to SSRI Black Box," MedPage Today.

24. Sen. Charles Grassley, US Sen., to David L. Shern, president and chief executive officer, Mental Health America, May 4, 2011, http://grassley.senate.gov/about/loader.cfm ?csModule=security/getfile&pageid=34269 (accessed September 26, 2011).

25. Dan Childs, "Some Experts Blame FDA Labeling for Child Suicide Increase," *ABC News*, February 5, 2007

26. Benedict Carey and Gardiner Harris, "Antidepressant May Raise Suicide Risk," *New York Times*, May 12, 2006.

27. "Experts Question Study on Youth Suicide Rates," *New York Times*, September 14, 2007.

28. Ibid.

29. Alison Bass, "Suicide Rates as a Public Relations Tool," *Boston Globe*, September 24, 2007.

30. Robert Gibbons et al., "Relationship between Antidepressants and Suicide Attempts: An Analysis of the Veterans Health Administration Data Sets," *American Journal of Psychiatry* 164 (July 2007): 1044–1049.

31. Ibid.; Robert Gibbons, Sharon-Lise T. Normand, and Joel B. Greenhouse, comment on "Risk of Suicidality in Clinical Trials of Antidepressants in Adults: Analysis of Proprietary Data Submitted to US Food and Drug Administration," *British Medical Journal* 339, no. 7723 (September 22, 2009); Center for Science in the Public Interest, Integrity in Science Watch, press release, September 10, 2007, http://www.cspinet.org/integrity/press/200709102.html (accessed February 2, 2012).

32. Jeffrey A. Bridge and Joel B. Greenhouse, "Suicide Trends among Youths Aged 10 to 19 Years in the United States, 1995–2005," letter, *Journal of the American Medical Association* 300, no. 9 (September 3, 2008): 1025–26.

33. Ibid.

34. Sarah Rubenstein, "Elevated Rate of Teen Suicide Stirs Concern," *Wall Street Journal*, September 3, 2008.

35. Carroll Hughes et al., "Texas Children's Medication Algorithm Project: Update from Texas Consensus Conference Panel on Medication Treatment of Childhood Major Depressive Disorder" (Texas Children's Medication Algorithm Project), *Journal of the American Academy of Child & Adolescent Psychiatry* 46, no. 6 (June 2007): 667–86.

36. Carey and Harris, "Antidepressant May Raise Suicide Risk."

37. Peter Pitts, "The Truth Hurts," *DrugWonks.com*, September 3, 2008, http://www.drugwonks.com/blog_post/show/6314 (accessed September 26, 2011).

38. Sam Dunbar, "What Are Antidepressants Doing to Our Children Now?" *Collegian*, September 9, 2008, http://media.www.smccollegian.com/media/storage/paper841/news/2008/09/09/Opinion/What-Are.Antidepressants.Doing.To.Our.Children.Now-3421468-page2.shtml (accessed September 26, 2011).

39. Martha Rosenberg, "Pfizer: The Drug Giant That Makes Bank from Drugs That Can Kill You," *AlterNet*, July 10, 2010, http://www.alternet.org/story/147467/pfizer:_the_drug_giant_that_makes_bank_from_drugs_that_can_kill_you/.

40. Ibid.

41. Kaiser Foundation Health Plan, Inc. et al. v. Pfizer, Inc. et al., United States District Court, District of Massachusetts, (Nov. 3, 2010).

42. Rosenberg, "Pfizer: The Drug Giant That Makes Bank."

43. *Pfizer, Inc. et al.*, United States District Court.

44. "FDA Requests Anticonvulsant Suicide Data Analysis," *Boston Globe*, April 20, 2005.

45. Ibid.

46. Margaret Cronin Fisk, Jef Feeley, and Cary O'Reilly, "Pfizer Faces First Trial on Neurontin Suicide Claim (Update1)," *Bloomberg*, July 24, 2009; Jim Edwards, "What Docs Didn't Know about Pfizer's Neurontin," *BNET*, July 24, 2009, http://www.cbsnews.com/8301-505123_162-42842249/what-docs-didnt-know-about-pfizers-neurontin/.

47. Parke-Davis, Neurontin in Psychiatric Disorder, Drug Industry Document Archive, University of California–San Francisco, http://dida.library.ucsf.edu/pdf/rba00a10 (accessed September 26, 2011).

48. Public Citizen Health Research Group, "Food and Drug Administration's Request for Comment on First Amendment Issues, Docket No. [02N-0209]," September 13, 2002, http://www.fda.gov/ohrms/dockets/dailys/02/Sep02/091602/80027d27.pdf (accessed May 28, 2011).

49. Ed Stannard, "Drug Trial Raises Ethics Questions, *New Haven Register*, June 28, 2011, http://www.nhregister.com/articles/2011/06/27/business/doc4e08fdb3df22b773134599.txt.

50. Carl Elliot, "Useless Studies, Real Harm," *New York Times*, July 29, 2011.

51. Ibid.

52. Kristina Fiore, "Journals Aided in Marketing of Gabapentin," MedPage Today, September 11, 2009, http://www.medpagetoday.com/MeetingCoverage/PRC/15928 (accessed September 26, 2011); United States District Court, District of Massachusetts, Report on the Use of Neurontin for Bipolar and Other Mood Disorders, In Re Neurontin Marketing Sales Practices, and Products Liability Litigation, Jeffrey S. Barkin, October 6, 2008, http://dida.library.ucsf.edu/pdf/oxx18u10 (accessed September 26, 2011).

53. "Scott Reuben," *Wikipedia*, http://en.wikipedia.org/wiki/Scott_Reuben; Scott S. Reuben, "Preventing Postmastectomy Pain Syndrome," International Research Foundation for RSD/CRPS, August 20, 2009, http://www.rsdfoundation.org/en/Preventing_RSD_Mastectomy.html (accessed September 26, 2011).

54. P. J. Wiffen et al., "WITHDRAWN: Gabapentin for Acute and Chronic Pain," *Cochrane Database Systematic Reviews and Protocols* 16, no. 3 (March 16, 2011); P. J. Wiffen et al., "WITHDRAWN: Anticonvulsant Drugs for Acute and Chronic Pain," *Cochrane Database Systematic Reviews and Protocols* no. 1 (January 20, 2010); D. J. Millington et al., "Effects of Gabapentin or SCP-123 in the Rat Chronic Constriction Injury Neuropathic Pain Model," *Pain Medicine* 11, no. 4 (April 29, 2010): 477–633.

55. Martha Rosenberg, "Son of Neurontin Meets the Fibromyalgia Epidemic," *Counter-Punch*, January 27, 2009, http://www.counterpunch.org/2009/01/27/son-of-neurontin-meets-the-fibromyalgia-epidemic/.

56. Core Marketing Team Meeting, April 8–9, 1997, Drug Industry Document Archive, Parke-Davis, University of California–San Francisco, http://dida.library.ucsf.edu/tid/vcb00a10 (accessed September 26, 2011).

57. Rosenberg, "Son of Neurontin"; I. Selak, "Pregabalin (Pfizer)," *Current Opinion in Investigational Drugs* 2, no. 6 (June 2001): 828–34.

58. L. J. Crofford et al., "Pregabalin for the Treatment of Fibromyalgia Syndrome: Results of a Randomized, Double-Blind, Placebo-Controlled Trial," *Arthritis & Rheumatism* 52, no. 4 (April 2005): 1264–73; L. J. Crofford et al., "Fibromyalgia Relapse Evaluation and Efficacy for Durability of Meaningful Relief (Freedom): A 6-Month, Double-Blind, Placebo-Controlled Trial with Pregabalin, *Pain* 136, no. 3 (June 2008): 419–31; Scott Reuben et al., "The Analgesic Efficacy of Celecoxib, Pregabalin, and Their Combination for Spinal Fusion Surgery," *Anesthesia & Analgesia* 103, no. 5 (November 2006): 1271–77.

59. Background Package for July 10 Advisory Committee, Analysis of Suicidality from Placebo-Controlled Clinical Studies of Neurontin® (Gabapentin) and Lyrica® (Pregabalin) Capsules, Pfizer, http://www.fda.gov/ohrms/dockets/ac/08/briefing/2008-4372b1-02-Pfizer.pdf (accessed September 26, 2011).

60. Ibid.

61. S. J. Hadley, F. S. Mandel, and E. Schweizer, "Switching from Long-Term Benzodiaz-

epine Therapy to Pregabalin in Patients with Generalized Anxiety Disorder: A Double-Blind, Placebo-Controlled Trial," *Journal of Psychopharmacology* (June 2011), 0269881111405360; J. D. Gale and L. A. Houghton, "Alpha 2 Delta (α(2)δ) Ligands, Gabapentin and Pregabalin: What Is the Evidence for Potential Use of These Ligands in Irritable Bowel Syndrome," *Frontiers in Pharmacology* 2, no. 28 (June 9, 2011).

62. David Healy, Andrew Herxheimer, and David B. Menkes, "Antidepressants and Violence: Problems at the Interface of Medicine and Law," *PLOS Medicine* 3, no. 9 (September 12, 2006): e372.

63. Robert Whitaker, *Mad in America* (New York: Basic Books, 2002), p. 187.

64. Healy, Herxheimer, and Menkes, "Antidepressants and Violence."

65. Edward S. Friedrichs, e-mail correspondence with author, September 26, 2011.

66. Martha Rosenberg, "Before You Take That Antidepressant, Visit this Web Site," *OpEdNews*, January 3, 2010, http://www.opednews.com/articles/Before-You-Take-That-Antid-by-Martha-Rosenberg-100103-313.html.

67. Ibid.

68. Joel M. Kauffman, "Selective Serotonin Reuptake Inhibitor [SSRI] Drugs: More Risk Than Benefits?" *Journal of the American Physicians and Surgeons* 14, no. 1 (Spring 2009).

69. SSRI Stories, http://www.ssristories.com.

70. Ibid.

71. Angela K. Brown, "Yates Found Not Guilty Due to Insanity in 5 Drownings," Associated Press, July 27, 2006.

72. SSRI Stories.

73. Mark Thompson, "Army Suicide Rate Hits New High," *Time*, August 12, 2011; "Health Promotion, Risk Reduction and Suicide Prevention Report," United States Army, July 28, 2010, http://www.army.mil/article/42934/ (accessed September 26, 2011).

74. Andrew Tilghman, "Any Soldier Can Deploy on Anything," *Military Times*, March 17, 2010.

75. Andrew Tilghman and Brendan McGarry, "Medicating the Military," *Military Times*, March 17, 2010.

76. Gregg Zoroya, "Thousands Strain Hood Mental Health System," *USA Today*, August 23, 2010.

77. John Ramsey, "Bragg PTSD Diagnoses Low, but Anti-Depressant Use Up," *Fayetteville Observer*, September 30, 2010.

78. Tilghman and McGarry, "Medicating the Military."

79. Andrew Tilghman and Brendan McGarry, "Psych Meds Spike among Younger Troops," *Military Times*, September 3, 2010; Tilghman and McGarry, "Medicating the Military."

80. Tilghman and McGarry, "Any Soldier Can Deploy on Anything."

81. S. Mohamed and R. A. Rosenheck, "Pharmacotherapy of PTSD in the U.S. Department of Veterans Affairs: Diagnostic and Symptom-Guided Drug Selection," *Journal of Clinical Psychiatry* 69, no. 6 (June 2008): 959–65.

82. Steven Reinber, "With Depression Vets Face Higher Suicide Risk," *Health Day*, January 12, 2009.

83. Tilghman and McGarry, "Medicating the Military."

84. Center for PTSD, Department of Veterans Affairs, *Iraq War Clinician Guide*, 2nd ed., http://www.ptsd.va.gov/professional/manuals/iraq-war-clinician-guide.asp (accessed September 26, 2011).

85. Martha Rosenberg, "Parents Fight Use of New Psych Meds for Kids," *San Francisco Chronicle*, September 13, 2009.

86. Miller, interview, June 20, 2009.

87. Ibid.

88. Martha Rosenberg, "Fraudulent Trials behind Asthma Drugs Cited," *Epoch Times*, May 29, 2009 (accessed January 7, 2012).

89. Ibid.

90. Ibid.

91. Jonathan M. Edelman, "Oral Montelukast Compared with Inhaled Salmeterol to Prevent Exercise-Induced Bronchoconstriction, A Randomized, Double-Blind Trial," *Annals of Internal Medicine* 132, no. 2 (January 18, 2000): 97–104.

92. Ibid.

93. Ibid.

94. Martha Rosenberg, "Are You Taking These Asthma Drugs?" *Huffington Post*, December 1, 2011, http://www.huffingtonpost.com/martha-rosenberg/asthma-drugs-research_b_1119163.html (accessed January 7, 2012).

95. Rosenberg, "Fraudulent Trials."

96. Ibid.

97. Ibid.

98. Ibid.

99. Ibid.

100. Ibid.

101. Ibid.

102. Ibid.

103. Ibid.

104. Ibid.

105. Ibid.

106. Rosenberg, "Are You Taking These Asthma Drugs?"

107. Peter K. Honig and John K. Jenkins, "Correspondence, Exercise-Induced Asthma," *New England Journal of Medicine* 339 (December 10, 1998): 1783–86.

108. Center for Drug Evaluation and Research, Application Number: 20-829, *Pharmacology Reviews*, January 28, 1998.

109. Center for Drug Evaluation and Research, Application Number: 20-829, *Medical Reviews*, January 12, 1998.

110. Tisha Thompson, "Fox 5 Investigates: Singulair," *Fox News*, November 9, 2010, http://www.myfoxdc.com/dpp/news/investigative/fox-5-investigates-singulair-110810.

111. Ask a Patient, http://www.askapatient.com/searchresults.asp?searchField=Singulair.

112. Ibid.

113. "Section 4, Managing Asthma Long Term in Children 0–4 Years of Age and 5–11 Years of Age: Diagnosis and Prognosis of Asthma in Children," *Expert Panel Report 3: Guidelines for the Diagnosis and Management of Asthma* (Bethesda, MD: National Heart, Lung, and Blood Institute, 2007), http://www.ncbi.nlm.nih.gov/books/NBK7229/#A2098 (accessed February 2, 2012).

114. Rosenberg, "Parents Fight Use of New Psych Meds for Kids."

115. Miller, interview, June 20, 2009.

116. Rosenberg, "Neurontin Killed Our Husbands, We Believe."

117. Ibid.

118. Miller, interview with the author, August 20, 2011.

119. Adam Klasfeld, "Pfizer Expert Can Testify on Neurontin," Courthouse News Service, March 28, 2011, http://www.courthousenews.com/2011/03/28/35270.htm (accessed September 26, 2011).

120. Robert Gibbons et al., "Gabapentin and Suicide Attempts," *Pharmacoepidemiology and Drug Safety* 19, no. 12 (October 3, 2010): 1241–47.

121. "FDA Approves Horizant to Treat Restless Legs Syndrome," Food and Drug Administration, http://www.fda.gov/NewsEvents/Newsroom/PressAnnouncements/ucm250188.htm (accessed September 26, 2011).

122. "Akathisia—Restless Leg Syndrome," definition, Medicine Online, http://www.medicineonline.com/articles/A/2/Akathisia/Restless-Leg-Syndrome.html (accessed February 2, 2012).

CHAPTER 6. PROTECTING BONES FROM PRODUCTS THAT PROTECT BONES

1. Merck Annual Report, 1999.

2. Diane Wysowski, "Oral Bisphosphonates and Oesophageal Cancer," *British Medical Journal* 341 (September 2, 2010): 516–17.

3. Marlene Cimons, "Shalala's Ads for Milk Leave Some with a Sour Taste," *Los Angeles Times*, July 2, 1998; Greg Barrett, "Hungry and Angry," Gannett News Service, March 30, 2000.

4. "USDA Panel Backs Doctors' Complaints against Milk Ads," Physicians Committee for Responsible Medicine, September 20, 2001, http://www.pcrm.org/media/news/usda-panel-backs-doctors-complaints-against-milk (accessed September 25, 2011); "67 of the Nation's

Top 100 Dairies Now All or Partially rBGH Free," NonGMO Project, http://www.nongmo project.org/2010/09/17/67-of-the-nations-top-100-dairies-now-all-or-partially-rbgh-free/ (accessed March 3, 2011).

5. John Morgan, "Meredith Vieira 'Bones Up' on Osteoporosis," *USA Today*, June 6, 3003, http://www.usatoday.com/news/health/spotlighthealth/2003-06-06-Vieira_x.htm (accessed September 25, 2011); "New Celebrity Drug Ads Have Subtle Twist," Associated Press, July 18, 2005.

6. "Vioxx (Rofecoxib) Questions and Answers," Food and Drug Administration, http://www.fda.gov/Drugs/DrugSafety/PostmarketDrugSafetyInformationforPatientsandProviders/ucm106290.htm (accessed September 25, 2011); "New Drug for Bone Disorders—Fosamax Approved as Treatment for Osteoporosis and Paget's Disease of Bone," *FDA Consumer*, December, 1995.

7. P. Groen et al., "Esophagitis Associated with the Use of Alendronate," *New England Journal of Medicine* 335 (October 3, 1996): 1016–21; John Simons, "Will Merck Survive Vioxx?" *Fortune*, November 1, 2004.

8. Alex Berenson, "Evidence in Vioxx Suits Shows Intervention by Merck Officials," *New York Times*, April 24, 2005.

9. Groen, "Esophagitis Associated with the Use of Alendronate."

10. Ibid.

11. "Fosamax (Alendronate Sodium Tablets): Proper Dosing and Avoidance of Esophageal Side Effects," letter from Louis M. Sherwood to doctors, March 15, 1996, Weitz & Luxenberg, P.C., http://www.weitzlux.com/fosamaxlawsuit/fdareport/deardoctor_402875.html.

12. Ibid.

13. S. L. Ruggiero et al., "Osteonecrosis of the Jaws Associated with the Use of Bisphosphonates: A Review of 63 Cases," *Journal of Oral and Maxillofacial Surgery* 62, no. 5 (May 2004): 527–34.

14. Michael Donoghue, "Bisphosphonates and Osteonecrosis: Analogy to Phossy Jaw," *Medical Journal of Australia* 183, no. 3 (2005): 163–64.

15. Ibid.

16. "New Drug for Bone Disorders."

17. Parish Sedghizadeh et al., "Oral Bisphosphonate Use and the Prevalence of Osteonecrosis of the Jaw," *Journal of the American Dental Association* 140, no. 1 (2009) 61–66.

18. Paul Harasi, "Osteoporosis Drugs Could Have Devastating Effect on Dental Work," *Review-Journal*, November 13, 2005.

19. Michelle L. Start, "Naples Woman Files Suit against Merck," *News-Press*, April 14, 2006.

20. Harasi, "Osteoporosis Drugs."

21. Dennis Black et al., "Once-Yearly Zoledronic Acid for Treatment of Postmenopausal Osteoporosis," *New England Journal of Medicine* 356 (May 3, 2007): 1809–22; Susan Heckbert et

al., "Use of Alendronate and Risk of Incident Atrial Fibrillation in Women," *Archives of Internal Medicine* 168, no. 8 (2008): 826–31.

22. "Severe Pain with Osteoporosis Drugs," Food and Drug Administration, http://www .accessdata.fda.gov/scripts/cdrh/cfdocs/psn/printer.cfm?id=851 (accessed September 23, 2011).

23. Ibid

24. Ibid.

25. Diane Wysowski, "Reports of Esophageal Cancer with Oral Bisphosphonate Use," *New England Journal of Medicine* 360 (January 1, 2009): 89–90.

26. Wysowski, "Oral Bisphosphonates and Oesophageal Cancer."

27. Deborah Gold and Stuart Silverman, "Compliance with Osteoporosis Medications: Challenges for Healthcare Providers," Medscape, http://www.medscape.org/viewarticle/503214 (accessed September 25, 2011).

28. Stuart Silverman et al., "Postmenopausal Osteoporosis: Putting the Risk for Osteonecrosis of the Jaw into Perspective," Medscape, http://www.medscape.org/viewarticle/552518 (accessed September 25, 2011).

29. V. Rabenda et al., "Poor Adherence to Oral Bisphosphonate Treatment and Its Consequences: A Review of the Evidence," *Expert Opinion on Pharmacology* 10, no. 14 (October 2009): 2303–15.

30. R. Recker et al., "Safety of Bisphosphonates in the Treatment of Osteoporosis," *American Journal of Medicine* 122, suppl. no. 2 (2009): S22–S32.

31. Thomas Weiss et al., "Underuse of Osteoporosis Treatment in Postmenopausal Women at High Risk for Fracture Differs by Age and Ethnicity: Observations from the National Osteoporosis Risk Assessment," poster abstract, National Osteoporosis Foundation, April 6, 2005, http:// nof.confex.com/nof/2005/techprogram/P186.HTM (accessed September 25, 2011).

32. Henry Bone et al., "Ten Years' Experience with Alendronate for Osteoporosis in Postmenopausal Women," *New England Journal of Medicine* 350 (March 18, 2004): 1809–22.

33. Nicholas J. Shaheen, "Long-Term NSAID Use and Acid-Related GI Complications: Improving the Outcomes," Medscape disclosures, http://www.medscape.org/view article/490253 (accessed September 25, 2011); "Doctor Questions Link between Fosamax and Esophageal Cancer," *NBC News*, January 8, 2008.

34. Janice Lloyd, "Long-Term Use of Osteoporosis Drugs Linked to Hip Breaks," *USA Today*, March 11, 2010.

35. Associated Press, "Increased Risk of Fracture with Bisphosphonates," *Drug Discovery & Development*, October 14, 2010.

36. "Possible Increased Risk of Thigh Bone Fracture with Bisphosphonates," Food and Drug Administration, October 2, 2010, http://www.fda.gov/NewsEvents/Newsroom/Press Announcements/ucm229171.htm (accessed September 25, 2011).

37. Tara Parker-Pope, "Drugs to Build Bones May Weaken Them," *New York Times*, July 15, 2008.

38. Jill Adams, "Take Bisphosphonates, Break a Leg?" *Los Angeles Times*, March 22, 2010.

39. G. Strewler, "Do Bisphosphonates Pose a Risk?" *New England Journal of Medicine* 350 (March 18, 2004): 1172–74; Susan Ott, "New Treatments for Brittle Bones," *Annals of Internal Medicine* 141 (September 7, 2004): 406–407.

40. Maja Visekrunacite et al., "Severely Suppressed Bone Turnover and Atypical Skeletal Fragility," *Journal of Clinical Endocrinology & Metabolism* 93, no. 8 (2008): 2948–52; E. Kwek et al., "An Emerging Pattern of Subtrochanteric Stress Fractures: A Long-Term Complication of Alendronate Therapy," *Injury* 39, no. 2 (February 2008): 224–31; A. Neviaser et al., "Low-Energy Femoral Shaft Fractures Associated with Alendronate Use," *Journal of Orthopaedic Trauma* 22, no. 5 (May–June 2008): 346–50.

41. "Patients Feel Painful Side Effects of Bone Drugs," *CBS News*, May 19, 2008.

42. "Drug Ratings for Fosamax," Ask a Patient, results page 3 of 17, http://www.askapatient.com/viewrating.asp?drug=20560&name=FOSAMAX&page=3&PerPage=60 (accessed September 25, 2011).

43. "Drug Ratings for Fosamax," Ask a Patient, results page 1 of 17, http://www.askapatient.com/viewrating.asp?drug=20560&name=FOSAMAX&sort=Timelength (accessed September 25, 2011).

44. "Drug Ratings for Fosamax," Ask a Patient, results page 6 of 102, http://www.askapatient.com/viewrating.asp?drug=20560&name=FOSAMAX&sort=timelength&page=6&PerPage=10 (accessed September 25, 2011).

45. "Drug Ratings for Fosamax," Ask a Patient, results page 68 of 102, http://www.askapatient.com/viewrating.asp?drug=20560&name=FOSAMAX&sort=timelength&order=1&page=68&PerPage=10 (accessed September 25, 2011).

46. "Drug Ratings for Boniva," Ask a Patient, results page 4 of 23, http://www.askapatient.com/viewrating.asp?drug=21455&name=BONIVA&sort=age&page=4&PerPage=60 (accessed September 25, 2011).

47. Ibid.

48. "Drug Ratings for Fosamax," Ask a Patient, results page 1 of 17, http://www.askapatient.com/viewrating.asp?drug=20560&name=FOSAMAX&sort=Timelength.

49. Alix Spiegel, "How a Bone Disease Grew to Fit the Prescription," National Public Radio, December 21, 2009.

50. Ibid.

51. Susan Kelleher, "Disease Expands through Marriage of Marketing and Machines," *Seattle Times*, June 28, 2005.

52. Simons, "Will Merck Survive Vioxx?"

53. Spiegel, "How a Bone Disease Grew."

54. Ibid.

55. Cimons, "Shalala's Ads for Milk Leave Some with a Sour Taste."

56. E. Michael Lewiecki, "Managing Osteoporosis: Challenges and Strategies," *Cleveland Clinic Journal of Medicine* 76, no. 8 (August 2009).

57. Ibid.

58. Ivy M. Alexander and E. Michael Lewiecki, "Prevention, Identification and Treatment of Postmenopausal Osteoporosis," Medscape, October 27, 2008, http://www.medscape .org/viewprogram/17528.

59. Morgan, "Meredith Vieira 'Bones Up' on Osteoporosis."

60. Ibid.

61. Lindsy Tanner, "More Bone Disease Cases Diagnosed," Associated Press, July 27, 2004.

62. Jennifer Washburn, "Rent-a-Researcher," Slate, December 22, 2005, http://www .slate.com/id/2133061/; "Actonel," Government Accountability Project, 2006, http://www .whistleblower.org/program-areas/public-health/actonel (accessed September 25, 2011).

63. "Actonel."

64. Washburn, "Rent-a-Researcher."

65. "Actonel."

66. Jack Neff, "Boniva Makers Slam P&G for Unethical Marketing," Advertising Age, June 12, 2006.

67. Jack Neff, "FDA Ruling Gives Actonel Boost in Osteoporosis-Drug War," Advertising Age, April 17, 2007.

68. "Procter & Gamble Pharmaceuticals and Sanofi-Aventis US, LLC, File Lawsuit against Roche Pharmaceuticals and GlaxoSmithKline," Sanofi, http://www.sanofi.us:80/l/us/en/search .jsp (accessed September 25, 2011).

69. Neff, "FDA Ruling Gives Actonel Boost."

70. Ibid.

71. Bruce Japsen, "Lilly Osteoporosis Prevention Drug Also May Be a Bone-Builder," Chicago Tribune, September 15, 1998.

72. Ibid.

73. Alison Young and Chris Adams, "'Off-Label' Drugs Take Their Toll," Pioneer Press, November 3, 2003.

74. "Eli Lilly and Company to Pay U.S. $36 Million Relating to Off-Label Promotion," United States Department of Justice, http://www.justice.gov/opa/pr/2005/December/05 _civ_685.html (accessed September 25, 2011).

75. Ibid.; "Newer Products Grew 45% to One-Fourth of Sales," PR Newswire-First Call, October 19, 2006.

76. Chris Adams and Alison Young, "Drug-Makers' Promotions Boost Off-Label Use by Doctors," McClatchy Newspapers, November 3, 2003, http://www.mcclatchydc.com/ 2003/11/03/28119/drug-makers-promotions-boost-off.html.

77. Scott Gottlieb, "Stop the War on Drugs," Wall Street Journal, December 17, 2007.

78. Ibid.

79. "Evista Approved for Reducing Breast Cancer Risk," Food and Drug Administration,

http://www.fda.gov/ForConsumers/ConsumerUpdates/ucm048474.htm (accessed September 25, 2011).

80. "Evista," Drugs.com, http://www.drugs.com/pro/evista.html.

81. "Evista Approved for Reducing Breast Cancer Risk."

82. "Drug Ratings for Evista," Ask a Patient, results page 1 of 5, http://www.askapatient .com/viewrating.asp?drug=20815&name=EVISTA (accessed September 25, 2010).

83. "Wyeth Receives Approvable Letter from FDA for Bazedoxifene for the Prevention of Postmenopausal Osteoporosis," PR Newswire-First Call, Drugs.com, May 1, 2007, http:// www.drugs.com/nda/viviant_071226.html (accessed September 25, 2011).

84. Thomas Gryta, "FDA Approves Amgen Osteoporosis Treatment for Postmenopausal Women," *Wall Street Journal*, June 1, 2010.

85. Ben Comer, "Amgen Deploys up to 1,000 Reps on Prolia Approval," *Medical Marketing & Media*, June 3, 2010.

86. Ibid.

87. Ibid.

88. Stephen Blythe, "Denosumab, Osteoporosis, and Prevention of Fractures," letter to editor, *New England Journal of Medicine* 361 (November 26, 2009): 2188–91.

89. Ibid.

90. Athanassios Kyrgidis, "Denosumab, Osteoporosis, and Prevention of Fractures," letter to the editor, *New England Journal of Medicine* 361 (November 26, 2009): 2188–91.

91. Advisory Committee for Reproductive Health Drugs, Background Documents, Food and Drug Administration, August 13, 2009, http://www.fda.gov/downloads/Advisory Committees/CommitteesMeetingMaterials/Drugs/ReproductiveHealthDrugsAdvisory Committee/UCM176605.pdf (accessed September 25, 2011).

92. Ibid.

93. Ibid.

94. Pamela Viale, "Management of Hypersensitivity Reactions: A Nursing Perspective," *Oncology* 23, suppl. 2 (February 1, 2009): 26–30.

95. Advisory Committee for Reproductive Health Drugs, transcript, Food and Drug Administration, August 13, 2009, http://www.fda.gov/downloads/Advisory Committees/CommitteesMeetingMaterials/Drugs/ReproductiveHealthDrugsAdvisory Committee/UCM187083.pdf.

96. Blythe, "Denosumab, Osteoporosis, and Prevention of Fractures."

97. B. Abrahamsen et al., "Patient Level Pooled Analysis of 68,500 Patients from Seven Major Vitamin D Fracture Trials in US and Europe," *British Medical Journal* 340 (January 12, 2010): b5463, http://www.fda.gov/AdvisoryCommittees/CommitteesMeetingMaterials/ Drugs/ReproductiveHealthDrugsAdvisoryCommittee/ucm126208.htm.

98. Richard Hyer, "Vitamin D Supplementation Prevents Breast Cancer Therapy-Related Bone Loss," Oncology Report, July 5, 2011, http://www.oncologyreport.com/news/clinical/

single-article/vitamin-d-supplementation-prevents-breast-cancer-therapy-related-bone-loss/1f 8771e9a1.html (accessed September 26, 2011).

99. "FDA Approves New Injectable Osteoporosis Treatment for Postmenopausal Women," Food and Drug Administration, http://www.fda.gov/newsevents/newsroom/press announcements/ucm214150.htm (accessed September 26, 2011).

100. "Report to Congress on National Dairy Promotion and the National Fluid Milk Processor Promotion Program," United States Department of Agriculture, Agricultural Marketing Service, July 1, 2002, http://www.ams.usda.gov/AMSv1.0/ams.search.do?q=congress (accessed September 26, 2011).

101. "The 'Milk Mustache' Ads Are All Wet," Physicians Committee for Responsible Medicine, http://www.pcrm.org/search/?cid=1473 (accessed January 7, 2012).

102. Milkads.net, http://milkads.net/view_ad.php?view_name=2000anthony01 (accessed January 7, 2012).

103. "Milk Processor Education Program," All Business, October 1, 2003, http://www .allbusiness.com/agriculture-forestry/animal-production-cattle/191259-1.html.

104. T. Colin Campbell, *The China Study* (Dallas: Benbella Books, 2006), p. 210.

105. Wynn Krieg, "Postgraduate Symposium: Positive Influence of Nutritional Alkalinity on Bone Health," *Proceedings of the Nutrition Society* 69, no. 1 (February): 166–73.

106. Dean Ornish et al., "Can Lifestyle Changes Reverse Coronary Heart Disease? The Lifestyle Heart Trial," *Lancet* 336, no. 8708 (July 21, 1990): 129–33; Dean Ornish, "Author's Response," *Journal of the American Dietetic Association* 150, no. 2 (February 2005): 202–204.

107. D. E. Sellmeyer, "A High Ratio of Dietary Animal to Vegetable Protein Increases the Rate of Bone Loss and the Risk of Fracture in Postmenopausal Women. Study of Osteoporotic Fractures Research Group," *American Journal of Clinical Nutrition* 273, no. 1 (January 2003): 118–22.

108. G. Mazziotti et al., "Drug-Induced Osteoporosis: Mechanisms and Clinical Implications," *American Journal of Medicine* 123, no. 10 (October 2010): 877–84.

109. Deborah Kotz, "Taking Antidepressants Leads to More Bone Loss in Elderly," *US News & World Report*, June 25, 2007.

110. Joe Graedon and Teresa Graedon, "Drugs May Increase Risk for Falls," *Spokesman-Review*, December 15, 2009.

111. T. Jarvinen et al., "Shifting the Focus in Fracture Prevention from Osteoporosis to Falls," *British Medical Journal* 336, no. 7636 (January 19, 2008): 124–26.

112. Emily P. Walker, "FDA Panel Waffles on Limiting Duration of Bisphosphonate Use," MedPage Today, September 9, 2011.

113. Ibid.

PART 2: BIG FOOD

CHAPTER 7. WE'RE DRINKING WHAT? THE RISE AND FALL OF MONSANTO'S BOVINE GROWTH HORMONE

1. Jerry Jackson, "Dairy-Herd Cuts May Not Have Solved Milk-Surplus Problem," *Orlando Sentinel*, June 19, 1988.

2. Ibid.

3. "Report to Congress on the National Dairy Promotion and Research Program and the National Fluid Milk Processor Promotion Program," Agricultural Marketing Service, United States Department of Agriculture, July 1, 2002, http://www.ams.usda.gov/AMSv1.0/getfile?d DocName=STELDEV3099963.

4. "Report to Congress on the National Dairy Promotion and Research Program and the National Fluid Milk Processor Promotion Program," Agricultural Marketing Service, United States Department of Agriculture, July 1, 2007, http://www.ams.usda.gov/AMSv1.0/getfile?d DocName=STELPRDC5065538.

5. Ibid.

6. "Report to Congress on the National Dairy Promotion and Research Program and the National Fluid Milk Processor Promotion Program," Agricultural Marketing Service, United States Department of Agriculture, July 1, 2005, http://www.ams.usda.gov/AMSv1.0/getfile?d DocName=STELDEV3099996.

7. Jane Brody, "Advice from Dr. Spock: Eat Only All Your Vegetables," *New York Times*, June 20, 1998.

8. Helen Salsbury, "Fat Kids and the Farm Bill, AMA and Agribusiness Battle over Kids' Obesity," *Wisconsin State Journal*, November 4, 2007.

9. Dinesh Ramde, "Minn. Congressman Proposes Dairy Subsidy Reforms," Associated Press, July 20, 2011.

10. Marjorie Garber, "Joe Camel, an X-Rated Smoke," *Baltimore Sun*, April 2, 1992.

11. Susan Thys-Jacobs et al., "Calcium Carbonate and the Premenstrual Syndrome: Effects on Premenstrual and Menstrual Symptoms," *American Journal of Obstetrics & Gynecology* 179, no. 2 (August 1998): 444–52.

12. Nanci Hellmich, "Got Milk—and Got Controversy," *USA Today*, March 8, 2006.

13. Report to Congress on the National Dairy Promotion and Research Program and the National Fluid Milk Processor Promotion Program," July 1, 2007.

14. "The Search Is on for America's Healthiest Student Bodies. National 'Got Milk?' Milk Mustache Campaign Launches Contest to Reward Teens and Schools for Encouraging Healthy Habits," PR Newswire, April 20, 2007.

15. Martha Rosenberg, "Milk Is Not a Diet Food," *AlterNet*, June 5, 2007, http://www.alternet.org/story/53102/milk_is_not_a_diet_food/?page=entire (accessed January 9, 2012).

16. Ibid

17. Ibid.

18. Hellmich, "Got Milk."

19. Ibid.

20. Ibid.

21. Robert R. Wolfe, PhD, letter to the editor, *Journal of the American Medical Association* 300, no. 15 (October 15, 2008).

22. "U.S. Government Calls for End to Dairy Weight Loss Ads," Reuters, May 12, 2007.

23. Rosenberg, "Milk Is Not a Diet Food."

24. Ibid.

25. "New Campaign Encourages Teenagers to Drink More Milk, Fewer Sodas," PR Newswire, August 30, 2006, http://finance.abc7news.com/abclocal.kgo/news/read/207751/new_campaign_encourages_teenagers_to_drink_more_milk (accessed January 9, 2012).

26. "Report to Congress on the National Dairy Promotion and Research Program and the National Fluid Milk Processor Promotion Program," Agricultural Marketing Service, United States Department of Agriculture, July 1, 2003.

27. Ibid.

28. "Unreported Financial Disclosures in the Recommended Dietary Allowance of Protein: A Misunderstood Concept," *Journal of the American Medical Association* 300, no. 12 (October 15, 2008): 1763, http://jama.ama-assn.org/content/300/15/1763.1.short.

29. Sharon L. Miller, Douglas B. DiRienzo, and Gregory D. Miller, "New Frontiers in Weight Management," *Journal of the American College of Nutrition*, 21 no. 2 (April 2002); Robert R. Wolfe and Sharon L. Miller, "Protein Metabolism in Response to Ingestion Pattern and Composition of Proteins," *American Society for Nutritional Sciences* 132, suppl. (2002): 3207S.

30. Douglas R. Bolster et al., "Dietary Protein Intake Impacts Human Skeletal Muscle Protein Fractional Synthetic Rates after Endurance Exercise," *American Journal of Physiology—Endocrinology and Metabolism* 289, no. 4 (May 2005); Robert R. Wolfe, "Protein Summit 2007: Exploring the Impact of High-Quality Protein on Optimal Health," *American Journal of Clinical Nutrition* 87, no. 5, suppl. (May 2008): 1583S.

31. Robert R. Wolfe, Sharon L. Miller, and Kevin B. Miller, "Optimal Protein Intake in the Elderly," *Clinical Nutrition* 27, no. 5 (October 2008): 675–84; Wayne W. Campbell et al., "The Recommended Dietary Allowance for Protein May Not Be Adequate for Older People to Maintain Skeletal Muscle," *Journals of Gerontology* 56, no. 6, (June 2001): M373–80; "Seniors Need More Protein Rich Food to Decrease Muscle Loss, Improve Quality of Life," *Medical News Today*, August 11, 2007.

32. Robert R. Wolfe et al., "Dietary Fat Composition Alters Pulmonary Function in Pigs," *Nutrition* 18, nos. 7–8 (July–August 2002): 647–53.

33. Jane L. Levere, "Body by Milk: More Than Just a White Mustache," *New York Times*, August 30, 2006.

34. "Report to Congress on the National Dairy Promotion and Research Program and the National Fluid Milk Processor Promotion Program," July 1, 2007, http://www.ams.usda.gov/AMSv1.0/ams.search.do?q=AMS.

35. Ibid.

36. "Got Milk? Seeks Next Big Idea," press release, Got Milk? http://www.gotmilk.com/Print_Html/Print.Php?Id=56 press release (accessed January 9, 2012).

37. Martha Rosenberg, "California Schools to Receive In-Class Milk Huckstering," *YubaNet*, October 8, 2008, http://yubanet.com/opinions/Martha-Rosenberg-California-Schools-to-Receive-In-Class-Milk-Huckstering.php (accessed January 9, 2012).

38. Ibid.

39. Martha Rosenberg, "Milk on Trial as Cornell Expert Testifies at Fired Teacher's Hearing," *Common Dreams*, June 24, 2008.

40. Ibid.

41. Ibid.

42. "Veganism's New Martyr," *Chicago Tribune*, September 12, 2007.

43. Dave Warwak, *Peep Show for Children Only*, Lulu.com, May 14, 2008.

44. Ibid.

45. Vaughn Stewart III, "Local Dairy Farmer Continues to Say No to Controversial Growth Hormones," *Anniston (AL) Star*, August 2, 2009.

46. Ibid.

47. Henry Miller, "Udder Nonsense about Milk," *Washington Times*, September 3, 2008, http://www.washingtontimes.com/news/2008/sep/03/udder-nonsense-about-milk/.

48. Stewart, "Local Dairy Farmer Continues to Say No."

49. "Await Consumer Reaction to bST," *Acres U.S.A.*, April 1994.

50. Norm White, "rBGH Supported by Convoluted Logic," *Acres U.S.A.*, February 1994.

51. Ibid.

52. Mark Harris, "Cloudy Judgment," *Vegetarian Times*, July 1994.

53. Melanie Warner, "Obama Gives Former Food Lobbyist Michael Taylor a Second Chance at the FDA," *BNET*, January 15, 2010, http://www.cbsnews.com/8301-505123_162-44040110/obama-gives-former-food-lobbyist-michael-taylor-a-second-chance-at-the-fda/ (accessed January 9, 2012); Lyndsey Layton, "New FDA Deputy to Lead Food-Safety Mandate," *Washington Post*, January 14, 2010.

54. Harris, "Cloudy Judgment."

55. John Schwartz, "Probe Clears 3 at FDA Who Approved Cow Hormone," *Washington Post*, October 29, 1994.

56. Stewart, "Local Dairy Farmer Continues to Say No."

57. Keith Schneider, "Despite Critics, Dairy Farmers Increase Use of a Growth Hormone in Cows," *New York Times*, October 30, 1994.

58. Ibid.

59. Ibid.

60. Danny Postel, "Mad Cow, U.S.A: Could the Nightmare Happen Here?" ZNET, December 25, 2003, http://www.zcommunications.org/mad-cow-u-s-a-could-the-nightmare -happen-here-by-danny-postel (accessed January 8, 2012).

61. Report of the Canadian Veterinary Medical Association Expert Panel on rbST, November 1998, http://www.hc-sc.gc.ca/dhp-mps/vet/issues-enjeux/rbst-stbr/rep_cvma-rap _acdv_tc-tm-eng.php (accessed January 8, 2012).

62. "*Lancaster Farming* Speaks with Michael Pollan," *Lancaster Farming*, February 22, 2008.

63. "Await Consumer Reaction to bST," *Acres U.S.A.*, April 1994.

64. Ibid.

65. William J. Cromie, "Growth Factor Raises Cancer Risk," *Harvard University Gazette*, April 22, 1999.

66. June Chan, "Plasma Insulin-Like Growth Factor-I and Prostate Cancer Risk: A Prospective Study," *Science*, no. 5350 (January 23, 1998): 563; "Study Finds Link between Hormone, Breast Cancer," Associated Press, May 8, 1998.

67. "Opposition to the Use of Hormone Growth Promoters in Beef and Dairy Cattle Production," American Public Health Association, November 10, 2009, http://www.apha.org/ advocacy/policy/policysearch/default.htm?id=1379; Marian Burros, "A Hormone for Cows," *New York Times*, November 9, 2005.

68. Burros, "A Hormone for Cows."

69. J. C. Juskevich and C. G. Guyer, "Bovine Growth Hormone: Human Food Safety Evaluation," *Science* 249, no. 4971 (August 34, 1990): 875–84.

70. Susan Gilbert, "Fears over Milk, Long Dismissed, Still Simmer," *New York Times*, January 19, 1999.

71. Gar Smith and Peter Montague, "The Monsanto Roundup: Did Monsanto Fake rBGH Science?" *Earth Island Journal* 14, no. 1 (Winter/Spring 1998–1999), http://www.earth island.org/eijournal/winter99/wr_winter99rbgh.html (Note: page no longer active at time of publication).

72. Gilbert, "Fears over Milk."

73. Greg Barrett, "Hungry and Angry," Gannett News Service, March 30, 2000, http:// home.intekom.com/tm_info/rw00407.htm.

74. Marlene Cimons, "Shalala's Ads for Milk Leave Some with a Sour Taste," *Los Angeles Times*, July 2, 1998.

75. Peter Hardin, "FDA, Monsanto Need to Reveal Truth about Growth Hormone," *Capital Times*, December, 18, 1998.

76. Ibid.

77. Letter from Michael Hansen, senior scientist, Consumers Union, to Governor Kath-

leen Sebelius, Office of the Governor, Consumers Union, Topeka, Kansas, April 8, 2009, http://www.consumersunion.org/pub/core_food_safety/010910.html, (accessed January 8, 2012); "Think before You Pink Campaign," Breast Cancer Action, http://thinkbeforeyoupink.org (accessed January 8, 2012); "Opposition to the Use of Hormone Growth Promoters in Beef and Dairy Cattle Production," American Public Health Association.

78. Gary Steinman, comment on "Twinning and Higher Intake of Dairy Products," letter, *Journal of Reproductive Medicine* 52 (February 2007): 81–86.

79. Trent Loos, "Hormones 101," Stop Labeling Lies, May 1, 2006, http://www.stop labelinglies.com/news/Hormones-101.html (Note: site no longer active at time of publication).

80. Leland B. Taylor, "Simple Statements Are Misleading," *Acres U.S.A.*, February 1994; "Ben & Jerry's in Food-Safety Fight," Associated Press, February 6, 2008; Martha Rosenberg, "Milk, rBST, & Monsanto's Rats," *CounterPunch*, November 18, 2006, http://www.counter punch.org/2006/11/18/we-re-drinking-what/ (accessed January 9, 2012); Brian Robert Lowry, Monsanto Counsel, to Sheldon Bradshaw, FDA chief counsel, February 22, 2007, International Dairy Foods Association, http://www.idfa.org/files/exhibit_003.pdf.

81. Lowry to Bradshaw.

82. Ibid.

83. "Creamery Group Bans Monsanto's Growth Hormone," *Columbia (MO) Daily Tribune*, February 21, 2005; Noel K. Gallagher, "Maine Dairy 'Somewhat Vindicated' as Monsanto Leaves Bovine Hormone Business," *Portland (ME) Press Herald*, August 11, 2008; Taylor, "Simple Statements Are Misleading"; Lowry to Bradshaw; Julie Deardorff, "Hormone-Free Milk Ads Not Misleading," *Chicago Tribune*, August 29, 2007.

84. Lowry to Bradshaw.

85. Andrew Martin, "Fighting on a Battlefield the Size of a Milk Label," *New York Times*, March 9, 2008.

86. Andrew Martin, "Consumers Won't Know What They're Missing," *New York Times*, November 11, 2007.

87. Voluntary Labeling of Milk and Milk Products from Cows That Have Not Been Treated with Recombinant Bovine Somatotropin, Interim Guidance, Federal Register, February 10, 1994, http://www.fda.gov/Food/GuidanceComplianceRegulatoryInformation/GuidanceDocuments/FoodLabelingNutrition/ucm059036.htm (accessed January 9, 2012).

88. "'Simple Statements Are Misleading,' says Monsanto," *Acres U.S.A.*, June 1994.

89. Ibid.

90. "rBGH- (rBST-) Free Dairy Processors Top 100 List," Physicians for Social Responsibility, http://www.psr.org/chapters/oregon/assets/pdfs/top-100-rbgh-free-dairies.pdf (accessed September 29, 2011).

91. Martha Rosenberg, "Downer Cows in Slaughter Video Were Products of Profit Happy Dairy Industry," Common Dreams, February 28, 2008, http://www.commondreams.org/archive/2008/02/28/7353 (accessed January 9, 2012); Naomi Starkman, "Grade 'A': Getting

rbGH Out of School Milk," Civil Eats, March 9, 2009, http://civileats.com/2009/03/09/grade-a-for-getting-rbgh-out-of-school-milk/ (accessed January 9, 2012).

92. "Rampant Animal Cruelty at California Slaughter Plant," Humane Society of the United States, January 30, 2008, http://www.humanesociety.org/news/news/2008/01/under cover_investigation_013008.html (accessed July 29, 2011) (Note: page no longer active at time of publication); Rosenberg, "California Schools to Receive In-Class Milk Huckstering"; Neil Nisperos, "Dairies' Helper," *Inland Valley (CA) Daily Bulletin*, March 10, 2008.

93. Andrew Martin, "Agriculture Dept. Vows to Improve Animal Welfare," *New York Times*, February 29, 2008, http://www.nytimes.com/2008/02/29/business/29food.html?fta=y.

94. Julie Schmit, "Meat Plant Concerns Raised for Years, USA Today Updated," *USA Today*, March 6, 2008.

95. Technical Briefing—Hallmark/Westland Meat Packing Co., transcript, United States Department of Agriculture, February 21, 2008, http://www.usda.gov/wps/portal/usda/usdahome?contentidonly=true&contentid=2008/02/0054.xml (accessed July 29, 2011).

96. "USDA Officials Hold Technical Briefing Regarding Inhumane Handling Allegations," transcript, United States Department of Agriculture, January 31, 2008, http://www.usda.gov/wps/portal/usda/usdahome?contentidonly=true&contentid=2008/02/0028.xml (accessed July 29, 2011).

97. Ibid.

98. Ibid.

99. Victoria Kim, "Questions Raised on Meat Safety," *Los Angeles Times*, February 7, 2008.

100. "'Downer' Cattle Not a Problem for One Livestock Hauling Company," *Land Line*, February 29, 2008.

101. Scott A. Yates, "Cattle Group Appalled by Meatpacker Video," *Capital Press*, February 2008.

102. "Darker Side of Dairy Farming," *ABC News*, January 26, 2010.

103. Department of Health and Human Services, Public Health Service Food and Drug administration, Inspections, Compliance, Enforcement, and Criminal Investigations, Letter to Dennis H. Eldred from Jerome G. Woyshner, district director, Warning Letter NYK 2005-06, February 23, 2005.

104. "Diary," Dairy's Dark Side: The Sour Truth behind Milk, Mercy for Animals, January 26, 2010, http://www.mercyforanimals.org/dairy (accessed September 29, 2011).

105. Holly Zachariah and Alan Johnson, "Dairy-Farm Worker Fired, Arrested over Video," *Columbus Dispatch*, June 3, 2010; Meghan Barr, "Conklin Dairy Farms Video Shows Dairy Cows Being Violently Abused, Says Mercy for Animals," *Huffington Post*, Associated Press, July 25, 2010.

106. Martha Rosenberg, "Pitchfork Wielder on Dairy Farm Receives Light Sentence," *Food Consumer*, September 10, 2010, http://www.foodconsumer.org/newsite/Politics/Politics/pitchfork_wielder_on_dairy_farm_0910100254.html (accessed January 9, 2012).

107. Gary Chittim, "Television Icon Bob Barker Takes on Costco," *KING 5 News*, September 1, 2010.

108. "Country Icon Joins over 22,000 Petition Signers in Pushing for Dairy Farm Reform," Animal Legal Defense Fund, March 26, 2008, http://aldf.org/article.php?id=512 (accessed January 9, 2012).

109. Noel K. Gallagher, "Monsanto Leaves Bovine Hormone Business," *Portland (ME) Press Herald*, August 11, 2008.

110. "Monsanto, Eli Lilly and Company to Acquire Monsanto's POSILAC Brand Dairy Product and Related Business," press release, August 20, 2008.

CHAPTER 8. "EGGSPOSÉS" AND TEFLON CHICKEN DONS

1. "Whistleblower Tell[s] of Deliberate Torture of Birds at Tyson Plant," United Poultry Concerns, formal complaint, http://www.upc-online.org/broiler/022403tysons.htm (accessed June 3, 2011); *Wikipedia*, "Tyson Foods, Use of Slaughtering Methods," http://en.wikipedia.org/wiki/Tyson_Foods#Use_of_slaughtering_methods (accessed June 3, 2011); "YUM! Brands," Sourcewatch, http://www.sourcewatch.org/index.php?title=YUM!_Brands (accessed June 3, 2011); "Tyson Workers Torturing Birds, Urinating on Slaughter Line," People for the Ethical Treatment of Animals, https://secure.peta.org/site/Advocacy?cmd=display&page=UserAction&id=1121 (accessed June 3, 2011); "Animal Rights Group Pursues Complaint against Perdue Farms," Associated Press, October 28, 2004.

2. Mark Bittman, "Banned from the Barn," *New York Times*, July 6, 2011.

3. Andrew Adam Newman, "Good/Corps Aims to Help Business Meet Social Goals," *New York Times*, May 12, 2011.

4. Caroline Gammell, "Jamie Oliver Campaigns for Chicken Welfare," *Telegraph*, April 12, 2008.

5. Julia Moskin, "Chefs' New Goal: Looking Dinner in the Eye," *New York Times*, January 16, 2008.

6. Daniel Zwerdling, "A View to a Kill," *Gourmet Magazine*, June 2007.

7. Ed Edelson, "Millions More Americans Might Be Placed on Statins," *Washington Post*, January 13, 2009.

8. Luc Djoussé and J. Michael Gaziano, "Egg Consumption and Risk of Heart Failure in the Physicians' Health Study," *Circulation* 117 (January 14, 2008): 512–16.

9. J. D. Spence, D. J. Jenkins, and J. Davignon, "Dietary Cholesterol and Egg Yolks: Not for Patients at Risk of Vascular Disease," *Canadian Journal of Cardiology* 26, no. 9 (November 2010): e336–39.

10. Z. Shi et al., "Egg Consumption and the Risk of Diabetes in Adults, Jiangsu, China," *Nutrition* 27, no. 2 (February 2011): 194–98; Luc Djoussé et al., "Egg Consumption and Risk

of Type 2 Diabetes in Men and Women," *Diabetes Care* 32, no. 2 (February 2009): 295–300, http://care.diabetesjournals.org/content/early/2008/11/18/dc08-1271.abstract.

11. Sandi Pirozzo et al., "Ovarian Cancer, Cholesterol, and Eggs. A Case-Control Analysis," *Cancer Epidemiology, Biomarkers & Prevention* 11, no. 10 (October 2002): 1112–14.

12. T. Mehta, "Industry-Sponsored Egg Supplement," *Canadian Family Physician* 56, no. 7 (July 2010): 634–36.

13. *Akin's Healthy Edge*, August 2011, http://issuu.com/hfai/docs/akins_healthy_edge_aug_2011 (accessed February 3, 2012).

14. Rod Smith, "'Good Egg' Going to School," *Feedstuffs* 82, no. 18 (May 3, 2010).

15. Ibid.

16. "New Animal Drugs; Cephalosporin Drugs; Extralabel Animal Drug Use," order of prohibition, Food and Drug Administration, *Federal Register* 73, no. 129 (July 3, 2008), http://edocket.access.gpo.gov/2008/E8-15052.htm (accessed June 3, 2011).

17. L. Jackson et al., "Antimicrobial Residue Detection in Chicken Yolk Samples Following Administration to Egg-Producing Chickens and Effects of Residue Detection on Competitive Exclusion Culture (PREEMPT) Establishment," *Journal of Agricultural and Food Chemistry* 48, no. 12 (2000): 6435–38.

18. Martha Rosenberg, "Free Antibiotics—in U.S. Food and Water: The FDA Has Quietly Revoked a Ban on the Routine Dosing of Farm Animals with Antibiotics," *AlterNet*, February 11, 2009, http://www.alternet.org/water/124265/free_antibiotics_--_in_u.s._food_and_water/ (accessed January 10, 2012).

19. Mary Clare Jalonick, "Iowa Farm Ok'd to Resume Shell Egg Sales," Associated Press, December 1, 2010.

20. Elizabeth Weise, "Cage-Free Hens Pushed to Rule Roost," *USA Today*, April 10, 2006.

21. "Experts," Hatchery Horrors: The Egg Industry's Tiniest Victims, Mercy for Animals, http://www.mercyforanimals.org/hatchery/expert-statements.asp (accessed September 28, 2011).

22. Ibid.

23. "United Egg Producers Animal Husbandry Guidelines for U.S. Egg Laying Flocks, 2006 Edition," Feedstuffs FoodLink, http://www.feedstuffsfoodlink.com/Media/MediaManager/2006UEPAnimalWelfareGuidelines.pdf (accessed September 28, 2011).

24. Sara Shields, PhD, to Nathan Runkle, Executive Director, Mercy for Animals, September 30, 2008, http://www.mercyforanimals.org/norco/Shields.pdf (accessed September 28, 2011).

25. "United Egg Producers Animal Husbandry Guidelines."

26. Ibid.

27. Ibid.

28. Alexei Barrionuevo, "Egg Producers Relent on Industry Seal," *New York Times*, October 4, 2005.

29. "What Does the 'UEP Certified' Logo Mean?" Humane Society of the United States, http://www.humanesociety.org/issues/confinement_farm/facts/uep_certified_logo.html (accessed September 28, 2011).

30. Adam Parker, "Mepkin to Close Egg Farm," *Post and Courier*, December 21, 2007.

31. Scott Morris, "Save the Chickens (from Hell)," *Decatur Daily*, June 11, 2007.

32. Bill Mattos, "Passage of Prop. 2 Would Be Devastating to Crucial Central Valley Industry," *West Side Index and Gustine Press-Standard*, October 9, 2008.

33. Stacy Finz, "Prop. 2: Caging of Farm Animals under Debate," *San Francisco Chronicle*, September 30, 2008.

34. Mattos, "Passage of Prop. 2 Would Be Devastating."

35. Kelly Lecker, "University Switching Suppliers," *Columbus (OH) Dispatch*, May 9, 2006.

36. "Ohio Poultry Producers Protect Flocks from Bird Flu," *ABC News*, April 25, 2006.

37. Martha Rosenberg, "Do You Really Want to Eat Turkey?" *Providence Journal*, November 19, 2007.

38. "Trader Joe's Stops Buying Eggs from Gemperle," KGO-ABC, May 8, 2008.

39. "What the Experts Say," Egg Industry Exposed! Mercy for Animals, http://www.mercyforanimals.org/caeggs/expert-statements.asp (accessed May 8, 2011).

40. "Investigator's Diary," Egg Industry Exposed! Mercy for Animals, http://www.mercyforanimals.org/CAEggs/field-notes.asp (accessed May 8, 2011).

41. Egg Industry Exposed! Mercy for Animals, http://www.mercyforanimals.org/CAEggs/ (accessed January 10, 2012).

42. Jia-Rui Chong, "Wood-Chipped Chickens Fuel Outrage," *Los Angeles Times*, November 22, 2003.

43. Temple Grandin, "Corporations Can Be Agents of Great Improvements in Animal Welfare and Food Safety and the Need for Minimum Decent Standards," National Institute of Animal Agriculture, April 4, 2001, http://www.grandin.com/welfare/corporation.agents.html (accessed September 28, 2011).

44. "Ernie Gemperle and Family to be Honored," *Council News*, Greater Yosemite Council, Boy Scouts of America, 2006.

45. "Local Egg Farmer Pioneer and Philanthropist Ernie Gemperle Passes Away," *Turlock City News*, November 16, 2008.

46. "Farms Accused Of Animal Cruelty, Abuse," KCRA News, May 6, 2008.

47. "Gemperle Investigation Reveals 'Staged, Manipulated' Video; Group Disputes Claim," *Feedstuffs*, May 12, 2008.

48. Dan Noyes, "Abuse on the Egg Farm," *ABC News*, May 5, 2008.

49. "Gemperle Investigation Reveals 'Staged, Manipulated' Video."

50. "Tyson, PETA Clash over Chicken Slaughter," Associated Press, May 25, 2005.

51. Victoria Kim, "Questions Raised on Meat Safety," *Los Angeles Times*, February 7, 2008.

52. Undercover at a California Factory Egg Farm, Mercy for Animals, http://www.mercy foranimals.org/norco/ (accessed June 3, 2011).

53. Frederic J. Frommer, "AP Exclusive: Video Shows Chicks Ground up Alive," Associated Press, September 1, 2009.

54. "Diary," Hatchery Horrors: The Egg Industry's Tiniest Victims, Mercy for Animals, http://www.mercyforanimals.org/hatchery/field-notes.asp (accessed January 10, 2012).

55. Hatchery Horrors: The Egg Industry's Tiniest Victims, Mercy for Animals, http://www.mercyforanimals.org/hatchery (accessed January 10, 2012).

56. Frommer, "AP Exclusive."

57. "Diary," Mercy for Animals.

58. Nathan Runkle, Executive Director, Mercy for Animals, to S. Robson Walton, Chairman, Walmart Supercenters, August 31, 2009, http://www.mercyforanimals.org/ hatchery/walmart_letter.pdf (accessed January 10, 2012).

59. "Whistleblower Tell[s] of Deliberate Torture."

60. Daniel Zwerdling, "A View to a Kill," *Gourmet Magazine*, June 2007.

61. "Tyson to Pay $6 Million in Espy Case," Associated Press, December 30, 1997; Neil A. Lewis, "Clinton Issues a Pardon to Ex-Rep. Rostenkowski," *New York Times*, December 23, 2000.

62. "Law and Illegals," *Christian Science Monitor*, December 27, 2001, http://www.cs monitor.com/2001/1227/p8s1-comv.html (accessed January 10, 2012).

63. David Barboza, "Chicken Well Simmered in a Political Stew; Tyson Fosters Ties to Officials but Is Unable to Avoid Scrutiny," *New York Times*, January 1, 2002.

64. *Wikipedia*, "Tyson Foods," http://en.wikipedia.org/wiki/Tyson_Foods (accessed February 3, 2012).

65. Brian Barber, "State AG Sues Poultry Firms," *Tulsa World*, June 14, 2005.

66. James B. Stewart, "Bribery, but Nobody Was Charged," *New York Times*, June 24, 2011.

67. Ibid.

68. Ibid.

69. Ibid.

70. Ibid.

71. "Tyson in Chinese Joint Venture," February 4, 2008, Poultry Site, http://www.the poultrysite.com/poultrynews/14013/tyson-in-chinese-joint-venture (accessed September 26, 2011).

72. Ibid.

73. Mitch Lipka, "Chinese Chicken: Which Fast Food Chain May Serve You This Scary Import?" *Daily Finance*, October 29, 2009.

74. Tim Lundeen, "Tyson Told to Revise Chicken Labels over Ionophore Debate," *Feedstuffs* 79, no. 49 (November 26, 2007).

75. "USDA Says Tyson Used Antibiotics on Chicken," Associated Press, June 3, 2008.

76. Ibid.

77. Avery Yale Kamila, "Natural Foodie: Pass Law That Helps Egg Farm? Consider History First," *Portland (ME) Press Herald*, May 4, 2011.

78. William Neuman, "An Iowa Egg Farmer and a History of Salmonella," *New York Times*, September 21, 2010.

79. Ibid.

80. Ibid.

81. Alan Clendenning, "Fine Gives DeCoster Workers Hope Deplorable Conditions Have Improved since a Massive OSHA Probe of the Turner Egg Farm, but Further Monitoring May Be Needed, They Say," *Maine Sunday Telegram*, July 14, 1996.

82. Ibid.

83. Michael J. Crumb, "Iowa Egg Producer Separates Business, Charity Work," Associated Press, September 20, 2010.

84. Ryan J. Foley, "Iowa OK'd Egg Farm Tied to 'Habitual Violator' DeCoster," Associated Press, August 27, 2010.

85. "Investigator's Diary," The Rotten Truth: Egg Industry Cruelty Revealed, Mercy for Animals, http://www.mercyforanimals.org/maine-eggs/field-notes.asp (accessed July 12, 2011).

86. Ibid.

87. The Rotten Truth: Egg Industry Cruelty Revealed, Mercy for Animals, http://www.mercyforanimals.org/maine-eggs (accessed February 3, 2012).

88. Scott Thistle, "OSHA Mum on Visit to Turner Egg Farm," *Sun Journal*, April 14, 2009.

89. Lindsay Tice, "Probe Goes on Day after Raid at Turner Plant," *Sun Journal*, April 3, 2009; Nathan Runkle, "Iowa Egg Recall: One Link in a Thirty-Year Chain of DeCoster Abuses," *MFA Blog*, August 24, 2010, http://www.mfablog.org/2010/08/iowa-egg-recall-one-link-in-a-thirty-year-chain-of-decoster-abuses.html (accessed January 10, 2012).

90. Bob, April 3, 2009, comment on Scott Taylor, "Egg Farm under Pressure: Local Stores Selling Products from Facility Targeted during Raid," *Sun Journal*, April 3, 2009, http://www.sunjournal.com/story/310802-3/LewistonAuburn/Egg_farm_unde...re_Local_stores_selling_products_from_facility_targeted_during_raid (accessed April 20, 2009).

91. Scott Taylor, "Egg Farm under Pressure," *Sun Journal*, April 3, 2009.

92. Anonymous undercover employee, telephone interview with the author, April 6, 2009; "Stores Urged to Boycott Turner Eggs," Associated Press, April 2, 2009.

93. Eggland's Best advertisement, unidentified magazine, 2011.

94. Tice, "Probe Goes on Day after Raid."

95. Ibid.

96. Scott Taylor, "Egg Farm Settlement Totals $36,947 in Fines and Restitution, $100,000 to Aid Inspections," *Sun Journal*, June 7, 2010.

97. Ibid.

98. Ibid.

99. Ibid.

100. Ibid.

101. Alec MacGillis, "Before Salmonella Outbreak, Egg Firm Had Long Record of Violations," *Washington Post*, August 22, 2010; "Egg Recall Investigation Widens," United Press International, September 16, 2010.

102. P. J. Huffstutter, "Eggs from Ohio Farm Are Recalled Over Salmonella Concerns," *Los Angeles Times*, November 9, 2010; "Product Recalls," Food Chemical News, November 12, 2010, http://www.morrisanderson.com/resource-center/entry/Decoster-again-Cal-Maine-Foods-Inc-Brief-article/ (accessed June 3, 2011).

103. Jenn Abelson, "Inquiry on Egg Farms in Maine Ties to Tainted Iowa Operation," *Boston Globe*, September 16, 2010.

104. Rep. Bart Stupak, House Committee on Energy and Commerce, US H.R., US Cong., to Austin ("Jack") DeCoster, September 14, 2010.

105. Ibid.

106. US House of Representatives, Subcommittee on Oversight and Investigations, *Hearing on the Outbreak of Salmonella in Eggs* (Washington, DC, September 22, 2010), http://democrats.energycommerce.house.gov/index.php?q=hearing/hearing-on-the-outbreak-of-salmonella-in-eggs (accessed September 28, 2011).

107. MacGillis, "Before Salmonella Outbreak."

108. Michael Schulman, "Cracked," *New Yorker*, September 6, 2010.

109. Elizabeth Weise, "Egg Industry Resorts to Blaming the Victim in Recall, Critics Say," *USA Today*, August 30, 2010.

110. Andrew Zajac and P. J. Huffstutter, "Filthy Conditions Found at Egg Producers," *Los Angeles Times*, August 31, 2010.

CHAPTER 9. THE DRUGSTORE IN YOUR MEAT

1. Daniel R. Verdon, "Pfizer Begins Integration of Fort Dodge," *DVM Newsmagazine*, October 26, 2009; Jennifer Fiala, "Pfizer Seeks to Unload Animal Health Division," VIN News Service, July 8, 2011.

2. "Sales of Pain Drugs Help Pfizer's Profit Beat Forecasts," *Bloomberg*, August 2, 2011.

3. Ransdell Pierson, "Eli Lilly to Buy J&J's Animal Health Business," Reuters, March 14, 2011.

4. Ibid.

5. Ibid.

6. Janet Reynolds, "The Chemicals in Your Poultry," *Hartford (CT) Advocate*, May 16, 2001.

7. "MICOTIL® 300—Tilmicosin Phosphate Injection, Solution," Elanco Animal Health Company, Food and Drug Administration, http://www.accessdata.fda.gov/spl/data/7985f116 -6909-4968-b0a4-214fee8c0b1e/7985f116-6909-4968-b0a4-214fee8c0b1e.xml (accessed January 11, 2012).

8. Ibid.

9. "Drugs Found in Dairy Cattle Meat Spurs Questions about What's in Milk," WBNS-10 TV, July 21, 2011.

10. Audit Report 24601-08-KC, FSIS National Residue Program for Cattle, Department of Agriculture, Office of Inspector General, March 2010.

11. Jeff Tietz, "Boss Hog," *Rolling Stone*, December 14, 2006.

12. Moira Herbst, "Beefs about Poultry Inspections," *Bloomberg Businessweek,* February 6, 2008; Chris Serres, "IL Girl's Family Sues Cargill," *Minneapolis Star-Tribune*, December 24, 2008; "American Foods Group Recalls Ground Beef on E. Coli Report," *Progressive Grocer*, November 26, 2007; David Beard, "More on Whole Foods's Nationwide Recall," *Boston Globe*, August 10, 2008; "U.S. Beef Recall Expanded, 18 Illnesses Suspected," Reuters, June 28, 2009.

13. Audit Report 24601-08-KC.

14. Ibid.

15. Ibid.

16. Ibid.

17. David Schoetz, "Darker Side of Dairy Farming," *Nightline*, ABC News, January 26, 2010; Department of Health and Human Services Public Health Service, Food and Drug Administration, Inspections, Compliance, Enforcement, and Criminal Investigations, letter to Dennis H. Eldred, NYK 2005-06, February 23, 2005.

18. Linda Cline, "Think Twice before Using Gentamicin," *FDA Veterinarian Newsletter* 18, no. 3 (May–June 2003).

19. Audit Report 24601-08-KC.

20. Ibid.

21. Ibid.

22. Department of Health and Human Services Public Health Service, Food and Drug Administration, Inspections, Compliance, Enforcement, and Criminal Investigations, letter to Raymond Wright, partner, The Wright Place, LLC, April 2, 2010.

23. Department of Health and Human Services Public Health Service, Food and Drug Administration, Inspections, Compliance, Enforcement, and Criminal Investigations, letter to Raymond L. Martin, owner, Corner View Dairies, April 28, 2010.

24. Department of Health and Human Services Public Health Service, Food and Drug Administration, Inspections, Compliance, Enforcement, and Criminal Investigations, letter to Rodney R. Land, owner, Land Dairy, April 21, 2010; Department of Health and Human Services Public Health Service, Food and Drug Administration, Inspections, Compliance, Enforcement, and Criminal Investigations, letter to Michael D. Martin, owner, Martin Feed Lot, April

27, 2010; Department of Health and Human Services Public Health Service, Food and Drug Administration, Inspections, Compliance, Enforcement, and Criminal Investigations, letter to Hendrik G. Doelman, owner, Elma Dairy, LLC, April 24, 2010.

25. Department of Health and Human Services Public Health Service, Food and Drug Administration, Inspections, Compliance, Enforcement, and Criminal Investigations, letter to Alan J. Svajgr, president, Darr Feedlots Inc., April 30, 2010; Department of Health and Human Services Public Health Service, Food and Drug Administration, Inspections, Compliance, Enforcement, and Criminal Investigations, letter to Shirlee K. Jelwin, president, and Thomas E. Jermin Jr., vice president, Templeton Feed & Grain Inc., April 13, 2010.

26. The Preservation of Antibiotics for Medical Treatment Act of 2007, 110th Congress (2007–2008).

27. "Senator Edward M. Kennedy on Antibiotic Use in Food Supply," press release, April 30, 2008, Animal-Health-Online.com, http://www.animal-health-online.de/int/2008/04/30/senator-edward-m-kennedy-on-antibiotic-use-in-food-supply/59/ (accessed September 29, 2011).

28. Sally Schuff, "Drug-Resistant Salmonella Found in Recalled Ground Beef," *Feedstuffs*, August 10, 2009.

29. The Preservation of Antibiotics for Medical Treatment Act of 2007.

30. Ibid.

31. Nicholas Kristof, "When Food Kills," *New York Times*, June 11, 2011.

32. Ibid.

33. Matthew Cimitile, "Crops Absorb Livestock Antibiotics, Science Shows," Environmental Health News, January 6, 2009, http://www.environmentalhealthnews.org/ehs/news/antibiotics-in-crops (accessed September 29, 2011).

34. Ibid.

35. Ibid.

36. Ibid.

37. "Soil Study Shows Rise in Resistance Genes," *Feedstuffs*, January 4, 2010.

38. Tara C. Smith, "Methicillin-Resistant *Staphylococcusaureus* (MRSA) Strain ST398 Is Present in Midwestern U.S. Swine and Swine Workers," *PLoS ONE* 4, no. 1 (January 6, 2009).

39. Katie Couric, "Animal Antibiotic Overuse Hurting Humans," *CBS News*, February 10, 2010.

40. Ibid.

41. Dale Keiger, "Farmacology," *Johns Hopkins Magazine*, June 2009, http://www.jhu.edu/jhumag/0609web/farm.html (accessed September 26, 2011).

42. Martha Rosenberg, "MRSA with Your Sunscreen? Death on the Half Shell?" *Epoch Times*, February 27, 2009.

43. Reynolds, "The Chemicals in Your Poultry."

44. Keiger, "Farmacology."

45. Ibid.

46. Ibid.

47. Cliff Gauldin, "Antibiotics in Ag Debate Gains Momentum," *Feedstuffs* 82, no. 3 (January 18, 2010).

48. Hector M. Cervantes et al., "The Influence of Virginiamycin on the Live and Processing Performance of Nicholas Turkey Hens," *Journal of Applied Poultry Research* 20 (2011): 347–52.

49. Lee Howard, "Moving Pfizer Antibacterials Unit May Delay Critical Research," *The Day*, April 8, 2011; Shahla Masood, "Why Women Still Die from Breast Cancer," *Jacksonville Medicine*, January 1999.

50. "PAMTA Introduced in Senate," American Veterinary Medical Association, July 2011, http://www.avma.org/advocacy/avma_advocate/jul11/aa_jul11.asp (accessed September 29, 2011).

51. Ibid.

52. Katie Couric, "Denmark's Case for Antibiotic-Free Animals," *CBS News*, February 10, 2010; Ralph F. Loglisci, "Can Hog Industry Kick Low-Dose Antibiotics Habit?" *Food Safety News*, April 7, 2011; Martha Rosenberg, "The Overuse of Antibiotics in Livestock Feed Is Killing Us," *AlterNet*, January 26, 2010, http://www.alternet.org/health/145272/the_overuse_of_antibiotics_in_livestock_feed_is_killing_us (accessed January 11, 2012).

53. Hector M. Cervantes, "Banning Antibiotic Growth Promoters: Learning from the European Experience," Elanco, June 2006, http://elanco.jp/market/pdf/200608_tp1_01.pdf (accessed February 5, 2012).

54. Ibid.

55. Ibid.

56. Reynolds, "The Chemicals in Your Poultry."

57. Keiger, "Farmacology."

58. Reynolds, "The Chemicals in Your Poultry."

59. "Animal Antibiotics: Keeping Animals Healthy and Our Food Safe," Animal Health Institute, 2009, http://www.ahi.org/wp-content/uploads/2011/04/Animal-Antibiotics-Keeping-Animals-Healthy.pdf (accessed August 29, 2011).

60. Ibid.

61. Jay P. Graham, John J. Boland, and Ellen Silbergeld, "Growth Promoting Antibiotics in Food Animal Production: An Economic Analysis," *Public Health Reports* 122 (January–February 2007), http://www.jhsph.edu/bin/s/a/antibiotics_poultry07.pdf (accessed January 11, 2012).

62. Ibid.

63. William A. Dudley-Cash, "Flawed Assumptions Result in Incorrect Conclusions," *Feedstuffs* 79, no. 6 (February 5, 2007).

64. Ibid.

65. Gardiner Harris and Denise Grady, "Pfizer Suspends Sales of Chicken Drug with Arsenic," *New York Times*, June 8, 2011.

66. "Pfizer Will Voluntarily Suspend Sale of Animal Drug 3-Nitro," Food and Drug Administration, June 8, 2011 (accessed January 11, 2012).

67. Harris and Grady, "Pfizer Suspends Sales of Chicken Drug with Arsenic."

68. Couric, "Denmark's Case for Antibiotic-Free Animals."

69. Ibid.

70. "Texas Governor Orders STD Vaccine for All Girls," Associated Press, February 3, 2007.

71. "Bayer Pulls Baytril," *Journal of the American Veterinary Medical Association* (October 15, 2005); Enrofloxacin for Poultry, Withdrawal of Approval of Bayer Corporation's New Animal Drug Application (NADA) 140-828 (Baytril) Docket No. 2000N-1571, Food and Drug Administration.

72. "Questions and Answers, Cephalosporin Order of Prohibition," Food and Drug Administration, July 16, 2008, http://www.fda.gov/AnimalVeterinary/NewsEvents/CVMUpdates/ucm054434.htm.

73. Ibid.

74. Reynolds, "The Chemicals in Your Poultry."

75. *Hearing before the Subcommittee on Livestock, Dairy, and Poultry of the Committee on Agriculture*, US H.R., 110th Cong. 2nd Session, (September 25, 2008), http://www.gpo.gov/fdsys/pkg/CHRG-110hhrg51478/html/CHRG-110hhrg51478.htm (accessed September 29, 2011).

76. Ibid.

77. Ibid.

78. Ibid.

79. Ibid.

80. William Neuman, "F.D.A and Dairy Industry Spar over Testing of Milk," *New York Times*, January 25, 2011.

81. Ibid.

82. W. Ron DeHaven, executive vice president, American Veterinary Medical Association, letter to Food and Drug Administration, Food and Drug Administration Docket No.-N-0326, "New Animal Drugs, Cephalosporin Drugs, Extralabel Animal Drug Use, Order of Prohibition," October 30, 2008, http://www.avma.org/advocacy/federal/regulatory/practice_issues/drugs/cephalosporin.asp (accessed January 11, 2012).

83. Ibid.

84. Sally Schuff, "Antibiotic Statements Stun Ag Groups," *Feedstuffs*, July 17, 2009.

85. Margaret A. Hamburg, "America's Innovation Agency: The FDA," *Wall Street Journal*, August 1, 2011; Jim Edwards, "Bad Medicine: If FDA Lets Drug Company Docs Advise It, Safety Will Suffer," *BNET*, July 26, 2011, http://www.cbsnews.com/8301-505123_162-42849230/bad-medicine-if-fda-lets-drug-company-docs-advise-it-safety-will-suffer/?tag=bnetdomain (accessed January 11, 2012).

86. "Opinion of the Scientific Committee on Veterinary Measures Relating to Public Health Assessment of Potential Risks to Human Health from Hormone Residues in Bovine Meat and Meat Products," European Commission, April 30, 1999, http://ec.europa.eu/food/fs/sc/scv/out21_en.pdf (accessed February 5, 2012).

87. Ibid.

88. Ibid.

89. Ibid.; Cimitile, "Crops Absorb Livestock Antibiotics, Science Shows."

90. "Paylean™ and the Canadian Pork Industry," *Bacon Bits* (Alberta) 19, no. 4 (November 25, 2005); Information conveyed from Elanco to Evanston (Illinois) Public Library, January 28, 2010.

91. Wes Ishmael, "New Gains on Old Money," *Beef Magazine*, October 1, 2005.

92. Jason Cleere, "The Facts about Optaflexx™ Ractopamine for Cattle," AgriLife Extension, Texas A&M System, http://animalscience.tamu.edu/images/pdf/beef/beef-optaflexx.pdf (accessed February 8, 2012); "Ingredient Can Help Reduce Feed Costs," *Feedstuffs* 78, no. 53 (December 25, 2006): 12.

93. "China's Quality Standards Obstacle for Import of U.S. Pork," *China Business News*, September 14, 2007.

94. "China Fights Back, Goes After U.S. Meat," Associated Press, July 14, 2007.

95. Hermia Lin, "Swine Farmers Get Rowdy over Ractopamine Issue," *Taiwan News*, August 2, 2007.

96. Ibid.

97. Ibid.

98. "The Codex Perspective on Ractopamine," *Beef Site*, August 2009, http://www.the-beefsite.com/articles/2082/the-codex-perspective-on-ractopamine (accessed February 5, 2012).

99. Peng Zuo et al., "Determination of Beta-Adrenergic Agonists by Hapten Microarray," *Talanta* 82, no. 1 (June 30, 2010): 61–66.

100. Len Ritter, "Ractopamine," Bureau of Veterinary Drugs Health Protection, Branch Health and Welfare Canada, Ottawa, 1987.

101. "OPTAFLEXX 45 (ractopamine hydrochloride) granule [Elanco Animal Health Company] label, Veterinary Medicine Labels," Daily Med, http://dailymed.nlm.nih.gov/dailymed/drugInfo.cfm?id=19100 (accessed August 29, 2011).

102. Department of Health and Human Services Public Health Service, Food and Drug Administration, Inspections, Compliance, Enforcement, and Criminal Investigations, letter to Patrick C. James, president, Elanco Animal Health, September 12, 2002, http://www.fda.gov/ICECI/EnforcementActions/WarningLetters/2002/ucm145110.htm (accessed September 29, 2011).

103. Ibid.

104. "News & Events: Officials' Calendar of Meetings," United States Department of Agriculture, Food Safety and Inspection Service, July 28, 2009, http://www.fsis.usda.gov/News_&_Events/Officials_Calendar_Jan2009/index.asp (accessed August 29, 2011).

105. Approvals: January 1, 2010, to April 5, 2010, Original New Animal Drug Applications (NADAs), Food and Drug Administration.

106. "Follow Label When Using Feed Additive on Show Pigs," Ohio State University Extension, July 18, 2002.

107. Jeremy Marchant-Forde, "The Effects of Ractopamine on the Behavior and Physiology of Finishing Pigs," *Journal of Animal Science* 81, no. 2 (February 2003): 416–22.

108. Ractopamine, Sec. 558.500, Subpart B, Specific New Animal Drugs for Use in Animal Feeds, chap. 1, Department of Health and Human Services, Food and Drug Administration, pp. 458–59 (rev. April 1, 2004).

109. Temple Grandin, "The Effect of Economics on the Welfare of Cattle, Pigs, Sheep, and Poultry," Colorado State University, 2009, http://www.grandin.com/welfare/economic.effects.welfare.html (accessed August 29, 2011).

110. Rosangela Poletto et al., "Aggressiveness and Brain Amine Concentration in Dominant and Subordinate Finishing Pigs Fed the Beta-Adrenoreceptor Agonist Ractopamine," *Journal of Animal Science* 88, no. 9 (September 2010): 3107–20; Rosangela Poletto et al., "Effects of a 'Step-Up' Ractopamine Feeding Program, Sex, and Social Rank on Growth Performance, Hoof Lesions, and Enterobacteriaceae Shedding in Finishing Pigs," *Journal of Animal Science* 87 no. 1 (January 2009): 304–13; Zuo et al., "Determination of Beta-Adrenergic Agonists."

111. Yan Zhang et al., "Rapid Determination of Ractopamine Residues in Edible Animal Products by Enzyme-Linked Immunosorbent Assay: Development and Investigation of Matrix Effects," *Journal of Biomedicine and Biotechnology* 579175 (October 11, 2009).

CHAPTER 10. FARMER JONES: DO YOU KNOW WHO YOUR EMPLOYEES ARE? NOT *THOSE* EMPLOYEES!

1. Trent Loos, "It's All a Part of Cycle of Life," *Feedstuffs* 80 no. 8 (February 25, 2008).

2. Steve Tarter, "Farming Activist Is Now the Target Being Singled out by Factory Farm Advocates," *Peoria Journal Star*, April 6, 2004.

3. Dan Murphy, "Five Minutes with Trent Loos, Rancher-Activist-Advocate for Farmers & Producers," *CattleNetwork*, February 27, 2008, http://www.cattlenetwork.com/templates/newsarchive.html?sid=cn&cid=628694 (accessed August 29, 2011).

4. Trent Loos and Kelli Loos, "Rancher Goes Undercover," *High Plains Journal*, April 8, 2004.

5. Trent Loos, "How Hungry and Homeless Would Vote," *Feedstuffs* 79, no. 53 (December 24, 2007); Trent Loos, "Cured Meats Found to Hold Health Benefits," *Feedstuffs*, July 11, 2009; Trent Loos, "Uncle Sam Not a Good Horseman," *Feedstuffs* 80, no. 47 (November 17, 2008); Trent Loos, "Flushing out the Facts," *Truth Be Told*, August 2, 2007, http://loostales.blogspot.com/2007/08/flushing-out-facts-i-am-quite-sure-that.html (accessed January 12, 2012).

6. Consumer Freedom, http://www.consumerfreedom.com/about/ (accessed January 12, 2012).

7. "Standing Up for the Right to Eat Meat (and Foie Gras)," *Better Farming*, June 2007, http://www.betterfarming.com/2007/june/st2.htm (accessed August 29, 2011).

8. "Animal Welfare Should Be Based on Reason, Science and Experience," Animal Agriculture Alliance, http://www.animalagalliance.org/current/home.cfm?Category=Press_Releases&Section=2007_0416_Animal (accessed August 29, 2011).

9. "In Dairyland, Pollan's 'Food' Book Sparks Debate," Associated Press, September 25, 2009.

10. Nick Penzenstadler, "7,000 Attend Talk by Controversial Food Author," *Milwaukee Journal Sentinel*, September 24, 2009.

11. John Oncken, "Farmers Have No Real Beef with Pollan, but Don't Blame Them for Obesity," *Capital Times*, September 25, 2009, http://host.madison.com/ct/business/article_5702383e-aa1e-11de-a8a3-001cc4c03286.html#ixzz1VWAAxWF4 (accessed August 29, 2011).

12. Trent Loos, "There's a Wolf Knocking at the Door," *Feedstuffs*, April 19, 2010.

13. Ibid.

14. "Food Industry Must Coalesce or Lose War," *Feedstuffs*, April 2, 2007.

15. Ibid.

16. Jim Provance, "As Ohio Considers Livestock Treatment, Michigan Crafts Law," *Toledo Blade*, October 11, 2009.

17. "Standing Up for the Right to Eat Meat."

18. "Dairy Farms Have 41% Foreign Workers," *Feedstuffs*, March 15, 2010.

19. D. A. Daley, "How to Lose the Argument on Animal Welfare," *Feedstuffs*, March 1, 2010.

20. "Videos Explain Production Practices," *Feedstuffs*, March 22, 2010.

21. "Farm Visits Influence Foie Gras Vote, Delegates Decide Issue on Science, Current Practices," American Veterinary Medical Association, September 1, 2005.

22. Ibid.

23. Mark Caro, "Liver and Let Live," *Chicago Tribune*, March 29, 2005.

24. Russ Parsons, "Chicago Says No to Foie Gras," *Los Angeles Times*, May 3, 2006.

25. Ibid.

26. Janet Rausa Fuller, "Foie Gras Ban Unites Chefs against Politicians," *Chicago Sun-Times*, May 17, 2006.

27. Josh Noel, "Let 'Em Eat Foie Gras, They Declare," *Chicago Tribune*, December 21, 2006.

28. Phil Vettel, "Has City Council Finally Quacked?" *Chicago Tribune*, May 4, 2006.

29. Noel, "Let 'Em Eat Foie Gras."

30. Janet Rausa Fuller, "Chef Thumbs Nose at Ban: 10 Courses of Foie Gras," *Chicago*

Sun-Times, May 7, 2006; Sandy Thorn Clark, "Controversy on the Menu," *Chicago Sun-Times*, May 17, 2006.

31. "Chef Wolfgang Puck Bans Foie Gras," Associated Press, March 23, 2007.

32. "Israel's Chief Rabbinate, Orthodox Union Refute Charges against Agriprocessors," PR Newswire, LUBICOM Marketing Consulting, http://dhengah.org/agri/agpprn.htm (accessed August 29, 2011).

33. Cliff Gauldin, "Film Prompts Look Back At Hog Farm Trial," *Feedstuffs*, March 19, 2009.

34. Andrea Zippay, "Ohio Pork Producers Help Wiles Farm," Farm and Dairy, August 9, 2007, http://www.farmanddairy.com/news/ohio-pork-producers-help-wiles-farm/901.html (accessed February 5, 2012).

35. Gauldin, "Film Prompts Look Back at Hog Farm Trial."

36. *10 News Morning*, I News Network, May 13, 2008; "Gemperle Investigation Reveals 'Staged, Manipulated' Video; Group Disputes Claim," *Feedstuffs*, May 12, 2008.

37. Martha Rosenberg, "Would This Video Make You Stop Eating Beef? Futures Traders Think So," *AlterNet*, April 22, 2011, http://blogs.alternet.org/speakeasy/2011/04/22/would-this-video-make-you-stop-eating-beef-futures-traders-think-so/?utm_source=feedblitz&utm_medium=FeedBlitzRss&utm_campaign=alternet.

38. Rod Smith, "Michael Foods Disputes COK Video," *Feedstuffs*, October 16, 2009.

39. Ibid.

40. Rod Smith, "Film Misses Key Messages," *Feedstuffs*, April 26, 2010.

41. "Police Guard Ohio Farm Target of Cow Cruelty Case," Associated Press, May 31, 2010; Gauldin, "Film Prompts Look Back at Hog Farm Trial"; Donna Willis and Tom Brockman, "No Additional Charges to be Filed in Animal Abuse Case," *NBC 4 News*, July 6, 2010; "Union County Animal Abuse Trial Is Continued," Farm and Dairy, August 12, 2010, http://www.farmanddairy.com/news/union-county-animal-abuse-trial-is-continued/15551.html (accessed August 29, 2011).

42. Susan Crowell, "We Deserve Truth in Conklin Dairy Farm Animal Cruelty Case," Farm and Dairy, June 1, 2010, http://www.farmanddairy.com/columns/we-deserve-truth-in-conklin-dairy-farm-animal-cruelty-case/15052.html.

43. "New Video Alleges Animal Cruelty at Veal Farm," *ABC News*, August 31, 2010.

44. Assessment of USDA's Controls for the Beef Export Verification Program for Japan, Report No. 50601-11-HQ, US Department of Agriculture, Office of Inspector General, Food and Marketing Division Audit Report, February 2006.

45. Chris Kick, "Bob Barker, MFA Call for Action against Veal and Dairy Farming," Farm and Dairy, August 31, 2010, http://www.farmanddairy.com/news/bob-barker-mfa-call-for-action-against-veal-and-dairy-farming/15660.html (accessed August 29, 2011).

46. Sarah Skidmore, "Costco Speaks out on Veal Supplier's Tactics," Associated Press, September 1, 2010.

47. Dan Murphy, "Beating the Anti-Industry Activists at Their Own Game" (speech, Agriculture and Agri-Food Canada 16th Annual Conference, Saskatoon, SK, December 12–13, 2007).

48. Ibid.

49. Daley, "How to Lose the Argument on Animal Welfare."

50. Ibid.

51. Rod Smith, "Grandin: Clean Up; Show Off," *Feedstuffs* 8, no. 32 (August 10, 2009).

52. Ibid.

53. Ibid.

54. Ibid.

55. Charlie LeDuff, "At a Slaughterhouse, Some Things Never Die: Who Kills, Who Cuts, Who Bosses Can Depend on Race," *New York Times*, June 16, 2000; "Interview: Charlie LeDuff of the *New York Times*," www.JournalismJobs.com, March 2001, http://www.journalism jobs.com/interview_leduff.cfm (accessed August 29, 2011).

56. Andrew Martin, "At Some Farms, It's 'Hog Hell,'" *Chicago Tribune*, March 24, 2004.

57. Ibid.

58. Jeff Tietz, "Boss Hog," *Rolling Stone*, December 14, 2006.

59. Ibid.

60. Daniel Zwerdling, "A View to a Kill," *Gourmet*, June 2, 2007.

61. "Undercover at a California Factory Egg Farm," Mercy for Animals, http://www
.mercyforanimals.org/norco/ (accessed August 29, 2011); "Aaron," telephone interview with the author, October 7, 2008.

62. "Aaron," telephone interview.

63. Ibid.

64. Martha Rosenberg, "Do You Really Want to Eat Turkey?" *Providence Journal*, November 19, 2007.

65. "Sam," telephone interview with the author, May 17, 2007.

66. Ibid.

67. "Worker's Diary," Mercy for Animals, http://www.mercyforanimals.org/hor/diary.aspx (accessed September 17, 2011).

68. "Diary," Breeding Misery: Inside the Pork Industry, Mercy for Animals, http://www
.mercyforanimals.org/pigs/field-notes.asp (accessed September 17, 2011).

69. Ibid.

70. Ibid.

71. "Experts," Breeding Misery: Inside the Pork Industry, Mercy for Animals, http://
www.mercyforanimals.org/pigs/expert-statements.asp (accessed January 12, 2012).

72. Ibid.

73. Ibid.

74. Breeding Misery: Inside the Pork Industry, Mercy for Animals, http://www.mercy foranimals.org/pigs/ (accessed January 12, 2012).

75. Dairy's Dark Side: The Sour Truth behind Milk, Mercy for Animals, http://www.mercyforanimals.org/dairy/ (accessed September 17, 2011).

76. "Diary" Dairy's Dark Side: The Sour Truth behind Milk, Mercy for Animals, http://www.mercyforanimals.org/dairy/field-notes.asp (accessed January 12, 2012).

77. Ibid.

78. Ibid.

79. "Pete," telephone interview with the author, January 12, 2009.

80. Ibid.

81. Ibid.

82. Ibid.

83. "Diary," Dairy's Dark Side: The Sour Truth behind Milk.

84. Dairy's Dark Side: The Sour Truth behind Milk (video; see note 75).

85. "Diary," Breeding Misery: Inside the Pork Industry.

86. Holly Zachariah, "Cow Puncher Gets 18 Months," *Columbus Dispatch*, September 25, 2010.

87. Nitasha Tiku, "Something Biblical Seems in Order for the Guy Convicted of Cow-Punching," *New York Magazine*, September 27, 2010, http://nymag.com/daily/intel/2010/09/post_35.html

88. Willis and Brockman, "No Additional Charges to Be Filed In Animal Abuse Case."

89. "Grand Jury Considers Conklin Dairy Case," news release, Office of the Union County Prosecuting Attorney, July 6, 2010; Katerina Lorenzatos Makris, "District Attorney Says He Needed Undercover Video to Make Calf Abuse Case," *Examiner*, May 27, 2011, http://www.examiner.com/animal-policy-in-national/district-attorney-says-he-needed-undercover-video-to-prosecute-calf-abuse-case (accessed January 12, 2012).

90. Martha Rosenberg, "No Charges Filed Yet in Dairy Atrocity Seen on *Nightline*," *Food Consumer*, March 24, 2010, http://www.foodconsumer.org/newsite/mobile/Non-food/Miscellaneous/no_charges_filed_yet_in_dairy_atrocity_seen_on_nightline_2403100.html (accessed January 12, 2012).

91. Scott Taylor, "Factory-Like Efficiency Key to Egg Plant," *Sun Journal* (Lewiston, ME), April 12, 2009.

92. Rod Smith, "Michael Foods Disputes COK video," *Feedstuffs*, October 16, 2009.

93. Loos and Loos, "Rancher Goes Undercover."

94. Trent Loos, "Change Names, But It's Still Ag," *Feedstuffs* 80, no. 9 (March 3, 2008).

95. A. G. Sulzberger, "States Look to Ban Efforts to Reveal Farm Abuse," *New York Times*, April 13, 2011.

96. Ibid.

97. Ibid.

98. Michele Simon, "Big Ag's Latest Attempt to Chill Free Speech," *Food Safety News*, July 7, 2011.

99. Sulzberger, "States Look to Ban Efforts."

100. Ibid.

101. Ibid.

102. "Victory: Ding Dong, the Bills Are Dead!" People for the Ethical Treatment of Animals, June 30, 2011, http://www2.peta.org/site/MessageViewer?em_id=82298.0&printer_friendly=1 (accessed January 12, 2012); Nathan Runkle, "Victory! Efforts to Ban Undercover Investigations Fail," Mercy for Animals, July 5, 2100, http://www.mfablog.org/2011/07/victory-efforts-to-ban-undercover-investigations-fail.html (accessed January 12, 2012).

103. Jesse McKinley and Julia Preston, "Farmers Oppose G.O.P. Bill on Immigration," *New York Times*, July 30, 2011.

104. Ibid.

105. Ibid.

CHAPTER 11. SLAUGHTER TRANSPARENCY AND ITS DOWNSIDES

1. David Firestone, "Sarah Palin's Alaskan Rhapsody," *New York Times*, December 8, 2010; Maureen Dowd, "Pass the Caribou Stew," *New York Times*, December 7, 2010.

2. Beth Fouhy, "Obama Turns Table on Clinton," Associated Press, April 13, 2007.

3. Barry Massey, "Richardson Reveals His Love of Hunting," Associated Press, June 8, 2007.

4. "Bill Richardson: I'm a 'Recreational' Hunter," FOX News, June 7, 2007.

5. James Oliphant, "Hunting with Huckabee," *Baltimore Sun*, December 26, 2007.

6. Michael Isikoff, "A Son's Past Deeds Come Back to Bite Huckabee," *Newsweek*, December 15, 2007.

7. Mike Glover, "Huckabee Bags a Bird in Iowa," Associated Press, December 26, 2007.

8. Sam Youngman, "McCain Has 'Work to Do' with Gun Owners: NRA," *The Hill*, April 9, 2008.

9. Jeannette Walls with Ashley Pearson, "Cheney Faces Heat for Canned Hunt," MSNBC, December 18, 2003.

10. Martha Rosenberg, "Dick Cheney's Sadistic Passion for Shooting Tame Animals," *AlterNet*, November 14, 2007, http://www.alternet.org/story/67663/ (accessed January 12, 2012).

11. Ibid.

12. Ibid.

13. Jim Davenport, "SC Gov Sought More Time in Argentina," *Fort Mill Times*, June 26, 2009.

14. "Argentina Dove Hunting," Cordoba Doves, http://www.cordobadoves.com.ar/ (accessed September 26, 2011).

15. "Argentina Dove Hunting," Rod & Gun Resources, http://www.argentinadovehunting.com (accessed September 26, 2011).

16. "Country Star Accused of Killing Tame Bear," Associated Press, August 16, 2006.

17. Gen. JC Christian, "Killing 'Cubby,'" *Jesus' General* (blog), August 17, 2006, http://patriotboy.blogspot.com/2006/08/killing-cubby.html (accessed September 27, 2011).

18. Maurice Chittenden, "Madonna's Baby Pheasant Targets Ruffle Feathers," *Sunday Times*, September 3, 2006, http://www.timesonline.co.uk/tol/news/uk/article626701.ece (accessed September 27, 2011).

19. Michael Pearce, "They May Not Admit It, but Several Celebrities Are Hunters," *Wichita Eagle*, December 10, 2001.

20. Alex Williams, "Slaughterhouse Live," *New York Times*, October 23, 2009.

21. Ibid.

22. Christine Muhlke, "A Movable Beast," *New York Times*, May 20, 2010.

23. Ariel Kaminer, "The Main Course Had an Unhappy Face . . . ," *New York Times*, November 19, 2010.

24. "Fury over BBC Plan to Screen the Slaughter of Lambs and Piglets," BBC, September 7, 2007.

25. Ibid.

26. Unidentified contractor, interview with the author, September 17, 2006 Chicago, Illinois.

27. Marv Lavin, chemist, undated interview with the author.

28. Charlie LeDuff, "At a Slaughterhouse, Some Things Never Die," *New York Times*, June 16, 2000; Joby Warrick, "They Die Piece by Piece," *Washington Post*, April 10, 2001.

29. "Whistleblower Tell[s] of Deliberate Torture of Birds at Tyson Plant," formal complaint, United Poultry Concerns, February 24, 2003, http://www.upc-online.org/broiler/022403tysons.htm (accessed September 26, 2011).

30. Frances Russell, "The Costs of Factory Farming," *Winnipeg Free Press*, November 26, 2004.

31. Frederic J. Frommer, "Film Prompted First Humane Slaughter Law," Associated Press, February 27, 2008.

32. Ibid.

33. Ibid.

34. Temple Grandin and Gary C. Smith, "Animal Welfare and Humane Slaughter," updated November 2004, http://www.Grandin.com (accessed February 6, 2012).

35. Ibid.

36. "Whistleblower Tell[s] of Deliberate Torture."

37. "Humane Slaughter Systems," Docket No. 04-013N (Lisa Baker), US Department of Agriculture, Food Safety and Inspection Service.

38. Grandin and Smith, "Animal Welfare and Humane Slaughter."

39. Ibid.

40. Ibid.

41. Ibid.

42. Toby Sterling, "Dutch Approve Ban on Religious Animal Slaughter," Associated Press, June 28, 2011.

43. Ibid.

44. John Tagliabue, "Bill on Humane Slaughter Yields New Front for Muslim Tensions," *New York Times*, June 26, 2011.

45. Ibid.

46. Jonathan C. Randal, "Brigitte Bardot's Ewe and Cry Protest of Ritual Slaughter Draws Charges of Racism," *Washington Post*, May 22, 1996.

47. Michele Linck, "Demand Grows for Kosher Food," *Sioux City Journal*, April 17, 2011.

48. "Continuing Problems in USDA's Enforcement of the Humane Methods of Slaughter Act," US House of Representatives, Subcommittee on Regulatory Affairs, Domestic Policy Subcommittee Oversight and Government Reform Committee (March 4, 2010) (statement of Jerold R. Mande, deputy, undersecretary for food safety), http://oversight.house.gov/index .php?option=com_jcalpro&Itemid=20&extmode=view&extid=133 (accessed September 26, 2011); US House of Representatives, US Government Accountability Office, Domestic Policy, Committee on Oversight and Government Reform, Testimony before the Subcommittee on Humane Methods of Slaughter Act Weaknesses in USDA Enforcement (March 4, 2010) (statement of Lisa Shames, director natural resources and environment), http://www.gao.gov/new .items/d10487t.pdf (accessed September 26, 2011); Jennifer Ross-Nazzal, *Societal Impacts of Space* (Washington, DC: National Aeronautics and Space Administration, 2007), p. 17.

49. Melanie Warner, "Obama Gives Former Food Lobbyist Michael Taylor a Second Chance at the FDA," CBS News, January 15, 2010, http://www.cbsnews.com/8301-505123_162 -44040110/-obama-gives-former-food-lobbyist-michael-taylor-a-second-chance-at-the-fda/.

50. Ibid.

51. Nicole Johnson, "Food 'Safety' Reform and the Covert Continuation of the Enclosure Movement," *OpEdNews.com*, April 28, 2010, http://www.opednews.com/articles/Food-Safety -Reform-and-t-by-Nicole-Johnson-100426-437.html.

52. Ibid.

53. Ross-Nazzal, *Societal Impacts of Space*; R-CALF USA, Policy of Ranchers-Cattlemen Action Legal Fund, United Stockgrowers of America, 2010, http://www.r-calfusa.com/policy .pdf (accessed February 6, 2012).

54. Janet Reynolds, "The Chemicals in Your Poultry," *Hartford (CT) Advocate*, May 16, 2001.

55. Ibid.

56. Ross-Nazzal, *Societal Impacts of Space*.

57. Continuing Problems in the USDA's Enforcement of the Humane Methods of Slaughter Act, US H.R., Committee on Oversight and Reform, (March 4, 2010) (testimony from Dean Wyatt), http://www.gpo.gov/fdsys/pkg/CHRG-111hhrg65127/pdf/CHRG-111 hhrg65127.pdf (accessed September 26, 2011).

58. Ibid.

59. Ibid.

60. Ibid.

61. Ibid.

62. Ibid.

63. Ibid.

64. Ibid.

65. Ibid.

66. Julia Preston, "Vermont Slaughterhouse Closed amid Animal Cruelty Allegations," *Los Angeles Times*, November 3, 2009.

67. Employee of Bushway Packing Plant Pleads Guilty Aggravated Cruelty to Animals, Office of the Attorney General of Vermont, November 18, 2010.

68. Continuing Problems in the USDA's Enforcement of the Humane Methods of Slaughter Act.

69. "Kosher Plant Is Accused of Inhumane Slaughter," *New York Times*, September 4, 2008.

70. Marissa Brostoff, "Activists Who Exposed Meat Industry Reveal Their Own (Kosher) Identity," *Forward*, April 30, 2008.

71. Nathaniel Popper, "In Iowa Meat Plant, Kosher 'Jungle' Breeds Fear, Injury, Short Pay," *Forward*, May 26, 2006.

72. "US Certifiers of Kosher Slaughter Defend Schechita Practices," Statement of Rabbis and Certifying Agencies, OKS, http://okskosher.com/certifiers.html (accessed September 26, 2011).

73. "Israel's Chief Rabbinate, Orthodox Union Refute Charges against Agriprocessors," PR Newswire, December 10, 2008.

74. Popper, "In Iowa Meat Plant."

75. Ibid.

76. Ibid.

77. "Sholom Rubashkin Responds to Forward Allegations," letter to the editor, *Philadelphia Jewish Voice*, July 13, 2006, http://www.pjvoice.com/v13/13104iowa.html.

78. Martha Rosenberg, "Need 400 Meat Workers; Start Immediately; Make up to $6 an Hour!" *CounterPunch*, May 31–32, 2008; Julia Preston, "27-Year Sentence for Plant Manager," *New York Times*, June 21, 2010.

79. Agriprocessors Report, May 28, 2008, United Food and Commercial Workers, http://www.bibdaily.com/pdfs/Agridoc1.pdf (accessed September 26, 2011) (Note: page not active at time of publication).

80. Alicia Ebaugh, "Search Warrants Detail Reasons for Postville Raid," *Cedar Rapids Gazette*, May 13, 2008.

81. "Obama Blasts Agriprocessors," *Des Moines Register*, August 25, 2008.

82. Ben Harris, "Orthodox Rabbis: Agriprocessors Iowa Kosher Plant Passes Muster," *Jewish Journal*, August 5, 2008.

83. Shmuel Herzfeld, "Dark Meat," *New York Times*, August 5, 2008.

84. Rabbi Neal Gold, "Rabbi Shimon vs. Agriprocessors Erev Rosh HaShana," http://www.shirtikva.org/PDF/Sermons/HHD98Sermons/Gold%20Sermons/Rabbi%20Shimon%20vs%20Agriprocessors.pdf (accessed September 26, 2011).

85. Jon Coppelman, "Meatpacking in Iowa: Not Exactly Kosher?" *Workers' Comp Insider*, May 27, 2008, http://www.workerscompinsider.com (accessed September 26, 2011).

86. Lynda Waddington, "Postville Tense after Evictions, Another Raid and Agri's Bankruptcy," *Iowa Independent*, November 6, 2008.

87. "Some Charges Dropped in Iowa Slaughterhouse Case," Associated Press, May 5, 2010.

88. Julia Preston, "Life Sentence Is Debated for Meat Plant Ex-Chief," *New York Times*, April 28, 2010.

89. Grant Schulte, "Former Postville Mayor Tried to Extort Money from Rubashkin," *Des Moines Register*, April 28, 2010.

90. Julia Preston, "27-Year Sentence for Plant Manager," *New York Times*, June 21, 2010.

91. Christopher Sherman, "Immigration Raids Are Boon to Texas Labor Recruiters," Associated Press, August 16, 2008.

92. Phred Dvorak, "Religious-Bias Filings Up," *Wall Street Journal*, October 16 2008; Kirk Semple, "A Somali Influx Unsettles Latino Meatpackers," *New York Times*, October 15, 2008.

93. Nazario Rodriguez Jr., "150 More Palauans Needed at Iowa Meatpacking Plant," *Saipan Tribune*, October 6, 2008; Mike Kilen, "Postville Sees Complex Picture," *Des Moines Register*, October 26, 2008.

94. Kilen, "Postville Sees Complex Picture."

95. Orlan Love, "Two Years after Agriprocessors Raid, Postville Is Flush with New Optimism, *Cedar Rapids Gazette*, May 12, 2010.

96. Ibid.

97. Kilen, "Postville Sees Complex Picture."

98. Elliot Resnick, "Agri Star Meat-Plant Owner: 'We Will Succeed,'" *Jewish Press*, October 28, 2009.

CHAPTER 12. MAD COW DISEASE— FORGOTTEN BUT NOT NECESSARILY GONE

1. Charles Weissmann et al., "Transmission of Prions," *Proceedings of the National Academy of Sciences of the United States of America* 99, suppl. 4 (December 10, 2002): 16378–83.

2. Ron Seely, "CWD Fear Recedes, but Risk Remains—DNR Still Urges Hunters to Toss Venison that Has Tested Positive for Chronic Wasting Disease," *Wisconsin State Journal*, July 27, 2009.

3. Perry Beeman, "Concerns at Ames Lab Delay Mad Cow Study," *Des Moines Register*, May 19, 2006.

4. "CSU Pinpoints Spread of CWD Research Shows Blood, Saliva Can Transmit Disease," *Fort Collins Coloradoan*, October 6, 2006.

5. Beeman, "Concerns at Ames Lab Delay Mad Cow Study."

6. Ibid.

7. Sandi Doughton, "Lawmakers Want USDA to Expand Mad-Cow Testing," *Seattle Times*, February 18, 2004.

8. "Epidemiological Investigation of Washington State BSE Case," summary report, March 2004, United States Department of Animal and Plant Health Inspection, http://www.aphis.usda.gov/newsroom/hot_issues/bse/downloads/WashingtonState_epi_final3-04.pdf (accessed September 26, 2011).

9. Review of the USDA's Expanded BSE Cattle Surveillance Program, Testimony of the Honorable Phyllis K. Fong, Inspector General, July 14, 2004, US Department of Agriculture, Office of Inspector General, http://www.usda.gov/oig/rptsigtranscripts.htm (accessed September 26, 2011).

10. Ibid.

11. Dan Morain, "Mad Cow Proposals Lead to Fight," *Los Angeles Times*, July 4, 2005.

12. Ibid.

13. Sabin Russell and Nanette Asimov, "State Can't Say Who Sold Beef Rules Bar Telling Which Stores, Restaurants Had Tainted Meat," *San Francisco Chronicle*, January 3, 2004.

14. Ibid.

15. Libby Quaid, "Feds Unable to Pin Down Source of Mad Cow," August 31, 2005, Associated Press.

16. Cathy Proctor, "Mad Cow Takes Bite from Exports," *Denver Business Journal*, November 28, 2004; George Raine, "Japanese Wrapping Up U.S. Beef Inspections Audit to Determine Whether Mad Cow Disease Risk Is Gone," *San Francisco Chronicle*, July 21, 2006.

17. Proctor, "Mad Cow Takes Bite from Exports"; "Timeline of BSE in Canada and the U.S.," CBC News, http://www.cbc.ca/news/background/madcow/timeline.html (accessed September 26, 2011).

18. Sam Hananel, "Government Asks Court to Block Wider Testing for Mad Cow," Associated Press, May 9, 2008.

19. A Review of the USDA's Expanded BSE Cattle Surveillance Program, July 14, 2004, US H.R. 108th Congress, 2nd Session, Joint Hearing before the Committee on Government Reform and the Committee on Agriculture.

20. "Fact Sheets," United States Department of Agriculture, Food Safety and Inspection Service, http://www.fsis.usda.gov/factsheets/fsis_further_strengthens_protections_againstbse/index.asp#10 (accessed September 26, 2011).

21. Michael Hansen (prepared by), comments on Food and Drug Administration Docket No. 2002N-0273: "Substances Prohibited from Use in Animal Food and Feed," Con-

sumers Union, December 20, 2005, http://www.consumersunion.org/campaigns//notinmy food/003031indiv.html (accessed September 26, 2011).

22. Mathias Heikenwalder et al., "Chronic Lymphocytic Inflammation Specifies the Organ Tropism of Prions," *Science* 307, no. 5712 (February 18, 2005): 1107–10; Rachel C. Angers et al., "Prions in Skeletal Muscles of Deer with Chronic Wasting Disease," *Science* 311, no. 5764 (February 2006): 1117; Candace K. Mathiason et al., "Infectious Prions in the Saliva and Blood of Deer with Chronic Wasting Disease," *Science* 314, no. 5796 (October 2006): 133–36.

23. Brent Race et al., "Detection of Prion Infectivity in Fat Tissues of Scrapie-Infected Mice," *PLoS Pathogens* 4, no. 12 (December 5, 2008), http://www.plospathogens.org/article/info%3Adoi%2F10.1371%2Fjournal.ppat.1000232 (accessed September 26, 2011).

24. Angers et al., "Prions in Skeletal Muscles of Deer."

25. Kevin Darst, "CSU Pinpoints Spread of CWD," *Coloradoan*, October 6, 2006.

26. Hansen, comments on FDA Docket.

27. Ibid.

28. "Evaluation of FSIS Management Controls over Pre-Slaughter Activities," audit report, Office of Inspector General, Great Plains Region, United States Department of Agriculture, November 2008, http://www.usda.gov/oig/webdocs/24601-07-KC.pdf (accessed September 26, 2011).

29. Ibid.

30. "Evaluation of FSIS Management Controls over Pre-Slaughter Activities," audit report.

31. Hansen, comments on FDA Docket.

32. Jon Bonné, "Banned Brains, Spinal Cords May Still Enter Food Supply," MSNBC, December 20, 2004.

33. Ibid.

34. Ibid.

35. Steve Mitchell, "Feds Probing Alleged Mad Cow Cover-Up," United Press International, May 3, 2005.

36. Ibid.

37. Louise McCready, "Recession Flexitarians," *Gourmet*, June 10, 2009.

38. "NASDA Offers Solution to Crisis Facing Dairy, Pork, and Poultry Producers," National Association of State Departments of Agriculture, http://www.nasda.org/cms/7196/7376/24287.aspx (accessed September 29, 2011).

39. Debora MacKenzie, "Swine Flu Myth: Once This Pandemic Is over We'll Be Safe for Another Few Decades," *New Scientist*, October 28, 2009, http://www.newscientist.com/article/dn18062-swine-flu-myth-once-this-pandemic-is-over-well-be-safe-for-another-few-decades.html (accessed September 29, 2011).

40. Martha Rosenberg, "Don't Breathe the Meat," *CounterPunch*, February 11, 2009, http://www.counterpunch.org/2009/02/11/don-t-breathe-the-meat/ (accessed September 29, 2011).

41. Patti Neighmond, "Study Links Red Meat to Cancer, Heart Disease," National Public Radio, March 24, 2009; "Eat More Chicken, Fish and Beans Than Red Meat," American Heart Association, January 13, 2011, http://www.heart.org/HEARTORG/GettingHealthy/Weight Management/LosingWeight/Eat-More-Chicken-Fish-and-Beans-than-Red-Meat_UCM _320278_Article.jsp (accessed September 29, 2011).

42. Amanda Gardner, "Eating Too Much Red Meat May Shorten Life," *Health Day*, March 23, 2009.

43. "Research, Education and Innovation," *Quarterly Update* 2, no. 4 (October 2008), newsletter published by National Cattlemen's Beef Association, http://www.beefresearch.org/ CMDocs/BeefResearch/October%201,%202008%20Vol%202%20Issue%204%20(October %202008).pdf (accessed February 6, 2012).

44. "Chemicals in Meat Cooked at High Temperatures and Cancer Risk," National Cancer Institute at the National Institutes of Health, October 15, 2010, http://www.cancer. gov/cancertopics/factsheet/Risk/cooked-meats (accessed August 29, 2011).

45. Cathy Proctor, "Mad Cow Takes Bite from Exports," *Denver Business Journal*, November 28, 2004; Art Hovey, "Cattlemen Leery of Reopening Border," *Lee Newspapers*, February 10, 2005; "Timeline of BSE in Canada and the U.S."

46. Hovey, "Cattlemen Leery of Reopening Border."

47. Betsy Blaney, "Cattle Herd Must Stay Put—Texas Ranch Where Diseased Cow Originated Is Quarantined," Associated Press, July 1, 2005.

48. Ed Howard, "USDA's Gutsy Inspector General Deserves Gratitude from Cattle Industry, Consumers," *Nebraska State Paper*, June 27, 2005.

49. Ibid.

50. Katie Fairbank, "Mad Cow Records Spotty," *Dallas Morning News*, November 2, 2005.

51. David Ivanovich, "Fed Testing Was Marked by Missteps," *Houston Chronicle*, June 24, 2005.

52. "New BSE Report May Hurt Market, Some Say," Associated Press, November 23, 2004.

53. Raine, "Japanese Wrapping Up U.S. Beef Inspections Audit."

54. Ibid.

55. "Assessment of USDA's Controls for the Beef Export Verification Program for Japan," Audit Report No. 50601-11-HQ, United States Department of Agriculture, Office of the Inspector General, Food and Marketing Division, February 2006.

56. Ibid.; Nathan Runkle, "Bob Barker Exposes Hidden Price of Veal in New MFA Investigation," Mercy for Animals, August 30, 2010, http://www.mfablog.org/2010/08/bob-barker -exposes-hidden-price-of-veal-in-new-mfa-investigation.html (accessed September 26, 2011).

57. "Japan Cites Concerns about Mad Cow Audit," Associated Press, February 15, 2006.

58. "Assessment of USDA's Controls for the Beef Export Verification Program for Japan";

"Packers Must Show Control of Supplies and Information" *Agri-vator* newsletter, Spring 2006, http://www.agribasics.com (accessed September 26, 2011).

59. David Ivanovich and Purva Patel, "Cattle Checks Called Flawed Inspectors Let Suspect Animals into Food Chain," *Houston Chronicle*, February 2, 2006.

60. Ibid.

61. Eiji Hirose (correspondent for *Yomiuri Shimbun/Daily Yomiuri*), "Johanns Claims Downer Cattle Did Not Have BSE," comment on Ranchers.net, February 18, 2006, http://ranchers.net/forum/about7761.html (accessed September 26, 2011).

62. Raine, "Japanese Wrapping Up U.S. Beef Inspections Audit."

63. Josh Funk, "Most Beef Plants Don't Bother with Japanese Trade," Associated Press, July 15, 2006.

64. "Creutzfeldt-Jakob Disease Fact Sheet," National Institute of Neurological Disorders and Stroke, http://www.ninds.nih.gov/disorders/cjd/detail_cjd.htm (accessed September 26, 2011).

65. Steve Mitchell, "Health Officials Probing CJD Cases in NJ," United Press International, March 13, 2004.

66. D. T. Max, "The Case of the Cherry Hill Cluster," *New York Times*, March 28, 2004.

67. "CJD Cases Unrelated to Jersey Racetrack, CDC Says Press Release from CDC," *CIDRAP News*, May 7, 2004.

68. "How Is CJD Diagnosed?" National Institute of Neurological Disorders and Stroke, http://www.ninds.nih.gov/disorders/cjd/detail_cjd.htm#186473058 (accessed February 6, 2012).

69. Ibid.

70. Steve Mitchell, "Calif. Man Had Human Mad Cow Symptoms," United Press International, January 5, 2005.

71. Ibid.

72. Ibid.

73. Ibid.

74. Ibid.

75. Ibid.

76. Ibid.

77. Ibid.

78. Ibid.

79. "Rare Disease Raises Questions—Idaho Cases of Creutzfeldt-Jakob," *Herald Journal*, October 23, 2005.

80. Ibid.

81. "Deaths Caused by Brain Disease? Four Northeastern Indiana Residents May Have Died from Rare Disorder," *South Bend (IN) Tribune*, June 4, 2007.

82. "4 Deaths from Rare Brain Disease in NE Indiana," Associated Press, June 6, 2007.

83. Bob Fowler, "One CJD Case Confirmed; 1 Investigated," *Knoxville (TN) News Sentinel*, March 24, 2009.

84. Ibid.

85. Martha Rosenberg, "Mad Cow in God's Country," *CounterPunch*, July 3, 2007, http://www.counterpunch.org/2007/06/26/mad-cow-in-god-s-country/ (accessed January 13, 2012).

86. "Kansas Man's Death Not Tied to Mad Cow: Officials," Reuters, January 16, 2008; Karen Shideler, "Kansan Contracts Disease Related to Mad Cow," *Wichita Eagle*, January 15, 2008.

87. Martha Rosenberg, "The Return of Mad Cow Disease?" *CounterPunch*, October 18, 2010, http://www.counterpunch.org/2010/10/18/the-return-of-mad-cow-disease/ (accessed January 13, 2012).

88. Cindy V. Culp, "2 Mysterious Cases of Disease in McLennan County a Rarity but No Cause for Alarm," *Waco Tribune-Herald*, July 9, 2010.

89. "CJD Cases by County 2000–2010," Texas Department of State Health Services, Infectious Disease Control Unit, http://www.dshs.state.tx.us/idcu/disease/creutzfeldt-jakob/data/ (accessed September 26, 2011).

90. Maki Becker, "Griffin Died of Very Rare Brain Disease," *Buffalo News*, November 13, 2008.

91. Rebecca Boone, "Elmore County Man Tests Negative for CJD," Associated Press, October 14, 2005.

92. "Texas BSE Investigation Final Epidemiology Report," United States Department of Agriculture, Animal and Plant Health Inspection Service, August 2005.

93. Barry Shlachter, "Mad Cow Undetected Thus Far," *Star-Telegram* (Fort Worth, TX), July 10, 2005.

94. "Texas BSE Investigation Final Epidemiology Report."

95. Ibid.

96. Ibid.

97. "Alabama BSE Investigation Final Epidemiology Report," United States Department of Agriculture, Animal and Plant Health Inspection Service, May 2, 2006.

98. Ibid.

99. Ibid.

100. Ibid.

101. Energy and Commerce Committee Subpoenas Hallmark/Westland Chief, US House of Representatives, Committee on Energy and Commerce, March 5, 2008.

102. "USDA Recalls 143 Million Pounds of Beef," Associated Press, March 3, 2008.

103. Nicole Gaouette, "USDA to Begin Naming Retailers in Meat Recalls," *Los Angeles Times*, July 11, 2008.

104. Kim Hyun, "S. Koreans Wave Candles against U.S. Beef as Gov't Strives to Quell Mad Cow Scare," Yonhap News Agency, May 9, 2008.

105. "Lee Myung-bak's U.S. Tour Confronts with Thorny Issues," Xinhau News Agency,

April 17, 2008; Shin Hae-in, "Parties to Wrangle over FTA at Hearing Tuesday," Xinhau News Agency, May 12, 2008.

106. "Bush, Lee Discuss N. Korea at Camp David," Associated Press, April 19, 2008.

107. Cho Jin-seo, "Scientists Refute Mad Cow Disease Myths," *Korea Times*, May 12, 2008.

108. Ibid.

109. Shin Hae-in, "Parties Collide over US Beef at FTA Hearing," Bilaterals.org, Yonhap News Agency, May 13, 2008, http://www.bilaterals.org/spip.php?page=print&id_ article=12089 (accessed September 26, 2011).

110. "S Korea, US Strike Deal on Beef Imports," AFP News, April 17, 2008.

111. Lee Joon-seung, "S. Korea, U.S. Agree on Revised Beef Import Rules," Yonhap News Agency, April 18, 2008.

112. Wayne Carter, "Virginia Woman May Have Human Form of Mad Cow Disease," WVEC-TV, April 8, 2008.

113. "Statement of Dr. Richard Raymond USDA Undersecretary for Food Safety Regarding the Safety of the U.S. Food Supply," United States Department of Agriculture, May 4, 2008.

114. "South Korean President Pledges to Suspend Imports of U.S. Beef If It Endangers Health," Associated Press, May 7, 2008.

CHAPTER 13. BRAVE NEW FOOD: SO SAFE IT'S NOT EVEN LABELED

1. "A Growth Industry," CBS News, February 11, 2009.

2. Andrew Pollack, "F.D.A. Approves Drug from Gene-Altered Goats," *New York Times*, February 6, 2009.

3. Alison L. Van Eenennaam and William M. Muir, "Transgenic Salmon: A Final Leap to the Grocery Shelf?" *Nature Biotechnology* 29 (2011): 706–10.

4. Colin O'Neil, "Congress, Public Not Fooled by Engineered Salmon," *Food Safety News*, August 2, 2011, http://www.foodsafetynews.com/2011/08/congress-public-not-fooled -by-engineered-salmon/ (accessed August 29, 2011).

5. Briefing Packet, AquAdvantage Salmon, Food and Drug Administration, Center for Veterinary Medicine, Veterinary Medicine Advisory Committee, September 20, 2010.

6. Ibid.

7. Ibid.

8. "Environmental Assessment for *AquAdvantage*® Salmon," AquaBounty Technologies, Food and Drug Administration, August 25, 2010, http://www.fda.gov/downloads/ AdvisoryCommittees/CommitteesMeetingMaterials/VeterinaryMedicineAdvisoryCommittee/ UCM224760.pdf.

9. Meeting Participants for AquAdvantage Salmon, Veterinary Medicine Advisory Committee, Food and Drug Administration, September 19–20, 2010, http://www.fda.gov/AdvisoryCommittees/CommitteesMeetingMaterials/VeterinaryMedicineAdvisoryCommittee/ucm224765.htm (accessed August 29, 2011).

10. Martha Rosenberg, reporter notes from Veterinary Medicine Advisory Committee hearings, Center for Veterinary Medicine, Rockville, Maryland, September 19–20, 2010; Martha Rosenberg, reporter notes from Center for Food Safety and Applied Nutrition hearing, Rockville, Maryland, September 21, 2010.

11. Transcript, Food and Drug Administration, Center for Veterinary Medicine, Veterinary Medicine Advisory Committee, September 20, 2010.

12. Ibid.

13. Ibid.

14. Ibid.

15. Ibid.

16. Transcript, Food and Drug Administration, Center for Veterinary Medicine, Veterinary Medicine Advisory Committee, September 19, 2010.

17. Transcript, Food and Drug Administration, September 20, 2010.

18. Ibid.

19. Ibid.

20. Ibid.

21. Ibid.

22. Ibid.

23. Ibid.

24. Briefing Packet, AquAdvantage Salmon.

25. Ibid.

26. Ibid.

27. Ibid.

28. Marian Burros, "A Hormone for Cows," New York Times, November 9, 2005; Peter Hardin, "FDA, Monsanto Need to Reveal Truth about Growth Hormone," Capital Times, February 2, 2004.

29. Transcript, Food and Drug Administration, Public Hearing on the Labeling of Food Made from AquAdvantage Salmon, (September 21, 2010).

30. Ibid.

31. Ibid.

32. "Environmental Assessment for AquAdvantage® Salmon."

33. Ibid.

34. Briefing Packet, AquAdvantage Salmon.

35. Ibid.

36. Transcript, Food and Drug Administration, September 20, 2010.

37. Caroline Scott-Thomas, "Eleven US Senators Have Signed a Letter to FDA Commis-

sioner Margaret Hamburg Urging the Agency to Find Another Way to Assess the Safety of Genetically Engineered (GE) Salmon," FOOD navigator-usa.com, September 30, 2010, http://www.foodnavigator-usa.com/Regulation/GM-salmon-assessment-inappropriate-say-Senators (accessed September 29, 2011).

38. "Senators Reintroduce Legislation to Ban GE Salmon," *FIS Worldnews*, February 2, 2011.

39. Ibid.

40. Scott-Thomas, "Eleven US Senators Have Signed a Letter to FDA Commissioner."

41. Elaine Watson, "Agro Groups: Derailing GM Fish Review Would Dent FDA's Credibility," FOOD navigator-usa.com, August 4, 2011, http://www.foodnavigator-usa.com/Regulation/Agro-groups-Derailing-GM-fish-review-would-dent-FDA-s-credibility (accessed September 29, 2011).

42. Ibid.

43. Ibid.

44. Ibid.

45. Van Eenennaam and Muir, "Transgenic Salmon."

46. Ibid.

47. Ibid.

48. Michael Hansen, comments of Consumers Union on Genetically Engineered Salmon, Food and Drug Administration Docket No. FDA-201034-N-0001, September 16, 2010.

49. Van Eenennaam and Muir, "Transgenic Salmon."

50. "Anti-Cancer Chicken Eggs Produced," BBC, January 14, 2007, http://news.bbc.co.uk/2/hi/science/nature/6261427.stm (accessed August 29, 2011).

51. Ibid.

52. Gina Kolata, "Cloning May Lead to Healthy Pork," *New York Times*, March 27, 2006.

53. Ibid.

54. Martha Rosenberg, "US Govt Hearings Go Swimmingly for GM Salmon," *Scoop*, September 27, 2010, http://www.scoop.co.nz/stories/HL1009/S00188/us-govt-hearings-go-swimmingly-for-gm-salmon.htm (accessed January 13, 2012).

55. "Myths about Cloning," Food and Drug Administration, http://www.fda.gov/AnimalVeterinary/SafetyHealth/AnimalCloning/ucm055512.htm (accessed August 29, 2011).

56. "FDA Issues Documents on the Safety of Food from Animal Clones," Food and Drug Administration, http://www.fda.gov/NewsEvents/Newsroom/PressAnnouncements/2008/ucm116836.htm (accessed August 29, 2011).

57. Pallab Ghosh, "Cattle 'Cloned from Dead Animals,'" BBC, August 12, 2010, http://www.bbc.co.uk/news/science-environment-10951108 (accessed August 29, 2011).

58. John Ross, "Cloned Animal Meat 'Already in UK's Food Chain,'" Scotsman.com, August 5, 2010, http://www.scotsman.com/news/health/cloned_animal_meat_already_in_uk_s_food_chain_1_819827 (accessed August 29, 2011).

59. Ghosh, "Cattle 'Cloned from Dead Animals.'"

60. Sarah Schmidt, "U.S. Unsure if Cloned Meat Has Been Sold in North America," *Montreal Gazette*, August 10, 2010.

61. Ibid.

62. Sharon Churcher and Annette Witheridge, "Farmer Who Sold Cloned Cow Embryos to Britain Claims He Fell for Sales Patter Promising Prize Animal Could 'Live Forever,'" *Daily Mail*, August 8, 2010.

63. "Animal Cloning: A Risk Assessment," US Department of Health and Human Services, Food and Drug Administration, Center for Veterinary Medicine, January 8, 2008, http://www.fda.gov/downloads/AnimalVeterinary/SafetyHealth/AnimalCloning/UCM124756.pdf (accessed August 29, 2011); "Food Safety, Animal Health and Welfare and Environmental Impact of Animals Derived from Cloning by Somatic Cell Nucleus Transfer (SCNT) and Their Offspring and Products Obtained from Those Animals," European Food Safety Authority, Opinion of the Scientific Committee/Scientific Panel, July 24, 2008, http://www.efsa.europa.eu/EFSA/efsa_locale-1178620753812_1211902019540.htm (accessed August 29, 2011).

64. Karen Kaplan, "FDA Standing in the Way of Montana Rancher's Leap into Cloning Revolution," *Los Angeles Times*, February 15, 2005.

65. "Animal Cloning: A Risk Assessment."

66. Ibid.

67. Ibid.

68. "Food Safety, Animal Health and Welfare and Environmental Impact of Animals Derived from Cloning."

69. Position Statement on the OIE Guidelines on Somatic Cell Nuclear Transfer in Production Livestock and Horses, Prepared by the International Coalition for Animal Welfare, September 2008, http://www.icfaw.org/Documents/ICFAW_cloning.pdf (accessed January 13, 2012).

70. "Animal Cloning: A Risk Assessment."

71. "Cloning," European Food Safety Authority, http://www.efsa.europa.eu/en/topics/topic/cloning.htm (accessed August 29, 2011).

72. "Animal Cloning: A Risk Assessment."

73. Ibid.

74. Ibid.

75. Ibid.

76. Ibid.

77. Ibid.

78. Ibid.

79. Ibid.

80. Scott Gottlieb and Matthew B. Wheeler, "Genetically Engineered Animals and Public Health," BIO, 2008, http://www.bio.org/node/2522 (accessed September 29, 2011).

81. Ibid.

82. Ibid.

83. Ibid.

84. Martha Rosenberg, "Is Meat and Milk from Clones in the Food Supply?" Food Consumer, August 22, 2010, http://www.foodconsumer.org/newsite/Watch-List/is_meat_and_milk_from_clones_in_the_food_supply_2208100140.html.

85. European Food Safety Authority Draft Scientific Opinion on "Food Safety, Animal Health and Welfare and Environmental Impact of Animals Derived from Cloning by Somatic Cell Nucleus Transfer (SCNT) and Their Offspring and Products Obtained from those Animals," Public Comments Received during Public Consultation, (Related to Question No. EFSA-Q-2007-092), July 24, 2008, http://www.gencat.cat/salut/acsa/html/ca/dir2955/pdf/sc_report_public_comments_animal_cloning_table_en.pdf (accessed August 29, 2011).

86. Ibid.

87. "FDA Needs to Reassess Risks and Proposed Management for Cloning," Union of Concerned Scientists, http://www.ucsusa.org/food_and_agriculture/solutions/sensible_pharma_crops/ucs-comments-to-fda-on.html (accessed September 29, 2011).

88. European Food Safety Authority Draft Scientific Opinion on "Food Safety, Animal Health and Welfare and Environmental Impact of Animals Derived from Cloning."

EPILOGUE

1. Kyle LaHucik, "A Return to the Top: Former FDA Commissioner Califf Reportedly Biden's Pick for Woodcock's Role," *Fierce Pharma*, October 14, 2021, https://www.fiercepharma.com/pharma/a-return-to-top-former-fda-commish-robert-califf-reportedly-biden-s-pick-for-woodcock-s-role.

2. Robert M. Califf and Richard Platt, "Embedding Cardiovascular Research Into Practice," *Journal of the American Medical Association* 310, no. 19 (November 20, 2013): 2037-2018, https://www.fiercepharma.com/pharma/a-return-to-top-former-fda-commish-robert-califf-reportedly-biden-s-pick-for-woodcock-s-role.

3. Ibid.

4. Ahmed Aboulenein, "U.S. Senate Narrowly Confirms Dr. Robert Califf to Lead FDA for Second Time," *Reuters*, February 15, 2022, https://www.reuters.com/world/us/us-senate-confirms-bidens-fda-nominee-califf-2022-02-15/.

5. Julie Appleby, "Klobuchar Says D.C. Has Enough Drug Lobbyists To Double-Team Lawmakers," *KHN*, July 26, 2019, https://khn.org/news/klobuchar-says-d-c-has-enough-drug-lobbyists-to-double-team-lawmakers/.

6. *Wikipedia*, "Opioid Epidemic in the United States," https://en.wikipedia.org/wiki/Opioid_epidemic_in_the_United_States#cite_note-:21-7 (accessed July 21, 2022).

7. *Wikipedia*, "Purdue Pharma," https://en.wikipedia.org/wiki/Purdue_Pharma (accessed July 21, 2022).

8. Ibid.

9. Joel Achenbach et al., "An Onslaught of Pills, Hundreds of Thousands Of Deaths: Who Is Accountable?" *Washington Post*, July 20, 2019.

10. *Wikipedia*, "Sackler Family," https://en.wikipedia.org/wiki/Sackler_family#Opioid_lawsuits (accessed July 21, 2022).

11. Ibid.

12. Brian Mann, "4 U.S. Companies Will Pay $26 Billion To Settle Claims They Fueled The Opioid Crisis," National Public Radio, February 25, 2022.

13. Andrew Kolodny et al., "The Prescription Opioid and Heroin Crisis: A Public Health Approach to an Epidemic of Addiction, *Annual Reviews,* January 12, 2015, https://www.annualreviews.org/doi/pdf/10.1146/annurev-publhealth-031914-122957 (accessed July 21, 2022).

14. House Committee on Oversight and Reform, "Chairwoman Maloney Releases Comprehensive Staff Report Culminating the Committee's Sweeping Drug Pricing Investigation," December 10, 2021, https://oversight.house.gov/news/press-releases/chairwoman-maloney-releases-comprehensive-staff-report-culminating-the-committee.

15. Ibid.

16. Benita Lee, "How Much Does Insulin Cost? Here's How 28 Brands and Generics Compare," Goodrx.com, January 26, 2022, https://www.goodrx.com/healthcare-access/research/how-much-does-insulin-cost-compare-brands.

17. Shefali Luthra, "'Pharma Bro' Shkreli Is In Prison, But Daraprim's Price Is Still High," *KHN,* May 4, 2018, https://khn.org/news/for-shame-pharma-bro-shkreli-is-in-prison-but-daraprims-price-is-still-high/.

18. Jim Zarroli, "Martin Shkreli Takes The Fifth, But Can't Resist Firing Back," *NPR,* February 4, 2016, https://www.npr.org/sections/thetwo-way/2016/02/04/465596177/martin-shkreli-takes-the-fifth-but-cant-resist-firing-back.

19. Fox News, "What's Being Done About EpiPen Price Hike, From $100 to $600?" *Fox 9*, August 24, 2016, https://www.fox9.com/news/whats-being-done-about-epipen-price-hike-from-100-to-600.

20. Ryan Grim, "Heather Bresch, Joe Manchin's Daughter, Played Direct Part In EpiPen Price Inflation Scandal," *Intercept,* September 7, 2021, https://theintercept.com/2021/09/07/joe-manchin-epipen-price-heather-bresch/.

21. FDA, "FDA approves Sovaldi for chronic hepatitis C," FDA, December 9, 2013, https://www.hiv.gov/blog/fda-approves-sovaldi-for-chronic-hepatitis-c.

22. HHS, "Viral Hepatitis in the United States: Data and Trends," *HHS,* June 7, 2016, https://www.hhs.gov/hepatitis/learn-about-viral-hepatitis/data-and-trends/index.html.

23. Ricardo Alonso-Zaldivar, "Maker of $1,000 Hepatitis C Pill Was Focused On Profits, Not Patients, Report Finds," Associated Press, December 1, 2015, https://www.pbs.org/news hour/health/maker-of-1000-hepatitis-c-pill-was-focused-on-profits-not-patients-report-finds.

24. Ibid.

25. Fierce Pharma, "To Boost Sales, Gilead's Hep C Awareness Ad Focuses On Baby Boomers," *Fierce Pharma*, February 23, 2017, https://www.fiercepharma.com/marketing/baby -boomers-targeted-gilead-hepatitis-c-awareness-campaign-even-as-drug-s-fortunes-drop.

26. Our Partners: Corporations, *CDC Foundation*, 2020, https://www.cdcfoundation.org/ partner-list/corporations.

27. Michael Gabay, "The Prescription Drug User Fee Act: Cause for Concern?," *Hospital Pharmacy*, 53, no. 2 (2018): 88–89, https://www.ncbi.nlm.nih.gov/pmc/articles/PMC5863890/.

28. European Medicines Agency, "PRAC Warns Of Risk Of Hepatitis B Re-Activation With Direct-Acting Antivirals For Hepatitis C," European Medicines Agency, February 12, 2016, https://www.ema.europa.eu/en/news/prac-warns-risk-hepatitis-b-re-activation-direct -acting-antivirals-hepatitis-c.

29. FDA Drug Safety Communication, "FDA Warns About The Risk Of Hepatitis B Reactivating In Some Patients Treated With Direct-Acting Antivirals For Hepatitis C," FDA, October 4, 2016, https://www.fda.gov/drugs/drug-safety-and-availability/fda-drug-safety -communication-fda-warns-about-risk-hepatitis-b-reactivating-some-patients-treated.

30. Denise Grady, "Are New Drugs for Hepatitis C Safe? A Report Raises Concerns," *New York Times*, January 24, 2017.

31. Ibid.

32. Ibid.

33. Ibid.

34. Ibid.

35. Ibid.

36. E.J. Mundell, "Antidepressant Use In U.S. Soars by 65 Percent in 15 Years," CBS News, August 16, 2017, https://www.cbsnews.com/news/antidepressant-use-soars-65-percent -in-15-years/.

37. Jillian Mckoy, "US Suicide Rates Are Stagnant or Rising among Many Groups, Despite Overall National Decline," BU School of Public Health, April 14, 2022, https://www .bu.edu/sph/news/articles/2022/us-suicides-are-stagnant-or-on-the-rise-among-many-groups/.

38. Danielle DeSimone, "Military Suicide Rates Are at An All-Time High; Here's How We're Trying to Help," USO, June 27, 2022, https://www.uso.org/stories/2664-military -suicide-rates-are-at-an-all-time-high-heres-how-were-trying-to-help.

39. Sunyoung Kang et al., "Use of Serotonin Reuptake Inhibitors and Risk Of Subsequent Bone Loss In A Nationwide Population-Based Cohort Study," *Scientific Reports* 11, no. 13461 (2021), https://www.nature.com/articles/s41598-021-92821-9.

40. Mary A. M. Rogers et al., "Depression, Antidepressant Medications, and Risk of Clostridium Difficile Infection," *BMC Medicine* 11, no. 121 (2013), https://www.ncbi.nlm.nih.gov/pmc/articles/PMC3651296/.

41. Benedict Carey, "The Murky Perils of Quitting Antidepressants After Years of Use," *New York Times*, April 8, 2018, https://www.nytimes.com/2018/04/07/health/antidepressants-withdrawal-prozac-cymbalta.html.

42. Stuart Seidman et al., Letter to Editor, *New York Times*, April 11, 2018, https://www.nytimes.com/2018/04/09/opinion/antidepressants.html.

43. Avinash K. Nehra et al., "Proton Pump Inhibitors: Review of Emerging Concerns," Mayo Clinic Proceedings 93, no. 2 (2017): 240–46, https://www.mayoclinicproceedings.org/article/S0025-6196(17)30841-8/fulltext.

44. Sonia Hernandez-Diaz et al., "Topiramate Use Early in Pregnancy and the Risk Of Oral Clefts: A Pregnancy Cohort Study," *Neurology* 90 (2018): 342–51, https://www.epilepsy.com/stories/topiramate-and-risk-birth-defects-new-data-women-epilepsy.

45. FDA, "FDA Updates Warnings For Fluoroquinolone Antibiotics on Risks Of Mental Health and Low Blood Sugar Adverse Reactions," FDA, July 10, 2018, https://www.fda.gov/news-events/press-announcements/fda-updates-warnings-fluoroquinolone-antibiotics-risks-mental-health-and-low-blood-sugar-adverse.

46. Ibid.

47. Martha Rosenberg, "Black Boxes: Health Warning or Profit Warning?" *KevinMD.com*, February 1, 2020, https://www.kevinmd.com/2020/02/black-boxes-health-warning-or-profit-warning.html.

48. "FDA Requires Boxed Warning About Serious Mental Health Side Effects For Asthma And Allergy Drug Montelukast (Singulair); Advises Restricting Use For Allergic Rhinitis," FDA, March 4, 2020, https://www.fda.gov/drugs/drug-safety-and-availability/fda-requires-boxed-warning-about-serious-mental-health-side-effects-asthma-and-allergy-drug.

49. "FDA Requests Removal of All Ranitidine Products (Zantac) from the Market," FDA, April 1, 2020, https://www.fda.gov/news-events/press-announcements/fda-requests-removal-all-ranitidine-products-zantac-market.

50. Marilynn Marchione, "Breast Cancer Risk From Menopause Hormones May Last Decades," Associated Press, December 13, 2019, https://apnews.com/article/cancer-san-antonio-womens-health-health-menopause-a73f6e7c1e77711f3b620caffe8fbcd1.

51. Zlati Meyer, "Here's Why Milk Giant Dean Foods Just Went Bankrupt (Blame Millennials and Walmart)," *Fast Company*, November 12, 2019, https://www.fastcompany.com/90429619/heres-why-milk-giant-dean-foods-just-went-bankrupt-blame-millennials-and-walmart.

52. Ibid.

53. David Yaffe-Bellany, "A Milk Giant Goes Broke as Americans Reject Old Staples," *New York Times*, November 13, 2019.

54. Rachel Brill, "Rising Plant-Based Consumption Causes Milk Giant, Dean Foods to Close Major Facility," FoodTableTV, July 17, 2018, https://www.foodabletv.com/blog/rising -plant-based-consumption-causes-milk-giant-dean-foods-to-close-major-facility.

55. David Yaffe-Bellany, "The New Makers of Plant Based Meat? Big Meat Companies," *New York Times*, October 14, 2019, https://www.nytimes.com/2019/10/14/business/the-new -makers-of-plant-based-meat-big-meat-companies.html.

56. Cleveland Clinic, "What You Need to Know When Choosing Milk and Milk Alternatives," November 11, 2021, https://health.clevelandclinic.org/what-you-need-to-know -when-choosing-milk-and-milk-alternatives/.

57. Food Institute, "The Meteoric Rise of Dairy Alternatives: Will Cow Milk Substitutes Remain Unstoppable?" August 16, 2021, https://foodinstitute.com/focus/the-meteoric -rise-of-dairy-alternatives-will-cow-milk-substitutes-remain-unstoppable/.

58. *Wikipedia*, "Pink Slime," https://en.wikipedia.org/wiki/Pink_slime.

59. Ibid.

60. Ibid.

61. Ibid.

62. Ibid.

63. Ibid.

64. Wire Services, "Fines Await Sloppy EID Butchers, Authorities Offer Training," *Daily Sabah*, August 29, 2017, https://www.dailysabah.com/turkey/2017/08/29/fines-await-sloppy -eid-butchers-authorities-offer-training.

65. https://www.nytimes.com/2019/01/08/opinion/editorials/belgium-ban-animal -slaughter.html.

66. *Wikipedia*, "Legal aspects of ritual slaughter," https://en.wikipedia.org/wiki/Legal_ aspects_of_ritual_slaughter.

67. "Belgium Bans Religious Slaughtering Practices, Drawing Praise and Protest," *New York Times*, January 5, 2019, https://www.nytimes.com/2019/01/05/world/europe/belgium -ban-jewish-muslim-animal-slaughter.html.

68. Cnaan Liphshiz, "Belgian Lawmakers Ditch Bill to Ban Kosher and Halal Slaughter in Brussels," *Times of Israel*, June 18, 2022, https://www.timesofisrael.com/belgian-lawmakers -ditch-bill-to-ban-kosher-and-halal-slaughter-in-brussels/.

69. *Wikipedia*, "Legal aspects of ritual slaughter," https://en.wikipedia.org/wiki/Legal_ aspects_of_ritual_slaughter https://en.wikipedia.org/wiki/Legal_aspects_of_ritual_slaughter.

70. Ibid.

71. US Food Safety and Inspection Service, "Modernization of Swine Slaughter Inspection," FSIS, August 17, 2022, https://www.fsis.usda.gov/inspection/inspection-programs/

inspection-meat-products/modernization-swine-slaughter-inspection.

72. US Food Safety and Inspection Service, "Modernization of Poultry Slaughter Inspection," FSIS, June 9, 2022, https://www.fsis.usda.gov/inspection/inspection-programs/inspection-poultry-products/modernization-poultry-slaughter.

73. Louis Anthony Cox, "Higher Line Speed In Young Chicken Slaughter Establishments Does Not Predict Increased Salmonella Contamination Risks," *Poultry Science* 100, no. 2 (2021), https://www.sciencedirect.com/science/article/pii/S0032579120307367.

74. Letter to Deputy Under Secretary Eskin and Administrator Kiecker, Abetterbalance .org, March 1, 2022, https://www.abetterbalance.org/wp-content/uploads/2022/03/Letter -from-26-Organizations-on-Concerns-and-Requirements-for-Waivers-Increasing-Poultry -Line-Speeds.pdf.

75. Ibid.

76. US Food Safety and Inspection Service, "Modernization of Swine Slaughter Inspection," FSIS, August 17, 2022, https://www.fsis.usda.gov/inspection/inspection-programs/ inspection-meat-products/modernization-swine-slaughter-inspection.

77. Federal Register, "Modernization of Swine Slaughter Inspection," October 1, 2019, https://www.federalregister.gov/documents/2019/10/01/2019-20245/modernization-of -swine-slaughter-inspection.

78. The United Food and Commercial Workers International Union, "The UFCW Sues The Federal Government Over Dangerous Line Speed Rule," UFCW, October 10, 2019, https://www.ufcw.org/swinerule/.

79. Ibid.

80. Alan Clendenning, "Fine Gives DeCoster Workers Hope Deplorable Conditions Have Improved Since a Massive OSHA Probe of the Turner Egg Farm, but Further Monitoring May Be Needed, They Say," *Maine Sunday Telegram*, July 14 1996.

81. William Neuman, "An Iowa Egg Farmer and a History of Salmonella," *New York Times*, September 21, 2010.

82. Ibid.

83. Ibid.

84. Alan Clendenning, "Fine Gives DeCoster Workers Hope Deplorable Conditions Have Improved since a Massive OSHA Probe of the Turner Egg Farm, but Further Monitoring May Be Needed, They Say," *Maine Sunday Telegram,* July 14, 1996.

85. Michael J. Crumb, "Iowa Egg Producer Separates Business, Charity Work," *Associated Press,* September 20, 2010.

86. Avery Yale Kamila, "Natural Foodie: Pass Law That Helps Egg farm? Consider History First," *Portland Press Herald*, May 4, 2011.

87. Scott Thistle, "OSHA Mum on Visit to Turner Egg Farm," *Sun Journal,* April 14, 2009.

88. Scott Taylor, "Egg Farm Settlement Totals $36,947 in Fines and Restitution, $100,000 to Aid Inspections," *Sun Journal,* June 7, 2010.

89. United Press International, "Egg Recall Investigation Widens," *UPI,* September 16, 2010.

90. Joe Fassler, "Egg Mogul Jack DeCoster Sickened 56,000 people. He'll Serve Just Three Months In Prison," *The Counter*, June 30, 2017.

91. Edward D. Murphy, "Judge Lets Egg Baron Jack DeCoster Serve Prison Time In New Hampshire," *Press Herald,* June 28, 2017, https://www.pressherald.com/2017/06/28/judge-approves-new-hampshire-prison-for-jack-decoster/.

92. Ibid.

93. Travis Dorman, "Community Supports Families Affected by Immigration Raid at Grainger Slaughterhouse," Knox News, April 9, 2018, https://www.knoxnews.com/story/news/local/tennessee/2018/04/09/immigration-raid-bean-station-tn-slaughterhouse/499928002/.

94. Ibid.

95. Travis Dorman and Jamie Satterfield, "ICE raids Grainger County Meatpacking Plant Amid Charges Owners Avoided $2.5M in Payroll," Knox News, April 5, 2018, https://www.knoxnews.com/story/news/crime/2018/04/05/ice-raids-meatpacking-plant-grainger-county/490673002/.

96. Ibid.

97. "Safety violations found at slaughterhouse raided earlier," Associated Press, August 24, 2018, https://www.seattletimes.com/business/safety-violations-found-at-slaughterhouse-raided-earlier/.

98. *Wikipedia*, "Koch Foods," https://en.wikipedia.org/wiki/Koch_Foods.

99. Justin Vicory, "Job Fair After ICE Raids. Here's Who Showed Up For Koch Foods Plant Jobs," *The Clarion-Ledger,* August 12, 2019, https://www.usatoday.com/story/money/2019/08/12/ms-ice-raids-koch-foods-job-fair-forest-who-how-many-applied/1990473001/.

100. David Robinson Simon, *Meatonomics: How the Rigged Economics of Meat and Dairy Make You Consume Too Much* (San Francisco: Conari Press, 2013).